Breaking Story

BREAKING STORY

STORY

The South African Press

Gordon S. Jackson

Westview Press
Boulder • San Francisco • Oxford

Copyright © 1993 by Westview Press, Inc.

Published in 1993 in the United States of America by Westview Press, Inc., 5500 Central Avenue, Boulder, Colorado 80301-2877, and in the United Kingdom by Westview Press, 36 Lonsdale Road, Summertown, Oxford OX2 7EW

Library of Congress Cataloging-in-Publication Data
Jackson, Gordon S., 1949–
  Breaking story : the South African press / Gordon S. Jackson.
    p. cm.
  Includes bibliographical references and index.
  ISBN 0-8133-8453-2
  1. Press and politics—South Africa—History—20th century.
2. Press—South Africa—Political aspects.   3. South African newspapers—History—20th century.   I. Title.
PN5474.J33   1993
079'.68—dc20   92-38861
                                           CIP

Printed and bound in the United States of America

The paper used in this publication meets the requirements of the American National Standard for Permanence of Paper for Printed Library Materials Z39.48-1984.

10   9   8   7   6   5   4   3   2   1

For Mom and Dad,
the Gerries, and Sue

Like it or not, we must have the news. For if the people do not have the face of the age set clearly before them they begin to imagine it.

—Rebecca West

You say that freedom of utterance is not for time of stress, and I reply with the sad truth that only in time of stress is freedom of utterance in danger. No one questions it in calm days, because it is not needed.

—William Allen White

In order to enjoy the inestimable benefits that the liberty of the press ensures, it is necessary to submit to the inevitable evils that it creates.

—Alexis de Tocqueville

Contents

List of Tables   xiii
Preface   xv
Acknowledgments   xix
Abbreviations and Glossary   xxi

PART 1: ROOTS

1   The Freeze, the Thaw, and the Future   3

     Why the Press? 5
     The Period: 1976 to 1990, 6
     Pressures on the Press, 6
     On the Positive Side, 10
     "The Blackest Years," 11
     The Prognosis, 12

2   The Backdrop   15

     The Context, 16
     The Press, 30

3   The Alternative Press   46

     A Problem of Definition, 48
     Distinguishing Characteristics of the
        Alternative Press, 50
     Problems, 59
     The Contribution of the Alternative Press, 63
     Assessment and Evaluation, 67

4   The Realities of the Marketplace   70

     The Death of the *Rand Daily Mail*, 70
     The Rise of Times Media Limited, 81

The Onset of Winter, 84
The Response, 94
Conclusion, 101

5   The Law   103

The Main Laws Infringing Press Freedom, 107
Evaluation and Assessment, 123
Conclusion, 126

6   The State of Emergency   128

The Chronology, 128
The Regulations Themselves, 130
The Government's Rationale, 137
Implications and Evaluation, 142
Conclusion, 156

7   Other Environmental Hazards   159

Public Apathy and Ignorance, 160
Censorship, Intolerance, and Secrecy, 163
Conclusion, 170

PART 2: PROSPECTS

8   The Prospects for Press Freedom   175

Press Freedom in Context, 177
Prospects for Press Freedom, 182
Conclusion, 191

9   Other Vital Issues   194

The Economic Basis, 194
What Kind of Journalism? 202
The Profession, 206
The Legal Foundation, 209
Toward a National Media Policy, 212
Conclusion, 215

10   Rewriting the Map 216

What Kind of Press? 217
Toward a Committed Journalism—
    South African Style, 224
Conclusion, 231

Appendix 235
Notes 251
Bibliography 279
About the Book and Author 295
Index 297

Tables

2.1	Circulation of daily newspapers	32
2.2	Circulation of weekly newspapers	33
3.1	Circulation of alternative newspapers	48
4.1	Consumption of media by race groups	90
4.2	The value of the rand and currencies of selected trading partners, 1972–1990	92
4.3	Average annual inflation rates in South Africa and selected trading partners, 1970–1988	92
9.1	Projected population changes in South Africa, 1980–2020	202

Preface

SOMEONE DESCRIBED a critic as a person who comes down from the mountain after the battle and shoots all the wounded. In preparing this critique of the South African press, I have increasingly realized how well the label fits. It is easy for me, having stood aside from the conflicts the press has faced in recent times, to step forward and assess its performance. Finding fault with journalists and their papers is not difficult when one's claims, like those in this book, are written in comfort and safety, far from battle conditions.

Yet because the press is such an important institution in influencing social and political change in South Africa, its story is too important to go untold. Thus, better that the narrator be an outsider looking in than there be no narrator at all.

The story told here is of the South African press between 1976 and 1990, followed by speculation on the shape that newspapers and journalism may take in the future. This study comes amidst unprecedented change in South Africa and is based on the almost self-evident assumption that the 1990s will be vitally formative years for both the country and its press. The ensuing chapters do not presume to present the definitive interpretation of events in the press's recent history. Nor do they offer the final word on where the press may go from here. Rather, this study is but one contribution to the discussions that will help determine the character and quality of tomorrow's newspaper journalism and shape the thinking of those who practice it.

No book on the South African press can avoid taking one of several ideological positions that characterize the writing on that topic. So it would be helpful to the reader to know from the outset that this study flows from what is known in South Africa as the liberal tradition. Without uncritically accepting that tradition's premises, I conclude by reaffirming the continuing applicability of this perspective to the press in South Africa.

This study has its genesis in an eight-month sabbatical leave in 1989 and 1990, spent in Grahamstown and elsewhere in South Africa. It is based on library research as well as interviews with some sixty journalists, media scholars, and other academics. Interviews were conducted between August 1989 and January 1990 with the editors of almost all the country's daily and weekly newspapers. The study is also a product of my own background: I am a South African and worked as a journalist in Johannesburg from 1976 to 1979.

Inevitably, given the pace of change in South Africa, some aspects of this book will be dated by the time it is published. Also, some individuals have made career changes since I interviewed them. I have noted all the changes I was aware of but apologize for any outdated identifications that may have slipped through. Two areas in particular have been vulnerable to the rapid pace of change in South Africa. One involves the group of papers referred to in this study as the alternative press, which has subsequently become known as the independent press. In several respects, these papers have shifted closer toward resembling the mainstream press than Chapter 3 suggests. However, the intent of this study is also to capture accurately the nature of these papers in their infancy in the late 1980s. For that reason, and to reflect accurately the written sources and interviews on which this study is based, the term *alternative press* is used throughout this book. A second area affected by change is that of legislation affecting the press. Here too the intent has been to provide a snapshot of how things were on the eve of the 1990s, so the reader should be cautioned that much of Chapter 5 may now be dated.

A note is needed here on the thorny question of terminology of racial groups. Identifying these groups is a highly politicized issue that is impossible to resolve without risking offending someone. Yet the analysis demands that one set of terms or another be adopted. I have used "blacks" to include all groups that in earlier days were termed "non-whites," namely Africans, Asians (Indians and Chinese), and Coloureds (people of mixed race). This term is a useful and more neutral way of identifying the great majority of South Africans who are not white and who—generally speaking—have in common a status as victims of white domination.

Another issue of usage concerns editors and gender. Only men held top editorial positions in South Africa at the time of this study. Occasional references to a hypothetical editor as "he" or "him" reflect this reality.

Finally, my hope is that this study will help accomplish two things. The first is to secure for South Africa's journalists a climate that increasingly honors and protects free expression. The second is that as these journalists react to this study, they will be inspired, goaded, irritated, or in any other way moved to offer their society only their best. Postapartheid South Africa will need from them nothing less.

Gordon S. Jackson

Acknowledgments

THANKS ARE DUE to many individuals and institutions, without whose generous help this book would not have been possible. The Institute for Social and Economic Research at Rhodes University, in Grahamstown, South Africa, deserves special credit for providing me a research fellowship. The Faculty Research Committee at Whitworth College also gave me significant financial assistance.

Then there were the countless individuals who helped. They include librarians at Rhodes University and various other institutions throughout South Africa. Academic colleagues like Don Pinnock, Charles Riddle, Gavin Stewart, and Tony Walker at Rhodes University's Department of Journalism and Media Studies welcomed me warmly and gave generously of their time and ideas during my stay at Rhodes. Other media scholars, especially Arnold de Beer and Keyan Tomaselli, were similarly supportive. Particularly noteworthy for me was the level of cooperation I received from individual editors, journalists, and managers. Across the ideological spectrum, these people and others associated with the press were, almost without exception, enthusiastically cooperative. Space precludes me from listing them individually. Nor was it possible to reflect their individual views in this study. Collectively, however, they were indispensable in shaping the impressions that structured my research. Although I owe all of them a great debt, a handful of individuals nevertheless merit special recognition: Jeanette Minnie, formerly the organizer of the South African Society of Journalists; Syd Pote, of the Newspaper Press Union; and Bob Steyn, the conciliator of the Media Council. Jimmy McClurg and my Whitworth colleague John Yoder deserve thanks for their incisive comments on parts of the manuscript. And for their computing expertise, I owe much to Ken Pecka and Elizabeth Carras for their always cheerful, always effective responses to my problems.

Last, there was the support and encouragement of friends, notably Beddo Vermeulen, and family: my parents-in-law, Neville and Cynthia Matterson, whose gracious hospitality helped greatly in offsetting the costs of the research; my wife, Sue, who encouraged, critiqued, and babysat countless hours to make this book happen; and Sarah and Matthew, who will finally have less need to ask why Dad keeps going to the office.

G.S.J.

Abbreviations and Glossary

ABC: Audit Bureau of Circulations. An independent agency that certifies the accuracy of newspaper and magazine circulations.

ADJ: Association of Democratic Journalists. A multiracial group, founded in 1989.

Afrikaans: The language derived from Dutch that is spoken by about 60 percent of South African whites, who are known as Afrikaners.

Afrikaans press: The daily and weekly newspapers produced in Afrikaans. Originally committed to furthering the aims of Afrikaner nationalism, it became a progovernment press in 1948.

Afrikaners: Whites of primarily Dutch descent, whose home language is Afrikaans. Previously unified in supporting the National Party, Afrikaners became deeply divided in the 1980s over the government's waning commitment to apartheid.

Alternative press: A group of weekly or biweekly newspapers, founded in the 1980s and rooted in the extraparliamentary movement. In the early 1990s these papers became known as the independent press.

ANC: African National Congress. This predominantly black organization was founded in 1912 to voice black political concerns. It was banned from 1960 until February 1990 and is regarded as the largest political opposition movement in South Africa. Its supporters have often clashed with Inkatha members.

Apartheid: A formal system of racial segregation. Vigorously implemented by the National Party after it came to power in 1948, it entrenched white domination in virtually all sectors of South African life.

Argus: The larger of the two English-language newspaper groups.

Coloured: A person of mixed race. One of South Africa's four main race groups.

Conservative Party: The official opposition in the white parliament since 1987. It favors adherence to the traditional principles and goals of apartheid.

COSATU: Congress of South African Trade Unions. An umbrella organization of antiapartheid labor unions, founded in 1985.

Democratic Party: An opposition party in the white parliament, to the left of the government. Formed by a merger of the PFP and other groups in 1988, it represents mostly English-speaking whites and more liberal Afrikaners.

English press: The English-language daily and weekly newspapers that traditionally catered to white readerships. Almost all these papers are published by the Argus and TML groups.

Extraparliamentary movement: A loosely defined coalition of mostly black organizations and individuals opposing the government that arose in the 1980s. Many of these individuals are members of the UDF.

Freedom Charter: Adopted in 1955, this document calls for a nonracial society with a mixed economy. The Charter has greatly influenced the policies of groups like the ANC and UDF.

Inkatha Freedom Party: A major black political and cultural movement supported primarily by members of South Africa's largest tribal group, the Zulus. Inkatha has taken a more conservative stand on political issues than its main rival, the ANC. Its supporters have often clashed with ANC members.

Mainstream press: The Afrikaans and English newspapers.

MDM: Mass Democratic Movement. An informal coalition of antiapartheid groups and individuals, including the COSATU and the UDF.

Media Council: An independent body whose main functions are to mediate in disputes concerning the press and to promote press freedom. It was established by the NPU in 1983 to succeed a similar body known as the Press Council.

M-Net: A subscriber television service, operated by a consortium of the four large newspaper groups: Argus, Nasionale Pers, Perskor, and TML.

Muldergate: A scandal involving the attempt to cover up a secret, extensive government propaganda campaign in the 1970s to improve South Africa's image at home and abroad.

MWASA: Media Workers Association of South Africa. A black media workers' group founded in 1980, including but not limited to journalists.

Nasionale Pers: The larger of the two Afrikaans newspaper groups.

National Party: The ruling party in South Africa since 1948. Previously the vehicle for promoting Afrikaner nationalism through the policy of apartheid, the party opened its ranks to black members in 1991.

NPU: The Newspaper Press Union. A voluntary, private group of newspaper publishers.

PAC: The Pan-Africanist Congress. A black political organization, to the left of the ANC. Like the ANC, it was also unbanned in February 1990.

Perskor: The smaller of the two Afrikaans newspaper groups.

PFP: The Progressive Federal Party. Previously the official opposition in the white parliament, to the left of the government. It merged with other groups to become the Democratic Party.

Rand: South Africa's currency. In January 1993 R1.00 was worth approximately 33 U.S. cents.

SAAN: South African Associated Newspapers. Formerly the smaller of the two English newspaper groups. It became TML in 1987.

SABC: The South African Broadcasting Corporation. The state-controlled agency that controls almost all radio and television broadcasting.

SAPA: The South African Press Association. An independent cooperative of newspapers and broadcasters. Operates on a basis similar to that of the Associated Press.

SASJ: South African Society of Journalists. A multiracial organization representing mostly journalists for English-language papers.

SATV: South African Television. The SABC's television operations.

TML: Times Media Limited. The smaller of the two English-language newspaper groups. It succeeded the ailing SAAN group in 1987.

UDF: United Democratic Front. A coalition of more than 700 antiapartheid groups that arose in the 1980s. It formed the heart of the extraparliamentary movement until it was effectively banned in 1988. Individual UDF supporters are now allied with the ANC, PAC, and other organizations.

. . . .

Part One

ROOTS

1

The Freeze, the Thaw, and the Future

CAPE TOWN'S WINTERS can be awful, with a mix of pelting rain and winds so fierce that motorists and pedestrians alike move with caution. The grayness intensifies the cold, producing a miserable grimness one never sees in the tourist material touting what is also one of the world's most exquisitely beautiful cities.

The bleakness of a Cape Town winter symbolizes the political climate generated over the past half century from the parliament buildings located in the heart of the city. The apartheid policies formulated and enforced by successive National Party governments led to a political winter for the entire country. Then, beginning with the de Klerk presidency in late 1989, the weather changed. It was as if the rain and wind suddenly stopped, and the clouds slowly dissipated to allow enough sunshine through to begin easing the chill. For the first time in their memory, many South Africans began to see sunlight through the dense clouds of apartheid.

Watching this ongoing whirl of political change in South Africa as intently as anyone else are the country's journalists. For one thing, that is their business. But underlying their interest are other, more fundamental, questions: Is South Africa becoming a more tolerable place to practice journalism and publish newspapers? And what of the easing of restrictions on the media, the lifting of bans on groups like the African National Congress and the South African Communist Party, and the general shift toward openness and toleration of greater political diversity? Will this shift prove lasting or ephemeral, for the press in particular and the society in general? How will these political changes shape the quality of life in a postapartheid South Africa?

3

As South African journalists look to the fast-changing environment in which they work in the 1990s and beyond, they face only two certainties. One is that their future and that of their papers is highly unpredictable. The other is that their future operating environment could also range wildly, from the freedom of expression characterizing the best of Western democracies to that of oppression and intolerance that surpasses even the record of South Africa's apartheid era.

Merely the prospect, if not the assurance, of healthier days ahead for South Africa's press is itself a significant shift in the country's political culture. The political changes of the early 1990s were as encouraging a step toward openness and freedom as South African journalists had seen in more than a generation. The changing political climate took on a heightened importance for the press when contrasted with the extraordinarily grim years leading up to the 1990s.

In 1979, Joel Mervis, former editor of the *Sunday Times,* presented the following assessment of press freedom in South Africa. Metaphorically speaking, he said, it "has its left leg in plaster, its right arm in a sling, a patch over the left eye, deafness in the right ear, a sprained ankle and a number of teeth knocked out."[1]

Mervis was addressing a conference titled "Survival of the Press," and his point was simple: "Can press freedom, with all its existing disabilities, survive? And, taking into account its already weakened condition, will it be strong enough to survive the further bruising blows it can expect in future?"[2]

Mervis had good reason in the late 1970s to be concerned about the prognosis for a free press in South Africa. The next ten years, however, brought a barrage of body blows one after the other to the newspaper industry, to the point that editors may have looked back to the previous decade with envy. By the mid-1980s, it seemed the patient had twice undergone major heart surgery, was wearing a pacemaker, had had a kidney transplant—and lost his medical insurance. And worse was to come.

Without doubt, that decade saw a mix of forces that together constituted the most serious assault on the survivability of an independent South African political press since its establishment in 1829. Then came the events of early 1990 and the unmistakable signals that South Africa was moving inexorably into a new, as yet undefined, political order.

These latter two points—first, the contention that the South African press underwent unprecedented attack from the mid-1970s and, second, its prospects for the 1990s and beyond—form the basis of this book. This chapter outlines the main forces that the press faced in the 1980s in particular, setting the stage for more detailed analysis in later chapters.

WHY THE PRESS?

The scope of this book is the South African daily and weekly press. Included are those general-interest newspapers covering political news. A full list of these publications is included in Tables 2.1 and 2.2 in Chapter 2. Excluded from this study are the burgeoning number of specialized publications, such as financial or trade newspapers, and the widely read consumer or other magazines and printed media. Nor is this a study of the broadcast media, even though television and radio are critically important in South Africa.

Several considerations underlie this deliberately narrow focus on newspapers. The first is the enormously influential role newspapers are assumed to play in the political life of modern societies.[3] Although media scholars struggle to assess with any precision the political impact of newspapers in modern societies, none question that they have *some* impact. Neither, for that matter, do politicians and government leaders have any doubts about that. Judging from the zeal with which the South African government has tried to control the printed word, it is as much in awe of the power of the press as governments anywhere.

A second reason is related specifically to the South African press and its function in that society. Ever since the present government came to power in 1948, the English-language papers have filled the role of an opposition press. The country's newspapers have traditionally consisted of two groups: the antiapartheid English press, which has generally reflected the views of the country's English-speaking whites (about 40 percent of the white population), and the progovernment Afrikaans papers, which in turn have typically been a voice for the Afrikaans-speaking community. With varying degrees of conviction and effectiveness, the English papers uniformly opposed the government and its policies throughout the apartheid era.[4] These papers became such an effective dissenting voice against the government that Elaine Potter argued that the English press in reality became the official opposition in South Africa, replacing the weak and ineffectual voice of the English speakers in parliament.[5] Because the press is a potentially powerful avenue available to those opposing the government, it is an especially significant institution in South Africa.

By contrast, South Africa's broadcast media are with a few minor exceptions state controlled. The South African Broadcasting Corporation has traditionally operated faithfully in accord with government policies, if not actively propagating the administration's ideology.[6] Political opposition groups on both the Pretoria administration's left and right have accused SATV throughout its history of being so dramatically and

blatantly biased in favor of the government that they have little prospect of being fairly treated in news and other programs.[7] Because of the
government's monopoly on the broadcast media, and especially the
monopoly over television news, the press's role as a channel for dissenting views takes on particular importance.

A third reason for focusing on the daily and weekly press is that this
segment of the media underwent the most significant structural change
in the 1980s. The decade saw some stunning newspaper deaths, such as
that of the *Rand Daily Mail*, long the most trenchant critic of the government, and the *Friend*, the only English paper in the Orange Free
State. The births column recorded several notable arrivals, most outside the mainstream commercial press, as a new cluster of "alternative" papers arose. These included *Grassroots*, *New Nation*, *South*, and
the *Weekly Mail*.

THE PERIOD: 1976 TO 1990

For these reasons, then, the press merits analysis as a major South African institution that changed extensively in the period from 1976 to
1990. But why this time frame? This period, more than any other in the
press's history, ushered in an array of challenges to the survival of newspapers that led to extensive adaptation by managers, editors, and journalists. The press of the late 1980s was thus a markedly different
institution from the one South Africans knew a decade and a half earlier. Especially during the 1980s, the press faced an unprecedented
range of problems.

The press was subject to all the major forces buffeting the society at
large: massive political realignments; increasingly harsh steps taken
against government opponents, culminating in the declaration of successive states of emergency from 1985 onward; a steady seepage of professionals leaving the country; and economic hardship, in the form of
high inflation, a devalued rand, rising tax rates, heightened international economic sanctions, and a massive outflow of capital.

These changes alone would have made life grim indeed for the newspaper industry. The list continues, though, with additional pressures
unique to the press.

PRESSURES ON THE PRESS

From the Government

The declaration of the state of emergency on 21 July 1985 opened the
way for the most specific challenge to the press and its freedom to fulfill

its traditional role as a purveyor of information of the day's events. More accurately, it was only a year later, with the extensive emergency regulations promulgated on 12 June 1986, that the press was first subjected to a wide range of debilitating, media-specific constraints. Then followed a series of legal challenges to these regulations and a corresponding bout of loophole tightening by the government. Finally, several major legal rulings by the country's highest court left the emergency regulations virtually unassailable—whether on media issues or any others.[8]

The emergency regulations and the numerous other laws concerning the press effectively placed vast parts of the society off limits for reporters. Freedom to obtain and publish information was severely curtailed even before the state of emergency was imposed. Afterward, to return to Mervis's metaphor, the patient was reduced to life on a respirator: Its quality of life was severely curbed, and the life could be ended at a moment's notice. The powers granted to the ministers of law and order and home affairs under earlier legislation and under the emergency rules gave them virtually absolute power to pull the plug on any newspapers they wished to close temporarily or permanently.

Government intolerance and hostility toward opposition papers, already widespread in the late 1970s and early 1980s, intensified as the decade unfolded.

From Television

Another devastating blow to the press had resulted from the arrival of television in 1976. Two years later, advertising was allowed on South African television, and so began the seemingly unstoppable inroads into the newspapers' previously impregnable advertising stronghold. Daily and weekly newspapers' share of the total amount spent on advertising dropped from 46.1 percent in 1975 to 29.4 percent in 1985.[9] In 1987, the latest year for which figures are available, the figure for the press was 26.6 percent; for television, it had reached 30.0 percent. Radio revenues pushed the broadcasting share in that year to 41.6 percent.[10]

Television's capacity to colonize advertising territory previously under undisputed press control was not the only damage the electronic medium imposed. Other dents resulted from the power of the television medium itself and its offer of easy, effortless media companionship. This impact was on the time readers would spend on papers, formally measured as readership,[11] and on actual sales—or circulation.[12]

Yet another, and more subtle, threat to print came from the inherent power of the television medium. Television's capacity to convey vivid visual images gives it an air of credibility that print can never claim, whatever advantages it may have over electronic media. For the South African press, this meant that more and more of its readers said they trusted television more than their papers. This was especially the case among whites, but blacks too said they felt similarly.[13] Whatever the problems in understanding the meaning of these findings—and some important questions arise in particular with those concerning black views—the result for the press is plain. Like the press in the United States and elsewhere in the Western world, it too has to accept that television as a medium has a head start in the competition for credibility among mass audiences.

From the Advertising-Reader Equation

Compounding its problems with television's appetite for advertising revenues, the press took a beating when the economic downturn of the mid-1980s led to severe cuts in total advertising spending. The twin problems of soaring inflation, as noted earlier, and the imposition of sales tax on all advertising meant that the money advertisers spent dropped 26 percent in real terms in 1985.[14]

Finally, several developments in the broader society served to complicate life still further for the press. One was increasing literacy among blacks. As the number of blacks able to read papers rose steadily throughout the 1980s, the proportion of white readers steadily dropped. By the end of the decade, the majority of readers of several English papers such as the *Star*, the *Argus*, the *Daily News*, and the *Cape Times* were Africans, Coloureds, and Asians, the country's three other racial groups.[15] The implications of this development on advertising are far-reaching indeed, as the *Rand Daily Mail* found in its desperate, and failing, fight to survive. A large circulation, the *Mail*'s experience showed, was not necessarily enough to woo advertisers if most of those readers were black.[16] The income levels of most of these blacks made them less attractive readers for advertisers seeking to reach the higher-income households represented predominantly by whites.

From the Alternative Press

Another major media-specific change in the 1980s stemmed from the rise of the Mass Democratic Movement (MDM), a coalescing of a wide range of antigovernment forces within the society. An increasing politicization of huge numbers of South Africans, coupled with political unrest throughout the decade, led to a hunger for information among many allied to the MDM. For a variety of reasons, critics of existing newspapers increasingly saw them as unable or unwilling to provide authoritative and pertinent information sympathetic to the groups forming the MDM. The mainstream press, the argument went, was too proestablishment, too concerned with the interests of monopoly capital and too concerned to please its white readers to cover issues like extraparliamentary politics, labor, and life in the townships with any credibility.[17] This discontent spawned one new alternative publication after the other, each focusing specifically on the areas largely untended by the mainstream press.

These alternative publications, though eating only minimally into the circulation or advertising base of the mainstream papers, nevertheless had an important impact. The very presence of a new press perspective more in tune with the views of MDM supporters reinforced their conviction that the mainstream press was out of touch with South African reality.

In addition, the alternative press practices a style of journalism dramatically opposed to that of the mainstream press. Ridiculing the established papers' claims that they practice an "objective" approach to gathering and reporting news, the newer publications embrace a "committed" or "advocacy" journalism. Far from regarding themselves as neutral observers of the scene, these papers openly embrace a viewpoint. They say that journalistic neutrality or objectivity is a myth under any circumstances; to claim to practice such journalism in South Africa is naive self-deception at best and outright dishonesty at worst.[18] A second implication of the arrival of these publications, therefore, is their challenge to the prevailing journalistic conventions of the traditional newsroom.

The third and possibly the most significant of the implications of the alternative or emerging press concerns the traditional role that the English papers have played as an opposition voice, as noted previously. This opposition function of the English press began fading. Increasingly, the alternative papers became more and more recognizable as the most vigorous antigovernment critics.

From the Public

Not helping the English papers in their self-proclaimed role as an opposition was the growing awareness that they were preaching to an audience less and less interested in hearing their message of dissent. By the end of the decade, evidence abounded of widespread apathy among whites in particular regarding negative news. The conciliator of the Media Council, Bob Steyn, argued that public apathy is one of the major threats to press freedom in South Africa.[19]

The apathy took two forms. The first was what Steyn and journalists noted was a conscious decision by readers to be spared whatever grim news today may bring. One reporter, commenting on his paper's coverage of unrest, said: "People do not believe it is happening and say we make a far bigger issue out of it than we should. Our feeling is that we are battling a readership that doesn't want to know."[20]

The second kind of apathy was the public's low commitment to press freedom and its general unwillingness to support the press when it was attacked. Decades of government attacks on the English press have encouraged a callous, disdainful public attitude to the value of press freedom. As one editor put it, "The public have been conditioned to the view that we are vagabonds and ne'er-do-wells. They have not got a commitment to free expression."[21] Coupled with the society's high levels of intolerance and a generation of government obsessed with secrecy,[22] the press faced an often hostile readership when bearing bad news. The press was thus forced to grapple with a "psychosis of silence."[23]

ON THE POSITIVE SIDE

Were the 1980s, then, a time of unmitigated pressure for the press, a time of gloom and darkness without respite? Was there anything positive to report? Undoubtedly, the answer is yes. In the second half of the decade, the economic picture improved markedly for the four main companies that dominated the press, especially for Times Media Limited (formerly South African Associated Newspapers). That company's financial turnaround, described in Chapter 4, was dramatic indeed: from a loss of R19.4 million in 1986 to profits in 1987 and 1988 of R10 million and R26.8 million respectively.[24]

Also in the economic realm, some relief came for the press with its ability to diversify into the lucrative television market. Also notable was the marriage of convenience in the mid-1980s between the English and Afrikaans papers. Forced by economic exigencies, the four major press groups (two English, two Afrikaans) cooperated to launch a subscription television service, M-Net. The service, made possible only with the grudging consent of the government-controlled broadcasting service, was specifically intended to help the press groups diversify their financial base and supplement their earnings from nonnewspaper sources.[25]

For the Afrikaans newspapers too the 1980s brought important change. Long seen as faithful handmaidens of the National Party, these papers began acquiring a previously unimaginable assertiveness and independence from the government. These papers were hardly about to dissolve their marriage with the party, and by no means have all of them begun to rattle the cage of the party establishment. Yet the questioning, prodding, and pushing of papers like *Beeld* and *Rapport* reached the level where former president P. W. Botha singled out *Beeld* for vicious attack[26]—the kind of treatment Nationalist leaders have typically reserved for what they have regarded as the unpatriotic, liberal English press. The Afrikaans press also sided with the English press in opposing various government moves against the press, including the emergency regulations themselves—further evidence of its having moved away from giving unqualified loyalty to government thinking.

A remarkably positive feature of the decade is that despite the emergency regulations and other legal press curbs, and despite the extensive harassment and intimidation that journalists continued to face, the mainstream and alternative press published as much significant news as they did.

"THE BLACKEST YEARS"

So the landscape was not utterly desolate. But no one had illusions on how to read the successive medical charts of the patient whom Mervis described earlier. The litany of claims by government leaders to favor press freedom rang more and more hollow as the state's vice of constraints squeezed the press ever more tightly. Shortly after the extensive press restrictions were outlined in the June 1986 renewal of the state of emergency, Foreign Minister Pik Botha "angrily denied there were widespread press restrictions in South Africa."[27] More reflective of reality is the comment of former *Cape Times* editor Tony Heard. Writing even before these far-reaching regulations were promulgated, he said: "What freedom there is exists in spite of, not because of, government."[28] He added: "The only encouraging factors in this repressive situation are the courage of some journalists and proprietors, the considerable room for dodging bureaucratic decrees ... and the incompetence of some of those attempting near tyranny."[29]

Whatever the successes that the management of the four major newspaper groups had in fighting the economic ravages of the mid-1980s (and these successes are widely recognized), they exacted a price. The closing of papers like the *Mail* and the *Friend*, and the loss of many mid- and senior-level English-language journalists through emigration, retrenchment, or early retirement packages, were part of the problem. Equally serious, though, were the side effects on journalists of these cutbacks, coupled with the toll exacted by the prolonged emergency regulations. Two Rhodes University researchers, John Grogan and Charles Riddle, said that "with some honourable exceptions, the South African press is being battered into submission. Many journalists are becoming demoralized, hypercautious and timorous."[30]

The problem was also reflected in the product of the mainstream press. Their coverage was seen to be tempered by self-censorship[31] and a weary resignation by some editors to increasingly give their white readers inoffensive, noncontroversial news. This diet of happy news constitutes what South African journalists cynically referred to as "sunshine journalism." One reporter on an English daily said, "Our paper is very much into sunshine journalism. Our reading market is not interested in black news; basically, they're interested in poodles and roadshows."[32]

The sweep of forces on the press thus extended from the heady levels of inflation and the international value of the South African rand to the individual reporters who resignedly wrote about the poodles rather than the perilous. The result was a press in grim straits. Notwithstanding a few shafts of light, Grogan and Riddle could legitimately write in 1987 that "the South African press is experiencing the blackest years since it was founded early in the last century."[33]

THE PROGNOSIS

All these factors combined to alter fundamentally the character of the South African press and its role in that society. That, in essence, is the first concern of this study. But if the primary focus of this book is "What shaped the press since 1976 to make it what it is today?" the question then arises, "What does all this imply for the press of tomorrow?" The developments of this period beg for at least some speculation on the future, and a prognosis is provided in the second half of the book. In brief, the shape of tomorrow's press will be inextricably bound up with that of the society itself. As Chapter 2 describes more fully, South African society is undergoing major sociopolitical change. The start of the de Klerk presidency in late 1989 introduced a new era in South African politics. The initial pronouncements of his administration were unambiguously committed to far-reaching changes in South Africa, giving an impetus to the reform policies that had been marked by a confused lethargy toward the end of the Botha administration. Just how committed the government is to fundamental political change, and how successful it will be in playing midwife to a new dispensation, were severely tested in the early 1990s. Various factors threatened the country's progress toward democracy that marked the initial phase of the de Klerk administration. But by mid-1992 continued and extensive black-on-black violence, primarily between ANC and Inkatha supporters, imperiled talks on a new constitution—because of the government's inability to control the bloodshed and because of charges that it was aiding or at least condoning attacks on ANC supporters. As the country moves toward some still undefined new political dispensation, the press too will simultaneously redefine its identity in and contribution to the society. In doing so, the press will be no different from other South African institutions in this regard. Many actors on the South African stage have for some time actively tried to stake out their claims in the "new South Africa." During this time of transition that lies ahead, the press, as an institution, must make plain to the other players how it wishes to function in a postapartheid South Africa and what it can contribute both to the process of political change and to the society it will serve in the future.

Fundamentally important issues need addressing. For example, what ought to be the nature of press freedom in a future South Africa? How ought the state's legitimate needs for security and a commitment to free expression be balanced? What of the traditional Western model of journalism, which commits itself to striving for objective and fair coverage; does it have a place in South Africa? And how ought the present highly concentrated ownership patterns of the press to change, if at all?

If questions like these were thrown to any half dozen South African journalists, to say nothing of their managers or publishers, furious disagreement would follow. The individuals who constitute the press in South Africa are hardly a monolithic group. On the contrary, journalists have major ideological differences among themselves: between English-speaking and Afrikaans journalists, between black and white journalists on the English papers, between journalists in the mainstream press and those in the alternative press. And then there is the often bitter rift between journalists and management on many of the country's papers. How, then, can such an ideologically diverse, fragmented group hope to present a coherent claim for the future of the press in South Africa?

Unquestionably, there will be no lack of interest in the society in seeking to prescribe the way the media ought to operate in the future. The newspaper community must, despite its diverse and divided nature, seize the moment and actively try to make the emerging culture more hospitable to their activities in postapartheid South Africa. Should they fail to do so, they can be sure that other forces will prescribe their operating conditions for them. Simply stated, if they cannot find enough common ground for some kind of united front, they will forfeit this opportunity to help shape their future working environment. Even more important, they may consolidate the expansion of press freedom that took place in the early 1990s and encourage further improvements.

Because the press is on the eve of receiving a new mandate or charter from South African society, two questions ought to be asked: "What is the press's present state of health?" and "What are its prospects?" The first question is answered in Chapters 2 through 7. In turn, these chapters deal with the social and political climate in which the press of the early 1990s finds itself and the overall media environment in which the press operates; the rise of the alternative press; the constraints caused by economic realities; the statute books; the state of emergency; and other limitations on the press.

The second question is addressed in Chapters 8, 9, and 10. Explored here are some of the key debates facing the South African press and the prospects for recovery from the battering it took between 1976 and 1990. As mentioned earlier, this prognosis is integrally related to the health of South Africa itself. The main possible directions of South Africa's future thus apply directly to the press as well.

The second part of this study demonstrates that South Africa's press, like the society it serves, has never before been so malleable and subject to major reshaping. The rest of the 1990s will be critical in determining the shape of Africa's most notorious country as it enters the twenty-first century. Likewise, the character, identity, and contribution of the press that must serve a postapartheid society are already being determined.

The patient whom Mervis described at the beginning of this chapter undoubtedly will join that society. The question is, in what condition? Understanding the circumstances that precipitated the patient's present critical status is vital for an accurate diagnosis. Only then can a prognosis be attempted. It is to these tasks that we now turn.

2

The Backdrop

N EWSPAPERS," Francis Williams has written, "are unique barometers of their age. They indicate more plainly than anything else the climate of the societies to which they belong."[1] Williams's contention is especially fitting in South Africa, as his elaboration makes clear:

> This is not simply for the obvious reason that they are a source of news about their time but because the conditions in which they operate, the responsibilities they are expected, or allowed, to fulfill, the pressures they have to meet, their circulation and economic base, the status of those who write for them and their relationship to their readers, all provide a direct insight into the nature of their communities.[2]

South Africa's media, like those anywhere else, reflect much of the character of their host society. Many of South Africa's features are mirrored in the structure of the press and broadcasting. Both are dominated by white finances and political interests; both have whites in almost all leadership and key staff positions; both are marked by deep cleavages and conflicting political and cultural values; both operate in a climate of secrecy and within a web of information-controlling legislation.

Like South Africa itself, the country's media are marked by distinct and often hostile ethnic, political, and linguistic cleavages. The country's mainstream press, comprising the urban and national daily and Sunday papers, is highly partisan. And the rise of the alternative press, representing as it does a strongly "antiestablishment" ethos, demonstrates the gap between two major political currents flowing through the society.

As a prominent South African institution, the press has been molded by four decades of apartheid and, inevitably, has taken on some characteristics of its society. Another question, of course, is how much the press, especially Afrikaans newspapers, helped shape South African so-

ciety and led the Afrikaner community to devise and then implement
the apartheid ideology. Nowhere are newspapers mere passive reflectors or mirrors of their society. Unlike the barometer of which Williams
wrote, the press has countless effects on the political climate and society it portrays. As it is, media researchers struggle to define the effects
of the press in the United States or Western Europe, where most effects
research has taken place. The press's effects in South Africa, by any
measure a highly abnormal society, are surely all the harder to measure.

Far more discernible, however, is the way the country's press reflects
the broader apartheid society at yet another level. Since 1976, South Africa has undergone massive social and political change. The press has simultaneously experienced unprecedented reshaping. Just as 1976 to
1990 were vitally significant years in South African history, so too were
they enormously formative for the press. The rest of Part 1 of this study
examines these changes.

Fuller accounts of recent changes and their implications for South Africa generally are available elsewhere.[3] But to understand the press's experience, and the context in which it occurred, it is vital to note the
main threads in the press's history, especially during the past decade
and a half.

THE CONTEXT

However much analysts of contemporary South Africa may debate the
causes of its turning away from apartheid and the route the country will
take to a postapartheid era, the 1970s unquestionably marked the beginning of this transition. This period of change, it is argued here, is of
fundamental importance to the press. Never in the South African
press's history has it been more open to reshaping than in the early
1990s. Of course, the changes that the press underwent between 1976
and 1990 did not occur in a void. What had happened to the press before
this period of crucial and often rapid transition?

The South African press had its beginnings on 16 August 1800, with
the *Cape Town Gazette and African Advertiser,* an official government
publication.[4] The paper contained mostly government notices but also
included news. Press freedom arose as a significant issue only a quarter
century later, however, with the arrival of the 1820 British settlers. William Hachten and Anthony Giffard have described how some of these
spirited, independent-minded settlers "arrived in South Africa fully ex-
pecting to continue their cherished rights as British subjects to voice
their grievances."[5] Some of the 4,000 settlers brought expectations
about free expression that were new to the Cape Colony and which

soon began to be claimed by men like Thomas Pringle and John Fairbairn. In 1824, Pringle and a Dutch clergyman, the Reverend Abraham Faure, started the *South African Journal* and the *Nederduitsch Zuid-Afrikaansch Tijdschrift*, which appeared alternately in English and Dutch each month. The *Journal* lasted only two issues because the second issue contained an article by Pringle that so infuriated the governor of the Cape, Lord Charles Somerset, that he closed it.

Also in 1824 Pringle and Fairbairn became coeditors of the *South African Commercial Advertiser*, a publication started by a printer named George Greig. The *Advertiser*, described as "South Africa's first actual newspaper,"[6] also incurred Somerset's anger and he closed it too.

Following sustained conflict with the governor, Fairbairn went to London and in 1828 persuaded the British government to grant "specific assurances regarding the rights of newspapers at the Cape."[7] The resulting "Press Ordinance" of April 1829 "must clearly be regarded as the Magna Carta of the press in South Africa."[8]

Since this stormy beginning, press freedom in South Africa has been jeopardized by numerous subsequent governments, both before and after the formation of the Union of South Africa in 1910. These initial conflicts with a reactionary British governor set the tone for an adversarial press that has marked government-press relations for much of the country's subsequent history—and certainly during the four decades of Nationalist rule. Many scholars and journalists have documented this ongoing struggle for press freedom.[9] Harvey Tyson, former editor of the *Star*, noted: "Every generation of South Africans, ever since that day in April 1829, has had to fight off major threats to the existence of their free press."[10]

During the period of British dominance in South Africa, between 1910 and the election of the Nationalist government in 1948, the English newspapers dominated the country. The South African English press has traditionally had strong ties with British papers. Many British journalists emigrated to South Africa and played formative roles in shaping that country's newspapers. In addition, South Africa's English speakers have deep-rooted cultural and family ties to Britain, further strengthening these papers' inclination to look to Britain for their spiritual and professional roots. Because South Africa's English press has functioned independently of British control for generations, in their own, unique environment, South Africa's journalists have increasingly developed a culture distinct from and independent of that of the "home country."

While this indigenous English press was establishing itself, Afrikaans papers were also taking root. These papers spoke a far more explicit political message, championing the hopes of Afrikaner nationalism. Then, with the electoral triumph of apartheid ideology in 1948, these papers switched from an opposition role to that of serving the government. The social engineering that the apartheid era introduced consisted of two broad themes that radically affected the society and the press. The most obvious change was structuring the entire social order on racial grounds, policies that engendered widespread opposition—especially from blacks but also from many English-speaking whites. Second, the government devised an awesome arsenal of security and constitutional measures to contain these challenges to implementing apartheid. These steps ranged from a series of constitutional maneuvers that empowered Parliament to pass laws immune to challenges in the courts to a bevy of measures curbing free expression and political protest. Subsequent chapters describe the impact and extent of these laws on the press and the toll they took by creating an increasingly secretive, information-poor, and intolerant society.

Early opposition to apartheid by the English papers aggravated already strained government-press relations and set in motion a series of confrontations and threatened government steps against these papers. Hachten and Giffard describe various instances in which the government has tried to assert its role as information broker. The first major example was the Press Commission, appointed in 1950 to investigate monopolistic tendencies in the press, reporting on South Africa published inside and outside the country, and advisability of "control over such reporting."[11] That commission took twelve years to present a report that predictably lambasted the English press for its unpatriotic reporting but led to no specific government actions against the press.

Press opposition in the 1950s came from the English papers, representing mostly whites, plus a small group of more harshly critical publications voicing mostly black concerns. These latter publications were repeatedly and ruthlessly attacked by the government, so that by the end of the decade they were largely a spent force. By then the government had not only effectively silenced these and other opposition voices, especially from blacks, but it had also implemented the main parts of the apartheid ideology. White protest was still tolerated, in Parliament, for example, and from various institutions of the English community, such as its newspapers, universities, churches, and other groups. Yet this protest was very much on the government's terms; Pretoria set parameters of what was permissible dissent and what was not. By the 1960s, the government had things going largely its way. Rumbles of discontent and political challenges at home were, to be sure, always present. In 1965, for example, the *Rand Daily Mail* was bold enough to run a series of stories exposing poor conditions in the country's prison system, a move that drew a harsh government response.[12] This confrontation sent the press a chilling message: that one did not lightly tackle the government on an issue it defined as off limits.

Abroad, the ideology of apartheid, which had never served to win friends and influence governments favorably, was slowly edging onto more agendas of interest groups and governments. Overall, though, the Pretoria administration saw no threats with which it could not cope. Writing in 1969, South African historian C. W. de Kiewiet accurately noted that the Nationalist government was "at the peak of confidence and self-assurance. It faces its critics and opponents with a level eye. It has the income to back bold decisions. It feels that the movement of events throughout the world has been predominantly in its favor and continues to be so. Its supporters, who grow in each election, breathe easily. ... The country is visibly relaxed."[13]

The following decade left that self-confidence badly shaken, to the point that the government itself recognized the need to change the existing order. Growing international sensitivity on human rights issues led to increased antiapartheid pressure from the world community, on issues as specific as the independence of Namibia and as general as South Africa's system of segregation.

In 1969 the World Council of Churches began funding guerrilla groups committed to overthrowing the South African government, and the United Nations instituted a mandatory arms embargo against South Africa following the death of black activist Steve Biko in 1977. Boycotts of sporting and cultural events grew in number and effectiveness.

Regionally, pressures on Pretoria came from the north, with the transformation in 1980 of Rhodesia into the black majority state of Zimbabwe. The transition from white rule in this country brought to South Africa's boundaries the process of African nationalism and independence that began in the 1940s. With the failure of Rhodesian whites to contain the force of black nationalism, South Africa and South African–controlled Namibia stood alone as Africa's white-dominated states. Black and white South Africans, the rest of Africa, and the world community now knew that South Africa was next to do battle over white domination.

The bloody guerrilla war leading to Zimbabwean independence was thus a critical event in shaping the climate of expected, or feared, change to which South Africans, black and white, grew accustomed in the 1970s. Zimbabwe's independence followed that of Mozambique and Angola after the collapse of the Portuguese colonial government in 1974.

Extensive pressures on the white establishment arose domestically, too. Among them were the unrest in Soweto and elsewhere in the country, which began in 1976, the ensuing widespread boycotts of black schools, consumer boycotts, and a dramatic increase in the number of sabotage attacks. Operating clandestinely and capitalizing on massive black discontent within the country, groups like the African National Congress and to a lesser extent the Pan-Africanist Congress encouraged resistance to the government. Business leaders likewise placed pressure on the government, urging the then prime minister (and later president) P. W. Botha to introduce changes designed to ensure political and economic stability.

As part of its cyclical attacks on the press, the government again threatened in 1977 to introduce legislation to curb what it saw as irresponsible journalism. The proposed legislation was withdrawn when the press undertook to set up more effective ways of addressing complaints against the press.[14]

But these pressures from abroad and at home were too serious for the government merely to attack the messenger of the bad tidings. It began making limited accommodations on racial issues, opening the way for a fledgling but fast-growing black trade union movement. Racial integration was permitted in areas where it was previously taboo, such as in certain hotels, theaters, private schools, and sports/athletic teams. The country's economy, chafing under various dysfunctional racial constraints, became more and more integrated.

In 1978 and 1979 the country was racked by the Muldergate scandal.[15] Revelations about improper use of clandestine government funds for domestic and international propaganda purposes ultimately ended several political careers, including that of former prime minister and state president John Vorster. The scandal demonstrated the government's growing sensitivity to its image problems, at home and abroad. Recognizing the importance of how it was portrayed in local and international media, the government spent more than R60 million[16] trying to influence news media, think tanks, and other opinion leaders, by buying or subsidizing existing organizations or establishing new ones. Its accomplishments included starting the *Citizen* newspaper in Johannesburg; its failures included secret attempts to buy a major stake in the now defunct *Washington Star* newspaper in Washington, D.C., and a 50 percent share in UPITN, then the world's second largest distributor of television news.[17]

For whites, the disclosures pointed to an aspect of their government's activities and character of which they were previously unaware. "South Africa has always prided itself on being a country with a clean administration," said Patrick O'Meara, adding that "Afrikaans-speaking South Africans, in particular, believed that their most trusted and

respected leaders were incorruptible and truthful and that the governing process in South Africa was precise and decent."[18]

The failure of Muldergate became a metaphor for the ills of the apartheid policy that spawned it. By 1980, South Africa stood alone in the
world as a country ruled by a racial minority government. In that year,
Philip Frankel, a political scientist, wrote that since the 1976 unrest the
internationalization of South African issues had "assumed a new momentum, ... with the country increasingly portrayed as one of the purer
and more recalcitrant examples of contemporary authoritarianism."[19]

The government's commitment to its apartheid ideology was crumbling fast. Beset by indecision, the government floundered in its inability to offer its supporters a clear vision or direction. Instead, Pretoria
gave the country an ad hoc mix of responses. It offered opposition
voices, especially those outside the parliamentary system, the traditional responses of a deaf ear and a heavy hand. Yet the duration, violence, and extent of dissent throughout the country proved both
embarrassingly difficult to contain and deserving of an explanation to
white supporters.

South Africa was thus primed for visionary and forceful leadership,
which many of the country's business and other white leaders hoped
would come from a reform-talking prime minister. Botha raised expectations with comments such as his much publicized charge to his fellow whites that the times and situation South Africa faced demanded
that they "adapt or die." Quite what sort of adapting Botha had in mind
never became clear, however, judging from his administration's responses in the early 1980s. A key part of the government's strategy was
to demonstrate that it had at least some idea of where it sought to take
the country. This pressure to present some policy initiative led it to introduce a new constitution in 1983. The proposal of this constitution
split the country's whites, the only ones who would be allowed to approve it. In quintessentially apartheid style, the new charter provided
for an executive president and three houses of parliament, one each for
whites, Coloureds, and Asians, yet completely disregarded the political
needs of Africans.

The new system introduced the concept of power sharing to a skit-
tish white electorate and was heralded by some white liberal opponents
of the government as a step in the right direction. Yet the constitution's
utter disregard for the fundamental problem of South African politics—
how to accommodate African aspirations—left other white liberals dis-
mayed at the government's cynicism in proposing such an obviously inadequate response to the country's constitutional needs. Most blacks
viewed the new dispensation with disdain, regarding it as simply a new
way of packaging white control, even though the system may have been

an advancement toward the beginning of a safe and tentative multira-
cialism in South African politics. Paradoxically, far from providing an
incremental improvement in the country's political environment following its adoption, the new constitution instead served as a major
force in causing additional unrest.[20]

In its bid to buy time, the government also invoked the concept of a
"Total Onslaught" against the country, which in turn called for a
"Total Strategy" to combat it.[21] The Total Onslaught concept posited
that South Africa was the target of revolutionary forces operating
within and outside of its borders. The West, the Soviet bloc, and the
Third World were all, according to the Total Onslaught theory, committed to overthrowing the established order in South Africa, by invok-
ing diplomatic, economic, and even military pressure against the
country.

The Total Strategy concept was repudiated by the official opposition
in Parliament and by many English-speaking newspaper editors, clergy,
and other intellectuals as well as Afrikaner dissidents. These critics regarded it as a device intended to divert attention from the need to make
fundamental accommodations in South African politics. They did not
deny the threats facing the established order, such as ANC guerrilla activities being supported by neighboring states. But they saw the threats
to South Africa's stability as emanating from the government's racial
policies and the international hostility they engendered.

From the government's perspective, all possible resources were
needed in responding to the Total Onslaught. The mass media took on
especial importance in this task. "Mass communication [was] seen as
one element in an interacting system of forces, all of which taken together determine the capability of the nation to meet threats to its security."[22] A substantial part of the press refused to accept the Total
Onslaught argument, thus aggravating the already poor relations between them and the government.

Arising from these tensions came the Steyn Commission of enquiry
into the media, whose 1982 report represented an important government attempt to control news and information. As Hachten and Giffard
pointed out, the South African government often appoints a commission of enquiry to pave the way for controversial action.[23] In this instance, the government sought recommendations for action against
what it had long seen as a disloyal and troublesome press. Not surprisingly, the commission handed down the indictment the government
wanted, with the added advantage of soundly endorsing the Total Onslaught theory at the same time. The government appointed the commission in June 1980 to "enquire into and report on the question
whether the conduct of, and the handling of, matters by the mass media

meet the needs and interests of the South African community and the demands of the times, and, if not, how they can be improved."[24] This mandate was later expanded and the commission was also required to propose legislation to implement its recommendations. This commission of enquiry was in fact the second led by a senior judge, Marthinus Steyn. The first dealt with press security matters; its relatively noncontroversial findings were published in April 1980.[25]

The commission's second and far more extensive report found that the performance of the country's media left much to be desired.[26] The faults that the commission laid at the door of the press included many that the government had complained about previously. To remedy what it saw as the press's shortcomings, the commission proposed several controversial steps. One was a plan to professionalize the activities of journalists, partly by establishing a register of licensed journalists comparable, the commission said, to those maintained by the medical and legal professions in South Africa and elsewhere. Another proposal was to establish a press council to watch over journalists and their performance and standards. Unlike the press council functioning at the time, the proposed body would have the force of legislation and newspapers would be compelled to join.

These proposals brought forth a storm of protest. Both progovernment and antigovernment newspapers attacked the recommendations. The press, especially the English papers, also assailed what they saw as a simplistic analysis of the media's role in society. The English papers in particular rejected the commission's view of the times in which South Africa found itself and its view of how the media ought to respond to this situation. The first two-thirds of the report's nearly 1,400 pages were devoted not to the media but to analyzing the political context. The report discussed at great length the phenomena of Soviet global aspirations, black consciousness, and black theology, among others, as part of the Total Onslaught. The report's conclusions resoundingly endorsed government thinking that a "Total Strategy" was the most suitable way of addressing this perceived threat. One example of the commission's thinking was its endorsement of a statement in its previous report:

> It can therefore be said that the security, preservation and welfare of the State, and consequently also the protection thereof, is the "Highest Law," which is accorded precedence when weighed against other rights and interests. If the interests of the State require that the rights of the individual or of certain groups in the community of State, for example the Press, be curtailed, it is consequently recognized that such curtailment must follow.[27]

This readiness to accord such power to the state was challenged by lawyers such as W.H.B. Dean as conflicting with traditional democratic values. The commission's approach lent support to a "fundamentally authoritarian" system of government, Dean wrote.[28]

The commission's report was attacked on various other grounds. Its members were regarded as not being representative of either the media or the public because the commission included no practicing journalists and included only whites.[29] Academics and journalists ridiculed the commission for its flawed methodology and selective use of data, numerous factual inaccuracies, and plagiarism.[30] The report was described elsewhere as "a rambling, self-indulgent piece of writing based on unscientific methodology and spiced with errata."[31]

What of the government's reaction? In his first public reaction to the report, then prime minister P. W. Botha told Parliament: "The Steyn Commission emphasizes with conclusive evidence the full-scale communist-inspired onslaught on the Republic of South Africa."[32] But even though the report supported the government's Total Onslaught thesis, the government did little to act upon its recommendations. Harvey Tyson, former editor of the *Star*, was probably correct when he wrote that the report "went too far, even for the Cabinet, in its bewildering deductions and in its specific recommendations for a communist-style register of journalists and the rest."[33]

The government took one tangible step in response to the commission's recommendations, however. Later in that year's parliamentary session, it introduced the Registration of Newspapers Amendment Act. This bill required all publications registered as newspapers under another law[34] to subject themselves to the discipline of a government-controlled press council. Following protests in the press and urgent consultations between newspaper representatives and the government minister concerned, the bill was toned down. The version passed by Parliament referred to "an independent and voluntary body (none of whose members shall be controlled by the government)."[35]

Curiously, the government announced the following year that it would not promulgate the provisions of the law following the newspaper industry's formation of its own regulatory body, the Media Council, in 1983. The reason, a government spokesman said, was "to give the Newspaper Press Union's media council a chance of 'proving itself.'"[36]

Because of its arising out of the Steyn Commission, the Media Council's birth was steeped in controversy. The dispute surrounding its origin was between those publishers and editors who said, in effect, "While we don't like being forced to establish another, more powerful agency to play watchdog over the media, it is better that we do this rather than have the government come in and do so for us." So the

Newspaper Press Union (NPU) agreed to revise the Press Council, take over its code of conduct, and devise a new body to meet the government's demand for stricter and more punitive measures. Journalists would be included under the new arrangement (and not just editors), which also allowed for greater public participation in the council's work than under the Press Council.

However, according to many journalists and others who regarded the new council with wariness, the NPU's stand appeared to be a sellout to the government. John Allen, representing the South African Society of Journalists (SASJ), one of two journalists' trade unions, listed several concerns. One was the secrecy that had surrounded the planning of the council and the discussions between the NPU and the government, although the NPU insisted it had made no secret deals with the government. A second concern was that the composition of the council was biased "towards managers and editors and the country's white and business establishment." Another was that "the inclusion of an important clause empowering the council to pass judgment on non-subscribing publications was in line with government wishes."[37] These and other concerns led the SASJ and the black union, the Media Workers Association of South Africa, not to take up the positions allocated them on the Council.

Among the objectives the council set for itself were to "uphold and maintain the freedom of the media"; to encourage adherence to the code of conduct; to "consider and adjudicate" possible violations of the code by organizations that had voluntarily placed themselves under the council's jurisdiction; and to encourage adherence to the code by those organizations that were not under its jurisdiction.[38] Only the mainstream press placed itself under the council's authority, thus exempting those papers from control under the Publications Act.

The council's detractors feared that newspapers that submitted to such control were compromising themselves by accepting yet another layer of government control. But the council's subsequent performance rendered these fears largely groundless. It proved to be a valuable avenue for venting and resolving disagreements between the press and members of the public and, especially important, government departments and officials. Having approved the council as the organization for handling disagreements with the media, the government was obligated to work with it. And it appeared that the government, like all parties that sought the council's help, generally received evenhanded treatment. Headed by a succession of distinguished judges, the council established a reputation for credibility and fairness. Overall, the council's performance set aside the fears of those who thought it would be a gutless body doing the government's dirty work. On the contrary, the council frequently irritated the government, which at times wanted it to take more initiative in aggressively pursuing what Pretoria saw as irresponsible press conduct.[39] Critics from the left, inclined to dismiss the council as a vehicle of the white establishment, have increasingly conceded that the council is indeed capable of advancing the interests of all media, including the alternative press. Particularly important has been the council's ability to serve as a mediator between complainants and members of the alternative press. Several of these papers now work with the council on a case-by-case basis yet decline to place themselves formally under the council's jurisdiction.

In the council's first years it has, as former *Cape Times* editor Tony Heard noted in 1986, "done good work and has managed to maintain its dignity and independence."[40] It came through the state of emergency with its reputation intact and, indeed, enhanced as a much-needed organization. It has done well in fulfilling its objective of serving as a mediator in disputes. Less publicly, it has played a crucial role in representing the media in negotiations with the government, a voice that can continue to be valuable as the press needs to establish a working relationship with a postapartheid government in the years ahead.

The Media Council has thus played an important part in South African journalism, despite its having arisen because of the discredited Steyn Commission. Ironically, the council has helped to lessen the impact of the Steyn Commission's emphasis on the Total Onslaught concept. Because of its close working relationship with the government, it has undoubtedly also helped reduce the gap between the massively different understandings of the government-press relationship that have prevailed in South Africa. The Steyn Commission, and those accepting its outlook, endorsed a media system that was subject at best to paternalistic control and at worst to authoritarian control. In the early to mid-1980s many whites accepted a Total Onslaught view of reality. The government's reluctance to act enthusiastically on the commission's recommendations was perhaps more in response to the protests they received and the report's embarrassing shoddiness and superficiality. There is no telling how readily the government might have acted on less heavy-handed suggestions, especially if they had been clothed with greater intellectual respectability.

The disturbing development was that a major government commission advocated an understanding of press freedom so obviously in conflict with the mainstream Western values that the government professed to embrace. Fortunately, enough of an opposition groundswell existed within the country, including among government supporters, to prevent the commission's understanding of the press from gaining greater credence in the society. Despite the years of National Party rule and the accompanying climate of indifference and outright hostility to freedom of expression, a commitment to this value still ran deep in many segments of society.

Total Onslaught thinking faded from prominence in government pronouncements in the second half of the 1980s. But by then President Botha had let the locus of decisionmaking shift from the cabinet to the defense force and the police.[41] In effect, he allowed policy to be dictated by a relatively small group of what came to be known as the "securocrats." One result of this development was the increasing license and lack of accountability given to the police officers and soldiers as they tackled unrest situations. Brutality and an almost cavalier disregard for human rights, long hallmarks of South Africa's style of coping with dissenting views, became commonplace as the unrest spread and particularly when the state of emergency was declared in 1985. In addition to security forces receiving a virtual carte blanche in dealing with dissenters, another result of South Africa's swing toward militarism was the creation of a climate that also encouraged unofficial or quasiofficial violence.

In mid-1989, for example, Amnesty International estimated that sixty-one government opponents and human rights activists had been singled out for assassination in the preceding ten years. In only one of these cases had identification and prosecution of those responsible resulted.[42] Long-standing suspicions that the government operated a death squad to eliminate critics took on substance in 1989, when former police officers and others charged that a special unit had assassinated numerous left-wing government opponents. A judicial commission of enquiry to investigate these claims found no firm evidence of government-sanctioned hit squads.

Official government figures demonstrated other symptoms of a society steeped in violent change, much of it in Natal province between supporters of the African National Congress and those of the Zulu political and cultural organization, Inkatha. A Bureau for Information official announced that some 5,000 people had died in unrest in the second half of the 1980s, all but two of them blacks. He said that in addition, "a total of 25,859 vehicles—11,654 private delivery vehicles, 10,082 ordinary vehicles and 4,123 police vehicles—as well as 8,034 houses, 110 of them the homes of policemen, 1,757 schools and 1,243 shops and factories had been damaged."[43]

The situation in the mid-1980s was markedly different from earlier waves of black protest, as one scholar noted at the time: "It is widespread, deep-seated and gives every sign of continuing indefinitely. It is unlikely to be continuous in any one area, given the strains and costs to the protestors themselves of continuous unrest; rather it is likely to wax and wane, but on a gradually rising plane."[44] Even though the unrest of the 1980s was like a forest fire that refused to be extinguished once and for all, it never threatened to topple the government. The importance of the countless conflicts between blacks and policemen and later the military lay in their wider repercussions. These were the greatly increased political awareness among blacks, and their consequently heightened political expectations; the growing stature of the ANC; the pressure to resolve the conflict that white business and other leaders placed on the government; and intensified international interest in and pressure on South Africa.[45]

Black protest in the 1980s was more successful than in the past, for several reasons. These included perceived vulnerability of the white government; the rise of black trade unions and their capacity to articulate their members' political aspirations; and the formation of groups like the United Democratic Front in 1983 that as part of the Mass Democratic Movement helped to articulate antigovernment opposition outside Parliament. Together, these factors helped mobilize opposition to the government on an unprecedented scale.

The conflict reached such intensity that the government proclaimed the first of a series of states of emergency in 1985. The state of emergency lasted, with a few brief intervals, until 1990. And it was in this period that the South African press underwent its darkest hours. The state of emergency and its impact on the press is discussed in Chapter 6. Although the impact of the emergency has yet to be measured, the government undoubtedly met one of its objectives: keeping as much unrest as possible from domestic and international eyes. How successful it was in restoring order, and at what cost, remain unanswered.

Amidst this sustained turmoil and political upheaval arose the alternative press. It grew because of the weaknesses in the mainstream press and the growing sense among elements in what became known as the extraparliamentary movement that they urgently needed their own media vehicles. The fuller explanation goes deeper and is integrally related to the changes of the 1970s and 1980s.

By the mid-1980s the extraparliamentary movement had enough political power to launch not one but a variety of papers. This growing political strength corresponded to the decline in Pretoria's ability to govern virtually as it pleased, essentially immune to any serious challenge to its power.

Media scholar Don Pinnock described the emergence of the alternative press as the voice of the widespread, grass-roots movement around which the extraparliamentary opposition forces coalesced.[46] As more and more township residents rejected the mainstream media as being out of touch with reality, "increasingly the information which informed their choices and *action* came from elsewhere."[47]

The alternative papers providing this information followed a lengthy tradition of dissenting journalism, which peaked during the 1950s with such publications as the weekly *Guardian* but was banned under this and in several subsequent incarnations. What is different about alternative publications like the *New Nation* and *South* is that they are more like newspapers than magazines. Also, they have for various reasons better withstood government pressures and show greater prospects for survival than their earlier soul mates. The alternative press's resurgence, stemming from this populist protest movement, was initially ad hoc and far removed in sophistication and organization from the newspapers that this chapter examines. Thus, Pinnock described how the growing availability of the plain-paper photocopy machine (unlike its treated-paper predecessor) allowed the protest movement to distribute information relatively cheaply, easily, and rapidly. Two consequences, he said, were "the sudden appearance of cheaply-reproduced facsimiles of books, articles and images" and "the discovery by artful innovators that with access to a typewriter and a photocopier one was in the pamphlet business."[48] The authorities, of course, had no hope of suppressing the ensuing flood of material, which Pinnock argued was critical in shaping a new political consciousness and self-confidence among the extraparliamentary opposition forces. It is noteworthy that except for *Grassroots*, the alternative press emerged during the state of emergency.

The relatively low-level technology of the photocopy machine significantly expanded the flow of information in the society—if not in actual volume compared with the society at large, then certainly in its impact on a crucial population group. But then came another nontraditional technological vehicle that added momentum to the alternative press: the computerized wonder of desktop publishing. As the alternative press grew stronger and more traditional newspaper or magazine formats were embraced, desktop publishing proved to be a godsend. With the new technology, papers like the *Weekly Mail*, which pioneered its application in South Africa, demonstrated that newspaper publishing was now within reach of a far wider range of would-be publishers. The result was that, in the realm of opposition politics, "the actors were becoming authors."[49] By the late 1980s the government and the largely black political opposition groups had reached a stalemate. The government had learned that its security forces could readily contain but not end political protest. Likewise, the opposition groups themselves learned with pride that they could organize extensive school and consumer boycotts, thoroughly discredit government-controlled black town councils, and render many black townships ungovernable. Yet despite delivering a succession of body blows against the government, they never came close to landing a knockout punch. This mutual recognition of their own and the other's strengths and limitations helped goad the government and the ANC toward the negotiating table.

Thus, in late 1989, came the shift that rewrote the rules of South African politics: the resignation of President P. W. Botha and the succession to office of F. W. de Klerk. Within months the de Klerk administration introduced extensive steps toward moving South Africa into the postapartheid era. The government's actions included lifting the bans on the African National Congress and other opposition groups and ending the state of emergency, which included the curbs on the media, freeing political prisoners and granting amnesty to others, and so on. The process of moving toward a postapartheid society then led to formal talks on a new constitution. This step, which included the government, the ANC, and other major groups, began in December 1991.

Other factors of course helped shape the developments from 1989 onward. Also playing a part were issues like the presence and subsequent easing of sanctions, the resolution of the Namibian independence question and a peace accord with Angola, South Africa's ailing economy, the collapse of communism in Eastern Europe and the Soviet Union, and the personalities of Nelson Mandela and F. W. de Klerk. The intent of this chapter is not to offer a comprehensive explanation of these events. It is more to paint the backdrop against which to understand the shape, recent history, and prospects of South Africa's press. That backdrop is of a society marked by various and intensely held ideological perspectives, views contending for dominance as South Africa wrestles with itself to seek a path out of the apartheid era.

THE PRESS

In all of this, the press was both an actor in the unfolding drama and a critic of the play itself. Particularly since 1976, a landmark year in South African history, the press has been shaped by the political, economic, social, and cultural forces buffeting the society. But the press's history is of less concern here than its present shape and the current atmosphere of change that it breathes. Especially important are the questions, What kind of press emerged by the early 1990s, and What might the air be like tomorrow?

Today's press is as extensive, sophisticated, and diverse as that of any comparably sized literate population in the Western world. Wherever permitted, the press tends to perform far more in keeping with the professional, production, and commercial standards of the West rather than of Third World nations. The country's mainstream papers and magazines are well financed and all the major publications are intended to be run as profitable ventures. In common with the press in the United States and elsewhere, they depend on a highly sophisticated capitalist economy for the major slice of a media advertising pie that in 1987 constituted an estimated R1,797 million—or about 1.66 percent of the country's total gross national product.[50] Comparable figures for other countries are 2.08 percent for the United States, 1.83 percent for both Australia and the United Kingdom, and 1.27 for Canada.[51]

South Africa was a relatively early adopter of computerized technology in the newsroom, and the alternative press in particular has enthusiastically embraced the wonders of desktop publishing. Front-page color photographs are common in the major dailies and Sunday papers. A national press agency, the South African Press Association (SAPA), operates on an extensive scale, transmitting some 100,000 words daily and serving scores of newspapers and other publications.

In addition to the impact of language and ethnic differences on the press, the considerable distances between the country's few major centers make geography another contributor to the media's fragmentation. As in the United States, which largely because of its size and geographical diversity lacks a national daily press in the British or European sense, in South Africa television, not the press, has become the main nationwide medium. In South Africa, even television does not reach a truly national audience, however, because the government-run service is split into separate channels for blacks and whites.

Hachten noted that the country's "press system seems to have been defined by apartheid and newspapers' circulations seem to follow rather than transcend the chasms erected by apartheid."[52] But it is more accurate to see the divisions in the press as corresponding to the three main newspaper markets: English, Afrikaans, and black. The existence of these readerships, rather than apartheid per se, is the determining factor underlying the division of the South African press.

The country currently has nineteen dailies, fourteen in English and five in Afrikaans. Their total circulation is some 1.3 million. Four-fifths of this amount is contributed by the English papers. Seven dailies are in the Johannesburg-Pretoria area, the two cities dominating the country's most populous region. The dailies are listed in Table 2.1. The largest of these dailies is the *Sowetan*, in Johannesburg, with a circulation of 208,591. The largest Afrikaans daily is *Beeld*, also in Johannesburg, with a circulation of 99,583.

The eight Sunday and other weekly papers typically have much larger readerships. The largest of these is the *Sunday Times* (circulation: 521,315). The total circulation for these papers is 1.4 million, with

TABLE 2.1   Circulation of Daily Newspapers

	City	Language	Ownership	Circulation
The Argus	Cape Town	English	Argus	100,137
Beeld	Johannesburg	Afrikaans	Nasionale Media	99,583
Die Burger	Cape Town	Afrikaans	Nasionale Media	72,619
Business Day	Johannesburg	English	TML	32,500
Cape Times	Cape Town	English	TML	59,030
The Citizen	Johannesburg	English	Perskor	133,601
Daily Dispatch	East London	English	independent	33,581
Daily News	Durban	English	Argus	92,544
Diamond Fields Advertiser	Kimberley	English	Argus	7,779
Eastern Province Herald	Port Elizabeth	English	TML	27,906
Evening Post	Port Elizabeth	English	TML	19,633
The Natal Mercury	Durban	English	Argus	60,063
The Natal Witness	Pietermaritzburg	English	independent	27,609
Die Oosterlig	Port Elizabeth	Afrikaans	Nasionale Media	8,846
Pretoria News	Pretoria	Afrikaans	Argus	24,299
Sowetan	Johannesburg	English	Argus	208,591
The Star	Johannesburg	English	Argus	204,347
Die Transvaler	Johannesburg	Afrikaans	Perskor	42,703
Die Volksblad	Bloemfontein	Afrikaans	Nasionale Media	26,309

Note: Saturday editions, which are treated separately in ABC reports, are not included.
Total circulation = 1,281,610
Source: Audited ABC circulation data for July to December 1991.

an average of 177,698. These papers are also divided into English- and Afrikaans-medium.[53] Five other weeklies, not published on Sundays, include two in black languages: *Ilanga,* in Zulu (circulation: 120,676), and *Imvo Zabantsundu,* in Xhosa (circulation: 34,533). The Sunday and other weekly papers are listed in Table 2.2.

No daily papers are published in a black language. However, the only daily addressing a black readership, the English-language *Sowetan,* has experienced dramatic growth in recent years, to the extent that in 1991 it displaced the *Star* as the largest-circulation daily in the country. By the end of 1991, its circulation stood at 208,591, up sharply from 111,306 in 1985.

All this is to assess the press in terms of its readership. The papers can also be categorized according to the political or philosophical bases from which they operate. One can thus refer to papers operating in the tradition of English liberal opposition to the government or one can refer to Afrikaans papers that have typically supported government policy, often a step ahead of the party leadership but never breaking rank with it. The English papers, with the exception of the progovernment *Citizen,* have a lengthy and often distinguished record of opposing apartheid and abuses perpetrated under the policy. Indeed, the role of the English papers attained such importance that media scholar Elaine

TABLE 2.2   Circulation of Weekly Newspapers

	City	Language	Ownership	Circulation
City Press	Johannesburg	English	Nasionale Media	134,389
Ilanga	Durban	Zulu	independent	120,676
Imvo Zabantsundu	King Williams Town	Xhosa	Perskor	34,533
Post Natal	Durban	English	Argus	48,141
Rapport	Johannesburg	Afrikaans	Nasionale Media & Perskor	355,675
Sunday Star	Johannesburg	English	Argus	83,975
Sunday Times	Johannesburg	English	TML	521,315
Sunday Tribune	Durban	English	Argus	122,880

Note: Alternative papers are listed separately in Table 3.1.
Total circulation = 1,421,584

Source: Audited ABC circulation data for July to December 1991.

Potter argued persuasively that it had in reality become the main opposition voice in the country, displacing an ineffective official opposition in Parliament.[54]

The Afrikaans papers, by contrast, have never pretended to be anything but a party press to promote the cultural and political interests of Afrikanerdom. As such, these papers have been integrally linked to the development of the National Party's policies, both before and after the party attained power in 1948. A former editor of the oldest Afrikaans paper, *Die Burger,* once described the relationship between his paper and the government "as a sort of marriage, in which the partners never really think in terms of divorce, but do think, sometimes, in terms of murder."[55]

In earlier times, the Afrikaans press was tightly controlled by the party and carefully followed the party line. James McClurg, a journalist who has long written on the Afrikaans press, said that in the past "one would have searched the columns of Nationalist newspapers in vain for the mildest dissenting opinion or for news that could embarrass the party."[56] He noted that the first signs of dissent were heard in 1959 and that over the past three decades the Afrikaans papers have considerably expanded the limits to their freedom.[57]

In the early 1980s a major split arose in Afrikaner ranks, with hardliners correctly fearing that the government was abandoning orthodox apartheid ideology. This division led to the formation of the Conservative Party, which displaced the Progressive Federal Party as the official opposition in Parliament in 1987. All the Afrikaans papers remained progovernment, however, and right-wing Afrikaners failed to launch a daily or other major paper despite attempts to do so.

The English and Afrikaans papers, or the "mainstream" press, have received close attention over the years, and more detailed accounts of their history and contribution are available elsewhere.[58] This is not the case with the alternative press. The papers composing this group are typically more sharply critical of the government and can be divided into either a "progressive-alternative" or "social democrat independent" press, according to P. Eric Louw.[59] Some in the alternative press tend to regard the English and Afrikaans papers as members of the same, establishment-supporting camp. The differences between them, it is argued, are superficial. The alternative papers therefore play a critical role by providing news and analysis from a political worldview distinctively different from that of the mainstream press.

Finally, in addition to these Afrikaans, English, and alternative papers that compose the larger daily and weekly urban newspapers discussed in this book, the country also has more than a hundred papers that make up the suburban or provincial press. Produced in the suburbs of large metropolitan areas or in small towns around the country, these papers are typically directed at white (and sometimes Coloured and Asian) readerships. Mostly weeklies, many of these papers are bilingual and typically avoid covering national politics. The suburban papers in particular have become an important economic influence, a point discussed elsewhere.

Other media include an extensive consumer magazine industry, which also avoids political issues. Twenty or so of these publications have circulations in excess of 100,000. Hundreds of other magazines and journals cater to professional, trade, and special-interest groups. Here too political issues are largely ignored or are irrelevant to the publications concerned.

Television and radio services are controlled by the government-run South African Broadcasting Corporation (SABC).[60] A few radio stations in countries or the quasi-independent homelands adjoining South Africa broadcast popular music to the country's major urban centers but these are the exception to the general pattern. The country has two bilingual TV channels for whites, one started in 1976 and the other in 1985. A similar single-channel service for blacks began in January 1982 and a year later split into two channels—one broadcasting in two black languages, the other in three. The white and black services are all national. The country has both national and regional radio services. The SABC transmits domestic programs in nineteen languages. The corporation's external service, Radio South Africa, was founded in 1966 and until recently broadcast in eleven languages to Europe, Africa, the Middle East, Latin America, and North America.[61]

Various writers have referred to the SABC's role as a political mouthpiece for the government. Hachten, for example, said, "Television is used as a propaganda instrument to espouse the political goals and aspirations of Afrikanerism. The government, meaning the National Party, keeps a firm hand on news and public affairs reporting, avoiding what it considers the distortions of the English-language press. Views opposing the government are largely ignored."[62]

Unlike the suburban or provincial press, the country's broadcast services do not shy away from politics. On the contrary, they make a vital, if ill-defined, contribution to the country's political process, at least among whites. In the second half of the 1980s, perhaps embarrassed over criticism of its unabashedly progovernment coverage, the SABC began to soften its bias. Gavin Stewart found in the 1987 election, for example, that SATV's political news gave time to a spread of political views. But there was a catch: Coverage was determined by what constituted "acceptable" political views. The acceptable political spectrum ranged from conservative white groups like the Conservative Party on the right to the Progressive Federal Party on the left.

Stewart's study found that even though views of white opposition groups were granted somewhat balanced treatment, "anything outside those limits is 'political extremism.' The political 'centre' is the National Party."[63] The election was strongly opposed by many blacks, and others, because blacks had no say in its outcome. Yet Stewart said that "none of the political organisations opposed to the elections was given any broadcast time at all. These include the United Democratic Front (UDF), probably the largest political grouping in the country, the Azanian Peoples' Organisation (Azapo) and others."[64] Content analysis suggested that the SABC fully adopted the National Party definition of political life in South Africa and that "The SABC does not question the existing political arrangements in South Africa."[65] The 1989 election similarly showed SATV's readiness to reflect various political views—but again only if they fitted into government-defined limits of "acceptable" positions.

These findings should have come as no surprise. As early as 1984, the former director general of the SABC, Adriaan Eksteen, outlined the corporation's policy on defining political reality: "Those groups and parties that, of their own choice, have either excluded themselves from the politics of consensus, or who intend to do so in favour of revolutionary and undemocratic methods, can make no claim on the SABC to reflect their views in any way."[66]

The SABC, despite its increased ideological flexibility, therefore remains an important tool of the Nationalist government as it seeks to direct political change in the 1990s. The result is that the mainstream and alternative press remain the single most important nongovernment media vehicles for recording, critiquing, and shaping political developments.[67]

What, then, are the distinctive features of South Africa's press? Ken Owen, editor of the *Sunday Times,* correctly identified the "fundamental problems" of the press as control and credibility.[68] Both of these factors are at the heart of the press's transformation into its postapartheid format. How these issues are addressed in the 1990s, by design and by default, will fundamentally reshape South Africa's papers and what they bring to their society. For now, the following five qualities are worth noting.

White Domination

South Africa's press accurately reflects the country's single most important political and economic reality: white dominance. The ownership, management, and editorial control of virtually all of South Africa's mainstream press is in white hands. Even the nation's only black daily, the *Sowetan,* is owned by the white-controlled Argus Company.

In the past decade, newspapers that more authentically represent black views have arisen in the form of the alternative press. The circulation and readership of these alternative papers are small, certainly when measured against the mainstream press. Their impact on the country and their capacity to influence thinking must necessarily be limited.

Willem de Klerk, now a communications professor and formerly editor of *Die Transvaler* and *Rapport,* correctly noted that little, if any, significant research has been done on the influence that South Africa's newspapers have on the political process.[69] Given the dominance of white control and ownership in the mainstream press, (by far the most powerful and influential papers), whatever influence the press has is filtered through predominantly white values, reflects white worldviews, and seeks to further white interests. A similar dominance of white perspectives underlies broadcasting, which is controlled from one particular white viewpoint—the government's.

By itself, this "whitening" of the country's mainstream press need not be bad. The difficulty, as with so much else in South African history, is that this white-controlled media platform has for all practical purposes stood alone. No comparably authoritative or influential press capable of articulating black views and aspirations has emerged. In part this is because of economic difficulties and government suppression of dissenting views.

But in the absence of a vibrant black press, the question arises, Could and would an institution dominated by whites fill the gap by catering to Coloured, Asian, and especially African interests? Obviously, one could not expect that from the Afrikaans press, whose raison d'être was the cause of white nationalism. That left the English press to carry out the task. How well did it do? That issue is addressed below. Regardless of its actual performance, however, the white domination of the English press hardly improved its chances of enthusiastic acceptance by blacks in a society suffused with racism. Moreover, if white ownership and control was one strike against the English press's credibility, another was the character of that ownership.

Monopoly

South Africa's papers are in effect controlled by four newspaper groups. The Argus Printing and Publishing Company and Times Media Limited (TML; formerly South African Associated Newspapers, or SAAN) dominate the English press. As will soon be demonstrated, however, Argus towers over the much smaller TML group. Nasionale Pers[70] dominates the Afrikaans press to the extent that its chief opposition, Perskor, is almost a token competitor. Only two dailies are independently owned, the *Daily Dispatch* and the *Natal Witness*, in the smaller cities of East London and Pietermaritzburg respectively. In reality, therefore, the South African press is dominated by only two companies: Argus and Nasionale Pers.

The South African press is far more frequently compared to the newspapers of the Western world rather than those of Africa or the Third World, and for good reason. Its history, values, and standards are all derived from Western Europe and, more recently, the United States. But the concentration of newspaper ownership in South Africa is extraordinarily high compared with that of other Western countries.[71] The purely economic dangers that arise in a minimally competitive environment are significant enough. In addition, the ownership structure of newspapers could itself constitute a threat to the free flow of information.[72] Virtually no papers of the same language face direct competition in the same time slot in the same city. In other words, no English or Afrikaans daily, whether distributed in the morning or the afternoon, faces direct competition on its own turf.[73]

The control of the four main groups is overwhelming. As can be deduced from Table 2.1, their papers account for 95.2 percent of daily circulation, with the Argus group alone controlling 54 percent.[74] In 1991 the independently owned *Daily Dispatch* and the *Natal Witness* controlled 4.8 percent of the circulation between them.

Recent history has witnessed some fierce competition between the two Afrikaans groups. By contrast, Argus and TML have traditionally had a cozy, cooperative arrangement, functioning in effect as a cartel.

Certainly occasional flurries of intense competition between them have erupted. One, described in Chapter 4, was the Argus group's successful raid on the *Sunday Express*'s lucrative property advertising that led to the paper's death. For the most part, though, the relationship between Argus and TML (and previously SAAN) resembled that of a family.

Referring to the English papers in the period leading up to the cost-cutting crunch that came in the 1980s, Owen offered a brutally incisive assessment of this chumminess between the two companies and its consequences.

> Competition is not the usual condition of the English newspapers whose publishers have operated for more than a generation in a neatly divided market which gave each company a genteel living. Challenges from outside were rare and, except for the State-backed special case of *The Citizen*, easily absorbed or contained.
>
> For most of the time since the Second World War, the English part of the newspaper industry has operated a cartel in which managements cooperated in pursuing joint interests. ...
>
> The symptoms of a cartel are those of monopoly: complacency, exploitation, inability to innovate or adapt, a gradual decline in standards, and in the end a vulnerability to more vigorous challengers. All of these were discernible, to a greater or lesser degree, in the comfortable milieu in which English journalism languished from the early Fifties until, perhaps, the late Seventies. At the end of this period, the industry was comfortable but the profession of journalism was close to ruin.[75]

The chief reason for this cartel arising in the first place is simple: ownership. Several analysts of the English press have reported the complex web of shareholdings that lie behind Argus and TML.[76] The simple explanation is that the large mining houses that constitute some of the country's largest corporations hold the controlling interests in each group. Journalist Paul Bell described their "common parent" as the massive Anglo American Corporation, and their "common guardian" as Johannesburg Consolidated Investments (JCI), nearly 50 percent of whose stock is owned by Anglo. Anglo has a controlling 50.94 percent interest in Argus and a 61.78 share in TML. The Argus Company, in turn, owns 40 percent of the stock in TML.[77]

This ownership pattern has long been a sore point with Afrikaners and, since 1948, the Nationalist government. Bell said that "to say that Anglo and JCI are sensitive about these holdings is an industry cliche, and an understatement. They have been attacked as monopolists by, at different times, government, journalists, and critics of the corporations."[78] Scholars approaching the press from a structuralist perspective are equally critical.[79] In describing how they see the media as supporting apartheid society, Keyan and Ruth Tomaselli, for instance, said: "Considering the composition of the holding companies and the directors who serve them, it is not surprising that the English-language press is closely associated with the aims, objectives and interests of the hegemonic bloc as a whole."[80]

Under these circumstances then, how can one understand those relatively few examples of head-to-head competition that occur between the two English newspaper groups? It is almost as if a parent watching over two children arguing decides to intervene only when they might harm each other. As Bell put it, "When those subsidiaries begin to fight among themselves to the extent that it threatens what Anglo and JCI consider the strategic interests of the industry, as happened in the early to mid-1980s, they step in and say: 'Enough.'"[81] Such obviously monopolistic elements in South African press ownership raise other issues: What implications does the ownership have for editorial independence, especially on the English papers? And what, in turn, are the implications for press credibility generally?

Credibility

If any segment of South Africa's press ought to deserve widespread credibility, it is the English papers. These papers are supposedly steeped in the British and U.S. models of objective, dispassionate journalism. According to the objectivity model, these papers ought to command a wide range of respect from across the political and social spectrum, assuming their reporting is fair, balanced, and complete. In theory, such reporting should ensure these papers high credibility ratings, even among groups holding divergent views.

In addition, the English papers enjoy an extraordinary degree of editorial independence. This is so despite the automatic correlation that many critics make that the mining houses significantly shape the papers' editorial content. One after the other, English newspaper editors have refuted this claim. With rare exceptions, editors are given free rein in controlling the content of their papers. Indeed, this autonomy greatly exceeds that of most U.S. editors, for example, who are likely to be much more subject to their publishers than English editors in South Africa are to their superiors. Owen, for example, said that being an English editor in South Africa is like being a ship's captain: He is totally in charge of the vessel and the only sanction his superiors have is to fire him.[82] And Gerald Shaw, a senior editor on the *Cape Times*, underscored this point in refuting critics' claims that business interests set the agenda for the English press. Not so, he said, adding that these

claims disregard the strength of a tradition that accords English editors
an exceptional level of editorial independence.[83]

Yet despite the traditions of objective reporting that the English press
claims to have espoused, coupled with a high level of editorial autonomy, these papers have serious credibility problems among many South
Africans. Even among their traditional constituents these papers' credibility has dropped.[84] More important here, however, is that the South
African press is inherently incapable of attaining an across-the-board
acceptance among politically diverse readers.

Regardless of their protestations about editorial autonomy, any English editor knows that each issue of his paper leaves the printing press
with two constituencies already wary of its contents. Whether from the
government on one hand or structuralist critics on the other, the link
between ownership and editorial control in the English press is readily
assumed. For many, merely to point to the "mining barons" who own
these papers automatically renders the editorial product suspect.

Until relatively recently, the government and the Afrikaans press
traditionally regarded the English papers with a mix of wariness, anger,
or outright hostility. Until the 1980s, when something of a rapprochement occurred between the Afrikaans and the English press, the mutually antagonistic relationship between the Afrikaner establishment and
the English press was a perennial feature of South African life. The government's distrust and dislike of the English papers have deep roots and
form "part and parcel" of South African history, according to Ton
Vosloo, now managing director of Nasionale Pers. These attitudes, he
wrote, go "back to the British mine lords who in the last quarter of the
previous century erected and maintained a press to promote a political
ideal—namely, to capture the independent Transvaal republic with its
gold for the British Empire. This they succeeded in doing, thereby giving Afrikaans nationalism its greatest impetus."[85]

Over the years, the government has seen the English press as a consistently hostile voice. When the Nationalist government came to
power in 1948, the decades of resentment between these two forces in
South African political life took on new dimensions, with the papers
becoming a highly partisan media opposition. The always strained and
often venomous relationship between them became a focal point for
much of the writing on the South African press.

In the course of this acrimonious relationship, the government has
repeatedly accused the English press of being disloyal, an irresponsible
abuser of its freedom, and so partisan that it long ago forfeited its authority and credibility. In addition, government representatives as well
as more detached critics say these papers are steeped in negativism and
so preoccupied with their opposition role that instead of serving a con-

structive critical role they play the part of a spoiler. Writing in the early 1970s, journalism professor Trevor Brown referred to this negativism when he said of the English press that it has been less inclined "to watch over government than to catch out the Nationalist Government."[86]

And writing at about the same time, Hennie Serfontein, an Afrikaans reporter who covered politics for the *Sunday Times*, expressed a similar view. Serfontein attacked English papers like his own for not being willing to criticize each other. Although the English press delighted in faulting their Afrikaans counterparts for constituting what they saw as a "servile party press," they in turn offered little other than a knee-jerk response of negativism in their coverage of government. The result: "Excepting the *Rand Daily Mail* that represented particular political ideologies," Serfontein wrote, "the overall impression is one of uninteresting, drab uniformity and almost deadly predictability of what the English press's view of a specific issue would be." Then he added:

> Whereas Afrikaans newspapers practically overturned their community from head to foot in merciless self-examination, even though they were supposedly party-bound, it is a shameful indictment against the English press that while claiming to be so "free" it did not take the lead in initiating a similar process among English-speaking people. ...
>
> If the English press had been less automatically anti-National, had remained critical and from time to time had rejected the views of opposition parties, then more notice would have been taken of its opinions.[87]

More recently, de Klerk also faulted the English papers for their negativism,[88] and even English journalists have faulted their own papers' failure to criticize rigorously the political parties they support.[89] Nevertheless, whatever the English press's flaws, only the most churlish critics would deny that these papers are in many respects accurate and authoritative chroniclers of South African life. In addition, English papers have long railed against government abuses and championed the cause of press freedom, the rule of law, and other civil liberties. For many Afrikaners, though, the English press is marked by fundamental character flaws—regardless of the virtues it brings to the South African political stage. The country's political matrix, therefore, has meant that far from the English press being able to win the respect of the Afrikaans community, these papers are instead seen as inherently untrustworthy and devoid of credibility.

Another significant group of South Africans is equally unenthusiastic about embracing the English press. Their views are incorporated in the dramatically different structuralist perspective and are forcefully

stated by writers like Howard Barrell; Jo-Anne Collinge, Herbert
Mabuza, Glenn Moss, and David Niddrie; Rob Davies, Dan O'Meara,
and Sipho Dlamini; Julie Frederikse; P. Eric Louw; and Keyan and Ruth
Tomaselli and Johan Muller.[90] Far from seeing the English press as challenging the government and apartheid society, these scholars see the
English press as supporters of the status quo. The English press, owned
as it is by the large mining houses that embody the forces of capitalism
in South Africa, cannot but reflect its owners' interests and views. And
those interests coincide markedly with those of South Africa's dominant ideology. A more accurate analysis of South Africa's press, they argue, is not to see the main division as lying between the English and
Afrikaans papers, as liberal scholars have long done, but "between the
so-called commercial press on the one hand—owned and controlled by
capitalist and allied interests—and, on the other hand, a range of progressive publications currently produced by community organisations,
the labour movement and student groups, as well as clandestine publications of the national liberation movement."[91]

Louw argued that despite their apparent conflicts, the English and
Afrikaans papers' common interests in preserving white interests is far
more significant. The differences between these papers, he said, are in
fact superficial.

> Both are owned and largely staffed by elements of the same (White) ruling
> elite. Both clearly paint a picture of the world that reflects the interests of
> the various White ruling elite "class fractions." Hence both (1) justify the
> status quo (though in marginally different terms in the English and Afri-
> kaans newspapers) to the White readership, and (2) both serve to exclude
> alternative perspectives (that is to say perspectives fundamentally at
> odds with those held by the ruling class). This latter point is important in
> terms of serving to keep the subordinate classes disorganised.[92]

Because of their ownership and consequent ideological bias, the English papers are riddled with major shortcomings, according to the
structuralists. Stated briefly, the main charges are that these papers present a biased and distorted view of reality that reflects only a highly selective and inadequate view of South African society. Some
structuralists concede that the English press has at times made notable
contributions in opposing apartheid or fighting for press freedom. Overall, though, these papers' contribution is seen as minimal or peripheral
at best and dangerously illusory at worst.

Frederikse encapsulated the concerns of millions of South Africans
when she said that "the majority of anti-apartheid activists define the
terrain of resistance politics as extra-parliamentary, and see both the

PFP [the Progressive Federal Party, which was the previous official white opposition in Parliament] and the liberal press as a token opposition, intextricably and unacceptably bound to the state."[93]

The result is that millions of government opponents who never saw the Afrikaans press as a credible voice in the first place have now also rejected the English press as a trustworthy and authoritative medium. This statement is of course a generalization. Some English papers, like the *Cape Times*, the *Star*, and the now defunct *Rand Daily Mail*, have traditionally had higher levels of credibility among government opponents than other publications. But even these papers have been accused of hypocrisy, preaching against apartheid while being steeped in racist values themselves. Ameen Akhalwaya, a former *Rand Daily Mail* staffer who now edits an alternative paper, said one reason the alternative press developed is that "black journalists were thoroughly disenchanted with apartheid in the newsrooms, even at newspapers which espoused a nonracial society."[94] Describing how he and other black journalists were treated, he said of his experience on the *Mail* that whites on this and other papers were "as racist as the racists they claim publicly to oppose."[95]

For these and other reasons, journalists like Akhalwaya joined the Afrikaans establishment—although for fundamentally different reasons—in rejecting the English press's credibility. Herein lies one of the vital realities of South African newspapers: Its journalism is composed of several mutually distrusting and apparently incompatible factions. No segment of the country's press can claim across-the-board credibility in the society.

Fracture

Perhaps in no way is South Africa's press more typical of its society than in the divisions and rifts that mark the papers themselves, the journalists who produce them, and the styles of journalism they embrace. This chapter has demonstrated the gaps between the English and Afrikaans press and between the mainstream and alternative press. It has also shown how the racial and language differences that mark the larger society are mirrored in the newspapers' target readerships.

The divisions in the press run deeper still. In the English press, for example, the gap between management and journalists is sizable and often bitter. Although differences arise from a natural tension between the two groups, a long history of mutual mistrust and antagonism between them has reinforced what has become a pattern of poor management-staff relations on many English papers. In times of heightened pressure, whether from threats of government crackdown or the state of emergency in the second half of the 1980s, or from intense economic pressures, the rift between these two groups invariably widens.

In numerous other areas the press reveals its fractured character. The training and educational options that equip aspirant journalists for a career vary widely in content, quality, and ideological orientation. No single model prevails. Similarly, the industry is split when it comes to organizations reflecting journalists' interests. The oldest and largest is the South African Society of Journalists (SASJ), which represents many journalists from the mainstream press. The Media Workers Association of South Africa (MWASA), founded in 1980, is a black union that also represents many nonjournalists in media positions. The most recent union is the Association of Democratic Journalists (ADJ). Launched nationally in 1989, ADJ draws its membership mainly from the alternative press. Few Afrikaans journalists belong to a union.

A similar split exists at the management level, although this has recently narrowed. Initially, only those in the mainstream press were members of the Newspaper Press Union, which the alternative press tended to view warily as a conservative, pro-owners industry group, but several of these latter papers subsequently joined the NPU.

Plainly, South Africa's press is far from a cohesive, coherent institution. At one level after the other, divisions exist. As South Africa moves into the 1990s, some of these divisions will decline in importance and others will undoubtedly arise. So it is the reshaping of the press, and its place in the society, that deserve attention.

Refining Its Identity

More so than at any other time in its history, South Africa's press is poised for change. As the country agonizes through the labor pains of a new society being born, so too the press is marked by unprecedented malleability. All in the press acknowledge that it is sure to undergo significant reshaping as South Africa's new political order emerges. Not only the political climate, however, provides the impetus for change. As ensuing chapters indicate, economic forces, changing life-styles, and differing demographic constraints are also requiring newspaper managers and editors to rethink the fundamentals of what they have done until now.

All groups of papers are sure only of the reality that their part in a postapartheid South Africa will differ from that which they have played in the past. The traditional opposition role of the English press, for instance, has already softened and to an extent been eclipsed by the alternative papers. What part will these English papers play in the future? And what of the Afrikaans press, long the vehicle for an Afrikaner nationalism that has now conceded the need to share power with a black majority? How much will these papers wane in influence as the country's proportion of Afrikaans speakers continues to shrink in the face of rapid black population growth? And will the alternative press become an establishment voice in a new South Africa or retain its present role as a government critic? Or, what is perhaps more likely, will individual alternative papers embrace a range of different functions and roles in the future?

Whatever the answers to these questions, they underscore the fluidity of the press. Part of the answer lies in the nature of a postapartheid South Africa and the climate it will offer journalism. Equally important, though, is the state of the press today. What in its recent experience speaks directly to the shape it may take tomorrow? The answer is "plenty."

3

The Alternative Press

T HE PROTAGONISTS and practitioners of the alternative press[1] regarded it as the most vibrant, influential, and heartening development in South Africa's media in the 1980s. Its detractors, most notably the government, took a different view.

In word and deed, the government subjected the alternative press to a vitriolic verbal onslaught, in Parliament and out. It used an extensive array of legal and administrative measures to threaten, silence, intimidate, and impoverish these publications—just short of closing them permanently.

What was it about these papers that evoked among their editors and journalists a level of passion, commitment, and purpose that once may have marked the English press but no longer does? And what evoked the kind of government wrath that was once reserved for the English press? Other questions also command attention. What, exactly, *was* the alternative press, and what brought it about? How did it differ from the mainstream press? What were its objectives? And, especially important, what was its contribution to the South African media mix, and how might that change in the future?

The alternative papers rapidly attained an influence greater than their limited size and circulation suggested. These papers mirrored and paralleled the major changes occurring in South Africa. At this level they illuminated shifts in South African society because these papers, like any other politically motivated publications, both reflected and shaped their constituencies' views. The alternatives also merit scrutiny because they provided an early indication of what an important part of tomorrow's press might look like. This is not to suggest that the alternative papers will necessarily displace their mainstream counterparts in such a society. Rather, it is to argue that they became a permanent

46

and significant feature of South Africa's press and are likely to become more important in the future.

The alternative papers analyzed here were in a sense the news vehicles of a much larger, highly diverse, and ever-changing set of publications. Of interest to us are the papers listed in Table 3.1.

These papers were only a small fraction of the overall alternative press, yet they were vitally important because of their wide distribution, high frequency of publication, and relatively large circulations and because they were among the most professionally produced alternative publications. They are highlighted here because they were both the newspaper component and flagship papers of the alternative press.

The *Weekly Mail* and the *Vrye Weekblad*, both based in Johannesburg, were unusual in that both were directed primarily at whites. Both weeklies, these papers were written for liberal, affluent readerships. Started in 1985, the *Mail* came to be regarded as the most professionally produced paper and consequently was highly respected as the premier alternative press—both within its ranks and by the mainstream press. The *Vrye Weekblad* was the only Afrikaans alternative newspaper and was produced primarily by Afrikaners. Each paper dealt with national political and social issues. Both were nationally distributed.

Two other Johannesburg-based papers were the *Indicator* (biweekly) and the *New Nation* (weekly). The former was located in an Indian residential area and concentrated on political coverage of interest to that community but also examined issues pertinent to the broader black community. The *New Nation* was more African oriented and openly allied itself with the African National Congress. This paper concentrated on coverage of labor issues, ANC and other opposition activities, and national politics generally.

South, another weekly, was based in Cape Town and was read mainly by Africans and Coloureds. Like its counterparts, *South* also emphasized extraparliamentary politics. Its tone was less somber and grim than that of *New Nation* and contained more popular material. In Durban, *New African* catered to a black and Indian readership. *Grassroots*, in Cape Town, did not fit into the same category as these other papers because it was more concerned with local community issues than national ones. *Grassroots* was the first of the alternative publications listed here and represented the populist, committee-oriented approach to writing and editing a publication in its purist form.[2]

Similar in its populist control was *Saamstaan*, a monthly published in the small, conservative, and intensely inhospitable town of Oudtshoorn. Published in Afrikaans, English, and Xhosa, *Saamstaan* faced perhaps more hostility than any other alternative paper. The paper and its staff were in constant trouble with the police. The barrage of harass-

TABLE 3.1   Circulation of Alternative Newspapers

	Place of Publication	Frequency	Circulation
The Indicator	Johannesburg	biweekly	27,000
New African	Johannesburg	biweekly	7,000
New Nation	Durban	weekly	80,862*
South	Cape Town	weekly	20,000
Vrye Weekblad	Johannesburg	weekly	10,000
Weekly Mail	Johannesburg	weekly	23,955*

Source: Asterisked circulations are based on audited ABC circulation data for July to December 1991. Other figures are publishers' estimates.

ment the paper experienced included death threats and three arson attacks on the newsroom (once with a reporter present). The paper had no formal owner but was run by a committee of local African and Coloured leaders.[3]

These papers were only a fraction of a much longer list. Writing in 1987, former *Cape Times* editor Anthony Heard said there were "200 or more" alternative papers.[4] But given the fluid character of this sector of the press, that number was constantly changing. Nor is an exact number really important. Far more significant is their character and their impact. Regarding their diversity, Leila Patel said: "These publications are aimed at different audiences, fulfilling different roles and meeting different needs. Some are literary and cultural; others theoretical and analytical; there is the student press, the community press, trade union newsletters and more recently, publications of political organizations."[5]

In addition to the newspapers examined here, well-known alternative publications included the journal *Work in Progress*, the literary magazine *Staffrider*, and the student publication *Saspu National*. These and scores of other publications are beyond this study's emphasis on newspapers. Yet they shared crucial features with the alternative newspapers that distinguished this press as a whole from other South African newspapers and magazines. Before these distinguishing characteristics are examined, however, some thoughts on the term "alternative" are in order.

A PROBLEM OF DEFINITION

The label "alternative" itself presents several problems. One was that several editors to whom it applied found it inaccurate or misleading. *Weekly Mail*'s coeditor Anton Harber, for instance, noted two difficulties. One was that "it suggests that we're fringe,"[6] an implication that several editors justifiably challenged. Compared with the press of Western Europe, for example, the alternative papers could hardly be regarded as peripheral and their editors correctly rejected the implication that they presented a minority or eccentric view in the overall spread of South African political opinion. This leads to another problem Harber had with the term: "It's a phrase used by the state to isolate us."[7] Judging from the government's tendency in the late 1980s to single out alternative papers for attack, grouping them together as witting or unwitting collaborators with the ANC,[8] Harber's fear was well founded. The negative connotations with which the government, in particular, colored the term is another reason to question its usefulness.

A further problem is that the term "alternative" suggested that these papers were somehow an exception or a deviation from the norm. That in turn raises the question, To what kind of press or style of journalism did these papers present an alternative? Without exception, editors of the alternative papers were in varying degrees critical of the mainstream press. For them, the very existence of their papers was an indictment against the mainstream press; if the latter group had been covering events as they should, the gaps that the alternative papers sought to fill would not have existed. The "alternative" label implies that these papers did not provide "standard" or "normal" journalism and that the mainstream press alone defined what good journalism in South Africa ought to be. Alternative papers strongly rejected both implications. To suggest that their publications were an alternative to some pure standard, from which the alternative papers differed merely in that they offered another perspective, minimizes the size of the gap between the editorial philosophies of these two groups.

Two promising possibilities for a term other than "alternative" came from Ameen Akhalwaya, editor of the *Indicator.* One was the "emerging press,"[9] which captures well the newness of the alternative papers and their still formative character. "Emerging is the best," he said, "because we're all beginning to find our feet."[10] Second, he suggested the "extra-parliamentary" press—or a combination of the two, as the "emerging extra-parliamentary press."[11]

The combined term is awkward, but "extraparliamentary" by itself deserves close attention. It has two notable strengths. One is that it best reflects the primary focus and indeed the raison d'être of these papers. Without exception, the editors of these papers saw the most significant political activity as taking place beyond the three chambers of Parliament in Cape Town. The emphasis of these papers was thus on what became known as the extraparliamentary movement. Not only were the ideas and activities of this segment of politics the primary focus of the political coverage of these papers, but the movement spawned these papers in the first place.

Yet despite the usefulness of this term and its greater precision, two overriding reasons argue against its adoption. The main consideration is the wide currency of the term "alternative press," in use since 1977.[12] The term is widely accepted, in South Africa and beyond, and people writing and talking about these publications use this term far more frequently than any other. To shift the terminology at this stage is likely to cause more confusion than clarity. The benefits of seeking to bring about a change, probably with little likelihood of success, simply are not worth the effort. Moreover, this is the term that many members of the alternative press themselves use to characterize their papers. Usage has accorded the term a permanence even among those who regard it as having serious weaknesses.

DISTINGUISHING CHARACTERISTICS OF
THE ALTERNATIVE PRESS

The assumption so far is that the great diversity and multiplicity of publications labeled "alternative" could realistically be placed in a single category. Doing so could easily lead to an oversimplification and a discounting of important differences among these papers. Harber wrote, for example, "We tend to lump all the alternative papers together. ... However, they are in fact a fairly diverse bunch of papers ranging from those who directly serve particular organisations or trade unions to those who strive for an independent position."[13] It is important, then, in defining the alternative press to seek those characteristics that set it apart from the mainstream press.

The first distinguishing characteristic of the alternative press was its genesis and grounding in the extraparliamentary movement. What characterized the alternative press was not simply its political emphasis, which was also a feature of the English and especially the Afrikaans newspapers, the latter having been founded expressly to promote the National Party and later the Nationalist government's programs. Rather, its distinctiveness was its roots in a lengthy tradition of opposition to apartheid and white domination. The alternative press represented a resurgence in the antiapartheid press, making them the heirs to a tradition of media opposition to the government that goes back to the beginning of this century.[14]

Like its forerunners, the contemporary alternative press also explicitly attempted to serve as a voice for the political cause that gave it birth. Akhalwaya said that "what sets the emerging press apart from the mainstream press is that we write from a different perspective—the liberation perspective, for want of a better description."[15] In addition, the alternative papers were generally identified by the close ties to the organizations and community groups from which they emerged. Mansoor Jaffer referred to this vital symbiosis:

> The alternative, community based newspapers are ... unashamedly partisan. Whereas the commercial press tends to adopt a tone of neutrality ... , papers like *Grassroots* locate themselves squarely within the community of oppressed people and all those striving for democracy, and report from their perspective. These papers report the facts truthfully and honestly, from a position irrevocably committed to the struggle against apartheid.[16]

The important difference between the alternative press and what Jaffer termed the commercial, or mainstream, press was this bond between publication and people. Perhaps the closest parallel in the mainstream press would be the ties between the present Afrikaans newspapers during their earliest days and the struggling, impoverished Afrikaner populace looking to its own nationalism for salvation. The depth and power of those ties, however, subsequently waned.

It was not so with the alternative press. These publications remained a "people's press" and were hence participants in a two-way process. First, they sought to articulate the political aspirations of the people whose views they shared, drawing heavily upon this segment of the population for the news and opinion that fill their pages. In addition, though, they placed themselves in a position of unusual accountability to their readers. Unlike the editors in the mainstream press, whose accountability was spread among management, readers, and ultimately shareholders, their alternative press counterparts felt far more obligated to accurately represent reality as perceived by their readers and the community leadership. Thus these publications tended to grow out of a need by a community or an organization for a vehicle of communication. This was especially so with community newsletters like the pioneering *Grassroots,* whose background was described by media scholar P. Eric Louw in detail. On its community links, he said:

> *Grassroots* developed from the premise that community issues were central to its raison d'être. From the very outset community organizations were involved in the *Grassroots* project: in December 1978 WASA [Writers Association of South Africa] approached about 50 community organizations, civic and worker groups in the Western Cape concerning the idea of starting such a newspaper. Only once endorsement was granted was the project set in motion during 1979.[17]

The participation typifying these papers must be seen more as an ideal or goal not always realized in practice. As Patel noted, "While we are committed to participation and decision-making by organizations in the entire operation, in reality the responsibility for bringing out our newspapers has rested on the shoulders of a few people."[18] Another caveat must be mentioned regarding this egalitarian, "editing by consensus" approach to publishing. On the more sophisticated weekly and biweekly papers that are the focus of this study, like *New Nation*, *South*, and the *Weekly Mail*, such high levels of consensus editing would have been cripplingly inefficient. Nevertheless, even these publications employed an egalitarian approach to producing their papers that was utterly alien to the mainstream press. Quite simply, the alternative newspapers manifested a common organizational culture markedly different from that of the mainstream press. This culture included a high level of commitment to a common purpose, a sense of unity and camaraderie (in no small measure heightened by the forces of commercial competition, limited resources, or government opposition), and a pervasive egalitarian ethos. This culture, with its own vocabulary, norms, and expectations, resembled that of a religious movement. Utterly convinced of the rightness of their cause, those in the alternative press banded together to continue "the struggle" regardless of the cost.

Generally, the extraparliamentary movement and its press were committed to far more fundamental sociopolitical change than the mainstream press and the white populace whose views it most closely reflected. In drawing the contrast between the mainstream and alternative press, Akhalwaya said: "The mainstream newspapers by and large believe in either supporting the government's political structures, or wanting these structures modified to include black people. All of them believe in the free enterprise system. The emerging newspapers believe that the political and economic structures must be radically altered in a society based on universal franchise irrespective of racial or other considerations."[19]

Not surprisingly, the depth of these differences formed the basis for other characteristics that distinguished the alternative press from the mainstream press. One of these was that the mainstream press was profit oriented whereas the alternative press was not. Although editors would have welcomed financial self-sufficiency and several worked toward this end, that was seen as incidental to their purpose: to present a message. The *Weekly Mail* was particularly successful, by alternative press standards, in attracting advertising, although its coeditor Harber said it remained an ongoing difficulty for the paper.[20] At one level, the problem for the more economically viable alternative papers was manifested in a deep wariness of being driven more and more by the marketplace rather than political values. These editors must at times have been tempted to sell their papers' soul for what they saw as a Faustian deal for financial security. So, when these editors saw the currency in which the market system required one to trade, the alternative press chose not to pay. As Howard Barrell said, these publications "have sought to free themselves from the political limitations which flow from the dictates of advertising and commercialism."[21]

But the alternative press's approach to commercialism went far beyond simply not accepting it. In keeping with the views of the extraparliamentary movement as a whole, the alternative press displayed views ranging from suspicion to outright hostility and opposition to South Africa's economic system and the mainstream press that embraced it. In discussing meanings of the term "alternative media," for example, journalism educator Clive Emdon said, "'Alternative' assumes a political and economic identity of its own. It is anti-capitalist. ... There is no half-way, we cannot use the same structures of organisation and control of the commercial press."[22]

Mansoor Jaffer, former full-time organizer for *Grassroots*, described the alternative press's problem with the capitalist structure of the mainstream press and its subjection to market forces.

The framework of the commercial press is by and large shaped by the need to pander to the most backward and reactionary sentiments in the market—the white readership who are the main target of most commercial newspapers. There are countless examples of this trend: from the vilification of the ANC and Bishop Tutu, to the editorial space regularly offered the SADF through the person of certain "Defence Correspondents."[23]

Then, in listing what he saw as the fundamental flaws in the mainstream press, Jaffer made explicit a vitally important connection between the commercial orientation of the mainstream press and its editorial content. Alternative editors differed in the degree to which they faulted the mainstream press coverage of crucial issues. But all agreed that this coverage and status quo orientation were crucial flaws and that the alternative press was needed to fill the resulting gap. Some alternative editors opposed the idea of a capitalist press in principle and probably all strongly reject the highly oligopolistic form the mainstream press takes in South Africa. For most of them, the immediate problem was the ideological roots and consequent editorial content of the mainstream press.

The deficiencies that alternative press leaders saw in the mainstream press lead us to another question, that of the style of journalism the newer papers practice. At issue was the very role of the journalist in a polarized society like South Africa. The editor of *New Nation*, Zwelakhe Sisulu, went to the heart of the matter: "The press cannot be neutral. When newspapers in this country claim to be neutral they are actually serving the interests of the ruling class. I would take the view that no reporter can be objective, no newspaper can be neutral, and that for newspapers to be acceptable to people, they must reflect their social reality. This is the bottom line. And they are not doing it."[24]

By itself, the alternative press's embracing of what could be termed advocacy journalism did not set it apart from mainstream papers. Joe Latakgomo pointed out for example that "the Afrikaans Press and the radio and television services are as good an example as any of 'advocacy journalism.'"[25] The difference was rather one of degree. What was noteworthy about the alternative papers, ranging from the most informal community newsletter to the sophisticated weekly newspapers examined here, was their conscious and unapologetic practice of advocacy journalism. This style of journalism was often fundamentally at odds with the traditional "objective" journalism typical of much Western and especially U.S. news reporting and interpretation.[26]

The alternative press's avowed editorial objectives and actual content also set these papers apart from the mainstream press. A proposal for the launch of *South* listed objectives typical of the alternative press. The aims and objectives included:

> To launch a weekly newspaper to articulate the needs and aspirations of the oppressed and exploited in the Cape and in so doing serve the interests of the working class people.
>
> To fearlessly keep the public informed; to vigorously oppose and campaign through media for an end to apartheid and exploitation; and to communicate important ideas for an alternative democratic society.
>
> To challenge and break the monopolistic control of newspapers by the State and private enterprise. To challenge through aggressive reporting and legal action government restraints and internal self-censorship of news.
>
> To act as a watchdog on government abuse of basic freedoms of the individual and to keep issues like detentions, harassments, repressions alive in the public mind.
>
> To support and promote through media political, community and worker campaigns like May Day, Release Mandela, end to pass laws, etc, and also to initiate through the paper campaigns on major issues.
>
> To aid and promote through development journalism issues like literacy, alternative education, health, and consumer and legal matters.[27]

Objectives like these, though overlapping with those of the mainstream press, were also plainly those of a crusading paper. No mainstream editors would ever define their task as seeking to "articulate the needs and aspirations of the oppressed and exploited," whether using those terms or not, to say nothing of the intention "to challenge and break the monopolistic control of newspapers."

Other, informally stated objectives emphasized the gap between the alternative and mainstream papers. One objective already referred to was that of supplementing the news coverage of the mainstream papers. The alternative papers were concerned with both the mainstream press's sins of commission and omission. So the alternative papers tried to cover issues of importance that they believe were ignored or downplayed as well as to counter media portrayals and information they saw as inaccurate or distorted. Examples of addressing the gaps included greater focus on the activities of organizations in the extraparliamentary movement, the labor front and trade unions, rural areas, and the nonracial sport movement in South Africa. On the local or community level, community papers addressed issues "such as poor maintenance of the houses in the townships; electricity problems; women calling for maternity benefits at work and the demands of workers for protective clothing on the factory floor."[28]

Covering such issues made sense for a mainstream paper choosing to emphasize particular issues or seek a certain niche in the market, such as the Johannesburg financial daily *Business Day*. A mainstream paper, if it chose, could relatively easily improve coverage of these areas, which some mainstream editors concede are a present weakness. These sins of omission could relatively easily be remedied in the future and if the mainstream papers cover these areas better they will provide increasing competition for the alternative papers.

What the alternative press saw as the sins of commission, however, were different. These were typically rooted in the explicitly and implicitly held values of the mainstream press and closely reflected those of the white South Africans generally. They included such volatile and contentious issues as the sanctions movement, consumer boycotts, the end-conscription campaign, the ANC, and the international sports boycott against South Africa. Jaffer offered an example in this last category concerning the internationally known athlete Zola Budd.

> Most recently we have been treated by these newspapers to a wave of bile on the Zola Budd issue. "The Hunted Fawn" or "The little girl who only wanted to run," scream headlines above stories written as if to deliberately obscure the issues at stake.
>
> The fact that Zola Budd ... refuses to condemn apartheid—that is the salient reality of the Zola Budd issue. Apartheid is internationally regarded as a crime against humanity—anyone refusing to condemn it can-

not be expected to be regarded as a decent human being, let alone an acceptable guest at international athletic gatherings.

Yet, playing to their audience, the commercial newspapers (almost across the board) vilify those who have made a consistent and principled stand against apartheid in the form of a sports boycott.[29]

Many white South Africans could read Jaffer's words without even beginning to grasp the depth with which issues like these were viewed by many of their black fellow citizens. Clearly on certain issues the mainstream and alternative press approached their society and its potential solutions from quite different worldviews. This gulf indicated that the alternative and mainstream papers' very definitions of South African society often differ drastically.

Although the alternative papers' editors were well aware that they were preaching primarily to the converted, their dual task was to affirm the faithful and proselytize the unbelievers. A major challenge facing the alternative papers was to broaden their base and widen the constituencies to which they appealed. This was especially so for the two weeklies catering mostly to white readers, the *Vrye Weekblad* and the *Weekly Mail.*

By the early 1990s, the alternative press was still young and its constituent papers were still clarifying their individual and collective roles. Patel summarized this process by noting that "our watchword has been to learn, to propagandise and to organise."[30] The alternative press was plainly committed to politicizing its readership, educating them not only about the nuts and bolts of daily life but also raising their awareness of political issues and helping to equip them with an ideology with which to counter the status quo.

The discussion thus far has emphasized the alternative press's raison d'être as an openly declared participant in "the struggle." This emphasis ought not to obscure the high-quality journalism that some alternative papers sought to practice. To many in the mainstream press, it seemed mutually exclusive for alternative editors to shun traditional objective-style journalism and simultaneously claim to strive for fairness, accuracy, and honesty in their news coverage. Alternative press editors and journalists disagreed. Except for the community newspapers *Grassroots* and *Saamstaan,* the editors of all the alternative papers discussed in this book had experience working in the mainstream press. The result, Akhalwaya said, was that they "will not allow their reporters to get away with distortions. They have too much at stake to risk losing their credibility and self-respect."[31] These editors spoke forcefully of their commitment to factual, accurate reporting. Moegsien Williams, editor of *South,* said he tells his staff that life in South Africa is grim enough that there is never a need to exaggerate. "There's no need for us ever to say the thing is worse than it is; all we want is to accurately reflect South Africa."[32]

Despite their commitment to factual reporting and accuracy, alternative editors were well aware of the ideologically laden freight their papers carried and the undefinable line separating news coverage and propaganda. They were aware too of the danger of becoming propagandists for their cause. Akhalwaya said, "To counter the things that the SABC does, we at times become counter-propagandists."[33] Max du Preez, of the *Vrye Weekblad*, also acknowledged this danger. Yet given the unusual nature of South African society, embracing advocacy journalism was necessary, he said: "In a distorted reality like ours you sometimes need that."[34]

For the government and other critics of the alternative press, statements like these confirmed their insistence that these papers constitute a propagandistic press.[35] Someone like Akhalwaya pleaded guilty as charged, given his definition of propaganda: "We genuinely believe we are propagandists for a fair society and genuine democracy. But there's a danger here that we might not be able to see our own undemocratic actions." He added that the diversity of newspaper voices, both mainstream and alternative, "help[s] keep you honest."[36] Journalists like Akhalwaya and du Preez also contended that they are at least aware of their biases and values and that openly proclaiming them was a marked improvement over the supposedly neutral but equally ideologically committed mainstream press.

The concentration thus far on the differences between the mainstream and the alternative press is not to imply that the latter papers were some monolithic cluster of like-minded, generic left-wing publications. Akhalwaya described the different perspectives and target audiences of the alternative papers, their different attitudes to accepting advertising, and their different editorial tone and character. "The *New Nation*, for example, is probably the most serious of these papers in that it seldom sees the funny side of anything in South Africa. That is not a criticism, but an indication of its approach. ... *South* is also serious, but its approach is probably more British-style, it does take the mickey out of officialdom, it does cover a lot of entertainment."[37]

Louw differentiated the alternative papers on another basis.

Two main forms of counter hegemonic press have emerged: firstly, a progressive-alternative press (such as: *Grassroots* and *Saamstaan*), and secondly a social democrat independent press (such as: *Weekly Mail* and *Vrye Weekblad*). It is problematic to simply lump these two forms of counter hegemonic press together (as the state frequently does) because the social democrat independent press has emerged as something of a hybrid of both progressive-alternative and "conventional" libertarian media practices. The social democrat genre differs from the progressive genre in so far as the progressive-alternative press is: more partisan and rhetorical; is more "organically linked" (i.e. less independent from) to community or worker groups; and is less inclined to use a "legalistic" strategy to counter state pressures.[38]

This distinction is significant and in a more sustained analysis of the alternative press would deserve careful attention. The present point, however, is simply that the alternative press was not a monolithic group of look-alike publications. The *Vrye Weekblad* and *Weekly Mail*, constituting what Louw termed the social democrat independent press, had predominantly white readerships, unlike the rest of the alternative press. Some observers referred to the *Weekly Mail's* readers as "slumpies," or "Slightly Left, Upwardly Mobile Professionals," most of whom live in Johannesburg's affluent northern suburbs. *Vrye Weekblad's* readership was embarrassingly elite, said du Preez. Four out of five readers had a university education and half had more than one degree.[39]

Could papers like these be regarded as stablemates of a *New Nation* or a *Saamstaan*, for example? Yes, despite the large differences between them. As a group, the alternative papers had enough features in common for them to be viewed as an entity—at least at this stage in their history. Also, these papers saw themselves as sharing a common identity, despite their significant differences. Especially important in cementing their identity were the two final features of the alternative press that merit attention.

The first was the government's reaction to its political orientation and message; the second concerned its vulnerability. The government responded to the opposition and harshly critical message of the alternative papers with a series of attacks notable even in South Africa for their ferocity. Moreover, the techniques the government used to battle the alternative press, primarily under the emergency regulations, attained an astonishing new level of disregard for press freedom. The government's antipress measures in the latter 1980s applied of course to the mainstream and alternative press and to the foreign press. But the government made no secret that its primary target inside the country was the alternative press. Both the alternative and mainstream press were subject to sustained government attack but the former group got closest scrutiny and was hardest hit.

Then there was the question of these papers' vulnerability. Compared with the mainstream press, they had small circulations, drew little advertising, and were underfunded, understaffed, and at times unorganized. These and other weaknesses were hardly exclusive to the alternative press; other segments of the South African press experienced similar difficulties.[40] They took on particular importance for the alternative press in view of its being targeted for sustained government attack. Religious publications or small-town weeklies could, and did, plod along with these problems year after year. For alternative papers, however, a chronic shortage of funds took on ominous dimensions in the wake of sustained and costly legal battles. Nor could short-staffed newsrooms afford to have editors and other colleagues spend most of their working days addressing legal problems—or even worse, languish in jail month after month without charge. These problems were serious enough for large, financially secure mainstream papers, but when they affected the alternative papers they could quite literally be fatal. Inevitably, their transition was hardly without other difficulties.

PROBLEMS

The typical alternative paper faced an array of difficulties that separated it from the mainstream press. These are divided here into funding and advertising and other limitations.

Funding and Advertising

Because alternative papers were driven by motives other than profitability and generated only part of the money needed to establish and run a paper, each relied on outside funding. The money came mostly from foreign governments, international media organizations such as the International Federation of Journalists, church groups, and humanitarian organizations. The Canadian government, for example, donated R2.4 million in August 1988 to counter "South African propaganda and censorship" as part of an action plan that included "a legal advisory fund 'to help the alternative press cope with government-imposed impediments.'"[41] The Canadians also provided *Vrye Weekblad*'s computer system, worth R73, 000.[42]

The Roman Catholic church was the driving force behind launching and funding *New Nation. South,* in turn, relied on Scandinavian and other European donors,[43] and the Eastern Cape News Agencies were funded by a British relief organization.[44]

The *Weekly Mail* was started with minimal capital, consisting mostly of the severance pay its founders received when the *Rand Daily Mail* closed. Likewise, Akhalwaya's paper, the *Indicator,* began with the money he got on leaving the *Rand Daily Mail*, supplemented by shares sold to friends and family members and a mortgage on his house. Du Preez's *Vrye Weekblad* began with "an overdraft of R10,000. The first month the editorial staff got their salaries three days late."[45]

When *Vrye Weekblad* was struggling to receive government registration as a newspaper, it ran into a potentially insurmountable roadblock. One of South Africa's curious press laws allows the government to demand a deposit of up to R40,000 from a publisher to secure the paper's registration. Normally only a nominal amount is required. With the *Vrye Weekblad*, however, the government required R30,000, the largest amount ever paid by a publisher.[46] The money came from the paper's readers, who sent in more than twice what was needed.

These specifics lead to two conclusions. One is that compared with the commercial press, the alternative papers tended to be seriously undercapitalized. The other was that they were likely to need external funding for a long while yet. For that reason, several papers were striving for self-sufficiency, out of choice and necessity.

The most obvious benefit of self-sufficiency was autonomy in running a paper. Although there was no suggestion that donors made editorial demands on the alternative papers, the editors knew as well as anyone that the flow of funds was unlikely to last forever. Either the donors themselves could stop giving or the government could intervene at a moment's notice. Foreign governments could have become uneasy about supporting newspapers, an action that could be seen as political interference.[47] Donors were unwilling to fund papers indefinitely, hence providing added incentive to seek financial autonomy. The chief problem for domestic funders, present or potential, was the threat of government retribution. For that reason, together with the far greater resources available abroad, the alternative press continued to receive much of its funding from outside the country.

Funding opposition papers and causes in South Africa remained popular for some governments, which Louw noted were "increasingly concerned with gaining a toe-hold into what they see as potentially the future ruling hegemony in South Africa."[48] He added that the extraparliamentary movement, or what he termed "the South African counter hegemony," became especially skilled in the 1980s at attracting these external funds.[49]

These factors were important incentives for the alternative papers to attain financial independence. Barrell, tying in concerns like these to the overall cause of the extraparliamentary movement, said, "We continue to be dependent upon external funding for these newspapers at peril both to our more narrow objectives as journalists as well as our broader national democratic objectives."[50]

The most sensible alternative was to increase advertising revenues. But alternative papers found that attracting advertisers was often extraordinarily difficult. Harber stated the chief problem: "Advertising is a great difficulty because of a prejudice in the advertising community about the alternative papers."[51] He noted how advertisers were reluctant to advertise in his paper, which had a circulation of 28,000, but not in the specialized business magazine *Finance Week*, which had a circulation half that size. The alternative papers frequently found that advertisers feared being associated with their political positions. A dramatic example was *New Nation*, which despite its circulation of 80,862[52] attracted little beyond the staple advertising diet of the alternative press: job announcements from universities and from extraparliamentary organizations and paid political messages. Some papers ran lucrative full-page ads from a few major corporations such as the Anglo American Corporation and the Shell Oil Company, seeking to present a certain image to the extraparliamentary movement. Other sources were arts and entertainment announcements, classifieds, and a limited amount of retail advertising.

The wariness of advertisers to be associated with the political stance of the alternative papers was difficult to overcome. In addition, the alternative papers operated in an extremely tight market, not made any easier by these papers' newness on the scene. Another consideration was that the alternative papers may not have been the dazzling media opportunity that their editors liked to believe. Except for the *New Nation*, the papers typically had low circulations that were among fairly specialized readerships. Also, most were not audited by the authoritative Audit Bureau of Circulations (ABC), a crucial factor for advertisers. The inertia of advertisers who favored their traditional media channels aggravated the problem, as did the generally more modest, less sophisticated advertising sales forces available to the alternative press.

The alternative papers faced another challenge: political pressure. So did other antigovernment papers, of course. The difference lay in the greater degree of political opposition the alternative press encountered. Du Preez, for example, was convinced that the *Vrye Weekblad* lost revenue during its especially difficult early days because some potential advertisers were intimidated into not advertising in his paper.[53] Although this was certainly not the most important advertising or revenue problem facing the alternative press, it was linked to another problem these papers faced: harassment and intimidation, described later in this book.

Limited Resources

Living with tight budgets and often sparse advertising, alternative editors simply could not buy the things of which they dreamed. The list was long. Lower salaries meant great difficulty attracting and holding high-caliber journalists, assuming they can be found in the first place. Because of the constant threat of government closure, the alternative papers cannot offer the job security that journalists, and other employees, can get elsewhere. Williams said that *South* could offer few benefits and struggled to lure experienced people. "You're asking for good people," he said, "who're already employed. You're asking people to leave secure jobs."[54]

For most alternative papers, the shortage of skilled journalists was serious. As a result, the alternative press made training a high priority. On some papers, journalists tended to be rich in youthful enthusiasm but lean on experience. Notable exceptions were *Vrye Weekblad* and *Weekly Mail.* Small editorial budgets meant fewer journalists on staff; these individuals were stretched thin and overworked. Editors in particular were often diverted from building their paper by a seemingly unending flow of legal problems.

Language difficulties presented a set of deep-seated problems, such as those of black journalists for whom English was not their first language. The list of journalistic weaknesses continued: an inadequate grasp of the all important area of press law, the deficient system of black education in South Africa that in turn severely handicapped potential recruits, limited computer skills, and a lack of in-service training.

The problems were not limited to journalism. The alternative press found comparable difficulty in attracting and holding experienced personnel in advertising, administration, circulation, and marketing. Akhalwaya candidly recounted the administrative difficulties that the *Indicator* ran into in its infancy. Keeping track of the accounts payable proved to be a serious problem, with the result that "we wrote off R30,000 in the first year and R20,000 in the second."[55]

The alternative papers had curiously uneven resources. Generously funded computer equipment and desktop publishing software were often underutilized by ill-trained and inexperienced journalists. Or there were teams of dedicated journalists who, on *South,* for example, had to use taxis, buses, or their own cars to get to stories.[56]

Other weaknesses went beyond the newsroom. Referring to the community papers, for example, Patel said that many of them "find it extremely difficult to sustain the interest and commitment that is required of the organisations in keeping the project alive. Organisations have their own problems and often they are not able to spare people to work on the project or to go out and distribute on a door-to-door basis."[57] Like the mainstream press, the alternative papers were subject to the steadily increasing price of newsprint, the overall impact of South Africa's protracted double-digit inflation rate, and the hefty chunk of South Africa's advertising budget that went straight to the tax collector.

The alternative press obviously did not begin life with a silver spoon in its mouth. Yet the difficulties it faced took surprisingly little toll on its morale or its overall performance. It is this performance, finally, to which we turn. In the light of its mission, history, and the constraints under which it operated, how did the alternative press affect the South African landscape?

THE CONTRIBUTION OF THE ALTERNATIVE PRESS

The papers examined in this chapter, and the other papers of the alternative press, became a permanent part of the South African press. Barring the unlikely move of a complete government crackdown, they will remain so. What was their contribution and impact?

A Complement to the Existing Media

The alternative press's most evident contribution was that it offered South Africans another viewpoint. The limitations of the mainstream press, and its political and ideological bases, gave their readers a view of reality that many South Africans found incomplete at best or offensive and hostile at worst. As indicated earlier, the alternative press brought its own emphases and perspectives. The result was that important but previously neglected areas of South African life received coverage. Many mainstream editors said that they found the alternative press an important source of information that supplemented their own understanding of the country. Like many of his mainstream colleagues, Andrew Drysdale of the *Argus* thought the alternative papers were "preaching mostly to the converted," but he welcomed the diversity of opinion they provided.[58] And Kosie Viviers, editor of the *Cape Times*, said the alternative press was "a very important part of the information system, a very necessary one—but then I believe all sources of information are essentially positive things."[59]

The alternative press saw its task as both providing information that mainstream papers did not and countering incorrect information or impressions. For example, pointing to the gap in certain kinds of coverage left by the *Rand Daily Mail*'s death, Akhalwaya said:

The role of these independent newspapers has been not only to partially fill the vacuum created by the *Mail*'s closure, but also to go beyond what the *Mail* stood for. Our role has been to provide information—news or opinion—that the mainstream papers ignore. ... Our role has also been to counter the increasingly blatant—and increasingly sophisticated—propaganda of the National Party and its junior partners of all hues. And it has further been to counter the nonsense some newspapers give us about what black people are supposed to be thinking—and who is thinking for them.[60]

The alternative papers enriched the quality of South Africa's media in at least two additional ways. They helped keep the mainstream press on their toes, forcing them to take account of stories and issues of which they may previously have been ignorant or that they may have thought were not newsworthy. The *Weekly Mail* in particular became mandatory reading for any editor taking his job seriously.[61]

They also provided another vehicle for expression of public views, an invaluable contribution considering the high concentration of media ownership in South Africa. People in the rural areas, for example, acquired a channel to voice their concerns, whereas in the past they were virtually ignored by the mainstream press. Similarly, the community publications succeeded in localizing the newspaper medium, focusing directly on their readers' concerns in ways previously untried in South Africa.

The alternative press enriched the quality and range of information available to South Africans in important ways. Nevertheless, these papers could not, and did not, claim to provide news, information, or interpretation to most South Africans. None publishes more frequently than weekly.[62] Therefore the intensive and comprehensive news coverage that characterized a good daily newspaper was simply not within the mission or scope of the alternative press. Daily newspapering remained the exclusive bailiwick of the mainstream papers. Recognizing this reality, Akhalwaya wrote that the alternative papers "are complementary to, rather than an alternative to, the mainstream newspapers." He continued: "That is why all of us [in the alternative press], to whichever political ideology or prejudices we subscribe, rely on the commercial daily press . . .; and that is why the mainstream press is so vital—with or without its commercial and editorial slant."[63] Du Preez, comparing the *Vrye Weekblad*'s role with that of the largest-circulation Afrikaans daily, said: "We don't want to take the place of *Beeld*. We can coexist."[64]

Like salt, the alternative press added to and enriched people's media diets. Like yeast, it also began transforming that which it supplemented. And it was not only the mainstream press whose character it affected.

A Catalyst in the Political Process

Another contribution was "to open up the field of political debate," said Pat Sidley, a former president of the South African Society of Journalists. "Suddenly the ANC was written about; every loophole that could be found was used."[65] Similarly, the alternative press was in the forefront of covering the most contentious political issues of the day: the situation of political detainees, especially children; prison conditions; the conscientious objection campaign; police and military action against political protestors, including allegations of government-backed assassination squads; the growth of the trade union movement; and so on. These issues were also covered by the mainstream press, sometimes with distinction, but most often not. Unquestionably, covering these areas became the specialty of the alternative press.

The result was that the alternative press not only influenced the agenda for the mainstream press, but it also did so precisely on the hottest political issues of the day. Patel said, "The alternative press has been a catalyst for the initiation and the building of democratic people's organisations."[66] The extent of its effectiveness in the political realm per se is a question that goes beyond the scope of this study; that is a task for another day. But the government, at least, did not feel the need for in-depth research to be convinced of what it saw as the alternative press's political potential.

A Prototype for Tomorrow's Press

The alternative press modeled key features of what a growing segment of tomorrow's press in South Africa could look like. Certainly South Africa's press will be increasingly black: in ownership, control, and readership. It will also embrace political positions closer to those of the alternative papers than those of the mainstream press. The very existence of today's alternative press reveals a diversity in South African newspapers that did not exist in the early 1980s. This quality undoubtedly presaged the kind of diversity characterizing tomorrow's press, too, which might also be marked by continued subsidies and advocacy journalism.

In all, then, the alternative press offered something of a prototype of the kind of papers that are increasingly likely to make up tomorrow's press. This is not to say they are about to replace the mainstream press. Far from it. What *is* important was their role as a model for future alternative papers to follow, learning from the present papers' successes and mistakes.

A Commitment to Press Freedom

First, a disclaimer. Paying tribute to the fight for press freedom by alternative editors and other journalists is *not* intended to denigrate the long and costly battle their mainstream peers waged. The point simply needs to be made that the alternative press has shown a vigorous and even aggressive willingness to tackle the government on a succession of legal issues. In waging since their founding a series of challenges against restrictive legislation or administrative actions, the alternative papers have done much to keep the issue of press freedom in the public eye. Journalists on these papers, for example, played a leading role in launching the Save the Press campaign, launched in May 1988. This campaign was a nationwide attempt, primarily by journalists, to draw attention to government restrictions on the press.

A Contribution to the Profession

The alternative papers demonstrated an emphasis on and a contribution to training, especially for beginning journalists and recruits to other areas of newspaper work. This focus on the short-term and long-term needs of South African journalism, or at least the segment that the alternative press represents, was a unique development. Although fraught with deficiencies and running well below its potential, these training activities were notable because they went far beyond those of individual newspaper groups, like the Argus Company's highly regarded cadet school. Not only did the alternative press open the doors to young journalists who could otherwise never have entered this field, but these papers also took extensive measures to train these recruits. The alternative papers thus began addressing the country's acute shortage of black journalists in tangible ways, affording them hands-on experience. In doing so, leaders in the alternative press clearly sought to address their immediate staffing needs. But the commitment went deeper—to building up a group of journalists capable of running tomorrow's newspapers. By highlighting the shortage and addressing it head on, these papers made a salutary contribution to the larger profession.

A second contribution was that the growth of the alternative press raised questions about the nature and responsibilities of journalism in South Africa. Debates over objectivity and advocacy journalism, press responsibility, and the part of journalists in seeking political change began long before the rise of the current alternative press. These papers enriched discussion of these issues because either their journalists raised these questions directly or the journalism the papers practiced did so. Questions about the nature and practice of journalism in South Africa will never be resolved among a group as opinionated as journalists. But the alternative press's presence ensured that mainstream editors and journalists were more likely to wrestle with important issues than they otherwise might have been.

ASSESSMENT AND EVALUATION

Even more than the people involved in the alternative press, those admiring its work from the sidelines can easily romanticize the part these papers played in South Africa's political process. To the extent that many saw all participants in the extraparliamentary movement as heroic, valiant, and flawless warriors in a cosmic battle between the forces of good and the ultimate evil of apartheid, so too was the alternative press in danger of receiving such hallowed status. An editor's glowing introduction to Patel's article demonstrated the temptation of elevating the alternative press to instant sainthood: "A press which speaks of the demands of the people, of their joys, their hopes and fears in the struggle for national liberation. A press which speaks of the unity of the oppressed, of life in a free and democratic South Africa in which the people shall govern."[67] If one is honestly to assess the place of the alternative press in South Africa, it is vital to move beyond clichéd adoration of these papers. History may evaluate the alternative press's role glowingly, but a more immediate analysis demands a willingness to look at these papers' shortcomings.

By the early 1990s, this vibrant press had made a significant impact on the country's journalism and, though more difficult to assess, on its politics too. Akhalwaya offered an insider's view of the long-term value of the alternative press: "When history looks at South Africa, it will get much information from the alternative press. The papers are getting the debate about the new society going."[68]

That history will learn much from these barometers of South African society is unquestioned; that these papers deserve credit for "getting the debate going" is not. Whatever the mainstream press's weaknesses, it was not as if it had lived in a political vacuum. It too was a major player in setting the political agenda, although this was admittedly primarily among the white electorate. Indeed, as Akhalwaya and others in the alternative press would agree, the mainstream papers have long played an overwhelmingly dominant role in the South African press and will continue doing so. There is thus a danger, evident in the remarks of both those inside the alternative press and those sympathetic to it, of greatly overestimating its present journalistic and political influence. The total combined circulation of the *Indicator, New Nation, Saamstaan, South, Vrye Weekblad,* and *Weekly Mail* (all weeklies except the *Indicator* and *Saamstaan*) was less than 200,000 in 1992. Compare that with the average *daily* circulation of the country's largest paper, the *Sowetan,* of 208,591.[69] As Barrell conceded of the alternative press, "These organs remain still peripheral interventions in their size and distribution."[70]

Nor could the alternative papers offer the fully developed, day-to-day coverage of news that was the forte of the daily press. Consequently, readers seeking the full range of a typical daily's offerings found the alternative papers lacking. That is not to fault these papers for defining their editorial identity and mission as they did; it is merely to note that the mainstream press produced the bulk of South African journalism and *all* its daily papers.

Because the alternative press was still young, it experienced many of the problems typical of new institutions. The difficulties listed earlier, such as limited funding, ill-trained journalists, personnel shortages, and organizational and management weaknesses, all hindered these papers in reaching their potential.

Another weakness, paradoxically, stemmed from these papers' great strength. The depth of their commitment to a particular political perspective narrowed their journalistic vision in exactly the same way it led to myopia in the mainstream press. Like the mainstream press, whose failings they sought to redress, the alternative papers also viewed life narrowly, presenting their own partial and one-sided view of reality. Not surprisingly, this was the chief complaint of mainstream editors, even those sympathetic to the alternative press. To overstate the case, if the mainstream press were guilty of offering a frothy diet of sport, semi-naked women, and yet more ways to make quiche, then the alternative press offers a predictable stodginess that knew of nothing beyond the grimmest of South Africa's political realities.

Fortunately, neither extreme was accurate. In addition, the undoubtedly strong temptation for the alternative papers to view all of reality through the filter of extraparliamentary politics was offset by the realities of flesh-and-blood readers for whom life consisted of more than the antiapartheid struggle. Williams, for example, told how *South,* a paper serving both African and Coloured readers, needed to adjust to the realities of its marketplace. *South* found on launching the paper that Coloureds were less hungry for political news than Africans. This difference, as well as differences in economic development, presented a problem. "Our initial reading of the situation was wrong; we came out with a very political paper. It sold well in the African community but not in the Coloured community," Williams said. "It's a fact of life that squatters are living in the rain, but people don't want to keep reading this." The result? "We tried to integrate into the paper elements that would appeal to a wider range of people. We no longer have heavy social commentary all the way through."[71] Changes included an insert that contained crossword puzzles, recipes, and what Williams described as "soap opera" serials.

South's experience suggested that as the alternative press matured it would adjust to the demands of its environment, tempering a zeal for what editors believed people *ought* to read by adding what people actually *want* to read. *Vrye Weekblad's* du Preez said, "The alternative press should get more mature and sophisticated now. We should put our anger more in perspective, and have more of a sense of humor. We tend to be angry political agents, but I think we can now afford to become more complete newspapers."[72]

Despite such "growing up," the temptation and pressure for the alternative journalists to become propagandists remained, as Akhalwaya and du Preez admitted earlier. This was a difficulty that the journalists alone could combat. It was a serious one, for it was on this front that it was most vulnerable to government attack. Ready to condemn these papers as a revolutionary press, bent on unleashing violence in a highly volatile nation, the government repeatedly showed its willingness to act harshly against any voices it found intolerable. The future of the alternative press was thus highly dependent on the present government's claims that it would tolerate opposition views.

The alternative papers that survive the 1990s will increasingly entrench themselves as part of the South African press. In 1986 *New Nation's* Sisulu said, "The alternative media in this country are in the process of becoming the mainstream media."[73] Perhaps. Although that day was still far off, what had become a reality was a small but vigorous press taken more and more seriously by South Africa's other papers, the public, and especially the government.

4

The Realities of the Marketplace

The principal factor in the re-making of the media is the end of the ascendancy of the traditional newspaper. For hundreds of years this doughty, unspectacular product has been the freightship of humankind's culture of information; a cavalier, crusader and villain in its politics; the bulletin board of change. Now change itself is killing the newspaper.

—**Patrick Lee**

THE SOUTH AFRICAN press, like the country it reflected, had little idea in 1975 how turbulent a ride lay ahead. Financially complacent and smug, and overseen by often unimaginative managements, it was ill prepared for the storm to come. The 1980s ended with the press having grown up fast. It was as if an institution that dated its origins to the 1820s suddenly experienced adolescence, propelling the press to adulthood in a few intense but mercifully compacted years. With a swiftness that no one expected, and a degree of pain that all would have avoided, the country's newspapers and their managements suddenly became adults. This chapter is the story of that transition.

THE DEATH OF THE *RAND DAILY MAIL*

More than any other event in recent press history in South Africa, the death on 30 April 1985 of the *Rand Daily Mail* signaled this emergence of a new era in the country's mainstream press. The paper's closure encapsulated many of the shifts characterizing a rapidly transforming institution. The death of a paper as important as the *Mail* would command attention no matter the context; given the way it symbolized the heart of the press's problems, such attention becomes vital.

The *Mail* was South Africa's best-known paper in the international community because of its long and admirable record as a champion of human rights and its readiness to voice black interests and perspectives. The unabashedly liberal stance that Laurence Gandar adopted when he took over as editor in October 1957 soon pushed the paper to the top of the government's list of "most hated" voices in South Africa. Gandar's successors ensured that the paper retained this status until its death. The paper won international recognition for its contributions, which fell into two categories.

The first was its impact on the society. By steadfastly proclaiming a liberal political alternative to the status quo of the Nationalists, and by offering editorial support and succor to the liberal forces in white politics, the paper provided a vehicle for viewpoints that might otherwise have gone unheard by whites. Unquestionably, it was a stirrer and catalyst in South African politics, always to varying degrees of government displeasure. The *Mail*'s combination of critical oversight of government and unapologetic embracing of views well to the left of most white South Africans endeared it to growing numbers of blacks in Soweto and other townships near Johannesburg. Raymond Louw, who succeeded Gandar as editor, said the paper played a unique bridging role between black and white in South Africa, serving as one of the few institutions in a segregated land where ideas and views could meet across the color line.[1]

The *Mail*'s second major contribution was to South African journalism. In many respects it was a pioneer. It initiated many searching exposés of government abuses and stood firmly and unambiguously against what it saw as the travesties of the apartheid society. This is not to say that the other English papers were cowed into submission—far from it. Many displayed courage and coverage similar to the *Mail*'s. But it was the *Mail* that earned a deserved reputation for its consistently courageous and enterprising reportage and editorial stance. Accordingly, many blacks saw the *Mail* as set apart from other opposition papers. The late Percy Qoboza, one of South Africa's most distinguished black editors, said: "The *Mail* was not just another paper; it was an institution, a courageous crusader for justice and peace. Far ahead of white public opinion, it gave us the courage to go on."[2]

The paper's contributions include a series of exposés in the mid-1960s on prison conditions, which led to a protracted and enormously expensive legal battle under the Prisons Act.[3] Two other series of stories brought South Africans the finest in journalism that the country has seen: the paper's coverage of the Soweto riots in 1976, by its team of superb black reporters and photographers; and, together with another SAAN paper, the *Sunday Express*, its coverage of the Information Scandal.[4] At the other end of the scale were steps that now seem small but were significant and even daring in their day. One was the *Mail*'s pioneering insistence on equal treatment in reports of people, regardless of race. Thus, said Benjamin Pogrund, a former deputy editor of the *Mail*, "it led the way in getting away from the ugly South African custom of referring to 'Two miners, Mr X and Mr Y, and six Natives were killed yesterday.'"[5]

In numerous ways, the *Mail* was a trendsetter for the opposition press. Its stories were frequently picked up by other papers, especially the other morning papers in the SAAN group. Clearly, whatever other South African newspaper editors thought of the *Mail*, they could not ignore it. The international press corps also watched the *Mail* closely and commented on its contents for audiences around the world. The paper's impact thus rippled far beyond its immediate readership. When the *Mail* failed, Louw said that "by far the greatest loss was the catalytic effect on the news channels throughout the country."[6]

The paper's death ripped a piece out of the soul of South African newspaper journalism. The *Mail* was the flagship paper for SAAN and set a standard for much of what English journalists, white and black, sought to emulate in their papers. When the *Mail* sank, the pride of the fleet went down. The loss was all the heavier because it was so unexpected. As Paul Bell put it in his comprehensive analysis of economic changes in the press, "There had been talk of closure before, but such talk had always come and gone. Closure was unthinkable."[7] So the *Mail*'s death shocked its readers and its admirers in South Africa and beyond.

What caused the paper's death? Some initial explanations have been offered, among them the assessments of several journalists: Bell, Laurence Gandar, Anton Harber, and Joel Mervis. Academics Koos Roelofse, Gavin Stewart, and Keyan Tomaselli, Ruth Tomaselli, and Johan Muller have offered additional insights.[8] At the very least, a thorough postmortem on the paper remains to be done. More than that, though, a full-scale inquest is called for because the circumstances surrounding the *Mail*'s decline and death raise a cluster of questions with serious implications for South African journalism. Perhaps that kind of investigation will never be conducted. In the meantime, though, one can at least record the questions that prompted Gandar to remark that the *Mail* "vanished from the scene with the facts of its own demise shrouded in mystery."[9] And one can list some of the factors suggested as causes of the *Mail*'s end.

In each of these exercises, one thing becomes clear: The *Mail* had long been in serious trouble. The flagship had became increasingly waterlogged, having suffered a decade of rising losses and numerous other problems, before SAAN decided to scuttle the vessel. Doing so was the company's prerogative. Whether that was a wise or necessary move is another matter. Moreover, was the admittedly ailing *Mail* killed for political rather than purely business reasons? Several observers are convinced that the answer is yes. One view is that the *Mail*'s board of directors, long uncomfortable about the paper's liberal politics, finally ran out of patience. Perhaps the losses the *Mail* was incurring were simply a welcome rationale for shutting the paper. This is essentially Mervis's view.

A more devious possibility, raised by a source familiar with the *Mail*'s final days, is that SAAN's accounting procedures were deliberately loaded against the paper so that it carried a disproportionately high share of the group's overhead.[10] In other words, the poor financial situation at the paper was deliberately aggravated through accounting procedures to make the *Mail*'s plight seem even worse than it was.

Another, far more conspiratorial, view is that the *Mail* was shut as part of a behind-the-scenes agreement between SAAN and the government that led to the establishment of the M-Net subscription television consortium described later in this chapter. Whatever validity the theory may have, no one has been able to offer anything beyond circumstantial evidence that a surreptitious deal was indeed struck.

What seems far more likely is that the SAAN board, for years unable to control the message and the money of the *Mail*, needed no prodding from the government to close the paper. If the board needed any encouragement, it came from elsewhere. In October 1984, Johannesburg Consolidated Investments bought some SAAN shares that gave it control over both that group and Argus. JCI's chairman, Gordon Waddell, reflected an unprecedented proprietary interest in the goings-on at SAAN. Previously, the ownership had employed a hands-off attitude to the board and the publications it oversaw. Not so with Waddell. As Mervis described it, Waddell "took an instant, direct, lively, aggressive interest in the affairs of the company."[11] After watching developments for some three months, he visited the managing director of the SAAN board in January 1985 and announced that because of the *Mail*'s continuing losses the paper would have to be closed, along with the *Sunday Express*.[12] Waddell said the decision was necessary to save the rest of the company, and that the two closures had the approval of Gavin Relly, chairman of Anglo American—which owned JCI.

With the blessing of the Anglo American hierarchy, the decision to close the *Mail* was taken. Ironically, the decision came on the ides of

March, after the board gave a perfunctory hearing to Rex Gibson, the paper's final editor. The paper closed six weeks later.

> Everybody blamed everybody else. Gordon Waddell, then JCI chairman, was hammered for it. His boss, Anglo American chairman Gavin Relly, was, in his own words, "stridently belaboured from around the globe," although it is claimed that [former Anglo chairman] Harry Oppenheimer, overwhelmed by complaints about the *Mail*, told his successor to deal with it as he saw fit.
>
> [Progressive Federal Party leader] Van Zyl Slabbert and the Progs were pilloried for "not lifting a finger."
>
> SAAN MD Clive Kinsley was accused of incompetence. ... [A former editor,] Allister Sparks, was accused of arrogance for, as people claimed, using the paper as a vehicle for his own crusade. There were charges of complacency, financial profligacy and waste, lack of political will, and betrayal.[13]

There was plenty of blame to go around. If Mervis's authoritative assessment is accurate, most of it belongs to the SAAN leadership. His detailed narrative of the events leading up to the death of the *Mail* and the *Sunday Express* reveals a board that frequently "bumbled along on two left feet ... ,"[14] was indecisive, allowed editors to dictate terms to them and left doubts as to whether they "really knew what they wanted, or what they were doing."[15] It seems the board never came to terms with exactly what kind of editorial policy it expected of the *Mail*. Nor could they discover how to pressure an editor into implementing that policy while still honoring the long-standing SAAN (and Argus) tradition of according editors full editorial autonomy.

The paper's owners were not blameless either. Mervis said that "the board's authority was undermined or emasculated by a proprietorship that remained aloof and detached."[16] Elsewhere, he said: "The majority shareholders of the past were either somnolent, dormant, hibernating, indifferent, or downright neglectful."[17] When the ownership did become involved, with the vigorous interest of JCI's Waddell, the harm done and the losses already incurred were so severe that the drastic decision to close the *Mail* resulted. Whatever secret deals with the government or private political agenda may have motivated Waddell and Anglo American, no one questioned that drastic action was needed.

The *Mail*'s losses, in South African terms, grew like a geometric progression during its last decade. The first, an amount of R381,000, came in 1975. Unprecedented though that loss was, it was tame compared with what followed. The figure more than doubled the next year, to R843,000, and nearly doubled again in 1977—to R1,673,000. By 1984, the figure was R15,603,000.[18] The various factors causing this hemorrhage symbolize much of what afflicted the rest of the newspaper industry in the 1980s. For example, all papers were affected by the havoc wrought by the arrival of television and its prodigious appetite for advertising Rand, by crippling inflation, and by increasing sales taxes. The *Mail*, however, faced additional difficulties. Three call for brief mention here.

Management Errors

As if the SAAN board did not inherit enough problems with the *Mail*, its members added several of their own. A recession in the mid-1970s led them to cut the paper's advertising rates to attract customers, a move that its editor Raymond Louw was later to regard as the single most important cause of the *Mail*'s collapse.[19] That decision was taken in 1975.

Five years later came an increase in the *Mail*'s cover price, which another *Mail* editor, Tertius Myburgh, termed "the height of folly" and "calamitous."[20] Then in 1982 a dispute arose with Argus over an arrangement by which their newspapers were distributed by the same company, Allied Distributors. The disagreement reached such heights that Clive Kinsley, SAAN's managing director, pulled the company out of the agreement to set up its own distribution system. The new system was a disaster and cost SAAN millions before the company abandoned it and shamefacedly returned to Allied.[21] The *Mail* was not the only SAAN publication to suffer from this fiasco, but this situation compounded the paper's woes when it could least afford the myriad public relations and other problems that a newspaper experiences when copies are not delivered.

These three incidents reveal mistakes of commission. Mervis referred also to serious errors of missed opportunity. In 1980, the board rejected the chance to enter joint printing arrangements with the Argus Company, a move that would have brought considerable savings to an already strapped company. By not doing so, Mervis said, SAAN's managers "lost their greatest opportunity of saving the *Rand Daily Mail*."[22]

Another error of omission concerned the arrival in September 1976 of the *Citizen*. This progovernment newspaper was clandestinely funded with some R32 million of taxpayers' money as part of the Information Scandal.[23] At the time, the *Mail* was the undisputed leading morning newspaper in South Africa. The paper was either unwilling or unable to use its dominant position to tackle the *Citizen* head on and allowed the interloper into its territory to gain an increasingly secure foothold. This was not for lack of editorial effort: The *Mail* revealed, for example, that up to 30,000 copies of the *Citizen* were being dumped daily to boost circulation figures.[24] Yet this and other editorial coverage of the Information Scandal meant little in the absence of a shrewd marketing strategy to secure the *Mail*'s place in an intensely competitive environment. Former editor Gandar said: "Instead of treating the *Citizen* as a serious threat right from the start," SAAN's management "tended to behave as if it were a minor nuisance that would go away if ignored."[25]

The White Readership

Another entity that could have saved the *Mail* and did not was the paper's white readership. In addition to its core of committed white liberal readers, the paper had an uncomfortably large proportion of readers who, in varying degrees, disliked the paper's political stance. Mervis traced the *Mail*'s problems with its white readership to the beginning of the paper's liberal era, which began with Gandar's editorship in 1957. From then on, the paper began raising issues and asking questions that many white readers preferred not to hear. By 1960, Mervis said, English speakers opposed to the government had adjusted to Nationalist rule. Indeed, they enjoyed their material prosperity in an apartheid society. "They could make money, enjoy life and sit back in comfort while the Government did all the dirty work and got all the blame. This was the paradise the *Rand Daily Mail* was apparently trying to spoil by articulating black grievances, publishing black news, and virtually pleading for integration."[26]

Ultimately, the paper's liberal policies "so irritated the government and many others," Stewart said, "that it called into being its own chief assassin: *The Citizen*."[27] Whether one agrees with the role Stewart accorded the *Mail*'s chief competitor, there is no disputing the level of anti-*Mail* resentment that spawned South Africa's only progovernment English daily.

This resentment from white readers would only increase in the remaining quarter century of the *Mail*'s life. By 1985, many of these readers were businessmen who bought the paper for its strong business coverage, certainly not its editorial slant. Quite simply, according to one white business leader, "It was not popular with whites. It was unnecessarily vitriolic and not prepared to concede the government's good moves."[28]

The troubles with the white readership by themselves would not have caused the paper to go under. Overall circulation figures revealed the paper to be in good health. The problem lay in what was perhaps the supreme irony for the *Mail:* that its great contribution to bridging the racial divide—pulling in large numbers of black and white readers—

proved in large measure to be its undoing in the essential realm of advertising.

The Advertising Profile

Despite all its problems, what should have sustained the *Mail*, at least in theory, was its advertising base. The *Mail* operated in the largest market in the country. Unlike its direct competitor, the *Citizen*, the *Mail* was well established in the area and was the market leader in morning papers in the Johannesburg area and indeed in the country.

However, far from solving the *Mail*'s problems, the paper's potential advertising income presented it with another riddle that neither the board nor a succession of editors could solve. Two simple realities governed the *Mail*'s situation. The paper's circulation, and especially its readership, were becoming less white and more black, and advertisers found the particular racial mix of the *Mail*'s readers increasingly unappealing.

The *Mail*'s readership was 70 percent black when the paper folded, and most of its white readers were men. The paper seriously lacked the white women readers that supermarkets and other retail advertisers covet. The *Mail* was all too aware of the problem. An example of the paper's long struggle to confront the problem came in 1977, when *Mail* executives tried an imaginative approach to resolving the advertising profile dilemma. The paper held a one-day seminar in Johannesburg for the advertising community to promote the concept that "racial barriers were unimportant" and that "the market was developing a cosmopolitan segment with similar incomes and tastes."[29] The idea got nowhere. The group marketing manager blamed the advertising agencies' creative staffs, whom he said "could see no way to address so mixed a readership."[30]

Even if the agencies were guilty of a lack of imagination, the paper's readership profile remained a serious obstacle. Other papers were also steadily acquiring black readers. By 1988, for example, 56 percent of the *Star*'s readers were black. Somewhat surprisingly, so were 60 percent of the *Citizen*'s readers,[31] challenging the conventional view that blacks would not read a paper whose editorial line was strongly progovernment.[32] So why should the *Mail* have succumbed to this black-white split in readers? The answer, said one advertising agency's media director, is that "the *Mail* was neither fish nor fowl. It appealed to businessmen and blacks alike. Only a few products, such as beer and cigarettes, appealed to both areas."[33] Stewart found a recurring theme in the advertising community's attitudes to the split: "You wouldn't advertise a BMW in the *Rand Daily Mail*."[34] The gap between upmarket white businessmen and black clerical and industrial workers was simply too great a barrier, both real and perceived, for the *Mail.*

The head office's strategy on advertising also cost the *Mail* countless thousands in lost revenues. SAAN centralized its advertising sales rather than relying on representatives working directly for each SAAN publication. This strategy worked badly for the *Mail* because its readership was far from the easiest product to sell to advertising agencies or directly to advertisers. In contrast to SAAN's highly lucrative *Sunday Times,* the *Mail* "had to fight every inch of the way to get advertising. The paper had to compete with a powerful afternoon rival [the *Star*], the market available was relatively small, and at the end of the day not much was left for the *Rand Daily Mail.*"[35] The result was that sales staff understandably pushed the publications that would pull in the most commissions for the least effort.

Other Aggravating Circumstances

The combination of these three sets of problems, perhaps by themselves, could have proved fatal to the *Mail.* But there was more to the story, as the scathing comment of an unidentified businessman suggested: "They were communists. And they couldn't spell."[36] In addition to attacking the paper's values, he pointed to a more objective problem: Regardless of their spelling abilities, the *Mail*'s journalists and editors unquestionably compounded their paper's problems. The tales of profligate spending were legendary and abundant. Editors would, said a *Star* reporter, "send out reporters on 'missions impossible' and have a four-paragraph story to show for a five-day story."[37] *Mail* reporters were renowned for covering stories as if money were no object. At times, such as in its coverage of the Information Scandal, this readiness to spend money on gathering news was justified. Yet a culture of unaccountability emerged at the paper. In the paper's final years, with staff morale low, the perception of an increasing abandonment by its management led many *Mail* staffers to adopt hostile attitudes to the company and its property. Ken Owen, who edited the paper for a short while in the early 1980s, told how when he first took over he learned that two reporters requesting a company car overnight had been using one every night for a month and had wrecked two cars in the process. Yet they had been allowed to continue unchecked their private use of company property.[38]

Far from being the exception, this kind of conduct was widespread at the *Mail,* as another interim *Mail* editor, Tertius Myburgh, noted. Myburgh was charged with assessing the paper's health; his lengthy report to the SAAN board in August 1981 was ominous. "The damage to the *Rand Daily Mail* is far worse than I had imagined it. It is a shattered organisation, perilously close to ruin. There are no miracle cures available and we are long past the stage where the newspaper can be secured by clever improvisation or by simply muddling through."[39]

Among the problems he identified were those of a weak production system; an appalling physical environment for the staff—"unquestionably the worst" in South Africa, in a building having "a general tone of depressing and repellent squalor";[40] and the consequent impact on staff morale. But Myburgh's most scathing comments were for management-editorial relations. They merit quoting at length.

> SAAN—as a company, and not only its editorial departments—shows all the symptoms of a demoralised organisation: neglect of people and plant, abuse of resources, dispersal of authority, lack of goals, corporate guerrilla warfare, virtually no corporate loyalty or sense of true belonging by rank and file staff, executive strain, buck-passing and poor inter-departmental communication. The management-editorial interface is bedeviled by the inefficiency and insensitivity of those who handle administrative and personnel matters. The hostility between editorial staff and the personnel manager has reached such proportions, amounting to scorn, that the effectiveness of the incumbent has been wholly destroyed. The impression that nothing really *works* efficiently or according to any generally known set of rules has bred an equally unattractive reaction among staff, who respond by engaging in guerrilla tactics to exploit the company and its assets (cars, expenses, equipment, furniture etc). This morally corroding cycle of action (or inaction) and reaction between management and editorial daily becomes one of the most displeasing aspects of life in this company. It has gravely undermined discipline. The *Rand Daily Mail*'s editorial staff have become hopelessly demoralised and cynical by years of crises, pseudo-crises, ever more unsuccessful attempts to launch "new *Mails*," and decades of neglect and indifference.[41]

Conclusion

Whatever the faults that could be laid at the journalists' and editors' door, the ultimate responsibility for the long, steady, and eventually fatal decline of the *Mail* must lie with the paper's board and owners. Waddell, who was highly instrumental in the paper's closure, said in a 1986 magazine interview that the *Mail*'s death was unnecessary: "I say that because I have no doubt that the *Rand Daily Mail*, run by the present management of SAAN, would not have died. ... I think the problem with SAAN was always seen as the style of the editors. I don't think the problem lay there at all. The problem lay with the management of the business as opposed to the editorial side."[42]

That candid admission only confirmed what many journalists and editors had been saying all along: The *Mail* need not have died. Commenting on the steps SAAN took after April 1985 to restore its financial well-being, such as entering into long-overdue joint operating agreements with the Argus Company, Gandar said: "The story of the RDM can be summed up as a gross misreading of the nature of its 'ailments,' a killing off of the patient and only after that the adoption of remedial measures."[43]

One government official, Deputy Minister of Foreign Affairs Louis Nel, by contrast, saw the paper's demise as "a natural death. We all feel sad about an unnatural death," he said, "but not about natural death."[44] And that remains the issue: Did the paper in fact die a natural death? Or one can use the metaphor of the paper's final editorial cartoon, which showed a tombstone with an inscription: "*Rand Daily Mail.* Born 1902. Killed in the line of duty 1985." Was it a tragic victim in combat, or a soldier sent unwittingly on a suicide mission? The debate about the *Mail*'s closure will continue among the present generation of journalists and press people until another generation has succeeded them. Or perhaps someone privy to the inner circles of the Anglo American Corporation leadership in the mid-1980s will eventually deliver some explanations. For now, one must settle for a partial explanation of what led to the paper's closure. What is plain, however, is that the sinking of SAAN's flagship represented the bleakest episode in what Bell called the "long winter" that befell South Africa's newspaper industry.[45] Equally clearly, both for those who grieved and those who exulted over the *Mail*'s closure, life went on. The *Mail* was replaced by South Africa's only specialist daily newspaper, *Business Day*. In virtually every respect, *Business Day* is different from the *Mail*. It is far smaller, with a circulation of 32,500 in 1991,[46] than that of 115,993 for the *Mail* at its end. *Business Day* is also a finely targeted publication, aimed specifically at South Africa's business community. Notwithstanding its articulate and highly literate opinion pieces, the paper has little of the flair and color or extensive news coverage that marked the *Mail* at its peak. The most significant difference of all is that *Business Day*, virtually from the beginning, has run at a profit.

The transitions from the *Rand Daily Mail* to *Business Day* and that of SAAN to Times Media Limited, symbolize the move from adolescence to adulthood in the South African newspaper industry described at the beginning of this chapter. For although it was a less publicized and certainly less lamented change, the metamorphosis of SAAN into TML marked just as significantly a crucial turning point in South African newspapering.

THE RISE OF TIMES MEDIA LIMITED

In 1986 SAAN posted record losses of R19.4 million. In the early part of that year, its overdraft had crept up to R52 million, putting its debt-equity ratio at nearly 600 percent.[47] One year later, Times Media Limited, the company under whose name SAAN emerged from the valley of the shadow of death, posted a profit of R10 million. The new company's debt was cut to R3.4 million—dropping the debt-equity ratio to 15 percent.[48] This turnaround reveals far more than the "near-miraculous recovery" of a company on the verge of bankruptcy.[49] The transition from a deathly ill SAAN into a thriving, vigorous TML epitomized the coming of age of South Africa's mainstream press during the 1980s. What caused the turnaround? It resulted from massive pruning, new leadership, and radically different corporate philosophy, style, and practice.

Closing the *Mail* and the *Sunday Express* did not bring an instant turnaround in SAAN's fortunes. Indeed, as the rest of 1985 unfolded, the company's losses continued to pile up. In December alone the company lost R3 million.[50] Waddell, as chairman of JCI, the major shareholder, saw SAAN heading for bankruptcy unless drastic measures were taken. A major shakeup in the SAAN board had, by itself, not been enough to effect the desperately needed changes. Out of the changes to the board, however, plus a sequence of other developments that Mervis detailed, came the leadership and strategy needed to turn SAAN around.

Enter Stephen Mulholland, editor of SAAN's weekly business magazine, the *Financial Mail*. Mullholland emigrated to Australia in 1992. He had joined the board in May 1985. His drive and zeal, coupled with a grasp of the urgency of SAAN's plight that coincided with Waddell's views, prompted the JCI chairman to offer Mulholland the managing director's position. Waddell "could not, or would not, save the *Rand Daily Mail*, but was undoubtedly the man who inspired the rescue of the remainder of the group from collapse."[51]

Mulholland recalled that when he became managing director on 1 April 1986, SAAN's losses meant "the company had four months to live before it became technically bankrupt. I suppose there was an unspoken understanding that we wouldn't be allowed to go down the tube, but the way I saw it, we had four months to live. The main thing was action."[52] And, as Bell put it, "Action SAAN got."[53] Mulholland sold SAAN's Johannesburg building, a building in Cape Town housing the *Cape Times*, and its four printing presses. This massive pruning of SAAN's activities meant corresponding staff layoffs; 2,200 people lost their jobs.[54] TML's staff complement in 1989, by contrast, was a lean 1,300.[55]

The company was transformed within a few months from a conventional newspaper and magazine publishing house into an information brokerage. Mulholland set up South Africa's first joint operating agreement for newspapers with the Argus company, under which all the functions of the *Cape Times* except editorial were taken over by its Cape Town evening competitor, the *Argus*. Thus the latter paper was responsible for the *Cape Times'* printing, advertising sales, marketing and promotion, and administration. Comparable to arrangements in U.S. cities like Seattle, where competing dailies share all functions except editorial, the agreement between the *Cape Times* and the *Argus* greatly reduced overheads for the *Times*. It contracted out to the *Argus* services that it had previously undertaken at considerable cost. The move met with considerable suspicion by journalists who feared that the independence of the *Cape Times* would be undermined by what seemed to be a forced marriage. In the much larger and more complex Johannesburg market, SAAN entered similar agreements with Argus that rationalized printing and distribution arrangements.[56]

The company then concentrated on the few things it believed it could do well, limiting itself to four areas.[57] The first comprised the company's daily and weekly papers and the weekly business magazine *Financial Mail*. The second was the company's minority interests in other newspaper enterprises, such as its 45 percent share in the Argus company's *Pretoria News*. The third area was its interest in "niche publishing," reflected by its acquisition of special-interest magazines. Mulholland said he is confident that publications catering to smaller, carefully targeted groups will play an increasingly important role in South Africa, as they are doing elsewhere.[58] Finally, along with other newspaper publishers, the company showed growing interest in electronic media. Like Argus and Perskor, SAAN has a 23 percent stake in the subscriber television system, M-Net. At present, that is the company's major involvement in this area, but it is undoubtedly watching closely for other opportunities in South Africa's still fledgling electronic information industry.

Accompanying the fundamental rethinking in SAAN's mission was an equally different management style and philosophy. To reflect these changes, SAAN underwent a formal but important symbolic change on 9 March 1987: It became Times Media Limited. The reason, Bell said, is that "the old name was associated with failure and did not reflect the company's new thrust."[59]

Mulholland personifies much of the new company's drive and ethos. He is known for emphasizing open communications throughout the company and what Mervis calls his "furious, almost savage enthusiasm."[60] He is uncompromising about his demand for results, unapologetic about his role to make and keep TML profitable. Mulholland's, and by extension TML's, detractors argue that the profit figure has become all important for him and the company—at the expense of the courageous, pioneering journalism that typified the *Rand Daily Mail* and the *Sunday Express*. Mulholland is unbending in his insistence that profitability is vital for the mission of a free press in any society. "If attention to profit had been properly applied," he said, "perhaps the *Rand Daily Mail* would still be here today!"[61]

For any mainstream paper in South Africa, like most papers in Western countries, profitability is an indispensable requirement for editorial autonomy. Mulholland places a premium on that autonomy. In 1989 he told an interviewer, "I have been a journalist for 33 years and I hold as sacred the principle of editorial independence."[62] Salaries and training have also received renewed attention in the late 1980s. Mulholland is an unswerving disciple of the school that insists that you get what you pay for and is committed to paying for the best people he can hire. This practice may be most true of the company's specialist business publications, *Business Day* and the *Financial Mail*, which are not included in national wage negotiations with the South African Society of Journalists. Nor has the union made much headway on these publications.[63] Jeanette Minnie, formerly the SASJ's national organizer, said her comparative salary data do not show that TML journalists are necessarily better off than others.[64] But this finding could be more a reflection of upgrading of journalists' salaries generally.

Nor are all TML journalists impressed with Mulholland's boasts about training. The training opportunities tend to be mostly in the business or finance areas, said journalists from *Business Day* and the *Sunday Times*.[65]

Yet few question Mulholland's commitment to staff development. While editor of the *Financial Mail*, for example, he earned a reputation as someone who "has always fought for better salaries for his employees, and created opportunities for them to travel and experience a wide range of stimuli and training in the course of their work."[66] Nor is there any doubt that TML's corporate culture and work style are worlds apart from that of the old SAAN. Referring to the two modes of operation, Mervis talks of "the effective, dynamic pragmatism of the new regime, in stark contrast to the convoluted, tortuous, indecisive approach of the old."[67]

In making the leap from a tired, directionless entity to a vigorous company with a clear sense of purpose, SAAN's extreme case symbolized the "growing up" of South African newspapering more spectacularly than the experience of Argus, Nasionale Pers, or Perskor. The cause and extent of SAAN's plight, and the impressiveness of its subsequent turnaround, make it atypical. Yet even though much in the SAAN/TML case study is unrepresentative of the broader picture, the company's recent history is shaped largely by the same factors that affected its three counterparts. What were the problems that beset the industry and how did it respond?

THE ONSET OF WINTER

The economic and market forces that began to assail South Africa's press in the mid-1970s resembled a horde of disliked relatives who unexpectedly come to stay. They arrived with little or no warning, gave no idea how long they would intrude, and came as a busload all at once. The press was denied the luxury of being able to deal with these problems one or two at a time. The magnitude, range, and timing of the problems only aggravated the plight of press owners, managers, and editors. The serious challenges began to converge in the late 1970s, when, as Bell put it, "a long winter fell upon the newspaper industry."[68]

Those charged with guiding the press through the bleak weather ahead were ill prepared for its severity. Some of their difficulties were common to their counterparts in other countries, such as declining newspaper readership. Other factors were distinctly a product of the South African situation. Taken together, their impact was profound.

Advertising Revenues and Competition: Attacks on Two Fronts

Television

In 1977, the year before South African television began carrying advertisements, the country's daily newspapers received a generous 32.9 percent of total advertising spending. A decade later, that figure had dropped to 18.8 percent. Weeklies experienced a comparable drop: from 13.2 percent to 7.8 percent.[69] During this period, the total advertising spending increased from an estimated R325 million in 1977 to R1,797 million in 1987.[70] The magnitude of this increase is deceptive, however, because of the corrosive impact of high inflation throughout the 1980s, a point to be pursued later.

As television siphoned off an increasing proportion of the total advertising expenditures, newspapers were forced to sell advertising more aggressively than ever. Forced to match the high inflation rates, the papers needed to increase their rates year by year. Television also offered advertisers a mass national audience that previously only radio and some major Sunday papers could deliver. A national advertiser could now tell millions of viewers about a product with a single spot rather than needing to place ads in perhaps a dozen major papers around the country.

Then there was the enormous power and immediacy of the television medium. Television's initial appeal to the advertisers was so great that would-be advertisers lined up to buy time, and the South African Broadcasting Corporation (SABC) devised a quota system to attempt to cope with the demand.

Aggravating the situation was the government's policy in introducing television. A former chief executive of Nasionale Pers, Dawid de Villiers, outlined in a 1983 article why the SABC's ability to draw advertising revenue had greatly hurt the press.[71] The government set several ground rules when it authorized the SABC to launch a television service. One was that it be financially self-supporting. Another was that it be a state-controlled monopoly and not a partially or completely commercial system that would give newspaper and magazine publishers the chance to offset the advertising revenues they were sure to lose when television went commercial.

In the absence of a government subsidy, South African Television (SATV) could therefore rely on only two sources of revenue: license fees, which it set, and advertising, which it also controlled. De Villiers pointed out, however, what occurred in the first several years of SATV's operation. Even though these were years of high inflation rates, the SABC sought to avoid the politically unpopular step of increasing license fees, so it left fees unchanged. Only in 1982–1983 were the first, and modest, increases introduced, with more significant jumps following later in the decade.[72] The result was easy to predict: "In terms of the financing straight-jacket which has emerged, the SABC is in effect permitted and indeed called upon, with all the monopolistic advantage which it commands, simply to draw the additional money it requires for its ever-growing needs from the pool of total advertising expenditure—thus leaving a diminishing share of that pool for the printed and other media."[73]

Television's introduction of advertising on a full-scale basis in 1978 did not help matters either. If the introduction had come gradually, papers may have had more time to adjust. Yes, they had two years of grace in 1976 and 1977, when SATV operated on a noncommercial basis. Yet the capacity for any established medium to adjust is severely limited when a competing vehicle like television can enter the picture and claim 16.3 percent of the money spent on advertising, with one station, in its first year of commercial operation.[74] That station, TV1, catered to the white market, by far the country's most lucrative sector at that time. Then, in 1982, two new channels were added: TV2 and TV3. These were aimed at the large and increasingly prosperous black market. Three years later the SABC started TV4, an entertainment channel. All these channels broadcast commercials and have opened avenues for the frustrated advertisers who, in earlier times, bristled at having to fight for the few available slots on a heavily oversubscribed TV1. Moreover, each of these stations now allows 8 percent of its airtime for advertising, up from 5 percent when TV1 first went commercial.

In addition, two other services began in 1984 and 1986 respectively. The first was Bop TV, broadcasting from the homeland of Bophuthatswana to certain parts of the Transvaal metropolitan area. The second was M-Net, a subscriber service that concentrates on entertainment programming. Neither of these stations significantly challenges the SABC's dominance of broadcasting advertising revenues.

The arrival of television had a massive impact on newspapers' advertising revenues. The *SARAD Media Yearbook* 1989, an advertising handbook, noted that despite its late arrival in South Africa, television "lost no time in revolutionizing the local world of media."[75] It continued:

> South African media planners have been quick to exploit the extraordinary potential of television to the extent that proprietors of other media feel that television is over used and that [advertising] agencies have an irrational attachment to it. Growth over the first nine years, in terms of adspend, has been an incredible 69.5%, and now takes almost one third of all the adspend as measured by MRA's Adindex. It goes without saying that the advertising medium of the present and the future is television.[76]

That reality was not lost on the leaders of the newspaper industry, as the very existence of M-Net testifies. The channel represents an important strategic move by the newspaper industry in its battle for the advertising rand. Although M-Net is described more fully later, of note here is that it was founded by a consortium of the country's four major newspaper publishing groups, specifically to secure them a share of broadcasting advertising income. By the mid-1980s, the newspaper industry had accepted an inevitable course: If you can't beat them, join them. M-Net provided one important element of that new strategy.

Another was a major study conducted for the Newspaper Press Union that examined the interplay of advertising in the television and newspaper media. The "synergy" studies were intended to demonstrate to advertisers that they could maximize their advertising results by carefully using both media in a campaign. The research suggested that television and print would reinforce each other as advertising media to give better results than either could have produced alone.[77]

Undoubtedly, newspapers will remain a major advertising medium; that is not at issue. Nor, at this stage, is the cut television has made into readers' time an issue. The point here is that papers were forced to adjust to a newcomer sharing the advertising trough, one with a prodigious and expanding appetite. Television now claims close to a third of South Africa's spending on advertising and a senior SABC official predicted that figure will probably peak at about 45 to 50 percent.[78]

The Suburban Press

Attacking the papers on another flank were the growing number of shoppers or free sheets, distributed mainly to suburban households. Packed with advertising from local merchants who often find the advertising rates of major dailies prohibitively expensive, these publications mushroomed in the 1980s. So did their share of advertising. Whereas daily and weekly papers tripled their advertising income between 1977 and 1987, revenues for the country and suburban press increased 762 percent.[79] The *SARAD Media Yearbook* 1989 described this growth as the "print media success story of the past decade."[80]

The extent of their growth, and the damage they inflicted on the mainstream newspapers, are further highlighted by the following figures. In 1977, the smaller papers' advertising revenue was 12.3 percent of that of the dailies. By 1987, the figure had risen to 30.8 percent. Compared with the large weekly papers, the figures were 30.5 and 74.2 percent respectively.[81] What accounted for such growth? Why had such a disproportionate amount of advertising money gone to the smaller papers, which operated under the identical economic conditions facing their larger competitors? The answer, deeply disturbing to the daily and weekly papers, is local retail advertising. No longer are people shopping primarily in the central business districts of their towns and cities; increasingly, they have directed their retail buying to the local shopping malls. As a result, a local, suburban paper can deliver readers to advertisers far most cost-effectively. The owner of a boutique in a Johannesburg shopping mall, for example, no longer has to buy an ad that would go mostly to readers miles away from the store. The local paper offers a more sharply focused readership compared with the more diffuse and spread-out readership available, at a higher cost, in what is essentially a regional newspaper.

The story of the main suburban publisher, Caxton Limited, and the two men behind its success, Terry Moolman and Noel Coburn, is an extraordinary record of publishing prosperity during generally dismal economic times. Their formula was simple: offer advertisers assured high penetration—at competitive prices—in the markets they want, usually through free distribution; focus editorial content on the local community, typically a suburb or a small town for which the larger dailies provide minimal, if any, editorial coverage; and sell, sell, sell to the advertisers. Caxton's sophistication and skill in selling advertising have made the company the envy of the mainstream press and attractive enough for the Argus group to have acquired a 49 percent share of the company. Patrick Lee referred to Caxton's as "the fifth column of South African publishing" and noted that "although the two English and Afrikaans press groups are still much bigger, Caxton's growth rate, its innovation, its success in markets no one else took seriously, make the company a serious player in the media game."[82]

Purists in newsrooms in the mainstream press would sneer at the Caxton approach. Mainstream editors and journalists see editorial content as by definition being the raison d'être of newspapering. If they choose, they can easily dismiss the country and suburban papers as often poor, sometimes dreadful examples of what a real paper should be. The Caxton approach, by contrast, is "based on the concept that people in the suburbs want to read adverts."[83] Moolman and Coburn start from a perspective exactly opposite to that of mainstream journalists: They see their role unambiguously and unapologetically as entrepreneurs filling a niche in the market. As Coburn put it, "We're heretics."[84]

Their critics would charge that Moolman and Coburn are kindred spirits with Lord Thomson, who once described editorial content as the "stuff you separate ads with."[85] While the Caxton philosophy may not go quite that far, its attention to news and analysis is slim at best. For the mainstream journalists who have looked at Caxton's record, however, a blunt reality remains. The company has thrived on an approach that is embarrassing and threatening, testing as it does some fundamental advertising and editorial assumptions of traditional newspapering.

The advertising share that the suburban press has claimed at the local retail level is, admittedly, nowhere near the problem posed by television's voracious appetite. Still, newspaper advertising managers in the 1980s must have felt as if they were watching for alligators while trudging through a swamp—only to be attacked by an increasingly large swarm of mosquitoes. They survived the journey but surely would not want to relive it.

Penetration

The issue at stake here is simple: Is the daily newspaper fading in its appeal to readers in South Africa? The figures suggest it is. Not only are papers struggling to hold on to their traditional readers, but they are also losing the fight to attract the millions of potential new readers generated by South Africa's rapid population growth.

Penetration is the percentage of households in a given area that are reached by a particular newspaper.[86] It is a concept preoccupying newspaper managers in various countries with increased urgency. Conrad Fink described the problem of penetration in the United States as the "silent crisis" of the newspaper industry. "The statistics," he said, "are dismally clear: paid newspaper penetration of U.S. households is falling far behind household growth and, certainly, behind advertiser demands."[87] He noted that whereas the United States sold 124 papers per 100 households in 1950, that number dropped to 77 papers per 100 by 1980.

Change the figures only slightly and one could be talking about South Africa's newspapers—or, more precisely, the traditionally white press. If one excludes the rapidly growing *Sowetan,* the total circulation of the English and Afrikaans daily press rose from 681,424 in June 1959 to 820,772 in June 1988—an increase of 20.4 percent.[88] The Afrikaans press, with about a fourth of the circulation, rose more healthily: 58.1 percent during the three decades. Combined, the increase was 27.8 percent. But this circulation growth is cause for great concern when compared with the overall increase in population of whites, Coloureds, and Asians during that time. These three groups, the main readers of the traditionally white dailies, increased from 5.1 million to 9.2 million, or 80.5 percent.[89] Assume for a moment minimal or even nonexistent black readership of these papers throughout this period. (This assumption would be increasingly inaccurate toward the end of this period, when black readership of papers like the *Star* greatly increased.) But even disregarding this reality, one should have expected at least a comparable growth in circulation simply to keep even with that of the Coloured, Asian, and especially white groups. In other words, if blacks had not turned in increasing numbers to reading these papers, their circulation growth would have been even more stifled.

These figures reflect two realities. Newspapers' traditional readership base is eroding badly and papers are struggling to attract new readers. Fewer whites, still the most lucrative market for advertisers, are reading newspapers. In 1963 an advertiser could have reached 78 percent of the white market by advertising in all dailies. By 1989, that figure was down to 43 percent.[90] As for blacks, the burgeoning group to whom the industry as a whole must turn for its survival, the habit of reading newspapers was not coming nearly as quickly as the industry would have liked. Table 4.1 shows the consumption of media by adults in different race groups.

TABLE 4.1   Consumption of Media by Race Groups

	White Men	White Women	WCA Men*	WCA Women*	Black Men	Black Women
Newspapers						
Read any English daily	34.7	27.5	34.4	27.1	17.1	7.1
Read any Afrikaans daily	21.3	17.2	16.2	12.0	0.2	0.2
Read any daily	51.4	42.0	46.6	37.0	17.2	7.3
Read any English weekly	39.8	36.8	39.3	34.1	11.9	5.6
Read any Afrikaans weekly	34.1	30.2	28.2	24.3	0.3	0.3
Read any "white" weekly	66.1	61.6	60.8	54.1	12.0	5.8
Read any "black" weekly	0.4	0.1	3.7	3.5	17.9	10.5
Magazines						
Read any English magazine	65.6	69.0	55.0	56.9	10.6	8.6
Read any Afrikaans magazine	47.6	52.3	39.0	43.2	1.0	1.1
Read any "white" magazine	84.7	89.6	73.0	76.7	11.3	9.4
Read any "black" magazine	0.3	0.5	1.6	1.8	24.4	21.1
Cinema						
Went in the last twelve weeks	42.2	42.5	34.7	31.0	13.5	3.4
Radio						
Listened yesterday	78.3	75.4	69.0	66.3	58.1	52.9
TV						
Viewed yesterday	83.5	84.5	74.7	77.2	31.3	23.5

* AMPS no longer publishes separate information for Coloured and Asian persons. Also, the white, Coloured, and Asian sectors of the population are now regarded as a single target audience. Figures for this audience are in the WCA columns. Separate information is available for whites because their proportion of the sample is large enough to permit their extraction.

Source: All Media Product Survey (AMPS) 1992 Survey, conducted by the South African Advertising Research Foundation, Sandton, South Africa. Reprinted by permission of the publisher.

The reasons for these changes are complex and are linked to changes in life-style and the fading commitment among many people to the newspaper buying habit. But even though the overall industry picture does not look good, several individual papers are doing well. The viability of smaller papers in particular is tenuous, unless—like *Business Day*—they can assure themselves a particular niche in the market.

The Economy and Rising Costs

South Africa's economy faced serious internal and external pressure in the decade of the 1980s.[91] Continuing domestic political unrest, grave doubts among business leaders about the government's ability to control the economy, and a host of other difficulties led to two kinds of pressure from the international community. The first was the economic sanctions campaign, which gained momentum throughout Western Europe and the United States. On the political front, South Africa faced increasing pressure and embarrassment as one company after another withdrew from South Africa and as one university, city, or pension fund after another divested itself of stocks of companies dealing with South Africa.

On the business front too the country became less and less attractive. In August 1985 former president P. W. Botha gave his notorious "Rubicon" speech, which was highly publicized in advance as a major statement on reform. Instead, Botha bitterly disappointed those hoping for promises of reform by in effect telling the world to go to hell. The result was that the domestic and foreign business communities turned their backs on a government unwilling to commit itself irrevocably and unambiguously to ending apartheid. The outflow of foreign capital following Botha's speech dropped the rand to new lows, pushing up the cost of South Africa's considerable reliance on imports. Table 4.2 indicates the drop in the rand's value since the early 1970s.

The gold price, to which South Africa's economy is closely linked, rose from an average of $161 an ounce in 1975 to $613 in 1980. Then it began to slide, to $460 by 1981 and staying essentially in the $300 and $400 range for the rest of the decade. In 1984 the South African Reserve Bank raised its prime bank overdraft rate to 25 percent in an attempt to curb consumer spending and inflation. This move placed severe constraints on the economy and led to high personal and bankruptcy rates. Other problems included high taxation rates, low productivity, and increased government spending. Table 4.3 indicates the annual inflation rates from 1970 to 1988.

One useful summary measure to indicate the plight of the economy is the gross domestic product. Post–World War II growth rates averaged

TABLE 4.2   The Value of the Rand and Currencies of Selected Trading Partners, 1972–1990

	U.S. Dollar	UK Pound	Japanese Yen	West German Mark
1972	1.30	.52	400	4.12
1974	1.47	.62	434	3.80
1976	1.15	.64	344	2.89
1978	1.15	.59	243	2.30
1980	1.28	.55	294	2.33
1982	.92	.53	227	2.23
1984	.68	.51	164	1.96
1986	.44	.30	73	.95
1988	.44	.25	56	.77
1990	.39	.23	52	.62

Source: Business Futures 1991 (Bellville: Institute for Futures Research, 1991). Reprinted by permission of the publisher.

TABLE 4.3   Average Annual Inflation Rates in South Africa and Selected Trading Partners, 1970–1988

	1970 to 1974	1975 to 1979	1980 to 1984	1985	1986	1987	1988
South Africa	7.5	11.8	13.9	16.2	18.6	16.1	12.9
U.S.	6.1	8.0	7.2	4.8	2.0	3.6	4.1
UK	9.6	15.5	8.8	6.1	3.4	3.7	4.9
West Germany	5.6	4.1	4.6	2.2	−0.2	−0.2	1.2
Japan	10.6	7.3	3.8	2.0	0.4	−0.5	0.7

Source: Business Futures 1989 (Bellville: Institute for Futures Research, 1989). Reprinted by permission of the publisher.

4.8 percent annually until the early 1970s. Between 1973 and 1980 the rates dropped to 3.3 percent. But then, following the gold boom of 1980, they plummeted to an average annual rate of 1.1 percent between 1981 and 1988. So grim did things become in 1985 that the government suspended foreign debt repayments for four months, undermining even further domestic and foreign confidence in the economy.

All these factors played havoc with newspapers' traditional cost structures. To give one example, the cost of newsprint, one of the largest expenses for any sizable newspaper, rose sixfold, from about R250 a ton in 1975 to more than R1,500 in 1989.[92] The impact of this increase and others is starkly revealed in Mervis's observation that "in the sixty-nine years from 1906 to 1975 the cover price [of the *Sunday Times*] rose from threepence to 20 cents. In the next thirteen years it moved from twenty cents to R1.80."[93]

Certainly repeatedly raising advertising rates and the price of the paper helped contain the relentless onslaught of rising costs. But how was one to cope with surprises such as the government's decision to apply sales tax to advertising in 1984? Because the tax rate was then 12 percent (it subsequently went up another point), that decision effectively cut more than a tenth of the advertising pie that actually went to the media. Coming as it did in a year when inflation ran at 16 percent, newspapers and other media had to increase advertising revenues by 28 percent simply to maintain ground.[94]

Economic realities thus forced managers to scrutinize their cost structures as they had never done before. How they reacted to what they found is discussed in the next section.

Industry Wars

As if the industry did not have problems enough, it engaged in two internecine battles of its own. One involved the Cape-based Afrikaans chain Nasionale Pers, which sought to gain a foothold in the politically dominant Transvaal. Its competition there was the other Afrikaans group, Perskor.[95] The essence of the conflict was that Nasionale Pers poured millions of rand into securing the Transvaal base that it sought. In 1975 it established the Johannesburg morning daily, *Beeld*, to take on the Perskor paper, the *Transvaler*, with the explicit view of driving it out of the market.[96] Through its aggressive news reporting and a bolder, more politically enlightened editorial stance, *Beeld* soon muscled its way into what had been secure Perskor turf.

Perskor fought back. It made the mistake, however, of illegally padding its circulation figures, including claiming an additional 20,000 nonexistent sales for the *Transvaler*. The subsequent outrage among defrauded advertisers and criminal convictions for fraud of Perskor managers helped cement a complete victory for Nasionale Pers. In a series of complicated moves, Perskor merged *Oggendblad* into the *Transvaler* and *Hoofstad* into *Vaderland*. Subsequently it merged *Vaderland* into the *Transvaler*. Then, in a final retreat in 1983, the *Transvaler* moved to the smaller Pretoria market and gave up the more desirable morning slot to Nasionale Pers's *Beeld*, which remained based in Johannesburg.[97]

These moves resulted from the weaker group having to accept Nasionale Pers's terms, as part of a "market-allocation agreement ... forced on Perskor with a Versailles-type vengeance," as Tony Heard, then editor of the *Cape Times*, put it.[98] One estimate placed the cost to Nasionale Pers at R60 million.[99] The cost to Perskor, besides financial damage, was its standing as a major newspaper publisher. Nasionale

Pers became the unmistakably dominant Afrikaans newspaper publisher. Perskor continued with what became only a token presence in the Afrikaans marketplace, with its flagship paper, the *Transvaler*, run at a loss for reasons of prestige and political influence. Perskor had to content itself with its various other publishing activities, including a steady diet of profitable government printing contracts.

The second of the two showdowns occurred between the Argus and SAAN groups. As Chapter 2 indicated, these newspaper companies have a strange relationship of "competitive symbiosis." In 1983 the competitive dimension dominated as Argus launched a full-scale attack on the *Sunday Express* and its corner on Johannesburg's weekend property advertising. The threat came from the *Star*, which dropped its Saturday afternoon edition in favor of morning publication. Mervis noted that the *Star* moved against the *Express* "so effectively that within a matter of weeks it not only captured the market but also destroyed the capacity of the *Sunday Express* to make a profit."[100] Offering massive discounts to advertisers, the *Star* easily lured away the SAAN paper's lifeblood. But, as Mervis related, the task was made all the easier by SAAN and *Sunday Express* incompetence and arrogance. The malaise that was endemic in SAAN's management, as evidenced in its handling of the *Rand Daily Mail*, was also highly significant in bringing about the eventual death of the *Express*. It is easy to argue that a seriously overcrowded and overtraded daily newspaper market was healthier as a result of the shakedown and that the Johannesburg-Pretoria market could not sustain the bevy of Afrikaans newspapers that were eventually reduced to *Beeld* and the *Transvaler*. Similarly, events showed that there was not enough property advertising to go around for both the *Sunday Express* and the Saturday edition of the *Star*.

All these developments meant that by the mid-1980s perhaps only five of the country's twenty dailies were making a profit.[101] Some, like the *Rand Daily Mail*, were hemorrhaging badly. Management and editors alike faced what were quite literally life-and-death issues for their papers. How did they respond to the bitter chill of winter?

THE RESPONSE

As the SAAN/TML case study indicates, the newspaper groups adopted several strategies. One, unique to SAAN/TML because of its grave situation, was to trim indebtedness, which it did by selling buildings and equipment. Three other strategies emerged.

Cutting Costs and Increasing Profitability

As the SAAN/TML experience suggested, one way to get out of trouble was simply to spend less money. SAAN did so in various ways. The most drastic was to close papers, which SAAN did with the *Rand Daily Mail* and *Sunday Express*. Also in 1985, the Argus group closed the *Friend.* The only English daily in the Orange Free State province, the paper had a circulation of 8,383 at its death and had long cost the company money. As mentioned previously, three Afrikaans papers were merged earlier.

Another serious remedy, which fell short of actual closure, was for an ailing paper to enter a joint operating agreement with a stronger partner. This merging happened in two instances, as mentioned earlier, with the *Cape Times* and with the *Natal Mercury* in Durban. Each of these papers linked up with a larger, financially stronger Argus paper: the *Argus* in Cape Town and the *Daily News* in Durban. These agreements helped the weaker papers shed many or all of the enormous overhead costs associated with running a newspaper. So, for example, under TML's twenty-year agreement with the Argus group, the larger and healthier Cape Town paper took over the advertising, administration, marketing, distribution, and printing of the *Cape Times.* The TML paper was left owning only its name and contrólling only its editorial content.

As we saw earlier, such a move meant massive layoffs. But it was not only TML that cut back on staff; nor did it do so only in the *Cape Times.* TML's Port Elizabeth papers, the *Evening Post* and the *Eastern Province Herald*, experienced cuts in their newsroom staffs in 1986. The *Post* lost twenty of its fifty-five editorial staff, a drop of 36 percent. The *Herald*'s newsroom suffered a similar reduction.[102]

The *Post*'s editor, Neville Woudberg, described some of the cutbacks, which he said led to enormous savings. The two papers now share reporters for local court coverage and for reporting on parliamentary news from Cape Town. The situation is likewise for rugby tours: Each paper no longer sends its own correspondent.

After the initial rationalizations, which bit hard, the passion for cutting costs eased somewhat. For example, at one stage the papers combined newsrooms to cut costs further. But that did not work, Woudberg said, "because we lost our competitive edge," and they were separated again.

The *Herald*'s Derek Smith said the cost-cutting moves were vital in the industry: "The fundamentals weren't watched. Management allowed costs to get out of control." Moreover, the two Port Elizabeth papers, which form a division of TML, took too long to adjust to changing sales and distribution needs occurring in their marketplace, he said.

Smith and Woudberg agreed that the belt-tightening was indispensable in restoring the financial health and profitability of the papers and hence their longer-term viability. Woudberg said: "The savings we've made far outweigh the detrimental affect on the paper." But he also readily spoke of the toll that the rationalizations took on his paper. The staff reductions meant that "we are running at just about rock bottom," he said. "You've just got to have one or two people out of work and then you struggle to get the paper out on time."

No doubt management could have done some trimming without affecting these papers' editorial quality. Yet in papers like the *Herald* and the *Post*, the cuts were drastic enough to impair their news coverage.

The retrenchments in particular seriously affected newsroom morale, to say nothing of the impact on news coverage. Coming soon after the closing of the *Rand Daily Mail* and the *Sunday Express*, the layoffs left South Africa awash with unemployed journalists.

Enter the Australians. South Africa was an early adopter of the Atex newsroom computing system, which Australian newspapers introduced in the mid-1980s. When Australian newspapers sought journalists experienced on the system, it took little effort to recruit unemployed South African journalists. Demoralized about the condition of journalism in their country and with ample reason to despair over the country's political climate, journalists saw Australia as a heaven-sent alternative.

Nor did the recruiters limit themselves to the unemployed. On one occasion, the Australians signed up twelve mid-level editors at the *Star*. And at the end of October 1985, another three *Sunday Star* and seven *Star* journalists headed east. The threat became so pronounced that the editor of the *Star*, Harvey Tyson, wrote a letter to the *Australian* in August that year. He said that despite the seriousness of the country's political situation, it was not the press's greatest difficulty. Instead, he said:

> The biggest threat, apart from a sagging economy which is helping to kill unviable newspapers, is the sudden raid by some Australian newspapers (not yours) on our best technical journalists. Far from recruiting "the unemployed staff of the extinct *Rand Daily Mail* and *Sunday Express*," they are coming to where the best in the business are employed in essential jobs. They are recruiting key men on whom years of training in electronic editing have been lavished. ... Stealing at one blow a dozen junior executives with an aggregate of at least 100 years of expensive training and experience has already hurt.[103]

The departure for Australia of these experienced journalists constituted a double-edged sword for South African newspaper managers:

lower salary bills but a corresponding lack of experience in the newsroom. Unplanned though it was, then, English papers seeking cost-cutting opportunities found another in the Australian raiders. Overall, however, the journalists' emigration had more impact on the profession than on budgets. Yet although the resulting savings were small, the departure of many of the country's experienced journalists symbolized a harsh reality: Whatever benefits the cost-cutting steps brought, and however necessary they were, the quality of South African journalism suffered as a result.

A final measure was to shift a paper from an afternoon publishing time to the morning. This change took place with two papers, the *Die Oosterlig*, a Nasionale Pers publication in Port Elizabeth, and the Saturday edition of the *Star*. The *Oosterlig* did so largely to cut costs and align itself with Nasionale Pers's two major dailies, *Beeld* and *Die Burger*, which are both morning papers. The *Oosterlig* switched to a morning schedule in August 1989, allowing it to share copy prepared for the group papers more easily. Pierre van Manen, the paper's editor, said the switch was prompted by factors other than simply getting in step with the rest of the group. One was that because of the television era "nowadays people simply are not reading papers in the evening."[104] Also, a morning paper would not encounter the distribution and news cycle difficulties of an evening daily. For example, he said that previously the paper would reach some of the most distant distribution points after the stores had closed and economic activity had ended for the day. With morning distribution time, delivery trucks would now also avoid daytime traffic problems. The time difference between South Africa and the United States was another factor, van Manen said. Because much important news came from the United States, a morning paper could present news that seemed "fresher"; afternoon newspapers would have little new to add to morning reports because it would have been nighttime in the United States.

Thus far only the Saturday edition of the *Star* has moved fully into morning publishing, but the paper's management makes no secret of their long-term plan for the entire paper to shift as well. By the early 1990s, the paper had already begun moving its production schedules and distribution earlier in the day, and the *Star*'s general manager, Jolyon Nuttall, said the process will be complete before the end of the decade.[105]

Diversifying

Companies like Argus, Nasionale Pers, and Perskor have long and extensive involvement in nonnewspaper ventures. By the middle of the past decade, however, they and TML were more deliberately and carefully seeking other information-related business opportunities. Like their counterparts in North America and Western Europe, South Africa's newspaper industry had realized that to thrive in the future they must increasingly think of their product as information rather than newspapers.

South African publishers therefore began seeking other media- and information-related opportunities in that country's much smaller and less complex market. These include moves into the weekly free-sheet papers. The Argus group, with its large share in Caxton's, and Nasionale Pers are leaders in this area. The latter company has also had special success in publishing consumer magazines, including the phenomenally successful and profitable *Huisgenoot*, and English titles such as *Fair Lady*. Nasionale owns three of the top five consumer magazines. TML's *Sunday Times* magazine, published as a supplement to the newspaper, is on a par in circulation with *Huisgenoot*, each in the 510,000 range.

Envious of the SATV's corner on television advertising, the publishing groups pushed for their own piece of the broadcasting revenues. The SABC naturally resisted any possibility of having to share the television airwaves. But in 1985 the government overruled the SABC and opened up bids for a subscription television service. The winning bid came from a consortium of newspaper companies. Nasionale Pers has the largest stake in the consortium, with 26 percent, because of its role in managing what became known as the M-Net service.[106] Argus, Perskor, and TML each hold 23 percent. The remaining 5 percent of the shares are split between the country's two independently owned dailies, the *Daily Dispatch* and the *Natal Witness*.

The lack of news apparently has not bothered the target audience, however. By September 1989 more than 330,000 subscribers paid about R600 to buy a decoder, followed by monthly subscriptions of about R40.[107] These prices, in a country where the average monthly income in 1989 was R769,[108] preclude the great majority of South Africans from receiving the service. M-Net's audience profile thus holds little surprise: Its subscribers, according to audience research, are 80 percent English and are affluent. A third of the viewers drive either a Mercedes or a BMW—the leading symbols of automotive prestige in South Africa—in makes that are standard-issue company cars for senior executives.[109]

M-Net's arrival set two precedents. For the first time, the government permitted a crack in the SABC's monopoly on broadcasting. The reasons it did so are not clear. One reason was probably that the newspaper publishing industry had needed to diversify, so the Afrikaans groups in particular had placed pressure on the government to open up the airwaves. Another possible reason was that it was an attempt to deflect long-standing domestic and international criticism of the government's television monopoly.

The second precedent was that the country's English and Afrikaans papers collaborated in a large-scale commercial venture. The coming together of the four groups, and to a lesser degree the two independent papers, represented a victory of economic self-interest over ideological and political differences.

To some scholars, though, neither of these precedents is surprising. P. Eric Louw, for example, argued that the ideological rift between the Afrikaans and English press has long been overstated and that they are each part of a proestablishment, capitalist press.[110] He and Keyan Tomaselli described the rise of M-Net as the result of collusion between the government and the mainstream press.[111] The deal was simple: In exchange for being offered the M-Net license, the press, as represented by SAAN, undertook to kill the *Rand Daily Mail* and the *Sunday Express*, undoubtedly the most critical antigovernment papers.

The argument is tied to the political climate of the mid-1980s. In the wake of the country's new constitution and the government's growing talk of reform, a rapprochement between business and government arose.[112] Admittedly, this was short-lived. But for a while there were heady days when the business community hoped that President P. W. Botha would usher in reforms that would bring accompanying economic improvements.

During this time, the argument runs, the mining houses that effectively own the English papers agreed to shut down the *Rand Daily Mail* and the *Sunday Express.* In exchange, the government would keep business happy by continuing its reform program. As an added plum, SAAN and all other daily newspaper owners were allowed to form M-Net. The service was established over the protestations and resentment of the SABC. The government's permission for the publishing industry to set up a competitive system was unquestionably a major concession, especially to the two English newspaper groups, Argus and SAAN. The timing of these circumstances convinced some scholars that this "deal" was but an unusually blatant example of the collusion between government and the supposedly antigovernment forces of big business.[113]

Did the press groups in fact sell their soul for a place at the electronic media banquet? As noted earlier, there is no hard evidence to substantiate the claim of collusion between the government and the M-Net consortium. Yet the domination of this important additional media outlet by already powerful media interests raises important issues that command attention later.

Thinking Differently

Until the late 1970s editors and managers could to a great extent let business take care of itself. In a pre-television age, they could content themselves with thinking exclusively about newspapering if they chose, and the profits still came rolling in. As Heard put it, "For many years, the absence of the subversive little box in the corner of the sitting room ... gave newspapers a freeway to boosted turnover and profits. Complacency crept in. The life was pretty easy, if legal and political pitfalls could be negotiated."[114] The events described in this chapter changed that forever. By the end of the 1980s, the emphasis was far more on how to *earn* a living through newspapers. The concepts of marketing, positioning, and efficiency were added to the industry's day-to-day vocabulary.

TML's Mulholland, for example, delighted in pointing out the company's sophisticated reporting system that allows him to know within days full details of each paper's sales, advertising revenues, and other performance indicators. In the past, it took months to gather the data, he said.[115] His ability to get that information quickly, and—more important—his *insistence* that he get it quickly, typify one of management's new touchstones in South African newspapering: accountability.

This accountability and the accompanying sine qua non that newspapers be profitable form the backdrop against which all but a few papers now perform. An exception would be the *Transvaler,* Perskor's flagship paper that is run on a "keep-losses-to-a-minimum" philosophy: The paper is too important to the company for its political voice and prestige to shut down. The norm in the mainstream press, however, is that papers be financially secure and independent.

In the United States, the newspaper industry is generally in vigorous financial health and producing sizable profits year after year.[116] But these papers have long engaged in strategic planning and have begun emphasizing marketing to a degree that simply was not needed in earlier days. An article in *presstime,* a U.S. industry publication, noted that "a quiet evolution at newspapers around the country has transformed marketing from a mere concept to the most urgent and deliberate of missions."[117]

So too in South Africa. Industry executives now rely increasingly on the hard data provided by market research. The Argus group, for example, has its own research company, Marketing and Media Research, which helps interpret the realities of South Africa's complex and fast-changing marketplace to the company's management.

Nor is the new thinking of newspaper executives limited to strictly business issues. Nasionale Pers has relaxed the political and ideological guidelines that influence its activities. For instance, when it bought *City Press,* a black weekly paper in Johannesburg, it left the staff free to pursue their own editorial position. Percy Qoboza, who edited the paper until his death in 1988, was long one of the government's most articulate critics. He was, according to Bell, very happy with the management.[118]

His happiness would have been difficult to imagine in earlier days, when Afrikaans newspapers were influenced more by ideological considerations than pragmatism. Indeed, until 1978, when former prime minister P. W. Botha forbade the practice, the two major Afrikaans press groups had cabinet ministers serving on their boards of directors.

Nasionale Pers has other black publications, such as *True Love* and the legendary *Drum* magazine, which it bought from Jim Bailey. Not one is profitable, but Nasionale Pers's managing director, Ton Vosloo, said the company is committed to the long term in developing its publishing interests in the black community.[119]

Nor is such new flexibility limited to the Afrikaans press. Argus's managing director, Peter McLean, described a situation that demonstrates a break from traditional thinking.[120] Nasionale Pers's *Beeld,* the Johannesburg morning paper that is also promoted vigorously in the predominantly Afrikaans city of Pretoria thirty miles away, competes head on with the Argus paper in that city, the *Pretoria News.* Despite this competition, however, McLean said Argus was aware that *Beeld*'s printing press capacity was limited. As a result, Argus approached Nasionale Pers to sell them press time on Argus's far more extensive printing facilities—despite the help it might give *Beeld* in luring away some of the *Pretoria News*'s Afrikaans readers who might prefer an Afrikaans paper. Argus nevertheless felt it was better off trying to land the printing deal with *Beeld,* a collaborative move that probably would have been unthinkable in a less pragmatic past.

CONCLUSION

Until recently, newspaper leaders were able to think of their product narrowly. Now they cannot, and are not. But their new thinking about newspapers and the new watchword of profitability, crucial though this is for the mainstream press to survive, is not without dangers. Abraham Maslow said that "when the only tool you have is a hammer, you tend to treat everything as if it were a nail."[121] The threat inherent in the industry's profit-oriented thinking is that other models of funding papers in the country can too readily be overlooked or rejected. As de Villiers made clear in the context of newspapers' competition with television for advertising revenues, the papers are not ordinary commercial products on sale in a society; they have a crucial role to play in shaping political and social developments. For that reason, many Western societies accord the press special kinds of protection in the marketplace. It is important, therefore, that South Africa's newspaper industry leaders not let their changing vision of the press regard profitability as the highest good. Special treatment for the press, or segments of it, that conflict with a strict free-enterprise approach to newspapering may well have an important part in reshaping South Africa's postapartheid press.

Facing all it did in the 1980s, the press undoubtedly grew up much in that decade. In the economic realm, the mainstream papers went through a turbulent adolescence. But in the context of South Africa's fast-changing political environment, it is clear that plenty more growing up still lies ahead.

5

The Law

*We have reached a point where I cannot believe any
individual within government or without, knows how
to handle the mare's nest of rules on a rational efficient
basis. I don't believe anyone but God and Peter
Reynolds & Associates, (the latter are our legal
advisers) know how many regulations actually exist.
And I think God must have forsaken the subject.
The only certainty for newspapers is that, if they do
nothing to upset the government, they will be safe.*

—Harvey Tyson, former editor of the *Star*

IN 1984, Harvey Tyson learned in a singular way that even if God
may have forsaken the subject of South Africa's press laws, the government had not. Ever vigilant against possible threats to national security, someone in government must have sat bolt upright on detecting an
apparently clear violation of the law in an article in the *Star*.

This official's instincts were flawless. Whoever first set in motion the
prosecution of the paper under the Internal Security Act, part of which
forbade quoting any of several hundred people inside South Africa and
out, must have derived much satisfaction from the outcome. The paper's owner, the Argus Company, was fined R100 for quoting the
banned leader of the African National Congress, Oliver Tambo. Tyson,
as editor, was also charged under the law. If he had been convicted, he
would have faced up to five years in prison without the option of a fine.

What was the threat this paper posed to the very survival of the South
African state? The story concerned an interview that the SABC wanted
to have with Tambo in London. And what was the *Star*'s iniquity? It
"quoted Mr. Tambo as saying that he could not legally be quoted."[1]
Clearly this was the stuff of which political satire is made. But South

African editors and journalists have found little to laugh about in the vast web of legislation that shaped their lives and their work.

It is a deeply ironic feature of South African society that the government's sustained and systematic curbing of human rights occurred within a carefully constructed legal framework. Whatever the government needed to do to implement and maintain its policies was—at least for its supporters—accorded the legitimacy and hence the moral authority of "the law." So the government could legally prevent migrant workers from having their families accompany them to the cities; or detain men, women, and even children without trial; or forcibly relocate a group of blacks who had lived somewhere for generations to eliminate a "black spot"—or any other of the countless types of human rights violations that repeatedly outraged the world community.

The government relied on the legislative system more than anything else to engineer the society it promised its supporters. In doing so, it needed two types of laws. The first set up the mechanisms essential to move South Africa toward the ideal of a truly separated society. These were scrapped by mid-1991.

The second category of laws ensured that as little as possible would hinder the government, initially in implementing apartheid and then in dismantling it on its own terms. This latter cluster of laws, dealing mostly with controlling political opposition and safeguarding the government's political power base, is of most interest here.[2]

The plethora of laws that faced South African journalists is probably without equal anywhere. The number, complexity, and breathtaking comprehensiveness of this legislation was surely the envy of any government seeking to control politically troublesome or embarrassing information. The South African government supplemented this barrage of antipress laws and regulations together with other techniques of information control, such as the formal and informal harassment of the press and political attacks described in Chapter 8.

Decades ago an editor of the *Star* likened editing a South African newspaper to walking blindfolded through a minefield.[3] That phrase became threadbare from repetition over the years. The image not only grew stale; it no longer accurately captured the legal risks that editors faced. When that grim picture was first used, editors and their papers faced a high likelihood of unwittingly triggering a government explosion. Later, the odds of being injured in combat approached certainty for the paper doing its job as it ought. Whether the government chose to prosecute a given paper in a given circumstance was another matter. The point is that papers and journalists were now markedly more vulnerable than before.

Another well-worn phrase used to describe the plight of the press was that it faced "more than 100 laws." By itself, this claim meant little. Included among these were laws common to other societies and that were unobjectionable to South African editors. Examples included legislation protecting the interests of minors; upholding honesty in advertising; regulating banking, currency, and stock market dealings; and protecting copyright holders.[4] The problem was not the number of laws that journalists faced; it was with their nature—and their capacity to gut thoroughly the news-gathering and distribution mission of the press.

If, for simplicity's sake, one divided the laws affecting the press into two categories, "routine" or "unobjectionable," and those having no place in Western democracies, the latter group still made up a sizable chunk of *A Newspaperman's Guide to the Law,*[5] the main legal guide for South African journalists. These acts constituted the chief weapons in the government's assault on the press. For the most part, these laws were not directed specifically at the press. Journalists were simply caught up along with everyone else who fell foul of the government's curious definition of subversive activity and were likewise subject to the resulting administrative actions or legal penalties to deal with such supposed threats to national security.

Until the coming to power of the Nationalist government in 1948, common law provided the basis of legal control on the press. Common law in fact provided strong support for press freedom, as Gilbert Marcus emphasized.[6] He cited as examples two cases containing strong endorsements for freedom of speech. In one, an important 1965 case concerning censorship, the judge commented:

> When a court of law is called upon to decide whether liberty should be repressed—in this case the freedom to publish a story—it should be anxious to steer a course as close to the preservation of liberty as possible. It should do so because freedom of speech is a hard-won and precious asset, yet easily lost. And in its approach to the law, ... it should assume that Parliament, itself a product of political liberty, in every case intends liberty to be repressed only to such extent as it in clear terms declares, and, if it gives a discretion to a court of law, only to such extent as is absolutely necessary.[7]

Another example came from a 1973 case, in which the judge wrote: "Freedom of speech and freedom of assembly are part of the democratic right of every citizen of the Republic and Parliament guards these rights jealously for they are part of the very foundation upon which Parliament itself rests."[8]

Ironically, the parliament that guarded these rights for itself for decades enthusiastically denied them to others. It could do so because the common-law tradition in South Africa was subject to the overarching reality of the sovereignty of Parliament. This legal doctrine meant that Parliament could enact whatever laws it pleased, virtually free from challenge by the courts except on certain technical grounds. Yvonne Burns elaborated on the implications of this preeminence of Parliament.

> Freedoms, liberties and human rights are not constitutionally protected in South Africa and such protection as there is takes place via the common law. As a result, these freedoms, liberties and rights may at any time be validly amended by Parliament since, in accordance with the doctrine of the sovereignty of Parliament, it is at liberty to alter or even totally remove individual rights, freedom and liberties.[9]

Even if the country's judges universally endorsed the sentiments expressed by their two colleagues just quoted, their hands were tied.[10] This absence of a constitutional guarantee for press freedom or free expression, or other human rights, coupled with the parliamentary strength the Nationalist government had enjoyed, opened the way for the steady curtailment of liberties since 1948. This process was characterized by three particular difficulties: (1) the standards governing official actions or serving as the basis for prosecution were often vague or excessively broad, (2) much government action that affected the press was not subject to independent judicial review, and (3) officials enjoyed wide discretionary powers and a corresponding lack of accountability to Parliament. These difficulties permeate the various pieces of legislation, described here later.

John Grogan, a media law scholar, listed four ways in which press freedom in South Africa was curbed. He referred to foundation rights, entailing "the right to start and continue publishing a newspaper"; practicing rights, "the right to decide who may practise as journalists"; editorial autonomy, "the right to decide what to publish"; and access rights, "freedom of access to information."[11] In each of these areas the South African press was greatly circumscribed, both in normal circumstances but especially under the successive states of emergency that marked the second half of the 1980s. Two issues therefore concern us. What was the routine, or "normal" legal environment facing the press, and how was it aggravated during the state of emergency? Burns, Hachten and Giffard, Anthony Mathews, and particularly Kelsey Stuart[12] are among those providing excellent introductions to the main laws affecting the press, and they amply answer the first question. For this reason, and because most of this legislation predates the period that serves as the focus of this study, these laws are described only briefly here.

More important were the changes in the legal climate caused by the emergency regulations. The media regulations and their impact on journalism and news coverage in the country deserve close attention and are dealt with in the next chapter. The present survey describes the web of laws that journalists operated under during the last decade-and-a-half of the apartheid era.

THE MAIN LAWS INFRINGING PRESS FREEDOM

Below follow brief descriptions of the eleven laws that most dramatically limited one or more of the rights Grogan described earlier. The list includes only those laws that would be out of place in a typical Western democracy and ignores those that journalists themselves found essentially unobjectionable, such as those protecting individual privacy.

With few exceptions, the controversial legislation dealt with security and other politically sensitive matters. Like their counterparts elsewhere, South African journalists have no problems with the principle of national security and being sensitive to their country's legitimate security interests. As always, the debate centered on the degree to which the interests of the state and the government of the day overlapped. The "reasonableness" of the laws listed here and the difficulties they raise are assessed later.

The Internal Security Act (Act 74 of 1982)

Unquestionably, this act was the single most troublesome and inhibiting set of restrictions on newsgathering and distribution. A consolidation of several security acts dating from the early 1950s, this law was South Africa's most far-reaching and comprehensive security law. It had serious, sometimes devastating, implications for each of the four rights Grogan listed.

Foundational rights, which concern the ability to establish a publication, were contingent on the minister of law and order. In terms of another act, the Newspaper and Imprint Registration Act (Act 63 of 1971), all newspapers published in South Africa had to be registered with the Department of Home Affairs. A newspaper was defined as a publication that appeared at least monthly and was concerned with political or other current news. Although this requirement by itself was not a serious problem, it could become crippling if the minister of law and order entered the picture. The Internal Security Act empowered the minister to require the would-be publisher to deposit up to R40,000 if this official believed it might be necessary to ban the paper in the future. Should the paper be banned, the amount would be forfeited to the state unless the government decided otherwise. Normally the issue of the deposit was not a difficulty, and usually only a nominal amount was required. The problem arose for those who for some reason the government wished to deter from publishing. A recent example involved *Vrye Weekblad*, from whom the government sought R30,000. As noted earlier, the paper's supporters provided the money, constituting the largest deposit ever paid, and the paper's registration went ahead.[13] The Durban-based alternative paper, the *New African*, was required to pay R20,000.[14]

Others did not surmount this barrier. "A considerable number of proprietors from whom the money has been demanded have been unable or unwilling to provide it and have consequently abandoned their plans to publish. It goes without saying that the poorer black publishers will be the chief victims of this law."[15] The government did not indicate how many planned publications were thwarted in this way, but Mathews estimated it to be more than ten.[16] An example was the Eastern Cape News Agencies' bid in 1988 to register a newspaper title, only to be required to pay the full R40,000—thus killing the proposed paper.[17]

Even if a publisher paid the deposit, a second problem arose. Mathews said, "There will be a continuing apprehension that the newspaper may offend the minister and that a banning will follow with consequent loss of the deposited money. This constitutes a diabolical way for the government to keep newspaper criticism and revelations in line with its political requirements."[18] In addition, the minister could place great pressure on a publication during this process, as occurred with both the *Vrye Weekblad* and the *New African*. The minister warned these papers while they sought registration that action against them under the Internal Security Act was possible.

> Such a warning means that newspapers are threatened even before they have produced their first edition and this affects the newspapers' finances, advertising and subscriptions as well as its general stability. In this way, what appears to be an innocuous legal requirement is used as a form of pre-natal harassment and control. Perhaps the most disturbing aspect is that it is an arbitrary control—the Minister may use his discretion to prevent registration of newspapers, or to make registration as difficult and costly as possible.[19]

For a paper that the government regarded as politically troublesome, securing registration may have been only the beginning of its problems.

The act also empowered the minister of law and order to ban a single edition or ban a publication outright. These powers of silencing a paper, based on legislation since incorporated into this act, were first used in 1952 to silence a Communist newspaper, the *Guardian*. Subsequent reincarnations of this paper were also banned, until 1962.[20] The provision has been used only once since then, in 1977, to silence two sharply critical black papers, the *World* and *Weekend World*. This represented the first such steps against the mainstream press.

Even though this power was seldom used, it was all the more awesome because it was for all practical purposes unchallengeable in the courts. Moreover, a decision to close a paper was entirely dependent on the minister's judgment, made according to a set of highly subjective criteria.[21]

The act also seriously undermined the second category of rights, for journalists to practice their craft. Ways in which this occurred included detention without trial or banning, both devastatingly effective ways of keeping a journalist out of action. Like most measures under the Internal Security Act, these two were also virtually unchallengeable in court. The state thus had the power to remove from newsrooms, for indefinite periods, any journalists it chose. Unlike the outright bans imposed on papers, this measure was used frequently. Scores, and possibly hundreds, of journalists were detained under this act, as listed in the annual *Race Relations Survey*,[22] the monthly Anti-Censorship Action Group newsletter,[23] and elsewhere.[24] In 1976, when South Africa erupted in violence following the June 16 unrest in Soweto and elsewhere in South Africa, fourteen black journalists were held under the act, thus drastically stemming the flow of news from the townships.[25] A notorious case was that of Zwelakhe Sisulu, editor of *New Nation*, who was served with a three-year banning order in 1980; detained from July 1981 for eight months without trial, in solitary confinement; and subsequently detained for a prolonged period under the emergency regulations. His experience indicated how the government could silence a journalist using either or both of these techniques.

The act also severely curtailed the right of editors to decide what to publish in a critical area of political reporting: the views and other statements of many government critics. No banned person, nor those in several other categories, could be quoted without permission. The names of these people appeared on a "consolidated list" published annually by the government. The list was, of course, never entirely up to date because names belonging on it were being added and dropped constantly. The 1989 list, for example, contained 534 names, seventy more than the previous year.[26] It was the journalist's task to ensure that anyone else whose words were proscribed, but who was not yet on the official list, was not quoted. "The provisions of the Act effectively silence any person (and the press) from quoting any person whose name appears on the consolidated list; persons convicted of sedition, treason or sabotage; persons under house arrest; ... persons prohibited from attending gatherings; persons whose speeches have been restricted by the Minister of Law and Order; and persons under preventive detention."[27]

Perhaps more than any other feature of journalism in South Africa, this list represented an ever-present threat, carrying sobering penalties. Quoting someone in one of these categories carried a penalty of up to five years' imprisonment, without the option of a fine for individuals.

One case demonstrates the inordinate difficulties this law placed on editors.[28] In December 1988 the *Sunday Times* quoted an ANC activist, Harry Gwala. This story led to the paper's owners, Times Media Limited, being fined R2,000 for quoting a listed person. How the error arose is illustrative. The news staff checking the original story did not find Gwala's name on the government's consolidated list. Then a news editor phoned the South African Press Association to check a more comprehensive list that it maintained. SAPA confirmed that Gwala was not on its own list. But it was. The problem was that the style of punctuation used meant that the name "T H Gwala" did not appear. As a result, the *Sunday Times* ran the story.

A reporter told the court that the *Government Gazette,* the raw material from which the consolidated list was compiled, was not checked directly because doing so was very time consuming. Anyone with the slightest understanding of how a newsroom operates would regard the paper's actions as reasonable. The magistrate hearing the case, however, exacted a higher standard. He said that the paper had acted negligently. "I cannot understand the difficulty in consulting the *Gazette, "* he said. "If that had been done, the mistake would not have occurred."[29] Subsequently, four other journalists were also charged with quoting Gwala.[30]

It is noteworthy that in the *Sunday Times*'s case, and that of Harvey Tyson and the *Star* described earlier, the editors charged with the offense were acquitted. Because this offense did not carry the option of a fine for individuals, the least that could happen was that someone found guilty would receive a suspended sentence. Even a suspended sentence is a serious penalty, because a guilty verdict in the future means a mandatory prison sentence for an editor.

It was the rare journalist who deliberately and knowingly risked these penalties. The former editor of the *Cape Times,* Tony Heard, published an interview with Oliver Tambo in November 1985.[31] Having conducted the interview in London, Heard wrestled with the risks entailed in publishing it, but he "judged the interview too relevant to suppress."[32] Both the editor and the paper's owners were charged but after months of postponements the state dropped the charges against Heard and fined the company.[33]

Finally, the Internal Security Act also directly affected the access rights that were fundamental if journalists were able to gather information freely. A person held in preventive detention, for example, was removed from the public arena—and hence from the reach of journalists. A potential news source detained under the act was about as inaccessible as one can get. In addition, access could be limited by suppressing news by banning gatherings or by barring journalists access to any area that police did not want to get media coverage.

These curbs on newsgathering, though serious, were overshadowed by the more extensive problem of journalists being unable to publish what they knew. This latter type of constraint, much in evidence in the Internal Security Act, was the most pervasive information-control technique that the government relied on and was embodied in numerous other laws. The most important of these were the Defence Act, the Police Act, and the Prisons Act. Each of these acts contained provisions with which few would quarrel. The problems in these laws lay in the extent to which large areas of South African life were cut off from legitimate public scrutiny and how this was accomplished.

The Defence Act (Act 44 of 1957)

Three categories of information could be published only with government permission. Briefly, these were information concerning the composition, movement, or disposition of the country's military forces; any statement, comment, or rumor that may prejudice or embarrass the government in its foreign relations or alarm or depress the public; and any secret or confidential information regarding the country's defense.[34] The result was "a blanket ban on knowledge about defence matters."[35]

The difficulty for journalists was simply that virtually nothing could be published except that which the government authorized. Even if journalists learned of newsworthy developments in the defense force that by no stretch of the imagination threatened national security, they still would need permission to publish.

The most notable way the government prevented coverage of a vital issue concerned its invasion of Angola in 1975. While the rest of the world knew of South Africa's extensive involvement in Angola, South Africans themselves remained ignorant and the press was required by law to share in the conspiracy of silence.

During the 1980s, when the army was used to control unrest in the country's townships, the question of reporting on military activities took on a new hue. If ever there were a need for public discussion and press monitoring of military activities and the charges of excessive use of force, this deployment of the army surely merited it. Again, though, it was only an officially filtered version of events that could legally be presented.

The Newspaper Press Union, which represented the mainstream press, concluded an agreement with the Defence Force in September 1980 to facilitate reporting on military matters. By its very nature, though, the agreement favored the military. Mathews commented that "both in form and practice it is precisely the kind of agreement one would expect between two parties that are hopelessly unequal in terms of legal right."[36] He mentioned as an example the provision that the minister of defence was empowered, "when he has decided to gag the press on a military matter, to require the press not to publish the fact of being gagged."[37]

More important, he continued, the agreement itself was based on the government's view of the conflict in South Africa, which was of course highly disputed. As a result, "the information and reporting is controlled and directed by the false assumption of a national consensus on the issues of conflict in the society. Relations between the press and the government being conditioned by this false assumption, any defence reporting which radically rejects the 'national strategy' will simply not be tolerated."[38]

This agreement, it must be emphasized, was separate from the act itself. Although it enabled the press to have a working relationship with the military authorities, all reporting remained subject to the requirements of the act. To conclude, two other far-reaching provisions of the law merit mention. One was the state president's absolute power to censor any communications, including newspapers. In addition, the government was authorized to intercept mail or phone calls if it was thought to be necessary for state security.[39]

The overall impact of this law was that it offered minimal leeway for news coverage that did not have official approval.

The Police Act (Act 7 of 1958)

The overwhelming bias in favor of the official interpretation of events was also the chief problem of the Police Act. Of especial importance was an amendment, added in 1979,[40] that made it an offense to publish any untrue statement about police action without having reasonable grounds for believing it to be true. Although no editor quarreled with the desire for accuracy in reporting on the police, or any other facet of South African life, the requirement had serious ramifications. The first was that the act criminalized what could be a perfectly innocent reporting error, made in good faith by a paper. An offense was punishable by R10,000 or up to five years imprisonment, or both. The second problem concerned the onus and standard of proof. The onus was on the publisher, who had to prove that "reasonable grounds" existed for believing the report was true. The burden of proof concerning the report's untruthfulness lay with the state. Each requirement carried considerable difficulty.

Only two major press cases under this act have been tried. The way a guilty verdict was reached in the first case confirmed media lawyers' fears about the inordinate difficulty of meeting the standards of proof required of the press. This case, in 1987, involved a report carried in the *Eastern Province Herald* two years earlier, concerning the police action in the Cape Province town of Cradock. The *Herald* reported that, among other things, the police had disrupted a church service by firing a teargas canister into the church building. Police officials testified in the trial, however, that the canister had in fact only landed at the entrance to the church. Because of inaccuracies like this, in a story written under tight deadline pressure, both the reporter and the editor were found guilty.

Significantly, the guilty verdicts came despite an August 1981 agreement between the police and the Newspaper Press Union specifying that if a paper obtained and published police comment on proposed reports they would be free from prosecution. This agreement counted for nothing in the trial, in which the magistrate ruled that this agreement did not provide the paper with immunity. The *Herald* was still required to prove that it had reasonable grounds for believing the allegations to be true, and it had failed to do so.[41]

Another case in that year had a dramatically different outcome. The deputy news editor of the *Cape Times*, Tony Weaver, was charged with publishing untrue information concerning the killing of seven alleged ANC guerrillas in a conflict with the police near Cape Town. Weaver had claimed that some of the men had been shot in cold blood and that the police had then planted weapons on the dead men to make it appear as if they had been terrorists.[42] Weaver was finally acquitted, and the medical evidence in particular so conflicted with police testimony that the authorities filed charges of perjury against some of the police witnesses.

This latter case was much the exception to a general principle: "Courts tend to favour the official witnesses when confronted by unofficial counter-versions of what took place; the police badge is presumptively a badge of credibility."[43] Anyone charged under this provision of the act entered court with half the deck of cards stacked against the defense and the other half in favor of the prosecution.

Such protectiveness of the police was long a norm in South Africa, especially on security-related matters, and had implications for the country that cannot be explored here.[44] Simply stated, "The vital question is whether this inhibiting provision and the consequent virtual immunity of the police force from penetrating public scrutiny is beneficial to the functioning of the police force, the furtherance of good government and the maintenance of democratic principles in South Africa."[45] In large measure, the capacity of the press to perform such scrutiny was greatly limited.

The Prisons Act (Act 8 of 1959)

Covering South Africa's prisons could be as perilous as covering the activities of its police. This act had a similar provision for punishing untrue reports and similarly onerous standards facing the accused. The most celebrated case prosecuted under this act showed both the difficulty of meeting that standard and the effectiveness of the law in minimizing criticism of South Africa's prisons. In an attempt to expose poor prison conditions, the *Rand Daily Mail* published a series of stories in 1965 after taking elaborate steps to verify the information. All their informants except one gave sworn statements and were cross-examined by a lawyer before the stories were published.

Yet the court held that the paper had not done enough to take reasonable steps to verify the information, without making clear what the paper should in fact have done. But "the prosecution did not have too much difficulty in establishing before the court that things were basically rosy within the prison system, a proposition which acute observers at that time believed to be untrue and which subsequent revelations have stripped of credibility."[46]

The lesson of this trial for other editors and reporters was brutally clear, and coverage of prisons that lacked official blessing effectively stopped after the *Mail* case.

The act contained other limitations on the press, but none was as severe and stifling. Another Newspaper Press Union agreement operated in this realm. The prison service maintained a twenty-four–hour service for papers wanting to report on prison matters. The papers had to convey the information in full to the department, allowing it reasonable time to check the story and prepare a comment or response. In turn, the paper was free to print the story provided it gave equal prominence to the official response.[47] The agreement offered some relief for the press. Yet this agreement also represented a concession from the authorities and did not replace the law itself.

In each of the three security-related areas of defense, police, and prisons, the government erected formidable barriers to media coverage. The barriers were not impenetrable, and critical and negative stories appeared. Some editors were courageous enough to test the waters, knowingly risking prosecution. Sometimes editors published stories because for a variety of reasons they thought prosecution was unlikely. Finally, the state was willing to accept limited criticisms, up to a vaguely defined point beyond which it could be expected to react. The overall effect of these three acts, however, was that vitally important areas of South African life were cut off from public examination. Journalists' rights to decide what to publish were correspondingly curtailed. Although these acts, together with the Internal Security Act, were the main legal barriers in South African journalism, several other laws deserve attention.

The Advocate-General Act (Act 118 of 1979)

This law followed South Africa's greatest political scandal, known as "Muldergate," or the Information Scandal. It provided for the appointment of a judge to examine allegations of wrongful spending of state funds. It was questionable just how effectively this official could monitor the secret government activities of the kind that led to Muldergate.[48] That issue goes beyond the immediate concern of the press, however, whose role in exposing government corruption was hampered by various clauses in the act. The net effect of these clauses was to prevent anyone from reporting or commenting on a matter that had been presented to the advocate general. The press was still free to report on corruption in government, but "as soon as *anybody* submits the matter to the advocate-general the restrictive provisions of the statute come into operation."[49] The implications for newspapers were at least threefold: (1) they were prevented from covering the matter until the advocate general made a report, (2) the issue could be buried forever because the law enabled the advocate general to prohibit publication of a report in the interests of state security, and (3) the press could have unwittingly contravened this law if the advocate general had been investigating an issue of which the press was unaware.

In its original form, a clause also required the advocate general's written consent before papers could publish *any* report about maladministration or dishonesty in government, but this ruling was dropped after intense pressure from media and legal groups, among others.[50] Although the law was thus not as restrictive as it might have been, it still presented an important hurdle to the press.

The Protection of Information Act (Act 84 of 1982)

Based on an earlier act that in turn was modeled on the British Official Secrets Acts, this law provided comprehensive protection to the state over a wide range of security matters. Like some of the laws already discussed, this one contained provisions to which few people took exception. They were the standard safeguards that nations take to protect their national security interests. But as with the other laws, the problem here lay with the breadth of powers granted to the state. The concept of security was defined extremely broadly, a serious problem in itself. The drafters of this act went beyond that, however, forbidding disclosure of information that could harm what was simply called "other interests of the Republic."[51] The impossibility of knowing how to translate such vague standards into day-to-day decisions in a newsroom was highlighted in Mathews's comment: "If the accused should have realised that *any* interest of the Republic requires that the information be kept secret (by what criteria, it is not at all clear), the information is protected and may not be disclosed."[52]

In practice, this law had fewer of the migraine-inducing qualities of the Internal Security Act, for example. Yet problems arose. One was the foreign policy fiasco in 1981, in which the government was involved in an abortive attempt to overthrow the government of the Seychelles, in the Indian Ocean. The press was prevented from describing the full extent of the government's involvement in this venture. The reason was that when the mercenaries who fled back to South Africa after the coup attempt failed were tried in court, parts of the proceedings were held in camera. Mathews suggested that even if some of the trial had not been held in camera, for the press to have disclosed a key government document proving the government's involvement would have violated the act. He added: "It should not be a crime, assuming that the government was involved in this stupid and dangerous piece of opportunism, to disclose official documents and thereby make public the involvement of government officials. While such disclosure remains criminal, there is no real government accountability to the public and no incentive to avoid future acts of irresponsible military or foreign policy adventurism."[53] As it was, the incident led to convictions against the editors of the *Rand Daily Mail*, the *Sunday Times*, and *Rapport* for contravening the act.[54]

The National Key Points Act (Act 102 of 1980)

This act empowered the minister of defense to declare any place a "key point." Nobody could publish information concerning a key point. Publishing information about an attack on a key point, or other "incident" occurring there, was similarly proscribed. The result was that the public could be kept ignorant of events, such as an armed attack, that in most other countries would receive extensive news coverage.

The journalist's difficulties did not end there. For one thing, the act did not require the minister to indicate when a key point has been designated. Indeed, the spirit of the law shrouds the process with secrecy rather than drawing attention to facilities or buildings deemed especially strategic. The problem? "A journalist, for example, who writes about a key point is guilty if he should reasonably have known that it was one—but what steps he should have taken to avoid a court finding that his ignorance was unreasonable is something of a mystery."[55]

As with the Protection of Information Act, this law did not present a problem for journalists on a daily basis. Its very nature made it difficult to know how much the government had relied upon it. Even if this usage were minimal, its mere presence fueled South Africa's obsession with secrecy and withholding information from the press and the public.

The Petroleum Products Act (Act 120 of 1977)

Because of South Africa's total dependence on imported petroleum, and the various economic sanctions imposed on the country, the government had an understandable strategic interest in controlling information on this crucially important commodity. Once again, however, the problem lay with legislation that was so broadly drawn that it could easily be abused. The most dramatic example of such abuse involved a scam in which a ship off-loaded its oil cargo at the port of Durban. The vessel was then scuttled off the West African coast, supposedly with the oil still on board. "The British press reported the story in full, but Durban papers could not publish a word even though the tanker was seen unloading in Durban."[56]

The Criminal Procedure Act (Act 51 of 1977)

South Africa had no shield laws to enable journalists to protect confidential sources. Courts regarded journalists as ordinary citizens when it came to requiring them to provide information concerning a possible crime. Numerous legal decisions "have established that journalists do not have any privilege in the eyes of the law; they may claim the privilege against self-incrimination, but this is invariably over-ridden by an offer from the prosecutor of indemnity against prosecution."[57]

The state had an especially powerful tool at its disposal in compelling journalists to reveal the identity of their sources. Section 205 of this act allowed the use of a subpoena to require the recipient to appear in court and answer questions before a magistrate. Refusal to do so could lead to a prison sentence of up to five years.

The problem for journalists was acute indeed in a highly divided society like South Africa, where many blacks had a great fear of the police and a similar lack of trust for the judicial system's ability to protect them from abuses. Journalists knew that in this context even quoting an unidentified source could lead to a subpoena and a subsequent in camera appearance in court to identify the source.

Another problem arose with information that had not been published, such as photographs or notes, which the police sought. Heard explained:

> No sane citizen would deny the police a picture, say of a routine murder. But what about incriminating evidence showing young colored youths demonstrating in a highly political event? Quite apart from whose side the newspaper is on, a very practical consideration is that if photographers are known to hand over film to the police for use in possible prosecutions (clearly to identify the ringleaders), the next time they go out to film unrest they could be attacked and even killed by demonstrators.[58]

In the United States, for example, there is at least a recognition of the conflict between the rights of the judicial process to command information from a journalist and the journalist's ethical imperative to honor source confidentiality. The Supreme Court has laid down guidelines to ensure that police and prosecutors turn to journalists only as a last resort in seeking to gather information.[59]

By contrast, no such recognition of the journalist's conflict was acknowledged in South Africa. On the contrary, journalists and their lawyers strongly suspected that Section 205 was used as a tool to intimidate a paper or its editor or as an act of retaliation for an unpopular story. One writer referred to "a long history of such subpoenas being used to attack government critics, locate and plug government leaks and harass opposition journalists."[60]

A particularly blatant, recent example involved the *Sunday Star*. In February 1989, the paper published some economic statistics given to it by a government official. The figures were innocent enough and indeed constituted what the paper's editor, Harvey Tyson, said the state "would call a 'positive' report."[61]

The problem was that the paper had published the figures before they had been presented to the minister of economic affairs. Three months later, Tyson was subpoenaed under section 205 to reveal the source. He speculated on the reason in his paper.

> It seems that a middle-bureaucrat has been upset or has been criticised by his Minister for allowing information to reach the public before he has seen it. Worse, it may be that the Minister is miffed with the *Sunday Star* for attacking his Draft Bill, which still has not come before Parliament. It is hard to reach any other conclusion as to why the police feel called upon to threaten an editor with a "205" and its implicit prison penalty.[62]

The police sought information that apparently had nothing to do with a crime having been committed. Yet again the pattern was of considerable legal power that could readily be abused by the authorities. Newspapers at least had some defenses, Tyson noted, one being that unlike other members of the public, they could create their own publicity.[63]

The use of section 205 appeared to become an increasingly popular tool for the authorities and presented corresponding difficulty for journalists.

The Publications Control Act (Act 42 of 1974)

The laws outlined so far applied to all journalists and publications in South Africa. Between them, they placed an extensive range of information off limits to the press. These laws dealt mostly with official information, concerning matters of state security, the police, prisons, and so on. The Publications Control Act covered virtually everything else.[64] "By extending control to private information," Mathews said, "the authorities have closed the net entirely and all factual material is potentially subject to control."[65]

Paradoxically, despite the name of this act it had no direct impact on the mainstream press. This was because all newspapers published by members of the Newspaper Press Union were exempt from its provisions; these papers were instead subject to the disciplinary provisions of the Media Council. The act was nevertheless of great importance in South Africa because of the large number of non-NPU publications it affected, mainly the alternative press, and the law's more general impact on political debate in the country. The overall place of censorship in South Africa and the broader implications that the Publications Act posed for freedom of expression are raised in Chapter 7. Of immediate importance was the nature and scope of the act.[66]

The law replaced a 1963 act[67] that served as the foundation for present-day censorship in South Africa. The act provided for a Directorate of Publications to implement the censorship process. Anyone was entitled to ask the directorate to rule on the desirability of any publication or "object, film, public entertainment or intended public entertainment."[68] In practice, about four out of five requests for a ruling come from the police or customs officials.[69] The scope of items subject to censorship was extensive, including books, magazines, and newspapers; films and stage performances; and items such as T-shirts and posters. An item could be found "undesirable" if all or part of it:

(a) is indecent or obscene or is offensive or harmful to public morals;
(b) is blasphemous or is offensive to the religious convictions or feelings of any section of the inhabitants of the Republic;
(c) brings any section of the inhabitants of the Republic into ridicule or contempt;
(d) is harmful to the relations between any sections of the inhabitants of the Republic;
(e) is prejudicial to the safety of the State, the general welfare or the peace and good order;
(f) discloses with reference to any judicial proceedings
   (i) any matter which is indecent or obscene or is offensive or harmful to public morals;
   (ii) any indecent or obscene medical, surgical or physiological details the disclosure of which is likely to be offensive or harmful to public morals.[70]

As Marcus noted, this list posed "intractable problems of interpretation. ... The breadth of these concepts is potentially all-embracing depending largely upon subjective evaluation."[71] As with so much other information-related legislation in South Africa, the key issue became who it was that was empowered to put flesh to the law's highly subjective guidelines. Someone once said that "God never made a man wise enough to be a censor."[72] Presumably agreeing with this view, the South African censorship system called upon a higher source of wisdom: a committee.

When the directorate received a complaint about an item, the matter was referred to a committee that worked in secrecy, anonymity, and without giving a hearing to interested parties. Committee members were appointed by the minister of home affairs, the official in charge of implementing the act. Marcus described several problems associated with the work of these committees. Among them were their inadequate representation of broad community views and an overemphasis on white values; the anonymity of the committee members; and the closed nature of these committees' hearings and the consequent lack of accountability to the public for their decisions.[73]

When a committee found an item undesirable, it could ban the work outright, or, if it were a periodical publication, it could also ban all subsequent issues. In addition, mere possession of the item could be banned. Another option was to approve a work, subject to certain cuts being made—such as in films.

A committee's decision on a work could be appealed to the Publications Appeal Board. The board, also under the aegis of the directorate, had the final say in the matter, because the act prevented court review of the board's decisions.[74] The only parties entitled to appeal were those with a direct financial interest in the outcome, such as a publisher, the person who initially submitted the publication for review, and the Directorate of Publications itself. Unlike the initial decision, the appeal was conducted openly, and interested parties such as a book's publisher were entitled to legal representation before the board.

In the 1980s the Publications Appeal Board's approach became considerably more enlightened than that of the committees, as even critics of the system conceded. For example, Jo-Anne Collinge, Herbert Mabuza, Glenn Moss, and David Niddrie said that the board "adopted a less arbitrary and more judicial approach to the question of censorship, and has established guidelines and precedents which involve questions of likely readership, and whether material presents a 'clear and present danger' to state security or not."[75] And Marcus said that "decisions emanating from the Publications Appeal Board in the first five years of its existence were often farcical and consistently restrictive. When Professor J.C.W. van Rooyen was appointed Chairman of the Board in 1979, a greater sense of reality emerged."[76]

In spirit and practice, the situation improved much over the paranoid, puritanical, and arbitrary bannings in earlier years. But serious problems remained. For example, few bannings were in fact appealed to the board.[77] A second problem was that because the censorship system operated along quasijudicial lines, the committees were required to follow the guidelines that emerged in board decisions. But some committees apparently disregarded them, and although the resulting wayward decisions might have been corrected on appeal, in reality that option was an inadequate safeguard because relatively few decisions were challenged.[78]

Yet another difficulty was the ideological and philosophical bent of the board. Marcus showed how the board's views on political issues in several respects closely mirror government thinking.[79] "Despite these criticisms," he concluded, "it would be wrong to portray the Publications Appeal Board as a mere handmaiden of the government. In recent years, the Board has delivered a number of courageous decisions which must have done little to endear it to the government."[80]

Indeed, the board plainly failed to control information as rigorously as the more security-oriented elements within the government may have desired. This failure was quite likely part of the government's thinking in turning to the emergency media regulations to exercise swifter, more direct, and more predictable control over unwanted information. The alternative papers in particular operated far more freely under the Publications Act than under the more stifling media regulations.

Even in the absence of the media regulations, the Publications Act remained a formidable impediment to the alternative press and other publications. The relatively enlightened approach that marked formal censorship in the 1980s was largely a result of the leadership of the Publications Appeal Board's chairman. A different leader or a different sociopolitical climate could see the board return to its previously more conservative approach.

The Registration of Newspapers Amendment Act
(Act 98 of 1982)

Compared with the laws discussed so far, the last act reviewed in this chapter is an anomaly in that it had no direct impact at all on the press yet at the same time presented papers with their gravest threat to date. Despite all the legal limitations it faced, the South African press at least remained independent of formal government control. This act threatened to change that. The law's most important feature was that it set up a mechanism that the government could invoke, at any time it chose, to exercise greater "discipline" over the press. This mechanism was never invoked because of a compromise arrangement under which the press took steps to "discipline" itself. But more on that later.

The act's main feature was that it allowed the minister of home affairs to withhold the registration of papers, without which they could not exist, if they did not submit themselves to a "disciplinary body concerned with upholding journalistic standards."[81] Membership of this body, designed to be independent and have no government appointees, would be voluntary. The catch was that if the minister canceled a newspaper's registration, it might not be renewed unless that official were satisfied that in the future the paper would subject itself to the body for disciplinary purposes. In this way the minister could force papers into the fold of this agency. Despite the supposed independence of this disciplinary body, the law made it clear that it had to be "recognized" by the minister. If the minister thought it was not meting out discipline as it ought, recognition or approval could simply be withdrawn and steps taken to set up a body that would.

The act would have come into force only if and when the state president chose. This proviso, a compromise made by the government after a massive public outcry, took the immediate sting out of the law. Yet the law's continued presence on the statute books made it a potentially lethal weapon against publications that upset the government. It was like a loaded, high-powered rifle aimed straight at a publication, waiting only for the safety catch to be flipped and the trigger pulled. Although not a single shot was fired, the equivalent of a powerfully armed, plainly hostile guard watching his every move was hardly soothing to an editor's nerves.

In introducing this and similar legislation, the government's refrain was always that the press needed to "put its house in order" and "discipline itself." Five years earlier, in March 1977, the government introduced the Newspaper Press Bill, which aroused a comparable firestorm of protest. This bill was withdrawn after an intense and bitter row between the government and the press, and a compromise was reached. The government dropped the bill, in exchange for a new, tougher NPU code that was closer to what the government sought. The government gave the NPU a year to test the new code.[82]

The government's dissatisfaction with the results led to the 1982 law. In a rerun of earlier events, this government-press clash also ended with the press agreeing to tighten its self-disciplinary measures yet again. This time the outcome was the Media Council.

It is appropriate to conclude this catalog of laws with the Newspaper Registration Amendment Act. This act symbolized the most awesome feature of government-press relations in South Africa: No matter how tight the state's headlock on the press, it always had the power to squeeze harder.

Except for this anomalous law, all the legislation discussed in this chapter constituted the *routine* operating environment for South African papers. That the government deemed even these massive powers over the press inadequate, necessitating further powers under emergency legislation, is an enigma addressed in the next chapter. What are we to make of this panoply of laws and their impact on South Africa's press?

EVALUATION AND ASSESSMENT

No editor, and only the most unrealistic journalist, would question the South African government's need for security legislation. It is a sine qua non that a government has as one of its primary tasks the mandate to uphold the country's security. The problem that was endemic in South Africa, and remains a constant temptation for governments everywhere, was to confuse the true interests of the state with those of the government of the day. Mathews provided a scathing dissection of how Pretoria systematically blurred these interests,[83] to the point where "opposition and subversion are no longer distinguishable in South Africa."[84]

Like many others, he outlined how much more difficult it is for a society to move toward or sustain democratic values when security rights get unquestioned priority over individual rights. Elsewhere, he offered a grim prognosis: "It is not freedom that has got out of hand in South Africa, but security. Unless the rapaciousness of the security machine is brought under control, the prospects for liberty and reform are dim, if not non-existent. But security power has to be tamed, not eliminated."[85]

As we saw earlier, this power undercut each of the four kinds of basic journalistic rights. No one suggested that these rights should be absolute; clearly it was a question of balance, or, more correctly, imbalance.

One aspect of this imbalance involved the character of the country's legal and political system. The "sovereignty of Parliament" doctrine gave the executive powers that were essentially beyond challenge by the courts. Unlike the U.S. political system, which relies on various branches of government to counterbalance each other, South Africa was marked by an extraordinarily powerful executive. "The legislature is free to confer on officials of the government whatever powers it thinks fit, and to authorize their use where the administrative authority deems it necessary or expedient."[86] Because the Nationalist government so dominated Parliament, it was able to indulge a growing and increasingly insatiable appetite for powers that would be unthinkable in a Western democracy.

The judicial branch of government was greatly limited, constitutionally, in countering the government's excesses. In addition, it was hampered by its traditionally strict adherence to a positivist approach to the law. Like their counterparts in many other countries, South African judges were by training and professional culture heavily oriented to interpreting and enforcing the law as it was written, not as they believe it *ought* to have been written.[87]

Another limitation on the South African judiciary was that it had no independent power to review actions by the executive. Only if such a review were sought by someone with a direct interest in challenging an administrative action could the courts get involved. The absence in South Africa of a bill of rights or other constitutional safeguards to pro-

tect individual civil liberties eliminated another possible course of redress for those whose freedom of expression had been curtailed.

The result was that "by law, the South African executive has sufficient power to control the content of all the country's channels of public communication. Officers of the government have an almost
unfettered discretion to decide when controls should be implemented.
And no institution independent of the executive has any real authority
to restrain them."[88]

A second category of difficulties involved the nature of the powers
accorded to the government. The scope of such powers was in itself
breathtaking, ranging from silencing individuals with a blanket ban on
anything they may have said or written, to detaining journalists (or anyone else) indefinitely and without trial, to summarily closing down a
newspaper with no recourse to the courts. The extent of such powers is
utterly incompatible with democratic principles and a commitment to
upholding individual civil liberties.

Granted, states must have recourse to extraordinary measures in
times of crisis. The legislation just outlined, however, was intended
for *routine* or *normal* usage; it was plainly untenable to argue that the
South African state—not the government—was under such critical
threat since 1950, when the grandfather of these laws, the Suppression
of Communism Act, was enacted. Moreover, the government contin-
uously and flagrantly abused this legislation to attack those who in
any Western democratic society would be viewed as legitimate political opponents. Undoubtedly, some of the government's actions have
been against those actively seeking the violent overthrow of the state.
The right, indeed the duty, of the state to act in these instances is not
at issue. The difficulty is with the state actions against the countless
thousands of cases of people and organizations expressing opinions or
doing things that would be perfectly legitimate political conduct elsewhere.

Even if one conceded that South Africa indeed faced a fiendish Communist onslaught for more than four decades, and even if one insisted
that never during this time did the government yield to the temptation
of using its vast security powers against legitimate political opposition,
three crucial difficulties remain.

First is the lack of accountability. For example, Grogan noted regarding those times a government genuinely needs to suppress information
that "the danger is ... that such powers can also be used to serve partisan ends. This is why states which lay claim to adherence to the rule of
law place strict limits on the exercise of executive powers."[89] Yet the
government needed to demonstrate to no one that it acted in the state's
interests, and not for partisan ends. The rule of law, Grogan wrote, re-

quires strict limits on the circumstances under which these exceptional powers can be used.

The second issue involved the language in the laws. The extremely broad definition of "Communism" in the Internal Security Act, for instance, was so vague that it could be used to act arbitrarily against virtually anyone opposed to the government.[90] Other examples have been listed previously. Then there were subjective and often vague standards that officials were to follow and the amount of discretion they had in implementing the law.

Finally, procedural matters often presented great difficulties for the press. One example was the inordinately difficult standards that papers had to meet under the Prisons Act and Police Act to show they had taken reasonable steps to verify the accuracy of their stories. Another was the easily abused technique of questioning journalists subpoenaed under section 205 of the Criminal Procedure Act during in camera hearings.

CONCLUSION

The South African press carried a vast amount of legal baggage on its journey toward a postapartheid society. The burden imposed by the number of bags and their sheer weight was immense. Especially ironic was that for all the power these security laws granted the government, South Africa's security situation was far worse in the 1970s and 1980s than when the laws were introduced starting in the early 1950s. In the absence of a solution to the country's political problems, even the far-reaching South African security legislation could not hope to contain political opposition in the long term.

Acknowledging this reality, the de Klerk government soon launched initiatives toward broadening democracy. As this process continued, the press saw the first easing of the government's antipress hostility since 1948. At issue was how quickly and how far the government would go toward dismantling the laws described here. Until the change in political climate at the turn of the decade, these laws remained a massive restraint on the press's potential to cover in full the country's sociopolitical landscape. Defying the system could quite literally mean death to a publication; even vigorously challenging it could unleash untold difficulties, including huge legal bills. When the *Rand Daily Mail* published its prison exposés in 1965, for example, it faced a series of trials lasting four years, at a cost of some R250,000, a staggering sum in the late 1960s.[91] More recently, the *Vrye Weekblad* faced a succession of charges in 1989, including one for illegally quoting Joe Slovo, leader of the South African Communist Party. The paper received donated legal services that its editor valued at about R60,000, over and above funding from the International Federation of Journalists to cover other legal costs.[92]

More critical was the cost levied on a society kept in darkness about some of the most vital developments in its recent history. Legal scholar John Dugard wrote in 1978, "The threat of legislative, executive, or conventional sanction hangs heavily over all South African newspapers opposed to the Government. The disappearance of in-depth, critical feature articles about some of the greatest injustices of South African society, and the enlargement of the number of journalistically taboo subjects, testify to the effectiveness of this threat."[93]

Such was the stifling legal charter under which South Africa's press operated up to the early 1990s. By definition, the legal constraints were the ground rules that determine how the game was played; only with these clearly in perspective can we look at other facts of life South Africa's papers faced—like economic realities, a culture imbued with secrecy, and widespread public apathy. Or a special set of circumstances known as the state of emergency.

6

The State of Emergency

T HE RENOWNED English prime minister Benjamin Disraeli was once asked to explain the difference between a misfortune and a calamity. "Well," he said, if his archrival "Mr Gladstone were to fall into the Thames, it would be a misfortune; but if someone pulled him out, it would be a calamity."[1]

Similarly, if the standing legislation affecting South Africa's press was a misfortune for press freedom, then the states of emergency declared between June 1985 and February 1991 were a calamity.[2] The sporadic genuflections the government still made toward the altar of press freedom were stripped bare of any remaining traces of sincerity. The government's emergency powers over information, and the way it exercised them, subjected domestic and foreign media coverage to unambiguously authoritarian control. The years under the emergency constitute the darkest period yet in a history marked by a long twilight.

What brought on the darkness? And what did the state of emergency permit the government to do under cover of night? As with the laws just analyzed, the concern in this chapter is with the narrower impact of legal limits on one segment of society, the press. The meaning of the state of emergency for the broader society and especially the process of political change, critical though that is, does not concern us here. We are concerned with the government's rationale for curbing the media, how it did so, and what this meant to the country's press.

THE CHRONOLOGY

The continuous and seemingly uncontrollable violence throughout South Africa in the first half of the 1980s led the government to declare a state of emergency on 21 July 1985.[3] Under the Public Safety Act,[4] the

128

state president may declare a state of emergency for a specified period, to allow the government to cope with circumstances that cannot be dealt with under the ordinary law. The July declaration applied to thirty-six magisterial districts, covering the most turbulent parts of the country. These regulations were enacted primarily to facilitate swifter government action against dissidents than existing laws permitted. The security forces received "wide powers to detain, to search or to control movement and to promulgate further control orders in the affected areas. The exercise of each of these emergency powers had obvious implications for the gathering of news."[5] More important, though, were the regulations that specifically affected the control of information. These included a ban on reporting the names of any persons detained under the state of emergency and on writing that could cause anyone "any harm, hurt or loss, whether to his person or to his property or in any other way."[6] The latter provision was aimed at anyone encouraging economic boycotts, for example, which were a popular protest technique.

The real problem for the media began on 2 November 1985, when President Botha proclaimed the first set of regulations specifically affecting the media.[7] These dealt mainly with visual portrayals of unrest and police actions. Aspects of these regulations were successfully challenged in court the next month, but the victory was short-lived—for two reasons. The judgments were later overturned on appeal to the country's highest court, the Appeal Court. Also, the government issued new regulations closing the loopholes.

The November regulations were lifted along with the overall state of emergency in March 1986. This respite was brief, though, for three months later President Botha announced another state of emergency, on 12 June 1986, applying to the entire country. The basic November regulations were included in the new emergency regulations.

The government turned to the Newspaper Press Union and the disciplinary body it established, the Media Council, to help institute greater control in reporting of unrest. Before the government introduced the December 1986 media curbs, it offered the NPU newspapers a deal: Tone down your reporting of the unrest, through voluntary adherence to a stricter code of censorship implemented by the Media Council, and you will be spared the heavy hand waiting to descend on the alternative press. To their credit, the mainstream papers, through the NPU, rejected the offer.[8] Two days later, on 11 December, additional regulations were promulgated, dealing specifically with the media by pulling together the media-related regulations already proclaimed and adding others.[9]

When newspapers began to carry advertisements calling for the unbanning of the ANC, the government responded in January 1987 with regulations that empowered the commissioner of police to ban reports or advertisements improving or promoting the image of illegal organizations. These regulations were overturned in court later that month but the government promptly revised the regulations, thus closing the loopholes exposed in court.[10]

More regulations were overturned in April, but the legal challenges again presented little difficulty to the government. Once more it closed the loopholes: on 11 June 1987, when it renewed the state of emergency. At the same time, it reimposed most of the media regulations enacted on 11 December the previous year.

The final major media constraints came on 28 August 1987, with the proclamation of new censorship powers for the minister of home affairs, who could stop publication of a paper for up to three months. On 10 June 1988, the government again renewed the state of emergency, once more closing remaining loopholes. By this stage, the government must have regarded the media regulations as watertight because they were renewed virtually unchanged on 9 June 1989.

The regulations were lifted in 1990, initially in all of the country except in Natal province, which continued to be torn by violence, and later there as well.[11]

THE REGULATIONS THEMSELVES

The media regulations are analyzed here as a whole, in the form in which they were published in 1988.[12] As noted earlier, this was also the form in which they were renewed largely unchanged a year later.[13] The press was subject to this main corpus of regulations for most of the emergency period. The analysis here, it must be emphasized, is necessarily oversimplified. Important qualifications and provisions of various aspects of the regulations are omitted. This section is intended merely to survey the main aspects of the regulations, not to provide a definitive legal analysis.[14]

The four kinds of journalists' rights listed in Chapter 5 will serve here as a useful way to structure the discussion.

Foundation Rights

The right to start and continue a publication was severely undercut. Publications were broadly defined and included all forms of the print medium, ranging from daily newspapers to handbills or stickers. In addition to the powers the government had under statutory law, the regulations gave the minister of home affairs and the commissioner of police sweeping powers to close publications. For example,

> The Commissioner may, for the purpose of the safety of the public, the maintenance of public order or the termination of the state of emergency, and without prior notice to any person and without hearing any person, issue an order ... prohibiting a publication, television recording, film recording or sound recording containing any news, comment or advertisement on or in connection with a matter specified in the order, to be published.[15]

To emphasize the obvious, this meant that the commissioner could ban a publication without having to be accountable to anyone if it contained anything that he deemed to threaten public well-being. The content areas likely to attract the commissioner's attention are dealt with later. But the clause itself left this wide open; in theory, he could have banned any publications reporting the defeat of his favorite rugby team or those predicting rain over the weekend. Such was the commissioner's power over existing or would-be publishers.

His power was matched by the minister's. Although the minister's options were limited by some requirements, he too was in effect able to silence publications at will.[16] For instance, he could ban any publications officially registered as newspapers for up to three months.[17] Others could be banned for up to six months. In each case, the period could be renewed for another three or six months. Unlike the unlimited range of subject matter to which the commissioner might take offense, the minister at least had to limit himself to the specific problem areas listed elsewhere in the regulations. In addition, he had to warn a publication when it had broken the rules, as he interpreted them, allowing it to mend its ways. If it again contravened aspects of the regulations, he had to give written notice that he was considering action against the publisher, who in turn was allowed two weeks to make representations to the minister. If these representations failed to satisfy the minister, he could then suspend the publication.

A final point worth noting here concerns a provision for a publication in danger of being closed. The regulations offered an out: Closure might come "unless the matter to be published therein and the way in which it is to be published therein has previously been approved for publication by a person specified in the order."[18] The implication of this clause was grim indeed, as media law scholar John Grogan explained: "The newspaper concerned is thus given the choice between outright closure and submission to advance censorship. This is the first statutory provision for formal censorship to have appeared in this country."[19]

The minister and the commissioner were also empowered to seize any publication if either of them were "of the opinion" that any of its content contravened the regulations. Again, the grounds on which they may act were specified and these are described later.

In each of these ways, the regulations allowed the government to close a paper or to intimidate greatly anyone contemplating publishing serious political reporting or commentary.

Practicing Rights

In one sense, the media regulations themselves provided only a limited impediment to these rights. The government's power summarily to close one's paper certainly dramatically undercut one's ability to practice as a journalist. However, other emergency regulations constituted a graver threat to practicing rights. The regulations, which gave the government greater powers to detain individuals than are provided under the normal law, were readily used against journalists. One example involved Brian Sokotu, a free-lance journalist working in Port Elizabeth, who was detained for thirty-two months without trial. On his release, he was placed under a severe restriction order that made it extremely difficult for him to work as a journalist.[20]

Another, and especially ominous, threat to this right came with the June 1988 regulations but receded after extensive protests at home and abroad. The measure concerned the compulsory registration of news agencies, which in turn entailed a move to register all journalists working for a news agency. The regulations required anyone operating a news agency to register the organization, and all journalists working for it, with the government. The regulations provided that everyone initially listed with the government would in fact be registered; the trouble was that registration of journalists could be withdrawn if the minister deemed it necessary for the public safety, the maintenance of public order, or the termination of the state of emergency. The minister could "without prior notice to any person and without hearing any person summarily withdraw the registration"[21] of journalists—effectively shutting down an agency if enough individuals working there were affected. Further, a deregistered journalist or one who had been involved with a deregistered agency could be kept from reregistering.

"News agency" was vaguely defined. The major agencies, like Associated Press, Reuters, United Press International, and the local South African Press Association, were exempt from the proposed rules. So were persons working exclusively for one publication or broadcast station or supplying material on a "casual or isolated" basis. Yet media leaders believed that despite these qualifications they could "include everyone from 'the little old lady sending a few paragraphs every month to *Scope* [magazine]' to a major newspaper like *The Star* which supplies news to its sister papers in the Argus group."[22]

Grogan said "that the registration requirement amounts effectively to a system for licensing journalists. The government has therefore introduced by way of emergency decree the long-threatened system of registration designed to empower it to decide who may practice as a journalist."[23]

Because of the outcry against these implications, the government backed down and the minister of home affairs announced a few days before the system was to be implemented on 31 July 1988 that he would not do so.

This incident was critically important even though the regulations never were implemented. It showed the extent to which government was willing to go to curb the flow of information. Not content with the array of controls it already exercised over the gathering of information, the authorities also sought unprecedented control over the news gatherers and distributors. This move, wrote Anton Harber, coeditor of the *Weekly Mail*, "represents a qualitative leap in the level of government control over the flow of information."[24] Harvey Tyson, then editor of the *Star*, described the move as "*the single, most dangerous attack on freedom of information.*" The register, he said, "is the Rubicon marking, not the suspension, but the death of free speech."[25]

Unquestionably, the system was intended to have life beyond the emergency. As media lawyers noted at the time, it was odd indeed that "such formal and long-term measures—which involve a complex bureaucracy—are introduced in terms of Emergency regulations."[26]

Fortunately this threat was not implemented, but it represented the climax of the government's media onslaught under the state of emergency and, as Tyson indicated, the single most serious measure ever considered against the press. On this front, at least, journalists' practicing rights were spared. However, in the broader picture of the media's life under emergency conditions, that offered little solace.

Editorial Autonomy

The ability of editors to publish what they know, seriously undercut in the best of days, was badly aggravated by the emergency regulations. Many categories of information were proscribed, and they are most usefully described in terms of three sections in the regulations.

Section 3: Publication of Certain Material Prohibited

This section banned publication of eleven types of information. Some depended heavily on lengthy and complex definitions contained elsewhere in the regulations, which for brevity's sake are not repeated here. The interested reader can refer to the detailed definitions of key terms, which are listed alphabetically in the first section of the regulations reprinted as the Appendix. In the following ten pictures of each restricted category of information, terms that are defined in the Appendix are italicized.

Security Action. No *security action* by the *security forces* taken within the wide framework of the emergency regulations could be reported. This was directed mainly at any security forces involvement in suppressing *unrest*. Briefly, "unrest" consisted of any gathering of persons in contravention of the emergency regulations, which included all meetings held outdoors without the approval of a magistrate. The only exception was bona fide sports meetings. Unrest also included any attack on a member of the security forces or a member of a local authority or family members of either groups. For example, attacking the house of a black councillor or attacking the mother of a policeman both constituted unrest. The prohibition extended to actions such as arrests made under the emergency regulations. Grogan said, "The net effect of this prohibition is to prevent publication of all information relating to security operations aimed at the enforcement of the emergency regulations."[27]

Deployment of Security Forces, etc. A similar ban applied to any information on "the deployment of a *security force*, or of vehicles, armaments, equipment or other appliances, for the purpose of security action."[28]

Restricted Gatherings. An upcoming *restricted gathering*, defined more broadly here than in the Internal Security Act, could hold much interest for one's readers. No information about the time, date, place, or purpose of such a meeting could be given. The meeting itself need not have been illegal; it was simply one that would have taken place subject to restrictions placed upon it, either under the Internal Security Act or the emergency regulations. In covering the meeting itself, a paper could not report what was said by any "restricted" speaker, as will be defined later.

Boycott or Strike Action. The media could provide only a carefully sanitized version of information about boycotts against firms or educational institutions, two common protest techniques during the 1980s, or of civil disobedience generally or illegal strikes. It was legal to mention the bare facts concerning one of these developments. However, one could not indicate the extent to which such an action was successful or how the public might have been intimidated, incited, or encouraged to take part in or to support such action.

"Alternative" Structures of Local Government. This regulation was designed to deal with the problem of informal, "people's" agencies of government set up in black townships during the height of the unrest, such as "people's courts." The intention was clearly to prevent these agencies from receiving favorable publicity or credibility and to avoid conveying the impression that the state was no longer fully in charge of all aspects of township life.

Statements by Restricted Persons. Not to be confused with the list of persons proscribed under the Internal Security Act, this provision allowed for a much wider range of individuals' statements to be silenced. Numerous organizations were banned under the emergency regulations. No office bearer or representative for the organization could be quoted if, as the regulations put it, the person's statement "has the effect, or is calculated to have the effect, of threatening the safety of the public or the maintenance of public order or of delaying the termination of the state of emergency."[29]

Detention of Persons. Information about someone detained under the emergency regulations could not be revealed. This information included the circumstances under which the person was detained, although, curiously, not the fact that the person was indeed arrested,[30] and the treatment of that person while in detention.

Release of Detainees. No information could be provided about anyone who had been released following detention under the emergency regulations.[31]

Restricted Organizations. This provision dealt specifically with advertisements supporting organizations banned under the Internal Security Act or restricted under the emergency regulations. The regulations forbade "defending, praising or endeavouring to justify such organisation or any of such organisation's campaigns, projects, programmes, actions or policies of violence or resistance against, or of subversion of, the authority of the State or any local authorities."[32]

Anything Proscribed by the Commissioner. This catchall provision, referred to earlier, empowered the commissioner of police to issue an order prohibiting the media from publishing news, comment, or an advertisement on virtually any subject he chose.

Blank Spaces. The press was also forbidden from leaving blanks or gaps to show that it had omitted material in compliance with the regulations.

Section 4: Taking of Photographs, etc., of Unrest or Security Actions

The regulations also forbade taking any photograph, drawing, or any "other depiction" of unrest or security actions or their results. *Television, sound or film recordings* were similarly banned. Nor, of course, could such portrayals of unrest be published.

Section 5: Making, Publishing, etc., of Subversive Statements

By itself, this section was one of the shortest in the regulations, running to only fifteen lines. It was nevertheless an especially complex part of the regulations because it was based on a 101-line definition of *subversive statement*. These complex rules determined the way Section 5 was to be applied. This section's four clauses were plain enough. They forbade making a subversive statement either orally or in writing or publishing such a statement. Again, the media of print, television, radio, and film were all covered. Also outlawed was the importation into South Africa of "a publication or a television, film or sound recording containing a subversive statement."[33]

What is the understanding of "subversive statement" on which such a powerful ban rested? The definition comprised twelve clauses. The first eleven forbade statements that could encourage public participation in a wide range of actions. For example, nobody could encourage others to engage in unrest, oppose the emergency regulations, engage in civil disobedience, stay away from work, or boycott elections. Attempts to discredit or undermine the system of compulsory military service, a highly controversial issue in the 1980s, were also defined as subversive. In case this list had missed anything important, the commissioner of police was empowered to add to the list of proscribed conduct anything else he chose.[34]

Grogan made the important point that the mere publication of information in these areas was by itself not an offense; it actually had to have the effect of inducing people to do the kinds of things mentioned.[35]

Access Rights

The preceding pages show how the ability of journalists to report what they know was seriously impeded. Similarly deep cuts were made into their ability to gather news. One example, listed earlier, concerned the ban on taking photographs, a provision that particularly affected print journalists.

Another and even more serious emergency restriction on access rights concerned the mere presence of journalists at certain events or in certain situations. No journalist, print or broadcast, could be at the scene of any unrest, restricted gathering, or security action or even at a place where these activities were within sight.[36] What of journalists who were present at a peaceful scene where unrest breaks out? Or what of a reporter attending a "nonrestricted" meeting that suddenly became "restricted" because a participant began making certain statements? The journalist in this situation was required to leave the scene immediately and had to remove "himself within such time as is reasonably required under the circumstances to a place where that unrest, gathering or action is out of sight."[37]

Conviction for violating the media regulations was punishable by a fine of up to R20,000, up to ten years' imprisonment, or a prison sentence without the option of a fine.

THE GOVERNMENT'S RATIONALE

The restrictions were without parallel in South Africa's history. Their scope astonished both South Africans, who were long accustomed to Pretoria's fondness for ironfistedness, and the international community. The London *Observer*, for example, described the restrictions of November 1985 as "some of the most severe imposed in any country outside the Communist bloc."[38] That was early in the evolutionary process of the regulations, before some of the most powerful regulations were enacted.

Given the extensive powers already available to the state under the Internal Security Act, it was surprising that the government felt it necessary to invoke a state of emergency at all. The government's argument was that the country faced an extraordinary situation and that normal levels of freedom simply could not be allowed to prevail. (Not that normal levels of press freedom in South Africa were much to boast of, but that is another issue.) The country was plainly in serious trouble. Violence was endemic and showed little sign of abating. Nor did the government seem to be able to contain it adequately, with new outbreaks occurring constantly. The emergency regulations were introduced when the Total Onslaught theory was still much in favor in South African government circles and the theory offered much support for the drastic measures. President P. W. Botha's own affinity with the security establishment, coupled with the great influence of the securocrats in his government, led his administration to take the path of emergency rule rather than continuing the reform process.

Ever since the early 1950s, with the introduction of the Suppression of Communism Act, the first drastic measure to curb internal dissent, the government's tune was that the state faced critical threats to its security. Extraordinary measures were thus needed. In 1953 Parliament voted into being the Public Safety Act, on which the emergency regulations were based. This act was considered a radical measure at the time because it conferred powers on the government that were usually reserved for wartime.[39]

The melody and lyrics changed little over the years. By the mid-1980s, a few harmonizations had been added, and the words updated, but the song was still a hit with government supporters. Admittedly, by then the lyrics carried much more credibility: The fear for white voters was no longer of clandestine Communists, but it was of what they regarded as real-life terrorists and revolutionaries presenting an all-too-palpable threat to white well-being. Never mind that once again the government preoccupied itself with treating symptoms rather than causes. That distinction held little relevance for whites watching the violence and destruction brought to them in SABC TV footage, which let the country know that things were bad but not so bad that the government had lost control.

By 1985 the songwriters had written another theme into the government's chart-topping hit. Never a favorite of government, the opposition press had long been an unfailingly useful whipping boy. Now, with the English press's antigovernment message having been eclipsed by that of the more vituperative alternative papers, it was predictable that the government would shift its hostility to these latter papers.

The media regulations would, of course, have to fall on the just and the unjust. Andries Engelbrecht, the head of the Directorate of Media Relations, which was the body appointed to monitor newspaper compliance with the regulations, said: "Those dedicated to and qualified for their mission and profession now have to suffer a measure of statutory control, not only on account of the state of emergency but also on account of the hijackers of the journalistic profession or the newspaper method for their partisan objectives; the protagonists of subversive propaganda."[40]

Then there was the foreign dimension. In the mid-1980s, international interest in South Africa's woes was at its peak. Extensive television and print news coverage grievously compounded the problems of a government already under intense pressure at home. The sanctions and disinvestment campaigns steadily gained momentum, fueled by a seemingly endless succession of horrific television images and detailed print reports of a white minority government's actions against its internal, and overwhelmingly black, political opposition.[41]

Incalculable international damage was done to South Africa's image at a time when the Botha government was desperately trying to promote its reformist image.[42] The government saw the foreign press as a crucial player in undermining the way its domestic political program was perceived abroad. Government officials have long charged the foreign press with biased and distorted reporting, sensationalizing the news, seeking only the negative and ignoring the good, and failing to take account of South Africa's complex situation in frequently grossly oversimplified reporting.[43]

Sometimes the government would go further, accusing the press of engaging in outright fabrication. Two days before the antiphotography regulations were imposed in November, President Botha slammed foreign media coverage while addressing the Foreign Correspondents' Association. He said there was a "possibility that foreign journalists have paid black children and adults to burn books and repeat stone-throwing incidents for the purpose of filming them."[44] Botha charged journalists with frequently violating basic principles and ethics of journalism, drawing support from an article that appeared in the *Star* in September. Allegations in the article included those concerning the books and the stone throwing. Another was a claim that a U.S. diplomat had confirmed that a television crew from his country had paid a black family living in Crossroads, the squatter settlement near Cape Town, to demolish their shack because it was in the way of a scene the crew planned to shoot.[45]

A problem with the story, however, was that all the allegations had come from the government itself, and the reporter involved later said that none could be independently verified.[46] Indeed, the government itself never subsequently identified any individual journalists alleged to have fabricated stories. This was despite requests by the Foreign Correspondents' Association for specific information so that the claims could be examined and transgressing journalists be held accountable.[47]

How much "irresponsible" or dishonest journalism the foreign press may or may not have practiced is not the point. Of importance here is that it was taken as given in government circles that such abuse by foreign journalists was widespread, long-standing, and actually precipitating unrest in an already volatile situation.

It was ironic that elements of the local press readily accepted the government's arguments on this issue. This was despite a dearth of any hard evidence to back up claims, repeated often enough over the years that they were accepted by the government and many South African whites. So it was no surprise that television was singled out for blame when the November 1985 regulations were introduced. The minister of law and order, Louis le Grange, said that the government was "concerned with the presence of television and other camera crews in unrest situations which proved to be a catalyst to further violence."[48]

After the regulations were invoked, the government spokesmen repeatedly justified the need to control print media within the country in terms of the revolutionary climate it said existed. The views of Stoffel Botha, minister of home affairs, are worth noting at length:

> In this country freedom in general, and press freedom in particular, must be looked at in the context of an attempted revolution by such violent organisations as the ANC and its mentor, the South African Communist Party. When the leaders of these organisations themselves blatantly admit they collaborate with the mass media to further their struggle for the takeover of South Africa, it should be clear to everyone that the role of sections of the local and international press in this revolutionary process is no flight of the imagination on the part of the government. ... My government will not allow the South African press to be used as a tool of war in the hands of foreign or other aggressors. Freedom of expression will not be allowed to such extent that it fosters chaos, murder, confusion and revolt in South Africa.[49]

The government's view was always that legitimate criticism and opposition presented no problem; the difficulty lay with the papers that spread revolutionary propaganda. By Botha's own admission, propaganda was impossible to define. Nor was it defined in the emergency regulations. But this did not deter him and his colleagues from relying repeatedly on the concept to justify the regulations. Two examples make the point. First, his cabinet colleague, the deputy minister of information, Dr. Stoffel van der Merwe, said: "I don't ask anybody's pardon for the fact that we are doing our utmost to suppress revolutionary propaganda. I am quite happy about that."[50] And then Leon Mellet, the minister of law and order's chief liaison officer, explaining why journalists and photographers were being removed from unrest situations and why their cameras were being confiscated if they returned: "We cannot allow these propaganda efforts by the MDM [Mass Democratic Movement] to tarnish South Africa's image abroad where a destructive view is being created by totally slanted reports emanating from South Africa. We do not want to suppress the news, but we are determined to withhold MDM propaganda from the outside world."[51]

The extent to which the material troubling the government was in fact propagandistic is really irrelevant, as the government itself might concede; rather, the issue was, How significant a threat did this material pose to the security of the state? The government's view that the threat warranted the kinds of steps usually reserved for wartime is open to debate. What is beyond dispute is the dual reality of the mid-1980s of sustained bad news at home and continuous negative coverage abroad. Facing that reality, what was the government to do?

Political scientists Jarol Manheim and Robert Albritton described the difficulty a country has in promoting its international image if its news images in the international media simultaneously have two characteristics: high visibility and what they term "negative valence," or the negative quality of news coverage.[52] They predict that under these conditions a government will try to improve its image by reducing the visibility of its problems, by taking steps such as limiting access to information rather than engaging in "more active forms of promotional activity."[53]

This is precisely what occurred in South Africa. Manheim and Albritton examined the role of South Africa's public relations effort in the United States at this time. Not surprisingly, they concluded that the efforts of professional image makers who were working on Pretoria's behalf had limited value in the light of developments at home. "When all was sorted out, the *force majeure* in determining the news image of South Africa was the domestic political violence, not that of professional image-makers. And control of that *force majeure* was in the hands not of the government, but of the anti-regime insurgents."[54]

This finding linked the elements that most troubled the Pretoria administration: the foreign press and the voice of the "antiregime" forces within the country, namely, the alternative press. The government therefore defined these two segments of the media as witting or unwitting coconspirators with the forces of evil arraigned against South Africa. The technique of blaming the messenger was unchanged; only the identity of the bearer (or bearers) of bad tidings had shifted.

The government was unable to put pressure on the alternative press through the Newspaper Press Union, the main vehicle for dealing with the mainstream papers, because none of the alternative papers were members. Nor was there an easy way of coping with the foreign correspondents, short of denying them visas on a one-by-one basis or systematically deporting them en masse from the country. In government thinking, the threats that these two groups in particular posed, together with the mainstream papers, called for immediate and comprehensive action. Hence came a set of emergency regulations, which gave optimal flexibility in preventing existing and potentially embarrassing media coverage. The emergency regulations also took effect immediately; waiting for the parliamentary approval needed by conventional measures was not necessary. Finally, because they also carried the benefit of a temporary status, they could be more easily defended as "unpleasant but necessary short-term measures." Deputy Minister of Information Stoffel van der Merwe told the *Star*'s conference on conflict and the press in 1987, "I do not feel comfortable using methods like these. . . . We want this to be of a temporary nature, as short-lived as possible."[55]

He was not alone in feeling uncomfortable. Highly controversial from their inception, the regulations drew immediate international and domestic criticism from press and broadcasting communities. They were joined by civil liberties and opposition groups in South Africa, foreign governments, and numerous other constituencies. What were their chief complaints? And, as important, what was the impact of the regulations?

IMPLICATIONS AND EVALUATION

In examining the regulations as a whole, four major themes emerge.

1. **Their Weakness as Legal Guidelines.** Whatever other failings they had, the regulations were also poor law. On several counts, they failed to meet the standards that societies upholding the rule of law seek to embed in their legislation and administrative regulations. The vagueness and breadth of the legislation made it difficult for lawyers to know how to advise journalists or how to defend their clients if they were prosecuted. Grogan offered a scathing indictment of the regulations.

> Their prolixity and sheer volume may be viewed as a deliberate attempt to intimidate journalists into compliance by sheer confusion. The rapid changes in, and addition to, laws governing the media, coupled with the vagueness of the terms in which they are couched, renders it increasingly difficult for journalists to discern the dividing line between legality and illegality. The regulations contain many terms which are novel to lawyers and have not yet been interpreted by the courts.[56]

And the *Weekly Mail*'s Harber wrote that the regulations present a "nightmare of interpretation" for journalists. "Instead of having to bear in mind what the courts would consider a contravention of the regulations, they would now have to constantly think of what [Minister of Home Affairs] Stoffel Botha would see as a contravention."[57]

The provisions granting the commissioner of police sweeping powers to define subversion or prohibit publication on an ad hoc basis went far beyond the legitimate needs of government. The extent of powers accorded to the commissioner and minister echoed the problem of unfettered discretionary power described in the previous chapter.

Another standard of good legislation or administrative regulations is that they are justiciable. Here too the regulations were flawed because, ironically, the drafters took exceptional care to refine the regulations to the point of rendering them virtually "judge-proof."[58] The government succeeded in making the media regulations virtually unchallengeable. Several attempts made in late 1985 to challenge the media regulations met some initial success but were overturned on appeal. More important, though, were several key appellate-level cases dealing with main emergency regulations.[59] The nub of these cases, for our purposes, was that the court ruled that "Parliament has conferred on the State President an unfettered 'subjective discretion' in the exercise of which, in its view, the courts ought not properly to interfere."[60] The result was that the government's ability to implement such far-reaching regulations was ruled to be essentially beyond the purview of the courts.

That was precisely the government's intention. The head of the Directorate of Media Relations said: "Propaganda and publicity per se cannot be adequately dealt with in terms of definitive criminal law and criminal law procedures during a state of emergency."[61] And Stoffel Botha told the *Star* conference "Conflict and the Press" in October 1987 that South Africa's state of emergency required the courts to be dispensed with in resolving disputes between the government and the press. The realities of the situation meant that "our courts will be overcrowded if we follow this particular procedure. One must take into account the fact that the very reason why the legal system is such a sound one, makes it also a very drawn-out system. From the moment you start investigating, until the time when the judge decides on his judgment, there are many months' lapse of time. And that will not meet the situation which the government has to face."[62]

That statement—that the courts were a hindrance, not a help, in the government's quest to control the press—was as honest as one could hope for from the minister most involved in implementing the media regulations. It also showed how committed the authorities were to retaining discretionary powers over the press that would not be subjected to independent judicial scrutiny. Botha correctly said that the measures did not give him unlimited power to act against publications. "No discretion, including my own, is unrestricted. Any publication that objects to my action, has the right to test the validity of my decision in court. ... I must exercise my discretion honestly and in accordance with the rules of reasonableness and fairness."[63]

Yet what was the basis on which the minister was empowered to suspend or close a publication? In what was presumably an attempt to bestow an impression of objectivity and fairness on the procedure that could lead to a paper's closure, the government said it would use a system of "scientific evaluation" to determine whether papers were promoting violent revolution.[64] Shortly after the August 1987 regulations were introduced, Botha announced the introduction of a Directorate of Media Relations to monitor publications.

In itself, this was a curious and even ominous move. It involved the establishing of a fairly elaborate bureaucratic structure for what was intended to be the purely temporary measure of overseeing media conduct during a time of emergency. A panel of experts would advise the directorate in determining which papers served as revolutionary tools. These individuals included "political scientists, psychologists, sociologists, journalists and lawyers. ... The public, however, was not entitled to know the names of these 'experts.'"[65] Pushed to define what was understood by promoting revolutionary aims, Botha said this could not be done.[66]

Such subjectivity led the former editor of the *Rand Daily Mail*, Raymond Louw, to comment that Botha "cannot describe in advance what promotes revolutionary aims, but he confidently assures that he and his 'faceless ones' will know it when they see it. Even the Spanish Inquisitors explained beforehand what 'heresies' they were intent on punishing."[67]

Compounding the problem was another legal provision: indemnity granted to the authorities and the security forces for actions that may be illegal but supposedly taken in good faith. What is distinctive about the South African situation is that this indemnity was granted at the *beginning* of the state of emergency. "Parliament has encouraged them [the security forces] at the outset to take the actions they believe to be necessary and preferred the legal protection which in other societies *might* be granted after the event. This licence for official lawlessness has no place in a state that values the rule of law, humanity or democratic government."[68]

In countless incidents, journalists fell victim to this blank check of legal protection accorded the security forces, who arbitrarily destroyed photographers' cameras and roughed up and detained reporters, knowing they had the full protection of the law in doing so. Challenging such actions and proving in court that the authorities were acting with mala fide was extraordinarily difficult.

Although the regulations may have been marked by technically excellent draftsmanship, they reflected serious deficiencies in the legal morality undergirding them. Like the standing legislation facing journalists, the media and overall emergency regulations were suffused with problems of vagueness, immense discretionary powers accorded to the authorities, and a lack of accountability to the courts. Even as emergency regulations, which are admittedly extraordinary measures, these constraints on the media failed to offer the legal safeguards that one could depend upon in other societies.

2. The Government's Ability to Define and Control News. The government acquired the capacity to control what could not be published without explicit permission or protection of privilege. Initially, the government's concern was to control the images of violence shown in domestic and international media. It was highly successful in this exercise, virtually cutting off media access to the unrest. For someone who might have obtained photographs or footage, there was the additional barrier of a steep fine or lengthy jail term for daring to share the material with the public.

But then, "from about December 1986 the focus shifted to preventing internal communication around campaigns of mass resistance."[69] As is evident from the numerous activities like strikes or boycotts that the media could not easily cover, the authorities were vitally concerned to stifle domestic dissent and protest by various means, including denying it publicity. In both cases, the target of the regulations was not incorrect or distorted information—the "propaganda" that the government insisted was the problem. Rather, it was *accurate* information that the state sought to hide, initially in visual form and then in written form too.

How these curbs were implemented is important. Invariably, decisions on what journalists could or could not cover were determined by the security authorities in a given situation. It was a police officer, then, rather than a reporter or photographer, who determined what was appropriate material for tonight's news or tomorrow's front page. Journalism professor Gavin Stewart said after the November 1985 regulations came into force, "In most professions, the practitioners themselves decide who may practice, when, where and how. I wonder how my doctor would react if he was told he had to ask a policeman for permission to do his job."[70]

But it was not as if the government inflicted a total news blackout. Although it prevented the media from covering much of the unrest, there was a great deal else it could say. The government simply ensured that only its version of reality was portrayed. The Bureau of Information was established when the 1986 state of emergency was announced to provide news briefings for journalists. From early on, though, it was plain that the bureau was neither equipped nor motivated to meet even the elementary needs of the media community. The police handed the responsibility of clearing and confirming information to the bureau, which in turn said it was not there to clear information. Asked for help in understanding the complex regulations, the bureau said its role was not to provide legal advice and told journalists to consult their lawyers. Because the bureau's meetings were not privileged occasions, journalists were warned that "even questions they asked ... could land them in trouble with the emergency regulations."[71] Bureau briefings were disdainful of the media's needs, often providing information only long after events, and frequently inaccurately.[72] A former *Newsweek* correspondent in South Africa, who was deported during the emergency, described the briefings as consisting "mostly of government minions denying eyewitness reports of police violence."[73]

Elements of farce sometimes marked the briefings, such as the time a frustrated official announced, "I will not allow this news briefing to degenerate into a briefing for the dissemination of information."[74] Then from 24 June 1986 the bureau attained a new level of noncooperation, refusing to answer questions unless they related to the day's briefing or had been submitted four hours previously. Three months later, the exercise in futility mercifully ended when on 25 September the bureau announced that it was closing its media center and would henceforth respond only to telex requests for information.[75]

This development did not mean an end to the government's management of the news, of course. The regulations still required approval for unrest-related news; now the primary agency for granting it once again became the police.

By placing various clusters of newsworthy events in a journalistic never-never land, with reporters having to pretend that certain events had never occurred, coupled with the government's own supply of information, Pretoria made "itself the sole provider of news and comment on its own actions."[76] In describing the impact of the emergency regulations, it is easy to forget that only a relatively small part of South African life was immune to media coverage. The proscribed areas of coverage, however, were crucial to the political developments in South Africa. The taboo areas were precisely those that most dramatically affected the political opposition in the country. The government's claim that it was concerned only to stifle propagandistic and revolutionary rhetoric in the media was belied by banning coverage of strikes, boycotts, civil disobedience, or protests against the system of military service. As Collinge et al. put it, "Obviously these curbs do not relate in any way to 'terrorist' activity as Stoffel Botha would like to suggest but to campaigns which have gained mass support in townships across the country."[77]

Some of the most significant events and trends helping to shape South Africa's future were thus off limits to the press and hence to the public as well. Yet these were the very developments of which all South Africans needed knowledge if they were to make intelligent choices about their future.

3. **Their Abuse and Selective Application.** The regulations' deficiencies listed thus far were more than enough to discredit these measures

at home and abroad. But even if these problems had not existed, the government's abuse and biased application of the regulations would by itself have brought them into total disrepute.

The government hardly intended to apply the regulations evenhandedly. As described earlier, the main targets were the alternative press and the foreign media, especially broadcasters. When the August 1987 regulations were introduced, for example, the government indicated that they were specifically intended for use against the alternative press.[78] These and subsequent media regulations made no such distinction and they applied equally to mainstream, alternative, and foreign media. In taking action under the regulations, however, the government's main interest lay with the latter two groups.

Government actions taken against journalists and newspapers, described in publications like the annual *Race Relations Survey*, the Anti-Censorship Action Group monthly newsletter, or the *IPI Report*, show a strong preoccupation with steps against the alternative press. Countless actions have been taken against the mainstream publications too, especially English papers. Yet one would expect far more government activity against the mainstream papers. This is because the alternative press constitute only a few publications, employ far fewer journalists than mainstream papers, and appear less frequently. Two possible reasons account for the disparity. One was that because of their editorial slant, alternative papers were far more prone to falling foul of the regulations. This was certainly true. But by itself this did not explain the disparity, given the degree to which the government frequently ignored violations by the mainstream papers. A second reason is that when it came to detecting possible violations of the regulations, the government read the alternative press far more scrupulously than it did the mainstream papers. Starting with the assumption that these papers were the real "troublemakers" that deserved the most attention, the government easily found occasion to prosecute alternative papers and their editors. The question is, How easily could it have done the same with the mainstream press? The answer lies partly in a study of one of the *New Nation*'s encounters with the regulations.

The instance involved the use of the emergency regulations to suspend the paper for a three-month period in 1988. Marcus provided a detailed analysis of the documentation on which the minister of home affairs based the suspension, the first under the regulations.[79] The minister cited twenty-one articles that he said violated the regulations.[80] Marcus discussed several of these stories. One involved a photograph of a man at the funeral of his nephew, an executed prisoner. It carried a caption that read, "The battle is now on to save the thirty-one other activists presently on death row." The minister regarded the photograph and caption as helping to foment revolution because it reinforced "the campaign with regard to the so-called patriots sentenced to death for deplorable capital offences linked with unrest and ANC terrorism."[81]

Botha also condemned a brief report about a visit by ANC president Oliver Tambo to Yugoslavia for giving publicity to "the revolutionary leader, ... thereby reinforcing the promotion of the image of an unlawful organisation."[82] Note how far government concern had moved beyond the standing ban on quoting Tambo and other listed individuals;[83] now a report describing his travels was instrumental in helping close the paper for three months.

The reasons Botha provided confirmed the fears that people had when the regulations were first introduced. Lawyers and academic experts "expressed alarm at the 'hypersensitive and politically paranoid attitude' adopted by Mr Botha in applying the restrictions. ..."[84]

As noted earlier, the regulations allowed a paper to make representations to the minister. The *New Nation* did so, without effect, and the minister soon took the next step in the process: He issued a formal warning that he was considering closing the paper because he said it was continuing to publish propagandistic articles. He identified six stories that he said continued this trend.[85] The paper's publishers went to court to try to prevent the government from suspending the paper but its application failed. Then in March 1988 the government used the media regulations to silence the paper.

Another incident is illustrative. In November 1987 the *Sowetan* received a warning from the minister to toe the line. Among the minister's specified complaints against the paper was a report quoting an ANC leader. The leader condemned "necklacing," the grim practice of executing suspected police informers or "collaborators" by setting fire to a gasoline-doused car tire placed around a person's neck. This report, Botha said, "tends to legitimise a revolutionary leader . . . and to promote his and his organisation's image." The *Star* asked, "Must one deduce that the Minister would have been quite happy had the paper quoted the ANC in support of such acts?"[86] The *Star*'s editorial raised another issue: the minister's double standards. It said that most, if not all, the reports that the minister objected to in the *Sowetan* would have appeared in Nationalist papers like *Beeld* and the *Citizen* without troubling him. "In one publication," the *Star* said, "they are permissible; in another, seditious."[87] This problem of double standards was confirmed by Marcus, who said that many reports that Botha objected to in the *New Nation* case had apparently caused him no concern when they appeared in other papers.[88]

As it turned out, the *Sowetan* was not suspended, unlike its alternative press counterpart. *New Nation*'s experience, however, was shared by numerous other alternative publications. By mid-May 1989, Botha had warned the following publications that they might be closed under the regulations: *Al Qalam, Grassroots, New Era, Out of Step* (published by the End Conscription Campaign), *Saamstaan, South,* the *Weekly Mail,* and *Work in Progress.* In addition to the *Sowetan* being warned, *Die Stem,* a conservative Afrikaans paper, was also warned.[89] This paper voluntarily closed in January 1988 after an official in the Department of Home Affairs telephoned its editor to tell him that a censor would be appointed to the paper. The editor said it was "clear that the government wanted to suppress all right-wing publications."[90] In addition, the more serious step of suspension was taken against *Grassroots, New Era, South,* and *Weekly Mail.*

The emergency regulations also contained the lesser but nevertheless serious threat of prosecution for violating any of their numerous provisions. Here too the alternative papers got closest, but by no means exclusive, attention. What is curious, however, about the government's reliance on its powers to prosecute under the regulations is that they ignored them for the first few years of the emergency. Then in mid-1989 came a flurry of activity. Within a short time, the *Weekly Mail* faced two counts of violating the regulations by publishing details in 1987 on the circumstances and treatment of detainees, and the former editor of *South,* Rashid Seria, and the paper's publishing company were charged because of a May 1988 report on the success of a boycott in the schools. *Vrye Weekblad* faced six charges of undermining the system of military conscription.[91] Two former editors of the student newspaper at the University of Cape Town were also charged with publishing reports about school boycotts.[92]

The prosecutions represented a strategic shift in the government's application of the regulations. Now it turned to the courts to enforce them. When the *Mail* appeared in court in August 1989, the trial was held in camera. The paper headlined its report on the court case by saying, "The *Mail* in court ... but we can't tell you why."[93] In terms of a provision under the general emergency regulations, no evidence in the trial of someone detained under the emergency may be released until the judgment is given.[94] In the report, the *Mail* wondered if the state would address two questions: "Why have more than two years been allowed to pass before prosecution? If the damage to state security was as great as the charge sheet alleges, why was swifter action not taken?"[95]

It is not only actual prosecutions that presented problems for the press. Police repeatedly launched investigations against papers, requiring them to give statements and spend extensive amounts of time with lawyers responding to police inquiries. At one time, the *Natal Witness* faced seventeen charges under the regulations.[96] Editors strongly suspected that the government used these regulations, together with investigations under other laws, to harass their papers.

In steps taken against journalists, here too the same pattern emerged of the government concentrating on the alternative press. No one can estimate with any accuracy the number of incidents in which local and foreign journalists have been affected by the emergency regulations. Such incidents must run into the thousands. These are separate from the countless other actions taken against journalists under other powers at the government's disposal. The expulsion of eight foreign journalists in the first year and a half of the nationwide emergency included the BBC and *New York Times* correspondents. In addition, Stoffel Botha told Parliament in 1987 that in the preceding year 238 foreign journalists had been denied visas or not had them renewed,[97] an example of an important government technique to regulate South Africa's image abroad used in conjunction with the emergency regulations.

The South African Society of Journalists tried to keep track of the degree to which its members were hampered by the regulations. Yet journalists covering the unrest areas had run-ins with the law so frequently that some stopped telling the organization of their experiences, according to Jeanette Minnie, a former SASJ national organizer. Arrests of photographers in particular, she said, were so routine that these journalists no longer saw any point in notifying her office. She mentioned one news photographer who had been arrested about a dozen times in one month.[98]

Another organization, the Association of Democratic Journalists, described the toll on journalists in one particularly grim period, the month leading up to the election on 6 September 1989. The ADJ concluded that more than 100 journalists were arrested during this period alone.[99] With the election opposed by a nationwide defiance campaign organized by extraparliamentary groupings, the authorities were especially sensitive to media coverage of police action. The result was indiscriminate action against journalists, especially photographers and television crews. In the Western Cape, for example, police were ultravigilant in their watch for cameras. Thus on 2 September "most of the TV crews operating in Cape Town were arrested shortly before protest action began near Parliament."[100] The police dread of the camera reached astonishing levels, as the ADJ report indicated: "Anyone with a camera was simply arrested—including several bewildered tourists and a local hotel manager."[101]

The police actions against tourists were admittedly atypical, but the behavior against journalists followed a familiar pattern that was simply intensified during this period. The pattern was for police to announce at an unrest scene that the press should leave, although often no warnings were given. Because their equipment made them stand out in a crowd, photographers and television crews were more prone than newspaper reporters to being rounded up and removed from the area or else arrested and detained. Rarely were these journalists charged under the regulations; the objective was simply to get them away from the scene.

A leading Johannesburg media lawyer, David Dison, told of another way authorities abused the regulations. "The authorities have interpreted the prohibition on the reporting of unrest and security action as entitling them to exclude journalists from areas where unrest, as defined, is not even taking place. ... They generally bar the Press from reporting, with an invocation of the litany: 'It's a contravention of the emergency.'"[102]

That was the experience of countless journalists. A photographer working for a Johannesburg paper said, "We used to believe that our presence caused the police to act less harshly. But since the state of emergency, police move out photographers and soundmen before they do anything. Their operation has shifted from dealing with the situation to dealing with the press before dealing with the situation."[103]

He told of his own experiences under the regulations. In one instance, a student demonstration he was covering at the University of the Witwatersrand, in Johannesburg, led to a standoff between students and the police. The police said they would leave the students alone if the photographer left the scene. He agreed but as he was leaving he was

> pulled to one side, put into a car and taken to a police station, where I sat for a couple of hours. They took photographs of a colleague and me, as if we were huge criminals. Later a lawyer came to fetch us, no charges laid, and we were told to go. This is intimidating.
>
> A few days later, at another event at Wits, the officer who had arrested me previously pointed a finger at me, he actually warned me about being back again. It intimidates you, you feel scared, lose concentration, want to get out of the place.[104]

His story can be repeated countless times, as individual journalists paid a hefty physical and emotional price in working under the regulations. Understandably, a similar price was exacted of their profession.

4. **The Undermining of Journalism.** From the practicing journalist's perspective, the most repugnant aspect of the media regulations was their frontal onslaught on the most fundamental tenets of good journalism. They forced reporters, photographers, and their organizations to practice the very antithesis of ethical journalism. Journalists were thwarted in their ability to seek and report accurately and completely what was occurring around them. They were forced to flee scenes of unrest, exactly the opposite of what a good journalist ought to do. More

than merely repressing their instincts and suppressing what they knew to be the truth, they were also knowingly and unavoidably co-opted into presenting the government's version of reality.

The regulations had other negative effects on journalists and the profession. One was on the morale of journalists. Journalism researchers Gavin Stewart and Charles Riddle found in a survey of editors and reporters that "a sense of defiant resignation characterised most of the interviews. The typical senior journalist sounds like a person living with a tumour: sometimes it hurts terribly; at any moment it might prove fatal, but most of the time it must be ignored so that life can go on."[105]

A recurring theme in reporters' comments was the frustration they encountered under the media regulations. Stewart and Riddle found that many mainstream reporters covering sensitive stories practiced considerable self-censorship and that their subeditors or editors adopted cautious approaches to stories that might violate the regulations. The caution levels varied greatly from one mainstream paper to another but the result for any reporter who had one story after another rejected by his or her superiors was frustrating indeed. A reporter on the *Natal Mercury* described the process: "You find yourself not writing stories that might create trouble because you know it's just such a lot of fuss. It's like an ongoing war. ... Reporters here feel they are fighting the newspaper hierarchy."[106] Another, on the *Eastern Province Herald*, which faced several expensive lawsuits in the mid-1980s, said: "There's probably the inclination now to stay safely within the law, whereas the inclination some years ago might have been to push the law to its limits."[107]

A *Cape Times* reporter described the situation at that paper as follows:

> Self-censorship is happening in the newsroom at two levels. Obviously, at the level of the emergency regulations one feels that one should rather temper one's own story rather than allow the newsdesk or the subs to do it. We are told to write as if the regs don't exist—with the result that the stories get spiked or cut. If we do it ourselves we feel somehow we can get around the regs and get the story in the paper. At a more insidious level there is a strong belief in the newsroom that the paper ignores certain kinds of news relating to progressive political issues, the community, labour, extra-parliamentary politics. Some big names in extra-parliamentary politics get coverage. But the newspaper turns a blind, rather disparaging, eye to what is happening on the ground in the factories and in the schools.[108]

The point about reporters being told not to censor themselves is important. Several papers had this policy, among them the *Star*. The difficulty is that it did not work. A reporter on that paper observed that "besides the cuts the editors make, reporters—especially those who routinely deal with sensitive matters—now know how to write their stories to get around these things. ... The editor has stressed that we mustn't censor ourselves. But people are. They are doing it against strict instructions but it has become ingrained."[109]

No one doubted that the regulations curbed what could be reported, in some cases seriously. But editors differed on the extent to which the regulations undercut their papers' functions as monitors and reflectors of society. Some, like Richard Steyn, formerly editor of the *Natal Witness*, believed that their news coverage was seriously curtailed by the proscriptions. He said, "We run into problems regularly with the emergency regulations." Steyn's paper had a reputation as one of the most aggressive and courageous dailies in its reporting during the state of emergency, and he said that despite the regulations, "We're getting a lot out." He added, though, "We're not telling the whole story; we *can't* tell the whole story."[110]

Sharing his view was Kosie Viviers, editor of the *Cape Times*. He described the impact of the regulations as "significant and very severe." Even more serious, in his view, was one of the many ripple effects the regulations have had. "Under the emergency the information networks that the newspapers had in the townships collapsed," he said.[111]

Beeld's editor, Salie de Swardt, warned against the danger of overstating the effect of the regulations. He said that their impact was less than many people think, especially outside the country. He estimated that only "five percent of our normal news flow is affected" by the regulations themselves, as distinct from the impact of other laws.[112]

Another danger of the regulations was that some papers or journalists were quietly grateful to use them as an excuse for inadequate coverage. While the regulations were still in effect, Denis Beckett, editor of the award-winning monthly magazine of political comment *Frontline*, said, "If the state of emergency were lifted tomorrow, very few papers would look different the day after."[113] Most papers, he added, used the regulations as an excuse and a shield for their incompetence and unwillingness to conduct the rigorous reporting that he said previously characterized the mainstream press.

His view was shared by several alternative press editors and journalists, who believed that their publications were generally far more willing to seek ways of getting around the regulations. Louise Flanagan, of the East London News Agency, said that despite the emergency, "the alternative press is more likely to make an effort to publish stories."[114] As a generalization her claim seems valid but the mainstream papers, under a wide range of editors, took a correspondingly wide range of attitudes to the emergency regulations. Some showed considerable courage and willingness to push the regulations to the limit; others, especially some smaller dailies, were complacent and far more inclined to follow the lead set by larger papers.

Speaking in the context of the various political pressures facing the English press, Rex Gibson, former *Rand Daily Mail* editor and now the *Star's* deputy editor in chief, said some papers were cowed. But, he continued, "about 70 percent of the English press has met the challenge, and about 30 percent has become more timid." As for editors using the regulations as a shield, however, he said: "I don't get any impression that English editors have said, 'Thank God we don't have to make these decisions.'"[115]

A media scholar pointed to another facet of the "shield" role that the regulations could or did play for the mainstream press. He told of an editor of a mainstream English daily who mentioned his gratitude for the regulations and the rationale they provided for keeping some of his more radical reporters in line.[116] This remark symbolizes the gulf on many English papers between their senior and especially medium-level editors and the reporters, as referred to earlier. This split between reporters and management, a permanent and troubling quality of the English press, was notably widened by the pressures of the emergency.

Serious though this rift was on some papers, it could have been far worse. The reason was that the government had come nowhere close to using the regulations to their fullest potential. Then again, it did not need to, given some of the almost certainly unplanned results that the regulations had—like the self-censorship and heightened internal tensions they fostered on newspapers. In addition, the regulations also damaged newspaper credibility. Jocelyn Kuper, an authority on newspaper marketing, said that "as long as there are media restrictions, newspapers will have credibility problems. It is not just the SABC which has a credibility problem. In conducting research on the *Sowetan*, we found that readers blamed the newspaper as much as the government for the media restrictions, because what they experience in their backyards is different to what they read in the newspapers."[117]

How did the press respond to the emergency regulations? Early on, it mounted several direct legal challenges. As noted earlier, these led to short-lived successes when the government won important court victories on appealing the initial rulings or else simply refined the rules to close the loopholes. Another tactic was to highlight the effect the regulations had on their news coverage. Several papers ran notices telling readers that what they were reading was produced under the emergency restrictions, and they continued doing so throughout the state of emergency. Until the government stopped them, many papers also published extensive blank spaces or blacked out text or photographs, indicating dramatically through self-censorship the large chunks of material of which their readers were now deprived.

From early on, newspapers began testing the limits of the regulations, some more courageously than others. Gaps in the regulations were probed and prodded, and innovative attempts allowed the press to report stories that, in the context of the suffocating regulations, breathed unexpected puffs of information or understanding into the public arena. One tactic involved opposition members of Parliament making statements under the protection of parliamentary privilege. Remarks that were otherwise illegal suddenly became publishable, under the exemption the regulations themselves afforded. Another dealt with the publication of detainees' names. Papers discovered that when police informed detainees' families of their detention, this technically constituted official release of that information—and was thus usable by the press.

Papers throughout the country repeatedly violated the rules, especially on more obviously newsworthy stories such as the annual stayaways on 16 June, the anniversary of the unrest that began in Soweto in 1976. Breaking the regulations by covering a particular story was obviously easier when an editor knew most other papers were likely to cover the story. Decisions on whether to publish a story that probably broke the regulations were highly subjective. In addition to whatever legal advice editors may have received, they based their decisions to publish on such factors as the degree of perceived government hostility to their paper, the current political climate, the likelihood of the story in question offending the authorities, and the relationship with the police in one's area.

As stressed earlier, the regulations were not open to clear legal interpretation. Michael Green, editor of the *Daily News*, said, "Technically, they are very restrictive indeed. I take a fairly pragmatic view, and try not to interpret them too literally."[118] Another Natal editor, the *Natal Witness*'s Steyn, likewise did not adhere to the letter of the law. "We've gone well beyond the emergency regulations," he said, "but only if we've got an *arguable* defense—not necessarily one that would win, but arguable."[119]

The daily routine of editors and reporters consisted of thinking about things other than the emergency, however. Andrew Drysdale, of the *Argus*, said: "One has to live with it. We don't go around muttering the numbers of the rules; we have to get on with producing a newspaper."[120]

This "routinization" of the media regulations posed another threat to the press. Having lived with the regulations for several years, the press found it easier and easier to accustom itself to them and became tired of seeking loopholes to exploit. With the passage of time, elements in the government also greatly welcomed the added powers and convenience the regulations gave them. De Swardt, editor of the largest Afrikaans daily, *Beeld*, said he was "concerned that the rules worked so well that the government would want to keep them."[121]

De Swardt, who opposed the media regulations in principle, said "the only problem is that in some respects they worked, especially with respect to overseas television coverage."[122] He typified the views of Afrikaans editors, who were more inclined to agree with the government that international television reporting on the unrest was sensationalized and distorted. Yet he was typical too in his ambivalence toward the regulations.

Undoubtedly, the rules *did* work well in attaining the government's primary objectives of stifling international and domestic portrayals of political violence and depriving the internal political forces of media coverage of their actions. But at what price?

CONCLUSION

Just as the media regulations cannot be seen apart from the general emergency regulations, nor can the toll that each set of restrictions has taken be separately identified. Together, though, there is no doubt that the regulations further dented the rule of law and aggravated Pretoria's already abysmal image among many at home and abroad as an authoritarian government that cared little for human rights. More important, though, the media regulations inflicted incalculable harm on the country's long-term interests. Marcus's remarks in this connection are apposite:

> The wisdom and efficacy of the use of emergency powers to silence opposition is questionable. Heavy-handed security measures cannot bring lasting security. Indeed, they appear to be accompanied by the reverse: an escalating intensity of violence. Security is more fundamentally ensured by political, social and economic measures which are equitable and offer all South Africans a stake in their futures.
>
> ... Television footage of brutal security force action (which South Africans are precluded from seeing) have [sic] attracted justifiable outrage and condemnation from foreign governments. The perverse solution was not to curb security force excesses but to stifle the messenger. The clamps on reporting have also had the effect of lulling white South Africa into a false sense of complacency by creating the impression that order has been restored to the townships. Those who live in the townships know better

and no amount of censorship can ever remove the harsh reality of their conditions of existence.[123]

Once again, the government had responded to a crisis of dissent by addressing symptoms rather than causes, leaving the condition of the body politic to deteriorate still further. This only made more difficult and complex the healing process that, sooner or later, would have to be tackled. When the de Klerk administration took office and began changing the country's political direction, it had still to deal with the legacy of the emergency regulations—and the price they exacted. To his credit, de Klerk ended the regulations within months of taking office.

Another part of that price deserving special mention is the long-term harm done to press freedom in particular and civil liberties generally. The length of the emergency, plus its scope, further numbed a society already steeped in secrecy, silence, and censorship as the normal operating procedure for much of South Africa's public life. The standing curbs on free expression were so severe and had accumulated over so many years that South Africa could without exaggeration be regarded as a closed rather than an open society.

Reversing this impetus toward secrecy and government control of information is inordinately difficult. Indeed, in the early months of the de Klerk administration, it became clear to some in the press that the new minister in charge of the media regulations saw them as increasingly undesirable and urgently needing to be modified or dropped. However, Stoffel Botha's successor, Gene Louw, was handicapped in trying to liberalize or even scrap the regulations by some personnel in his department who greatly resisted such moves.[124]

The apparent will on the government's part to begin reversing the damage that the regulations had inflicted was of course to be welcomed. Assuming this commitment is genuine and that the government is not deflected from its course, it is impossible to predict how far the de Klerk administration might move the country toward a culture of openness.

Yet just when South Africans had most needed to know what was happening in their country and ought to have been exposed to the full range of ideas contesting for political recognition, the government chose to serve up ignorance. Pleading the crisis of the times did little to justify the media regulations, especially not in the form they appeared and the way they were applied.

President John Kennedy once said, "We are not afraid to entrust the American people with unpleasant facts, foreign ideas, alien philosophies, and competitive values. For a nation that is afraid to let its people judge the truth and falsehood in an open market is afraid of its people."[125] This fear of its own people, perhaps more than anything else, characterized the government's tragic decision to usher in the dark years of the media emergency regulations.

Dark though these times were, they were not without scattered shafts of light. Through the media at home and abroad, or through informal channels of communication, South Africans who wanted to know still learned what was happening in their country. And, in the end, the unpleasant facts, the foreign ideas, the alien philosophies, and the competitive values would all still be there when the state of emergency was merely an ugly memory.

7

Other Environmental Hazards

If you take a frog from its pond and put it in a pan of
cold water and heat it slowly on the stove, the frog will
sit there until it boils to death. The frog's senses are
equipped to measure only large differences in
temperature, not gradual ones. It has evolved that way
because it normally has no need to measure gradual
changes in temperature.

—**New Scientist**

B OB STEYN, the conciliator and registrar of the Media Council, was
on the phone with a woman complaining about a headline in that
morning's *Cape Times.* The headline dealt with an incident of police
beating schoolchildren in Cape Town's streets, a story she saw as yet
another fabrication by a troublemaking newspaper.

As they spoke, Steyn noticed out of his window a group of uniformed
black schoolchildren walking in single file in Darling Street below.
Then out of nowhere and for no apparent reason came a group of
policemen, batons flailing as they dispersed the children. Steyn described to the woman what he was witnessing.

"I don't believe it," she said. Then, referring to what she assumed
must be his political bias, she added: "What's more, you must be Prog
and shouldn't have the job you have."[1]

Steyn told this anecdote to illustrate how, during the state of emergency, countless white South Africans in particular simply did not
want to know what was happening around them. Far from resenting the
massive clampdowns on information described in the previous chapter,
many South Africans (by no means all of them white) took comfort in

159

ignorance. They did this to the degree that Steyn ranked public apathy as possibly the greatest obstacle to press freedom in South Africa. Three other obstacles he listed were the loss of media credibility, direct or indirect pressure from the government or other vested interests, and economic pressures.[2]

This chapter examines two sets of overlapping issues: (1) public apathy and ignorance and (2) censorship, intolerance, and government secrecy. Together they seriously undercut public support for newspapers and created an environment highly inimical to a vigorous, healthy press.

PUBLIC APATHY AND IGNORANCE

Steyn's anecdote about the angry woman reader provides a troubling starting point for this discussion. Her denial of reality is documented repeatedly by observers of white South Africans. These whites approached a feared reality with a mix of apathy and ignorance that varied in its levels of willfulness. Referring to South African whites in particular, Steyn said, "There are too many people who are not only disinterested but actively resistant to being informed—they do not want to know."[3]

This is not the place to examine how the psychology of denial in a siege climate affected the media in a society like South Africa, fascinating though that exploration might be. More pertinent here is the reality of this phenomenon. In their attempts to report and comment on the state of emergency, newspapers often encountered apathy, hostility, or both, especially from more conservative readers. This was most vehemently displayed toward English papers critical of the government and the state of emergency. Not surprisingly, papers that focused less on bringing bad news to their white or middle-class Coloured readers, for example, encountered less reader hostility. Understandably, many white readers were predisposed to seeing life about them through a government-shaped interpretation of reality. The many conservative Afrikaners who believed that the government had betrayed their cause were even less inclined to accept certain propositions. For example, they were less likely to accept that blacks had legitimate grounds for opposing the political system or that much black unrest was spontaneously generated out of deep and long-standing deprivation.

Even the English press, which traditionally prided itself on not getting caught up in the government's definitions of reality, was not immune to the wishful interpretation of reality that some of its readers wanted. Take the example of the end of white rule in the rest of southern Africa. Ken Owen, editor of the *Sunday Times,* described South African newspapers' reluctance to take seriously their own reporters' stories pointing first to the fall of the Portuguese colonies of Angola and Mozambique and then to the likely victory of Robert Mugabe in Rhodesia's last election. Readers similarly failed to take these predictions seriously. According to Owen, "We struggled to have our reports published, even if only on page 29 or 43; and when they were published they were seldom read, when read seldom believed."[4] Pretoria, he wrote, was so committed to supporting Mugabe's chief opponent that it "managed not only to manipulate public perceptions in South Africa but to deceive itself into malappropriate policies."[5] In both instances, South African whites were ill prepared for changes that reporters closest to the scene had viewed as inevitable.

When a paper presents information that is not easily accommodated by a reader's worldview, one of several responses results. One possibility is denial, which occurred when press coverage of domestic turmoil became increasingly unavoidable for South African readers. Another is to attack the press. Readers, or former readers, may rely on other defense mechanisms, such as withdrawal, repression, and rationalization. This avoidance of reality marked a conversation that Richard Manning, a former *Newsweek* correspondent, had with a white, English-speaking woman in Johannesburg during the state of emergency:

> This intelligent woman had only two sources of information: her maids and NP [National Party] propaganda. She knew nothing. Nor, it seemed, did she want to know anything. When I told her that the phones to Soweto had been cut off, she refused to believe me. When I told her about the idiocy of the press briefings, she said she thought the government was right to quash irresponsible rumors. And when I told her about the thousands of arrests, she said they were probably necessary.[6]

Manning made the important point that benign or willful ignorance was by no means limited to Afrikaners. Ignorance, he wrote, has long "been a way of life for South Africa's two million whites of English descent—the Anglos," whose "contribution to the South African drama had been to watch quietly from the sidelines. They had turned themselves into a giant irrelevancy."[7]

Manning overstated his case but his point is valid. For English speakers like the woman whose remarks he recounts, avoiding the truth has long been a grim feature of South African life. "Repression of realities, Anglo style, is above all else a frenzied immersion in privilege and luxury. I found it hard to watch, because nobody likes to watch futility— rearranging the furniture while the house burns down."[8] Here too Manning's remarks must be tempered, by the courageous and principled stand many English speakers and English papers have taken against apartheid. Yet the fact remains: People respond to the media's challenge to their worldview in varying ways.

At the 1987 *Star* conference on conflict and the press, Yehudi Litani, an editor on the *Jerusalem Post,* drew a parallel between South Africa and the plight of Northern Ireland and Israel. Societies facing high levels of violence and turmoil are prone to the "Belfastization" of their people, which Litani said leads the populace to tell the media: "Leave us alone. With so much politics, terror, war, bloodshed and agony—we do not wish to hear or read about it. We are too tired and confused. If grief does not come to me or my family, thank God. We don't need to hear of other people's troubles."[9] The parallel between white South Africa and Israel is clearer still. Litani said, "For most of the Israelis the situation is too complicated to live with constantly. They resort, naturally, to a process of psychological repression in which reality is kept hidden, deep down. They do not wish to be reminded of it. Yet here we, the journalists, come along and keep reminding them constantly, almost every day. Do you wonder why many of us are disliked? And that is an understatement!"[10]

South African readers are no different when it comes to news they would rather not hear. Besides denial and apathy, readers may also select the time-honored technique of stoning the messenger who bears bad news. The government has for decades cultivated a climate of antipress sentiment, targeted initially at the English papers and the foreign press and more recently at the alternative press. But it did not stop there. As Owen said, "The white public, including the business community, took up the Government's complaints. Denigration of newspapermen and newspapers became something of a national occupation."[11]

The English press was accustomed to attacks from the government and its supporters in the Afrikaans community. But then segments of the English press's own support base began turning on these papers. So it was not surprising that journalists and editors would question the value of their news-gathering efforts and commitment to conveying as full a picture as possible of South African life. To be sure, many white and especially African, Coloured, and Asian readers sought far more than these papers could or would publish. Their desires for a fuller account of events presented the opposite problem to the barriers of apathy, ignorance, denial, or hostility among other actual or potential readers. But by the later 1980s the values of a large portion of South Africa's English speakers were no longer in tune with those of the traditional liberal principles of the English press.

The response to censorship indicates how this is so among whites generally. For most of them, according to legal scholar Gilbert Marcus, censorship is not a burning issue.

> By and large ... censorship has become "acceptable." Perhaps the constant monotony of bannings over so many years has induced a complacency and lethargy. Perhaps the new "enlightened" standards of publications control have led people to believe that there are no longer severe restraints on the freedom of expression. The true explanation, however, is that censorship operates to shield and protect white South Africans from reality—the reality that the majority of the population are living in squalor and poverty and that years of oppression are giving vent to violent anger on an unprecedented scale.[12]

All this is to say that the big news story of 1976 to 1990, the shift to the country's postapartheid era, itself greatly influenced the press's acceptance by its readers. These years brought much grim news and presaged what many whites feared above all else: black majority rule. For them, the wisecrack about the smoker who read that cigarettes caused cancer and decided to quit reading newspapers makes sense. These readers cope with unpleasant newspaper reports about their society by rejecting the messengers bearing them. As T. S. Eliot wrote, "Humankind cannot bear very much reality"[13]—especially not in a society steeped in intolerance and secrecy.

CENSORSHIP, INTOLERANCE, AND SECRECY

Richard Steyn, editor of the *Star*, wrote in 1987, "I am continually surprised by the number of intelligent people, from both the right and left of the political spectrum, who hold no brief for a newspaper publishing views at variance with their own. Intolerance of opposing viewpoints is by no means the preserve of those in power; it is one of the characteristics of society under siege."[14] And that is the key: South Africa is not a country in which free expression has been allowed to thrive.

The government's strategy of introducing extensive media curbs in the latter 1980s was no surprise. Doing so was perfectly in character for an administration that had progressively cultivated a climate of censorship, intolerance, and secrecy since coming to power in 1948. By 1985 South Africans had grown accustomed to nearly four decades of increasingly authoritarian rule. As in other societies, authoritarianism South African style found support from an often compliant or even supportive white electorate.

Formal censorship, which eased in the 1980s, is one of three legs on which South Africa's approach to the flow of controversial or embarrassing information is built. The other two are intolerance and secrecy, both qualities embedded in South African culture. The formal censorship system, supplemented by various other information-related laws, both flowed from and reinforced these two other qualities. Direct and indirect censorship were, consequently, the codifications of a society steeped in intolerance and secrecy.

It was not always so. Before the apartheid era, South Africa may not have been noted as an incubator for controversial ideas or as a champion for intellectual tolerance. But nor was it known as the largely closed society that it subsequently became. Quite appropriately, describing that sorry journey long preoccupied analysts of the country's media. This theme of a move from openness toward a closed society runs throughout all the major works on the South African press.[15] Law professor Anthony Mathews's comparative treatment of government secrecy in South Africa, the United States, and Britain, *The Darker Reaches of Government*, is now dated but remains a masterful analysis.[16] His more recent contributions also offer rich insights into South Africa's culture of intolerance and secrecy.[17]

Although the direction South Africa took for its first forty-one years under the Nationalist government is plain, the issue now is whether this trend had peaked with the presidency of F. W. de Klerk and, if so, how readily this legacy of intolerance and secrecy can be overcome.

Beginning in the early 1950s, the government stitched a quilt comprising one piece of silencing, stifling legislation after another. By the mid-1980s, the quilt was large enough to smother much of the debate on crucial areas of South African life. Finally, Pretoria became so infatuated with the powers of secrecy that it passed the National Key Points Act, which afforded the government the curious power of designating installations so secret that it need not announce it had done so.

To be sure, voices opposing this trend were heard from early on but the government was set on its course. Like the development of these constraints on free expression, the reasons that the government invoked this strategy were complex. At the risk of greatly oversimplifying its objectives, one can point to several themes. The first was the government's oft-stated fear that the media would aggravate an always volatile security situation in the country.[18] Journalist Amanda Armstrong referred to this theme in connection with the state of emergency. Quite simply, "the state seeks to silence individuals and organisations resisting apartheid."[19]

The government sought also to address another constituency: the white community, which it wished to insulate from the uglier realities of South African life. Again, Armstrong's view: "The state seeks a form of political and ideological control where those forces which keep it in power, namely big business and the white electorate, remain ignorant about the levels of repression and resistance. The state is attempting to manufacture evidence of 'normality' within South Africa, and prevent publication of anything which would have detrimental effect on public morale."[20] Although this comment also referred specifically to the media curbs under the state of emergency, it applied equally to the government's long-term approach. Then there was the government's concern with its international image. As the discussion on the state of emergency made plain, Pretoria was greatly troubled by the images of violence on television screens around the world.

The result was that the government has steadily raised the temperature of the water, as if boiling would sterilize the water of all contaminants or threats to its health. As with the steadily warming water and its effect on a frog, the government's approach to controlling information also took a toll in South Africa. Without offering a detailed analysis of this impact, one can point to several negative effects of the government's three-part approach to information.

- Perhaps the single greatest impact was on the political and social system that emerged in South Africa. Restricting the information that the government has most diligently sought to control inevitably *hinders the democratic process*. If one accepts that a democratic society cannot function without high levels of access to information, to enable educated voter participation in the electoral process, then South Africa has long been thwarted—even among white voters—in its potential to do so. Put differently, South Africa is a society that has not prized openness of information, for which it continues to pay a price. Theo Coggin, formerly deputy director of the South African Institute of Race Relations, addressed this issue in 1988: "Always accepting that there are exceptions, I do not believe that South Africans can be described as an informed people." He added: "The free flow of information will indeed be critical in a future South Africa, because it is going to be important for the constituent parts of this society, not only to be told what each is saying and doing, but to be given a clear understanding of the reasons for the actions and decisions of the various institutions and organisations in society."[21] The cultural and political climate has made this openness impossible in the past.
- A corollary to inhibiting the democratic process was the *limited discussion of alternatives*. Until the de Klerk administration

lifted the bans on the African National Congress and other political groups, open and full debate of various political options facing South Africa was simply impossible.

- Limiting information not only undercut the democratic process in a broad sense, but it also *undermined faith in institutions* critical to the success of a democratic society, such as the army, the police, and the courts. These institutions were long held in low esteem by blacks. Whatever the weaknesses of these institutions, their flaws were more easily tolerated by the authorities or more easily exaggerated by their critics in the absence of the fuller, unconstrained discussion of these institutions that marks democratic societies.

- Mathews noted that another danger was that of the government *establishing an official truth.* He pointed to the government's attempts to portray highly controversial matters as having only one possible interpretation, the version officially handed down.[22]

- Another danger of limiting information was that *the government itself becomes ignorant of reality.* Just as its supporters succumbed in varying degrees to more than forty years of government propaganda, the government itself was at times seduced by the persuasiveness of its own single-voiced messages. An example was Pretoria's readiness in the 1980s to accept the Total Onslaught theory. Legal scholar Gilbert Marcus quoted the International Commission of Jurists as saying that "it becomes increasingly difficult for government officials themselves to be adequately informed about the extent of abuse of authority, the gravity of social problems and other matters which cannot be freely reported."[23]

- Another obvious danger included *the temptation to cover up incompetence and corruption.* Chapter 5 indicated how the government could, and did, use the protection of numerous laws as a shield from embarrassment. And even if the government were never to succumb to this temptation, "bureaucratic reluctance to impart information to the press and public often causes distrust and indeed a suspicion of malpractice or incompetence on the part of the government."[24]

- Finally, limiting information on controversial topics *opened the door to human rights abuses.* Anton Harber, *Weekly Mail* coeditor, rightly noted censorship's distinctive power: "Censorship is fundamental to all other forms of repression because it provides the veil behind which they can happen. It is censorship that allows the government to contravene human rights without the public scrutiny and the international attention that may inhibit their actions."[25]

As Pretoria increasingly depended on information control in its approach to governing, its intolerance of hostile views or facts soaked through the wider society. Following the government's example, other groups increasingly regarded intolerance of opposing views as the norm in South African political discourse. Paradoxically, this was less an issue when the government's clampdown on dissent was at its peak. But by the mid-1980s formal censorship had eased[26] and various antigovernment groups made bolder statements in a changing political climate. As more dissenting voices surfaced, however, it was plain that they shared some of the ugly qualities of the government they so vigorously opposed. Two incidents bear mentioning. The first is that of Irish academic and journalist Conor Cruise O'Brien. In 1988 pressure from militant student groups at the University of Cape Town and Johannesburg's University of the Witwatersrand forced the cancellation of public addresses on these campuses. In what became a cause célèbre, critics accused these universities of sacrificing the principle of free speech because of left-wing pressure.

The other example concerned British author Salman Rushdie, whose novel *The Satanic Verses* unleashed an outpouring of rage from the Islamic world in 1988, which culminated in a call for his death by the late Iranian leader the Ayatollah Khomeini. In South Africa too the book caused a furor among that country's Muslims.

The *Weekly Mail* and the Congress of South African Writers invited Rushdie to speak on an anticensorship panel at an annual book festival that the *Mail* and COSAW sponsored. A flood of death threats against Rushdie arrived at the *Mail*'s offices as outraged members of South Africa's 500,000-member Muslim community protested Rushdie's proposed visit. Many of these individuals were actively involved in antiapartheid movements, leading to "conflict in anti-apartheid circles whose unity had been polished up on the easily identified 'common enemy'—state censorship. Seasoned victims and opponents of censorship found themselves in the position of potential censors."[27] Ironically, COSAW is a leading voice of writers opposed to the government, many of whom are themselves victims of censorship. Moreover, COSAW had fought for an exemption from the cultural boycott imposed by the British Anti-Apartheid Movement to bring Rushdie to South Africa to address the censorship issue.[28] Now COSAW faced intense pressure to impose its own censorship and withdraw its invitation. Twenty-four hours before Rushdie was due to arrive in the country, COSAW gave in to the pressure.

The *Weekly Mail*'s Harber pointed to the hypocrisy in the UDF affiliates who sought to prevent Rushdie from visiting South Africa by asking the government to withdraw his visa and ban his book. Harber said that "people felt no qualms about making use of the state's censorship machinery when it suited them. For me that was the clearest indication yet that the democratic movement in this country has not given serious enough thought and commitment to the notion of anti-censorship with freedom of expression."[29]

Rushdie, particularly disappointed that it was a writers' organization that had yielded to this pressure, commented: "I am saddened that COSAW was finally unable to stand by *The Satanic Verses* as a work of literature. Part of my reason for coming to South Africa was to express my solidarity with those who fight censorship there. I am saddened by the fact that the same solidarity was not extended to me."[30]

Rushdie's situation was unique. Yet it provided a valuable test case demonstrating the double standards present in the antiapartheid movement. In an editorial, the magazine *Reality* referred to the threats of violent disruption if the O'Brien lectures had gone ahead and to the calls for Rushdie's death. "In the last two cases the threats came from groups which in other contexts claim to be committed to non-violence. The Government's censorship reminds us that we live in a society that is not free; the other that, if we are not careful, we may still not be after it has gone."[31]

Reality was responding not to an aberration in behavior by antiapartheid groups but to a systematic pattern noted with growing concern by others. Coggin put it bluntly when he said that "limitations on freedom of expression are not only imposed by government, but also by other organisations, to the left and right of government."[32] He mentioned the development in the black townships when contending factions sought "to impose thought control and its ideological ideas, through violence if necessary."[33] To illustrate further the climate in which extraparliamentary politics is played out, he quoted black journalist Joe Thloloe, who wrote in a column in the *Sowetan*

that arrogance and intolerance had crept into anti-apartheid politics. He said that many journalists got "flak" for even acknowledging the existence of some organisations. People who insisted on speaking up faced penalties, he said, ranging from the disruption of their meetings "right up to the fiery 'necklace' death." ... Simply put, some radicals have successfully bullied journalists in the press to toe the line—or else.[34]

Black journalists suffered enormous pressure in the 1980s as political views within the black community became more polarized. For a black journalist to be perceived as not supporting one faction or another could quite literally invoke the death threat Thloloe referred to.[35] The level of intolerance within the black community in particular reached such heights that the South African Institute of Race Relations held a conference in 1990 on this topic, inviting black journalists and others to describe the problem and explore ways of addressing it.[36]

Then there was the phenomenon of the "cultural desk" of the Mass Democratic Movement, the cluster of extraparliamentary groups that became a major antiapartheid force in the 1980s. In seeking to promote its ideological orthodoxy, the MDM established its own "approval mechanism." What became known as its cultural desk served as an informal, unstructured vehicle to provide (or refuse) a stamp of approval on cultural or other events; anything deemed incompatible with "the struggle" was unlikely to receive the cultural desk's blessing. Individuals involved in activities like dramatic performances and who desired to be taken seriously by a broad spectrum of South Africans had to jump through the hoop of the cultural desk or local "people's committees." Otherwise their contribution might be ignored or, worse, actively boycotted.

Dawn Lindberg, active in South African theater for more than two decades, lamented in a newspaper column that just as the government was easing its grip on censorship, "the focus has now turned instead to new problems facing SA theatre and film; the hardening in attitudes of the authors of the cultural boycott, and a new censorship body, the 'Cultural Desk' of the new left."[37] She described, for example, how when she was producing a play the previous year "we were ... under pressure and virtually obliged to submit the script for assessment by a faceless body who would judge its relevance to 'the struggle' before giving the green light to actors to audition and perform, or for audiences to attend."[38]

And a final example of this readiness to seek free expression for oneself but refusing to grant it to others: A group of students disrupted a campus dinner to be addressed by a white politician and prevented him from speaking. Asked why he had done so, one student said: "I can't comment until I have mandate from the people."[39]

As the *Reality* editorial suggested, the "cultural desk" concept and the groupthink syndrome underlying it were anathema to those who feared that the Nationalist government's successors would replace one set of constraints on free expression with another.

These problems were aggravated by another ingrained feature of South African life: government secrecy. Pretoria has repeatedly shown its enthusiasm for placing actual or potential embarrassments off limits from public scrutiny. Whether the issue was police or military conduct, treatment of prisoners, or general charges of government corruption, the government could shield behind powerful legislation that at worst flatly forbade revealing information or at best greatly dampened journalists' enthusiasm for doing what they ought.[40]

Government secrecy was an important strategy invoked to control information. As Mathews said, "By keeping information secret a government may increase its power over opponents and create a climate for the manipulation of its citizens."[41] Coupled with the extensive censorship of political views in the past, such as those of the African National Congress, the Pan-Africanist Congress, the South African Communist Party, and scores of other voices, tight governmental secrecy on opposition politics effectively stanched the flow of much sensitive information and opinion within South Africa. This veil of silence began to lift in the late 1980s with the rise of the alternative press. The unbanning in 1990 of the three aforementioned organizations and the major political changes at that time further helped move the society toward openness. Yet as the government allowed freer political discussion and stretched the range of what it considered tolerable opposition activity, the question arose: To what degree would it retain powers of secrecy that by Western standards are breathtakingly excessive?

The government's earlier reliance on secrecy represented a fundamental conviction that the society lacked the ability to handle various kinds of sensitive information. It must be recalled that the government's political power base was tenuous when it came to power in 1948. It undoubtedly felt highly vulnerable to opposition movements, white and black. As a result, it quickly and efficiently shored up its position with the legal arsenal that included careful attention to information control. Subsequent government-press relations were marked by a constant feud over who should define the appropriate level of information to which the public should have access: the government itself or the society? Having claimed greater rather than lesser powers in this realm, the government jealously guarded its ability to control much of the country's more volatile information. Inevitably, as in any other country marked by a similar government strategy, South Africa has paid a price for this approach.

CONCLUSION

Censorship, intolerance, and secrecy were cultivated among many white voters, who were all too ready to filter out the discomforting realities of an apartheid society. The residue of the government's information strategy was like toxic waste that increasingly contaminated the soil of white political discourse. Inevitably, even apartheid's racial barriers could not keep the soil of others from being tainted too.

Fortunately, government opponents of various stripes, and some government supporters themselves, recognized that the government had no monopoly on intolerance. The Association of Democratic Journalists, for example, committed itself in its constitution to fighting all censorship, whether by the government or "by those claiming to speak in the name of freedom and democracy."[42] And alternative press editors like Moegsien Williams, of *South*, emphasized the educational mission that they face: "We must impress on our own community the virtues of good journalism, that they may be persuaded that press freedom is worth having in the new society."[43]

That will be a significant task in a country where free expression was an unwelcome guest, resented and undermined for four decades by the government. Subsequently it came to be viewed by some of the supposed champions of freedom as a means to an end, to be invoked when convenient, ignored when political or ideological needs suggested otherwise. Just as the government's protestations about how much it values press freedom were rendered irrelevant by its actions, there emerged a similar gap between theory and practice regarding freedom by groups on the political left. The danger is that in a postapartheid South Africa free expression will not emerge as a cardinal value sustaining the society, to be treated as an end in itself and not merely an instrumental good.

Whatever the present standing of free expression in South Africa implies for the future, this chapter offers little solace to the press. South African society has in large measure espoused intolerance as the rhetoric of public discourse; it does not offer a congenial environment to newspapers or any other vehicle seeking to air or test contesting views and ideologies or present unpalatable realities. Yet forceful voices championing free expression have been raised throughout South Africa's history. In the more recent past, they have, on the one hand, responded to government action and attitudes against the press and have, on the other hand, responded to cultural censorship and intolerance by those on the left. The vitality of South Africa's postapartheid press will unquestionably depend on how successfully these voices set a new tone for public debate and free expression in a society primed for change.

Part Two

PROSPECTS

8

The Prospects
for Press Freedom

PERHAPS THE SINGLE most compelling question about the future of
South Africa's press is, What are its prospects for operating freely in
postapartheid South Africa? The first part of this book described the difficulties the press has encountered since 1976; it is now necessary to examine its prospects. The quick and noncommittal answer is to say that
its outlook is as good or poor as that of the country as a whole. Editors,
journalists, and academics agree that as the country goes, so will the
press. A more considered response, however, is that South Africa's press
is likely to end the 1990s with markedly more freedom than it began
the decade. This chapter identifies those factors likely to enhance freedom and those impeding it.

Like many societies in transition, South Africa is at a critical juncture
regarding its stand on press freedom. Inevitably, it must choose between two fundamentally different and incompatible positions. The
first, the assumption on which this study is based, is that press freedom
is indispensable in building and sustaining democratic societies. As
countless observers of the press have noted, that institution's health in
a society accurately reflects the well-being of the body politic. But the
press is not merely a passive indicator. It is more than a thermometer,
simply measuring the extent of genuine democratic practices in a society. For it can also play a vital role influencing and shaping events and
values—and ought to be highly prized precisely because of this potential. As Donald Trelford, editor of the *Observer* in London, has said,
"No matter what is wrong with a society, if the press is free, the facts
cannot be concealed forever. That is why press freedom ... is the key to
all other freedoms."[1] In the long run, the press is foundational to securing and maintaining other rights.

175

The second view, which has long characterized South Africa's experience, is that press freedom is a luxury, beyond the reach of politically unstable societies. In this view, a certain level of press freedom may be tolerable. But invariably the government's bias is toward decreasing that freedom or at least containing that which already exists. Hence the opinion of Louis le Grange, then minister of tourism, who told the annual congress of the Newspaper Press Union in 1979 that press freedom was not a civil liberty but a privilege that carried responsibilities. The public had a right to be informed only when the information was in the interests of the state.[2]

This view of press freedom emphasizes the harm that the press can do. Always, the discussion turns to themes of irresponsibility and sensationalism. The press is seen as an evil that must be suffered, one of the occupational hazards suffered by governments and politicians who also proclaim democratic values. This is the G. Gordon Liddy view of the press: "The press," he said, "is like the peculiar uncle you keep in the attic—just one of those unfortunate things."[3]

Accordingly, this view has little room for error on controversial issues; the granting of press freedom is seen as conditional on acceptable performance. Yet as Lord McGregor, a distinguished media leader in Britain, said in opening the *Star*'s conference "Conflict and the Press," "a free society which expects responsible conduct from a free press, must go on tolerating some—often shocking—irresponsibility, as the price of liberty."[4]

The point is that press freedom does not come with a manufacturer's warranty. Never can the authorities who permit a critical press know that journalists will act professionally or responsibly, however these standards are defined. Nor can they predict what impact the press will have in society, whether intended or not. That is the risk that Western societies by and large feel secure enough to take. Many South Africans are not yet confident enough to take that risk. The dilemma South Africa faces is shared with many other developing nations that also have both limited press freedom and fledgling or incomplete democracy: Does one wait until the country has a sufficiently democratic culture to tolerate a free press, or does one allow press freedom to help cultivate a democratic culture? The tension parallels the dilemma that developing societies face in deciding whether to grant priority to political or economic progress.[5]

In facing this choice over the past several decades, the South African government has decided that when faced with the two evils of democracy and press freedom the best course is to choose a third evil—and allow neither. Now that option is no longer sustainable for the Nationalist government. As South Africa enters a new era, the present government and its immediate successor will be mostly responsible for determining the vitality of press freedom in postapartheid South Africa.

As this chapter explores how press freedom might fare during this transition, and the shape it may take tomorrow, an exercise in definition is appropriate. What exactly is meant by press freedom, in the context of South Africa in the 1990s?

PRESS FREEDOM IN CONTEXT

One could say that South Africa's recent experience with press freedom at least helps define what it is not. It is more difficult to say what it is. Few people argue for an absolutist approach to press freedom; nor is that position adopted here. Whatever arguments are advanced in discussing the absolutist approach,[6] they become irrelevant when press freedom has to be lived out in real life. Such freedom is simply unattainable. More pertinent are the limits placed on press freedom: What are they, what is their impact, and who determines them? Do these limits reach such a level that freedom of the press can no longer be said to characterize a society?

Press freedom is understood here broadly and is defined as an environment that enables the press to function essentially unhindered in obtaining and providing a substantially complete, timely account of the events and issues in a society.[7] All societies place limits on the press, whether these concern libel law, fraudulent advertising, or matters of national security. Even the freest of newspapers are accountable to other agencies or individuals in society. Of course, the feud between governments and journalists over what constitutes acceptable limits to that freedom, and how the press's objectives and obligations ought to be understood, is another matter, to which we shall return presently.

Any society tracing its core values from Western European roots, as South Africa's government says it does, inherits high standards when it comes to practicing certain fundamental rights. The South African government therefore has had no choice but to embrace the value of freedom of expression and a free press—in theory, if not in practice. The reality is that the government's repeated endorsements of free speech rang increasingly hollow up to the beginning of the de Klerk administration. Remarks of prominent Nationalists over the years are rich in irony when measured by their performance. For example, Hendrik Verwoerd, the former prime minister and leading intellectual architect of apartheid, drew on his experience as a newspaper editor when he argued: "Not only has a government no right to take away freedom from the press, but the press itself may not give away this freedom. It is the duty of the press towards the nation to defend itself to the bitter end."[8] Another example is the view of a successor, prime minister and then president P. W. Botha: "Without a healthy, alert and critical press no government can give of its best. To curtail that role of the press is a certain road to disaster for the state."[9]

In practice, the government has at best grudgingly tolerated a relatively free press. At worst, it has acted with a brutal ruthlessness against the press. Earlier discussion of the standing legislation affecting journalists and their papers, as well as the state of emergency, demonstrated the extent of formal government opposition the press has faced in recent decades. In addition to these constraints, however, the press lacks support from the rest of society and faces informal and unofficial government pressures. Any catalog of hostile conduct against the press therefore includes a wide range of steps and pronouncements, official and unofficial, government and private. Lengthy and detailed lists of such actions, and status reports on press freedom in South Africa, mostly report formal police actions against journalists, such as arrests, threats of arrest, or acts of physical violence.[10] Harassment may take the form of being placed under police surveillance for extended periods, being followed or formally questioned by the police without any charges being brought, having one's telephone tapped, mail opened, and so on.

South, for example, told its readers of "security police visits to the newsroom and the home of the editor, harassment of staff, threatening phone calls to their families, tampering with the newspaper's mail, even regular checks through its dustbins [trashcans] by anonymous white officials."[11]

If anything, actions taken formally by the police at least allow journalists or their publications to seek some recourse by publicizing the incidents and publicly describing the authorities' actions. Although such a step only minimally embarrasses the government, if at all, it at least places these events in the public arena.

More problematic are the countless other unofficial actions, which their targets assume are conducted with either the official approval or connivance of the police or other government agencies. Journalists all round the country have their own war stories to recount, but those in the Eastern Cape—especially members of the alternative press—were repeated targets of this style of harassment. Incidents have included death threats and the fire bombing of a journalist's car.[12] Louise Flanagan, of the East London News Agency, suffered slashed tires on her pickup truck and later found her car's wheel nuts deliberately loosened.[13] In addition, she said, "Most of us have been briefly questioned [by the police] and followed around at night."[14] In another incident, three journalists at the Durban alternative paper, the *New African,* suffered burns to their eyes after opening chemically treated copies of the *New Nation* mailed to them from Johannesburg.[15]

Then there were the mysterious burglaries for which the Eastern Cape News Agencies became notorious. In August 1989, the Port Elizabeth News Agency was hit by the fourth in a succession of burglaries apparently calculated to shut it down. The agency lost all its equipment, including a fax machine, a photocopier, and two computers. There was no sign of forced entry.[16] A month earlier, the agency's counterpart in Grahamstown, eighty miles away, was similarly struck. In that burglary, also with no sign of forced entry, the Albany News Agency lost everything—down to their telephone directories, dictionary, and hot water kettle.[17] Peter Auf der Heyde, one of the agency's journalists, said of the theft, "Someone's making it very difficult for us to get back. We must be making an impact if they're trying to close us down."[18] For anyone familiar with the South African press and its treatment by the government, the incidents recorded here and in earlier chapters represent nothing new or surprising. They are only a recent sampling of formal and informal government harassment against dissident journalists and other opposition voices. This sorry catalog could be prolonged almost indefinitely but the point is clear: For decades, South African journalists and journalism have not known what the Western world would regard as a normal operating environment.

This begs the question of what would be a normal or healthy standard of press freedom. Specifically, what guidelines can one use to measure press freedom, whether in South Africa or anywhere else? Denis McQuail, a prominent European media scholar, lists seven principles that summarize this concept:

- Publication should be free from any prior censorship by any third party
- The act of publication and distribution should be open to a person or group without permit or licence
- Attack on any government, official or political party (as distinct from attacks on private individuals or treason and breaches of security) should not be punishable, even after the event
- There should be no compulsion to publish anything
- Publication of "error" is protected equally with that of truth, in matters of opinion and belief
- No restriction should be placed on the collection, by legal means, of information for publication
- There should be no restriction on export or import or sending or receiving "messages" across national frontiers.[19]

These criteria are helpful in focusing the discussion, for they plainly indicate South Africa's shortfall from acceptable standards. The issues arising then are what areas òf press freedom most need attention and how ought the present weaknesses be remedied.

As noted in Chapter 5, if media are to function freely they require four types of protection: foundation rights, practicing rights, editorial autonomy, and access rights.[20] The concept of press freedom advocated here thus goes beyond a mere cessation of government hostilities against the press. It extends to a call for a societywide acceptance of press freedom as a foundational value in postapartheid South Africa. And it goes further still. The Hutchins Commission on Freedom of the Press published several seminal studies on the press in the United States in 1947. It proposed an understanding of press freedom that is readily applicable to South Africa's situation more than forty years later. The commission defined the elements of press freedom as follows.

> An ideally free press is free *from* compulsions from whatever source, governmental or social, external or internal: from compulsions—not, of course, from pressures, since no press can be free from pressures except in a moribund society empty of contending forces and beliefs. An ideally free press is free *for* the achievement of its own instinct of workmanship and the requirements of the community combine to establish; and for those ends it must have command of all available technical resources, financial strength, reasonable access to sources of information at home and abroad, and the necessary staff and facilities for bringing its information and its judgments to the national market. An ideally free press would be free *to* all who have something worth saying to the public; and the selection of voices thus deserving to be heard must be a free selection.[21]

Emphasizing that these elements constituted an ideal view of press freedom, the commission readily conceded that these elements also were incompatible given the conflicting demands of real life. The first area it identified, concerning freedom from constraints, is the one immediately identified as most needing correction in the South African press. But that is only part of the picture. The second cluster of freedoms consists of "equipping" qualities. These questions of technical resources, financial stability, and professional skills are discussed in Chapter 9. The third segment concerns the question of public access to the press and the resulting implication that the press should accurately represent the public. *South*'s editor, Moegsien Williams, said that it is not enough for papers simply to be antigovernment. "It's going to be important for the majority of people in this country not only to get newspapers that reflect their views, but that they also get access to the media." He continued: "The key question for us is that if press freedom is to survive in the future, it must be accepted by the majority of the people."[22] Unless the great majority of South Africa's newspaper readers have confidence and trust in their publications and believe that in some sense these papers represent their interests and voice their concerns, press freedom is not so much imperiled as it would be pointless. To win this necessary degree of credibility among their readerships, papers in theory need do nothing more than what they already claim to. The trouble is that in South Africa's ideologically diverse society it is extraordinarily difficult for a paper to obtain a wide spectrum of readers who will enthusiastically regard it as "their" paper.

As the press moves from this point in its history, those capable of shaping its future health face three options. Those who will wield such influence, mostly the political leadership of the 1990s but journalists and others too, can maintain the unworkable and unjustifiable "dissension-on-our-terms" model that the Nationalist government has fashioned. The second option, advocated in this and subsequent chapters, is to restore the Western standards of free expression that the country, by and large, previously embraced. Or they can consciously and unapologetically choose to model South Africa's philosophy and practice of press freedom on that of other African and other Third World countries.

Much has been written on the reasons that Third World countries, including those in Africa, have failed to incorporate many of the protections for human rights that characterize the nations that colonized them. For example, political scientist Rhoda Howard, in her study of human rights in nine former British colonies, concluded that "Africa's colonial heritage, her absolute poverty, the newness and fragility of her nation-states, and her rapidly consolidating class structure all conspire to deny human rights to most of her citizens."[23] David Lamb, who has reported extensively on Africa for the *Los Angeles Times*, offered a similarly gloomy assessment of the continent's press. When black African countries gained independence, he said, assurances of a free and competitive press abounded. In fact, however, "the role of newspapers in black Africa has declined so dramatically that they have little significance in society."[24] His conclusion is more ominous: "But just as the free press was the first institution in black Africa to fall, I'm afraid it will be the last to be resurrected. Before one can contemplate a renewed role for newspapers, governments will have to become more secure, leaders more tolerant, the masses more educated. Only then will the African journalist have a chance to be a real journalist."[25]

This chapter is nevertheless based on the premise that South Africa's situation is sufficiently different from that of the rest of Africa so that it is not doomed to echo its experiences in human rights, specifically in the realm of press freedom. Despite the grim legacy of "unfreedom" that South Africa will carry into its postapartheid future, the country also enjoys another, and more positive, heritage. These positive forces greatly improve the odds that South Africa may achieve a standard of press freedom that has eluded the rest of the continent. The rest of this chapter examines that prospect.

PROSPECTS FOR PRESS FREEDOM

The political system that postapartheid South Africa acquires will determine the vigor of press freedom in that country. If the negotiations of the early 1990s lead to a government genuinely tolerant of freedom of expression and dissenting viewpoints, then the likelihood of a free press will be immeasurably heightened. Salie de Swardt, editor of *Beeld*, said the press's prospects are as "uncertain as those for South Africa" generally. The future hinges on how far reaching the political changes in the country will be and, as he put it, on "how democratic we'll really be."[26]

Because of the political changes that introduced the 1990s, South Africa now faces the best prospects for improving press freedom in more than a generation. As part of its overall political agenda, the de Klerk administration took what in the South African context were astonishing steps of liberalizing constraints on free expression. But it is how the broader agenda for political change is played out that will determine the foundation on which tomorrow's press can be built. To the degree that the National Party, the African National Congress, Inkatha, and other major constituencies can come to an accord on the country's direction, so will the rest of society's well-being be secured—including that of the press. How a new political order is attained, whether mostly by negotiation or violence, and the economic prosperity or hardship the new order might introduce, would also influence the climate facing tomorrow's press. A political solution acceptable to most South Africans and to the international community thus constitutes a necessary but not a sufficient condition for press freedom to prevail. A free press cannot prosper without a hospitable political climate and a government respectful of the right to dissent. But by themselves these conditions by no means assure a free press.

Thus, even if South Africa crafts a promising new political dispensation, much else needs to be in place if the press is to thrive. Among the elements that this mix demands are economic stability, a legal system that in theory and practice upholds the rule of law, a population more willing to accept diverse viewpoints than it is at present, and a press that simultaneously practices both shrewd and visionary management and a journalism that is courageous, thoroughly competent, and ready to transcend an often narrow sectionalism. The odds of such a diverse mix of elements coalescing by the end of this decade, if ever, are slim. Moreover, several arguments, to be discussed presently, weigh heavily against the press surmounting these odds.

Another cluster of arguments, however, points to a different possibility: that the press has a better than even chance of securing a markedly healthier future. Best understood perhaps as an overall momentum likely to broaden press freedom, the half dozen factors constituting this force call for identification.

Factors Favoring Press Freedom

A Lengthy Tradition of Press Freedom

South Africa's press has its roots in the libertarian traditions of Western Europe. The English press, which comprises the country's most economically powerful papers in the country, have consistently embraced and proclaimed this legacy. These papers, as a group, have constantly reaffirmed the value of a free press. But the editors of these papers do not necessarily regard the British system as the ideal for which they strive. Legal scholar Anthony Mathews has shown the penchant that both Britain and South Africa (and the United States, for that matter) have shown for secrecy.[27] Rather, the call is for a return to an ideal standard, one best implemented in the societywide acceptance of free expression generally characterizing countries like those of Western Europe, the United States, Canada, Australia, and New Zealand.

The British roots of South African journalism have faded over the years, especially since South Africa left the British Commonwealth in 1961. Yet the roots of their craft and the premium they place on their society's need for free expression remain a vital part of a legacy acquired from the 1820s onward. Today's English-language journalists regard the early British settlers who championed the cause of a free press as their "founding fathers." A comparable commitment to a free press remains a central theme in the raison d'être of the English press today. How faithfully they have honored this legacy is vigorously contested by the Left and the Right. Those in the alternative press, for instance, contend that the English press has repeatedly turned its back on freedom in exchange for a safer, more profitable life. Alternative papers see themselves as far more willing to take risks in the fight to regain lost freedom. Although the Afrikaans press (like the government) has long viewed the English papers as irresponsible abusers of press freedom, it has become increasingly emboldened and direct in its calls for press freedom. The entire range of the South African press, therefore, has in the past decade begun singing the same words—perhaps to slightly different tunes, but all conveying the same message: Press freedom is of paramount importance in South African society, and the press itself has formed something of a consensus on this point. The implication is therefore that South Africa's journalists, regardless of their deep divisions, are perhaps more in accord on this issue than at any time in their history. Of course, they disagree on exactly what a free press ought to look like in South Africa. But because the press so prominently places the value of a free press on the public agenda, newspapers themselves provide an important impetus for furthering free expression in the society. Moreover, despite the problems of public apathy and decades of abuse heaped on the press, the idea of free expression is not alien to South Africans. Even though many South Africans hardly view a diverse and vigorous press with warmth and fondness, they are at least well acquainted with the concept. Whether they like it or not, they also see considerable evidence of a free press in practice. The idea and implications of press freedom are therefore to a large extent already familiar to the public. Regardless of their attitudes toward press freedom—and many of them regard it highly—South Africans are far more teachable on this issue than they would have been if press freedom had been completely suppressed years ago. Press freedom, then, has to be revived in South African society, not reintroduced. That task will be all the easier because of the heritage to which an often beleaguered English press has clung throughout its history and which is now more broadly proclaimed by South African journalism as a whole.

A Broader Cultural Base

The press does not operate in a void, divorced from the rest of the society. On the contrary, many other institutions provide support for the newspapers and the value of press freedom. In this context, former *Cape Times* editor Tony Heard wrote that "there are powerful institutions such as churches, chambers of commerce and industries, universities, political parties, trade unions, and cultural groups that stand outside (and critical of) government and, combined, could play a transforming role in society in spite of a formidable-looking government."[28]

These agencies have in the past provided much support for the liberal ideals in which the South African tradition of press freedom is rooted. As noted earlier, South Africans by no means universally embrace the values of tolerance and freedom of expression, and support from institutions like these is thus far from assured or consistent. Yet institutions like the universities and churches in particular have similar roots in the West European heritage that was crucially formative in shaping the press's values. The ties that the universities, churches, and newspapers have with the rest of the English-speaking world have helped to sustain this broad commitment to values such as press freedom. The point is that the press can wage its fight for free expression from a much broader base: the cultural heritage of English-speaking South Africans. The press is therefore not the only voice seeking to secure freedom of expression. And just as the press has on occasion defended the freedoms of universities and the churches or the independence of the judiciary, so too have it and the cause of press freedom benefited from the support of these institutions and their international links in return.

An Established Press

South Africa's journalism benefits from a clear sense of history and a high level of connectedness to the rest of society. In more tangible ways, too, journalists do not step into a vacuum as they look to producing newspapers in the future. They have been doing so for nearly two centuries and the press's various segments have vast reservoirs of experience and skills in producing newspapers. This is less true of the alternative press but many of their staff were trained on mainstream newspapers and have the advantage of the accelerated learning that came with publishing under the intense pressures of the state of emergency.

The result is that despite difficulties, a wide range of newspapers have continued to appear in South Africa, and the people producing them have established a mostly virile, energetic press. A score of daily papers, plus the various Sundays and weeklies, place South Africa in a different category from the many other African countries whose more limited and fragile traditions of newspapering were more easily crushed with the onset of independence. South Africa's press is too deeply entrenched for it to be silenced easily by a postapartheid government. In addition, it has had decades of experience in learning how to cope with government hostility. This lesson is reinforced by the recent example of the alternative press, whose survival has demonstrated the resilience of opposition newspapers even in the face of a government armed with extraordinary powers. Because of the changes that facilitated the rise of the alternative papers, publishing is, as *Sunday Times* editor Ken Owen noted, "now beyond the capacity of any but a totalitarian government to control."[29]

Independent Ownership

Denis Beckett, editor of *Frontline* magazine, told the story of a friend who had lived for seven years in Zimbabwe and grown accustomed to reading its government-controlled press. On returning to South Africa she began reading *Business Day* and its scathingly antigovernment editorials. Her initial response, Beckett said, was that she was terrified she would be arrested for treason for exposing herself to such material.[30]

This anecdote points to a crucially important quality of the press: the tradition of independent ownership and control that has always marked the English and alternative press. Under a non-Nationalist government, the Afrikaans press too would most likely become an independent voice, not linked to the government of the day. In such a setting the press would not be in the vulnerable position that newspapers faced in most of postindependence black Africa. Presumably, some existing papers (probably among the alternative press) would become progovernment voices or other papers would be founded for that purpose. But as is the case today, most papers are likely to be independently owned.

To the extent that the existing papers retain their editorial autonomy, and remain vibrant, forceful publications, they have the potential to remain an important force for press freedom simply by continuing to present a voice independent of any future government.

Ideological Diversity

Linked to the previous point is that of the press's ideological makeup. Its diversity and polarization lend credence to the idea that at least a certain level of press freedom presently exists in the society, which of course it does. Such diversity, however, both reflects press freedom and helps sustain it. As noted previously, the mere presence of a vibrant, vital, and, of importance here, ideologically diverse press constantly models for the public some level of press freedom. In a postapartheid setting, such diversity would continue doing so; the question is whether such diversity would be permitted. Assuming it were, however, this factor provides additional momentum for press freedom.

World and Domestic Expectations

A final and crucially important element is that people inside and outside the country will hold high expectations for a postapartheid society to embrace greater press freedom. There is no guarantee that a future government will do so or do any better than its predecessor in assuring other human rights. Yet any postapartheid government will know that its human rights record will be closely compared, at least initially, with what came before. South Africa's ties with the international community, which began to be strengthened and renewed with the policy changes of the de Klerk government, will further heighten these expectations abroad.

At home, too, many will have high expectations of an improved human rights record. Again, this offers no guarantee that the new government will respect freedom of expression. Economic questions or its own political stability may push issues like press freedom to the side. But especially because of the poor record of its predecessors, the future government is likely to be highly sensitive to charges that it is simply serving up more of the same when it comes to human rights.

By itself, this consideration is unlikely to offer comfort to those pointing to countries like Zimbabwe. Heard noted that "the experience of Rhodesia was that when [President Robert] Mugabe came to power, he did not have to do much to control the press, because government control existed already; generally he could rely on [former prime minister Ian] Smith's emergency decrees for some of his drastic actions."[31] Yet a vitally important difference prevails in South Africa as the apartheid age comes to an end. It is that the de Klerk government has itself begun some momentum toward improved press freedom. By ending the state of emergency (including the curbs on the media), unbanning political opposition groups, and repealing some press-related legislation, de Klerk set in motion rising expectations about freedom of expression. These expectations cannot easily be reversed, whether by his government or its successor.

Although the six factors listed here are important individually, more significant is their combined potential. Working together they offer a relatively optimistic picture. Any future government will not easily be able to dismiss the combined weight of these six forces.

Factors Impeding Press Freedom

To look only at the preceding list, however, is to live in cloud-cuckooland. One can easily envision another scenario that could lead to a future for a free press even worse than its past.

Political Instability

The precondition for an optimistic scenario for press freedom is a relatively stable political climate. Without it, the chances for an encouraging future are poor indeed. The arguments favoring such a bleak alternative must begin then with the fragility of the political changes marking South Africa in the early 1990s. It is as if the leaders working toward a new political order are trying to build a house of cards with glue. If nobody hits the table accidentally or on purpose, and if the glue has time to set, the house might well stand. However, one wrong move could make everything collapse. Regardless of the goodwill brought to the political process, or the domestic and international pressures to devise a new political order, enormous barriers lie in the way of attaining a just, stable, and internationally acceptable political order.

The Government's Human Rights Legacy

Even if the cards stand long enough for the glue to set, and at least provide a sound foundation for subsequent political building, other barriers to press freedom will remain. Not the least of these is the National Party's legacy on human rights. As the example of Zimbabwe cited earlier made clear, any future government in South Africa would not have to look far to find a prescription for dealing with a dissident press. Much will depend on whether the momentum generated by scrapping the apartheid system will carry over into dismantling the country's security laws, many of which directly inhibit press freedom. If the government bequeaths this network of legislation to its successor, the temptation will be enormous for the new administration to retain these laws, especially if it attains power in a climate of significant political unrest or instability. Claiming to use these powers only on a temporary basis, the new leaders would assure the world that press curbs were an interim measure to deal with the extraordinary circumstances facing the country. The government homage to press freedom that marked the apartheid era would be echoed, and the situation would—from the press's perspective—simply be a matter of watching the same play with a different cast.

Intolerance of Free Expression

Even if the Nationalist government removes much of the restrictive legislation described earlier, a related problem will remain: the disturbingly high level of intolerance woven into South Africa's political cloth. Pulling out these strands will take time that the country can ill afford. Most of South Africa does not share the Western cultural traditions in which the values of press freedom and tolerance are rooted; nor have whites presented a compellingly attractive record as to why these values are worth embracing anyway. Indeed, just the opposite is true. Just as many in the extraparliamentary movement have understandably associated capitalism with white oppression, so too do Western-style pronouncements on tolerance come with a tainted pedigree. In a rejection of the libertarian theory of the press in the South African context, media scholar P. Eric Louw, for example, went to the extent of dismissing "the myth that tolerance is a virtue." The liberal press not only helps sustain the status quo, he argued, but the liberal ideology on which it is based "has it that everything can be sorted out in a 'civilized' manner 'if only' everybody would 'see the light' and accept the umbrella of liberal tolerance."[32] The tradition of press freedom that has marked the country's press since its beginning, coming as it does in a particular ideological context, is thus by no means embraced by all South Africans. On the contrary, for many it remains part of the baggage of white domination.

An Ill-Defined Commitment to Press Freedom

Another potential weakness is the absence of any clearly articulated stand on free expression by groups like the ANC, Inkatha, or other leading contenders for a share of the power in a postapartheid South Africa. Admittedly, with the more fundamental issue of political control paramount on the agenda of groups like these, it is unrealistic to expect them to have published detailed statements or position papers on the question of free expression. The ANC's Constitutional Guidelines, published in 1988, for example, notes that the state "shall guarantee the basic rights and freedoms, such as freedom of association, expression, thought, worship, and the press."[33]

What is disturbing is how few pronouncements on this question surface and that when they do they are predictable, superficial, and short on specifics. One of numerous meetings between South African whites and ANC leaders in Lusaka, before the Congress's unbanning in 1990, included lengthy discussion on the issue of press freedom. Harvey Tyson, former editor of the *Star*, recounted the discussions: "We strongly believe in press freedom. We also believe in responsibility and accountability," he quoted the ANC officials as saying. What did that mean? "It means we would not tolerate anti-Semitism, or Nazi propaganda in the media. But otherwise anyone could produce any kind of newspaper, from say the British *Guardian* to the conservative *Daily Telegraph*; from the girlie *Sun* to the *Independent*. Every political ideology (except racism) will be possible in the press." Tyson concluded, "The longer we debated, the more Apple Pie we were offered."[34]

In addition to Tyson's concern about a lack of specificity is another problem: A grave danger exists that the commitment to press freedom by groups on the political left in South Africa will in practice be narrowly defined and regarded only as a freedom that allows for the outworking of its own political vision. In other words, groups like the ANC may well regard press freedom instrumentally; it is valued only as long as it helps accomplish or maintain a broader set of political objectives. The danger is that if freedom of expression conflicts with a preordained view of the political order, then the right to expression becomes dispensable. Rather than having a value in its own right, and regarded as a human right in and of itself, press freedom can be defined as having meaning only within the context of a specifically defined political order. By definition, then, if one questions or rejects that political order, one's claim to free expression is rendered irrelevant. This thinking was exemplified following the Conference on Culture for Another South Africa, which took place in the Netherlands in December 1987. In an article referring to the conference, Brian Bunting, a former South African journalist living in Britain, presented a concept of journalism with disturbing implications. Writing in the ANC journal *Sechaba* about a freedom of the press campaign that South African journalists had launched, he wrote: "Our cadres engaged in various forms of organisation and action must remember that they are also propagandists, and that the purpose of all their work, in journalism and elsewhere, is to arouse, educate and mobilise the masses within South Africa to revolutionary activity."[35]

Some journalists are alert to the implication in this kind of thinking that, despite policy statements to the contrary, in practice only a coopted or subservient press would be tolerated under a new government. *Weekly Mail* coeditor Anton Harber said: "We all have a fear that the new government will transform a press monopoly that is part of the present status quo to that which is part of the next status quo. It's important for us to show people in the resistance movement that if they come to power it will not be in their interests to do that."[36]

A particular danger arises with journalists who ardently call for free expression but who view it instrumentally rather than as an end in itself. Put differently, their view rejects the concept of press freedom as something that is indivisible—that cannot be granted selectively to some groups and not to others. Thus, even among journalists in the extraparliamentary movement there arises the sense that their passionate calls for press freedom come with assumed limits. Sometimes these assumptions are made explicit. The ANC's Constitutional Guidelines, for example, say that notwithstanding the guarantee of free expression and a free press, "the advocacy or practice or racism, fascism, naziism or the incitement of ethnic or regional exclusiveness or hatred shall be outlawed."[37] Although this leaves wide open the question of what is meant by these terms, and who gets to define them, the limits are at least stated. Moegsien Williams, the editor of *South*, put what he saw as the problem in tangible terms when he asked: "Can the future society afford to have a paper like *Die Burger*," the Cape Town Afrikaans daily, "continuing to sprout racist theories?"[38] The danger is when these assumptions are left unstated or implicit. For even though no one expects a truly libertarian press to emerge in South Africa, a problem arises when differing groups do not make explicit what limitations they think are tolerable or even desirable. Those most likely to obtain political power in South Africa therefore have a special obligation to give the clearest possible statement of where they stand with respect to press freedom. Their failure to do so thus far is not encouraging; their apparent readiness to settle for a limited view of press freedom is more disturbing still.

How likely is it that this constrictive, doctrinaire understanding of press freedom could take hold in South Africa? It is impossible to say. Groups like the ANC, simply because they remain in political opposition, have not had the chance to demonstrate how their understanding of press freedom would be implemented in practice. Early indications are not encouraging. Several signals suggest that a move toward tolerance may not be rapid under a future black government. One example is the emergence of the "cultural desk" and the expectation that loyal followers of the "struggle" must accept uncritically some nebulously defined will of the people. Another is the intimidation and violence against black journalists, some of whom have been tried by kangaroo courts and "convicted" for writing stories that were presumably seen as critical of "the struggle."[39] The ANC denied responsibility for these incidents. But even those sympathetic to the political Left raised concerns about the ANC's stand on the press following its unbanning. Thus one observer wrote in the *Weekly Mail* that the ANC "should be concerned at how frequently the press-basher accusation is being made against it, not only from mainstream sources like *The Star*, but from 'alternative' media too."[40]

The ANC had not, at least by mid-1992, demonstrated that it could or would live up to its principles concerning press freedom. The ANC's performance could, unfortunately, be symptomatic of a serious impediment to press freedom in a changing South Africa. The intolerance manifested in its ranks, and that of other groups (on all points of the political spectrum), comes as no surprise, of course. Any future government will inherit a society steeped in intolerance; the question is therefore quite simply, How readily will the government resist the temptation to use this legacy to its advantage?

CONCLUSION

This chapter has described the potential for press freedom to thrive in a future South Africa or to be stifled. These considerations are overlaid with the same array of uncertainties and imponderables affecting all change in South Africa. Now that one set of factors has been weighed against the other, why then is it argued here that press freedom will leave the 1990s healthier than when it entered the decade?

Again, the basic assumption bears repeating: Without stable political change, press freedom in South Africa has poor prospects in the 1990s. So do the other human rights that the world community would like to see restored in the country. Yet if the political leadership succeeds in securing a reasonably calm transition to a stable, postapartheid society, then the prospects for improved press freedom are good. Several factors together provide a momentum that neither the present government nor a future government can easily dismiss: the deeply rooted traditions of freedom of expression, especially in a well-established press but in other sectors of the society too; the country's ties with the international community, whose expectations for greater freedom will be matched by many inside the country; and the fact that the country is already on a trajectory of change toward greater openness. Undoubtedly, there is a measure of wishful thinking in arguing that press freedom will indeed improve. To engage in such thinking, however, is not to wish merely for better pastures for the press. It is instead to call for the overall improvement in South African affairs for which millions inside the country and out have strived for decades. In the realm of press freedom, this calls for work on two fronts simultaneously: to secure a press freer from constraints and to secure a press more reflective of and accessible to the entire South African population.

The press is potentially its own best advocate in striving for these ends. The difficulty remains, however, that the press itself is divided on aspects of press freedom. Problem areas include the access question and consensus on the appropriate limits that a future government should place on press freedom. Although journalists remain deeply divided on basic issues of press freedom, they also share much common ground. To a large degree, they concur in rejecting much of the restrictiveness that has marked their recent past. The problems arise in agreeing on what kinds of limits ought to exist in the future. For until journalists and editors themselves can share a broader vision of press freedom, as well as a broader vision of their raison d'être in South African society, they will struggle to secure from the broader society the mandate they need.

The movement toward greater freedom of expression will also be helped or hurt by the public at large, with its myriad factions and interest groups. Together, the press and the public will be enormously formative in shaping government policies and practices that will ultimately determine how free or controlled South Africa's postapartheid press will be. Whether South Africans will enjoy a considerably freer press by the turn of the century is impossible to predict, although it is argued here that they will. But let there be no illusions:

Despite the signs of movement toward a freer press, and the significant pluses that can add to this momentum, daunting barriers remain. How well South Africa succeeds in restoring a free press will, as much as any other indicator, symbolize the country's long-term prospects.

Thomas Macaulay once wrote, "Many politicians ... are in the habit of laying it down as a self-evident proposition, that no people ought to be free till they are fit to use their freedom. The maxim is worthy of the fool ... who resolved not to go into the water till he had learned to swim."[41] By the early 1990s, South Africa had got its feet wet. The question now is, Will it wade safely close to shore, tread water perilously, or perhaps even learn to swim?

9

Other Vital Issues

ALTHOUGH THE FUTURE of press freedom is the overarching issue facing South Africa's newspapers, it is hardly the only one. Press freedom does not exist in the abstract; it needs to be lived out and exercised day by day in newsrooms, in debate on contentious issues, in readers' living rooms, and in courtrooms. Critical though it is to a vibrant press, freedom is never the only issue editors face. They think constantly of issues ranging from news selection and presentation to libel suits and readers' complaints about smearing ink. The ideal of press freedom is striven for and in varying degrees attained in the countless routine acts and decisions made each day. All these activities help transform the abstraction of press freedom into a newspaper in a reader's home.

Just as press freedom faces a highly formative period in South Africa, so too does much else that is associated with that country's press. This chapter examines five issues that command attention as the press moves through the transitional decade of the 1990s. First, on what kind of economic basis will tomorrow's press be run? Second, what kind of journalism will it practice? Third, what will be the professional status of journalists? Fourth, what kind of legal foundation will undergird the press? And fifth, what place might a national media policy have in South African society?

These are not the only questions the press must address, yet they are as important as any that need resolution. How they are answered will also suggest much about the press's shape and quality and its potential contribution to postapartheid South Africa.

THE ECONOMIC BASIS

The greatest fear of many mainstream newspaper editors and owners is that tomorrow's press will change notably from its present overwhelmingly private ownership model. The greatest hope of many others in the society is that it will. The press's existing structure will unquestionably be challenged and possibly changed in some important ways. Organizations like the African National Congress have always had economic issues central to their platforms, along with their call for political rights. ANC thinking draws much from the Freedom Charter, adopted in 1955, which takes as given that the country's economy will be subjected to major restructuring under a postapartheid government. The ANC's 1988 Constitutional Guidelines likewise reflect this emphasis. Thus a call is made for "corrective action which guarantees a rapid and irreversible redistribution of wealth" and for a mixed economy.[1] How these changes would be implemented is a fundamental bargaining point among the ANC, other predominantly black groups, and the government. This broader issue does not concern us here. Nor is it pertinent to examine here how the government monopoly on broadcasting might change in the future. Rather, the focus is on the implications for the press and its ownership and structure.

As the shift to black majority rule continues, publishing activities are likely to expand at all levels—from pamphlets at the local level to the possible launching of a national daily. Unlike the present alternative press, many of these news publications will be part of the new established order, which is only just starting to define itself. The number, purpose, and quality of these new publications will depend greatly on funding, which in turn will depend on how important the print medium is to the political parties and other groups seeking to promote their interests.

Until a black government gains power, and perhaps for a short while afterward, any additions to South Africa's newspaper lineup will almost certainly be funded for partisan political motives. This could also include a right-wing Afrikaans daily in Pretoria or Johannesburg, most likely launched by the Conservative Party. (Whether such a paper would be tolerated under a black government is another question.) But there are unlikely to be many additional daily or weekly newspapers, as defined in this study. Bankrolling even a new weekly publication is enormously expensive; trying to launch a new daily is dramatically more so.

If the de Klerk administration demonstrates a continued commitment to broadening democracy in South Africa, groups like the ANC will operate at a political disadvantage if they are unable to secure an adequate press voice. They will face considerable pressure, therefore, either to establish a newspaper, distributed nationally or at least in the highly populated Witwatersrand region. Acquiring such a voice would entail winning the formal endorsement of an existing publication like

New Nation, now a weekly, or to establishing a new one—possibly even a daily.

The financial base for the press will remain unchanged until a black government comes to power. The privately owned English-language papers will continue to dominate the press; the Afrikaans press will continue their affiliation with a metamorphosing National Party; and the alternative press will continue as a cause-oriented press, subsidized by those believing in the individual missions of these papers.

Far harder to predict is what will occur under a new political order. The worst case, from the perspective of the mainstream press's management, would be nationalization of the media. All papers would then serve as government voices. However, there is little indication that the ANC and other groups that may be part of a future government would choose this course—or find it politically wise to do so even if they wanted to. Far more likely is some kind of affirmative action program to address the economic imbalance reflected in the present ownership patterns. Assuming the ANC became part of the future government, any paper supporting it would in turn serve as a progovernment voice, just as the Afrikaans papers have filled that role under the Nationalist government. Some alternative papers would align themselves in varying degrees with the government or its various constituencies. Others, such as the *Vrye Weekblad* and the *Weekly Mail*, expect they would seek to maintain the independent role they now strive for.[2] Yet others may fold or drastically redefine their mission. What part the mainstream English and Afrikaans papers would play is unclear. It is easy to assume that they would fill an opposition role. That is not necessarily so, however, as it would depend on how much these papers reposition themselves in the marketplace by that time. Already the more astute managers and editors on these papers are well aware that their organizations' future lies with black readerships. Much will depend on how rapidly these papers stop thinking of themselves as oriented primarily to whites and start trying to appeal more deliberately to black readers, and how successfully they do so.

These white-owned, white-managed papers face an enormous task, assuming they are genuinely committed to shedding their identities as primarily white publications. Some of them, especially the smaller ones, either see no need to make this shift or else are content with predominantly white readerships. Even for those papers that do seek to appeal to a wider black readership, many blacks view these publications as part of the "system." Among many in the extraparliamentary movement, then, it is a sine qua non that additional press voices must be made available in postapartheid South Africa. Relying solely on the existing mainstream press would be out of the question. For some, even tolerating it at all is a problem. According to a senior ANC official, Pallo Jordan, "Monopoly control and ownership of the press correlate directly with the system of White domination and exploitation. The prerequisite for a truly free press to emerge in South Africa is the destruction of both the racist state and the economic interests it serves."[3] He added: "Only under a people's government, based on the principles enshrined in the Freedom Charter, will the stifling grip of racism and monopoly interest on the South African media be broken."[4]

How far an ANC government would be willing to go in attacking the monopolistic character of the press is unclear, as is the way it might do so. Undoubtedly, though, it would not accept the present ownership structure. Several reasons would compel a new government to act. One is simply to put into effect what groups like the ANC have long said they would do on coming to power. Another is to seek vehicles for building their own political base. A third is to reduce the political risks that the English and, to a lesser degree, the Afrikaans papers could pose. As Jo-Anne Collinge, Herbert Mabuza, Glenn Moss, and David Niddrie put it, the new government "will—if it plans to ensure that mainstream press does not become a weapon, as in Chile, to 'demobilise the masses'—have to give immediate attention to the media."[5]

How? Jonathan Hobday, editor of the *Sunday Tribune*, typified the views of mainstream editors when he considered the possibility of nationalization. "To avoid this disaster, for so it would be both in economic and democratic terms, is the greatest challenge facing the newspapers in the '90s." He added: "We have been told by some of the New Politicians [*sic*], that one of the first targets of nationalisation will be the Argus Newspapers. It is a threat we take extremely seriously."[6]

In reality, the option of nationalization seems slim. Actions against the mainstream press would draw a firestorm of criticism, both at home, from many whites and internationally. A politically safer and generally more defensible option would be to exercise the "affirmative action" approach mentioned earlier. The most likely way of doing this would be to devise some formula for arranging subsidies to papers that were less secure financially. In a concerted effort to increase press diversity, the government might follow the example of Sweden, whose subsidy system has generated considerable interest in South Africa. With good reason, the ANC argues that because blacks have for generations been deprived of credible media outlets, a compelling need exists for the state to help level the playing field in tomorrow's press environment. Trade union and other nonmainstream publications could receive funding generated perhaps by a tax on other papers' advertising revenues. The amounts received could be determined in accordance with the kind of formula used in Sweden, perhaps according to their viability, size, circulation, amount of space devoted to advertising, and so on.[7]

This perspective is underscored by the *Star's* editor, Richard Steyn. Arguing from a traditional liberal perspective, Steyn warned against the dangers of a monopolistic press. Then he added:

> If the needs of a liberal-democratic society are to be adequately served, the South African media will have to become more broadly based. Black-owned publications will need to be encouraged by means of establishment grants, by production subsidies to help the commercially disadvantaged or by tax concessions for publications in under-developed areas. Although it may be argued that subsidisation shores up the weak and discourages competitiveness and efficiency, it is difficult to envisage any other way of promoting diversity in the print media.[8]

Steyn is right. What is therefore likely to emerge is some kind of official, government-sponsored plan to redress the present imbalance. Because of South Africa's sorry experience with government attempts to regulate the media, it is imperative if a subsidy program were to have any credibility that it be administered fairly and neutrally, apart from partisan political concerns.

The new government will have the chance to establish a standard of impartiality in regulating the press that could serve as a model to other developing nations. But it will get that opportunity only once. The government should seize it by setting up a neutral body to encourage and initiate press diversity, comparable to the board governing the British Broadcasting Corporation. Endowing this body with similar independence and authority would considerably heighten the prospects of establishing a richer and more diverse press. Such a body could emerge as part of a comprehensive national policy on the media, as described later.

If the mix of developments hoped for in the previous chapter were to occur, the prospects for this approach are good. This system would "allow for a gradual levelling of the tilt towards white South Africans, as society gradually adjusts itself towards equality."[9] Implementing a subsidy program is not done without risk, of course. The system could easily be abused or subverted to favor the government of the day. But regardless of these and other risks, such as those Steyn noted, his concern remains: What other choices are there?

One option unlikely to be tolerated is that of the essentially laissez faire approach that has historically characterized the press: that the freedom to publish a newspaper belonged to anyone who could afford one. Especially because of the greatly skewed distribution of wealth toward whites, blacks in a postapartheid South Africa will be ill placed indeed to afford the high costs of launching daily and weekly newspapers. Until blacks control a significantly larger share of the country's wealth, their prospects of privately funding their own papers are bleak indeed. Not surprisingly, the strongest objections to moving from a strictly laissez faire, free market approach to funding newspapers come from people who already own them. Various mainstream editors and publishers dislike the idea of the alternative press being subsidized. The thinking is that if they cannot survive in the marketplace on an equal footing with the for-profit papers, they ought not to be there.

At least two responses to their objections are appropriate. The first is that the objections are based on a narrow understanding of press freedom. For the most part, they come from publishers who for years have pleaded for greater press freedom and often fought courageously to protect it. Now they are troubled by groups and individuals uninterested in profits and who are willing to subsidize papers that otherwise could not exist. Yet nowhere does Western thinking on press freedom suggest that the right to publish be limited to for-profit publications. Unquestionably, the right to publish ought to have nothing to do with who pays the bills—even if this means that papers need to rely on foreign funding. If publications are otherwise operating legally, why ought the fact that they have received British or Canadian help somehow make them less entitled than mainstream papers to the benefits of freedom?

A second response to these antisubsidy sentiments is that if South Africa were a relatively normal society, with a correspondingly normal distribution of wealth, the subsidy question would not be an issue. But of course South Africa is not a normal society. One measure of the country's economic disparities is the ratio of "white to other-than-white wage income." Between 1950 and 1954, each economically active white on average earned 11.6 times as much as someone in another racial group. By the period 1980–1985, that ratio had dropped to 7.0,[10] but the gap was still significant, as these figures illustrate. In 1985, four out of five whites (83 percent) earned R16,000 or more annually. Only 5 percent of Africans did; for Coloureds and Indians the figures were 14 and 42 percent respectively.[11]

Given the extent of this disparity, one returns to Steyn's point: It is difficult to envisage any way of remedying the situation without some form of affirmative action program. If a country like Sweden, whose policies have systematically tried to equalize the distribution of wealth, deems it necessary for the state to actively support media diversity, an infinitely more convincing case can be made in South Africa.

Regardless of the changes likely to take place under the new government, the present mainstream press is almost sure to continue dominating the media landscape. By every significant measure—number of

publications, circulation, readership, advertising revenues, total revenues, and so on, the mainstream press is far ahead of the alternative papers. Nor will this situation substantially change in the next decade or
two, barring highly unlikely steps such as a government ban on many or
all the mainstream papers.

Despite the argument here that a future government will not take
over the press, at least some in the mainstream press have called for pre-
cautionary measures. The best hope to avert nationalization, Hobday
said, is "a constitution that will make such economic plunder impossible"—because of a bill of rights combined with the checks and balances
and a firm commitment to democracy that he hoped would mark a new
political dispensation.[12] That would not be enough, though. He argued
that the mainstream press will have "to free itself of the image and reality that it is monopolistic and under the control of 'Big Business.' This
means undertaking a process of de-monopolisation."[13]

Hobday suggested several ways this could be accomplished. One is to
break up the close ties between the Argus and TML groups, as described
in Chapter 2. Another is to broaden the base of the papers' ownership by
selling shares to individual members of the public and newspaper employees. The objective? "It is much easier to steal big loot from a few
people than it is to steal lots of little items from a lot of people. The
power of private ownership will have to be harnessed to contest the
power of public ownership."[14] Yet another is the theme touched on repeatedly in this study: "The newspaper industry must do much, much
more to make itself more relevant to people of colour."[15]

Whatever changes the Argus group and other papers may make,
some things will remain constant—such as their continued relationship with and dependence on the advertising industry. No one expects a
diminished need for advertising; on the contrary, as the economy ex-
pands, continued significant growth in advertising expenditure is most
likely.

The present strength of the mainstream press holds another obstacle
for papers wishing to challenge its dominance. Unless two papers are
fairly evenly matched, it is inordinately difficult in the newspaper industry for one paper to displace the market leader in a city. Peter
McLean, managing director of the Argus group, said that "it would be a
brave decision to come into one of the three major urban markets."[16]
The reality of this difficulty was illustrated when the *Weekly Mail*
launched a daily paper in June 1990. Known as the best organized and
most professional of the alternative papers, the *Mail* was best posi-
tioned to enter the daily ranks. Its attempt lasted only several months.

What kind of marketplace will the established papers, and any
would-be challengers, encounter in the 1990s? The number of daily pa-

pers remains large and at least a few of these could fold in the next several years. The market will thus remain highly competitive, with some market leaders like *Beeld*, the *Argus*, and the *Star* continuing to do well. Weaker papers will struggle and at least a few could fold or merge in the first half of the decade, possibly employing a joint operating agreement like the one that has kept the *Cape Times* alive because of its relationship with the larger and healthier *Argus*. Almost all papers will have to address the issue of how best to draw the potential readers among a burgeoning black population. Few papers will have the luxury of being able to ignore the country's demographic realities. The country's black population grew from 15.3 million in 1970 to 20.8 million in 1980 and to an estimated 28.2 million by 1990 (see Table 9.1). This figure, according to one projection, will rise to 36.9 million by the turn of the century.[17]

How well will newspapers be able to tap into this huge potential readership? Indications so far are not encouraging. Although a paper like the *Sowetan*, which is aimed at black readers, is seen as a great success because of its rapid growth in the 1980s, it is far from typical. The overall picture reveals newspaper circulations lagging far behind population growth. Thus total circulation of English dailies, the papers most likely to be read by blacks acquiring the readership habit, rose from 681,424 in 1959 to 820,772 in 1988—an increase of 20.4 percent.[18] During that time, however, the population of Africans (not Coloureds or Asians) rose nearly 300 percent. Other figures point to similarly disturbing realities for newspaper editors and managers. No one doubts the critical need to halt and, ideally, reverse the problem of declining penetration.

The size and growth of the potential market is thus deceptive because the trick for the existing papers will be to turn these people into newspaper readers. That will not be easy. South Africa's blacks, who are the overwhelming majority of these potential new readers, do not have a strong tradition of newspaper reading. Several reasons account for this, including low but now improving literacy rates and poverty and language barriers. Then there is the impact of broadcasting. In the absence of any competing media, these potential readers might be much more likely to turn to newspapers for the information and entertainment needs. As a major advertising agency noted in a newsletter comparing the competition between print and electronic media in "the battle for black minds," print does not come out well. "All the elements that could contribute to the formation of a society with strong bias towards electronic media are in place."[19] The agency listed these factors as widespread illiteracy or semiliteracy, low socioeconomic status,

TABLE 9.1   Projected Population Changes in South Africa, 1980–2020

	Blacks	*Whites*	*Coloureds*	*Asians*	*Total*
1980	20,800,000	4,528,000	2,686,000	821,000	28,835,000
1990	28,192,000	4,997,000	3,189,000	972,000	37,350,000
2000	36,912,000	5,374,000	3,732,000	1,111,000	47,129,000
2010	47,328,000	5,674,000	4,170,000	1,226,000	58,398,000
2020	58,748,000	5,897,000	4,607,000	1,334,000	70,586,000

Note: These figures include the populations of the nominally independent homelands. The figures for 1980 are based on census data, and from 1990 onward on projections.

Source: Business Futures 1989 (Bellville: Institute for Futures Research, 1989). Reprinted by permission of the publisher.

lower education standards, and a measurable preference for electronic media.[20]

On any given day, the following percentages of black men or women use these media: 58.1 (men) and 52.9 (women) listen to the radio, 31.3 and 23.5 view TV, and 17.2 and 7.3 read a daily paper. For whites, the figures are 78.3 and 75.4 percent, 83.5 and 84.5 percent, and 51.4 and 42.0 percent respectively, as indicated in Table 4.1. Figures for the other population groups are also contained in this table.

One implication of these usage patterns is that the black market may skip the print generation and move straight to reliance on the electronic media. Whether it does or not, "the future path for print media in the black market is going to be a bumpy one."[21]

Aggravating the situation are the other economic realities described in Chapter 4, such as high inflation rates and competition for advertising revenue from the free shoppers and television. All these considerations place a premium therefore on prudent and visionary management of the country's mainstream papers if they are to survive as the apartheid era ends. Assuming these papers come through that transition financially stable, the next question is, How will the journalists producing them approach their task?

WHAT KIND OF JOURNALISM?

Just as the economic basis of the press will undergo some reshaping, so too will the product it produces. Newspapers at the turn of the century are likely to look and read differently in important ways. Editors and managers gave many of the same projections in interviews. They expect papers to be more visually oriented, following as they do the trend in the United States to place greater emphasis on layout and design. More color will be present. So will more charts, graphs, and other devices for presenting information visually. Papers will pay even closer attention to packaging the news into sections that are useful to readers. The possibilities of zoned editions will take on heightened importance, as the major metropolitan dailies will emphasize more parochial news for segments of their readers. A great deal of these changes will arise from an increased reliance on market research.

Not only the appearance of the papers will change, however. The approach to journalism itself will also shift. The tension between various approaches to newswriting could well reshape how the craft of journalism is practiced in South Africa. As earlier chapters made clear, a gulf exists between the philosophy and practice of journalism adopted by the mainstream press and the alternative papers. Simply stated, the debate is between adherents of the "objective" model of reporting and those adopting an "engaged" or "advocacy" stance. The former dominates the mainstream papers, although in the past decade a growing proportion of journalists on these papers have accepted at least some aspects of advocacy journalism. The alternative press, by contrast, is a direct response to the perceived inadequacies of the supposedly objective journalism of the mainstream papers.

A former president of the South African Society of Journalists, John Battersby, spelled out this tension soon after it surfaced as a significant issue among his organization's membership. Writing in 1981, he traced the debate to an address by black theologian Dr. Alan Boesak, two years earlier to a group of black journalists. Boesak told them, "Neutrality in the struggle is a crime which the community will not forgive."[22] This call for journalists to throw off claims to impartiality went to the heart of reporting as it had been practiced on mainstream papers and led Battersby to raise several key questions. More than a decade later, they remain unresolved. Some of the tensions he highlighted then are worth repeating now:

> Is objectivity an outdated myth being used by the "liberal Press" to subtly maintain the status quo while paying lip service to the need for fundamental reform and social change?
> Is the ideal of objectivity a worthy value which needs to be re-examined and redefined in a changing South Africa?
> Is it a value worth preserving and one which can serve the interests of all sections of the society?
> And are the only alternatives to objectivity the blatant dissemination of propaganda and ultimately a centrally administered system of thought control?[23]

The divide between the two traditions of journalism in South Africa has not narrowed in the decade since Battersby explained the tension with this set of questions. If anything, it has only deepened, as journalists who reject the objectivity model have found a welcome base in the alternative press for practicing the reporting and analysis they believe appropriate. Regardless of what traditionalists in South African journalism may think of the reporting in the alternative press, these papers' "advocacy" journalism is now firmly established. As the discussion on the alternative press concerning these different approaches made clear, the basic philosophies underlying approaches of these two schools of journalism have some overlap, for example, in their mutual respect for factual reporting. But they also have large philosophical differences, such as the extent to which journalists ought to see themselves as mere recorders of contemporary history or as people who help shape it. How will these two approaches to journalism coexist?

The answer is probably much as they have until now: uneasily, with varying degrees of mutual respect or mutual scorn. The mainstream editors interviewed for this study held the *Weekly Mail* in high regard. And some of their alternative press counterparts spoke with respect for what are regarded as the best mainstream journalists or papers, such as the *Star* or the defunct *Rand Daily Mail.* In looking at the *best* examples of how their counterparts across the ideological divide practice journalism, many editors admit to more common ground in their activities than one might assume exists.

In other words, the most pertinent features of each style of journalism, when practiced at their best, show remarkable overlap. True, the ideological or philosophical frameworks that underlie the practice of journalism on English, Afrikaans, and alternative papers unquestionably differ markedly. These differing foundations inevitably lead to often vastly different approaches to news selection and news treatment. Yet what is remarkable is that degree of overlap between each approach's ultimate objectives. Thus each has a commitment to values like truthfulness, accuracy, justice, and so on.

Still, journalists hold a wide range of views on what is the right, appropriate, possible, or morally defensible approach to practicing their craft in South Africa. As the country's press and its practices are reshaped as the country moves into its postapartheid era, the press faces both the "is" and "ought" questions regarding the practice of journalism: How is it likely to change, and how ought it to change? If the new government were to nationalize the press and allow only a developmental, nation-building kind of journalism, then the question would become moot. But the more likely outcome is that the present tensions would carry over to the new order. If so, what is likely to occur is a gradual rapprochement between the two styles. The more successful English papers are likely to practice a journalism that is more self-aware and open about its biases and ideological base than before. The Afrikaans papers, which have always done far better at wearing their ideological colors on their sleeves, are unlikely to change their basic approach to gathering and reporting news. Their need will be to define a new relationship with their traditional white, Afrikaner constituency, now irrevocably split over South Africa's political direction, and with the National Party that caused this split. At the same time, these papers will explore the growing potential of the predominantly Afrikaans-speaking Coloured market. No doubt, as Afrikaners relinquish political power, their papers will have to relearn what being an opposition press means. To this extent, these papers will need to rethink some of their editorial approaches.

Over time, most English and alternative papers will probably continue narrowing the gap between them. The English papers will increasingly become more oriented to their black constituencies and become better equipped to serve them as they hire more blacks. The papers with more farsighted managements will actively lessen their dependence on their white readerships because it is so plainly in their interests to redefine their constituencies. Other, less forward-looking managements, will eventually do likewise—for sheer survival. As they take these steps, the content of their papers will inexorably change. More news about blacks, written by blacks and edited consciously for black readers, will introduce an array of changes that will make these papers more, not less, like the alternative press.

For their part, the alternative papers are likely to become more like the present-day mainstream press. Already, the alternative papers find that even their politically aware readers seek more than a diet of unrelenting politics. Hence the broader approach adopted in editorial content described in Chapter 3. As these papers mature further, they will undoubtedly show more signs of responding to reader expectations. Heightened competition will come from the far better equipped mainstream papers, as they produce papers more appealing to the blacks who compose the bulk of alternative press readers. This development will compel alternative papers that wish to be competitive to offer the broader range of reporting that characterizes the traditional daily or weekly paper.

This is not to say that the ideological positions of either the English or alternative papers will substantially change as they refine their contents. Rather, these positions will simply be presented through a broader range of editorial content. As the topics of news coverage increasingly overlap between these groups of papers and the Afrikaans press—the ideological perspectives or worldviews that individual papers bring to their selection—the interpretation and presentation of news will of course take on heightened importance. What will continue to divide journalists and newspapers, then, will be their ideological bases and their philosophies of journalism. South African journalism, in other words, is not on the verge of becoming a homogenized, united enterprise.

Is there nevertheless a core of common, shared values that these journalists and their papers can take into their postapartheid society? And is there an approach to practicing journalism that does two things: (1) offers a substantive, coherent "philosophy" of journalism that accommodates these core values and (2) avoids being so broad and vague as to offer a collection of truisms or platitudes? The answer to both questions is yes, the concept of "Committed Journalism" described in the next chapter.

THE PROFESSION

Ken Owen recalled receiving a visitor when he was editor of the *Sunday Express*. The man, a millionaire, was obviously unacquainted with the constraints under which this SAAN newspaper was produced. He "stared in disbelief" at what Owen termed the squalid conditions in the newsroom before commenting: "So much power, and they keep you in a place like this."[24] This anecdote symbolizes much about how journalism was traditionally practiced in South Africa. Despite the potential and actual influence of the country's journalists, by and large they have never been accorded high status in South Africa. By almost any measure, journalism has long been seen as an occupational stepchild. Factors like the following did little to attract would-be journalists into the country's newsrooms: traditionally poor salaries; constant and often vicious political attacks from the government or its opponents, including physical assault; harassment and intimidation from the police; limited status in the community; and an overall environment (corporate, legal, social, and so on) that often tolerated substandard performance or allowed no better. Overall, journalism hardly constituted one of the top career options for the country's brightest and best. And if white journalists had problems, things were far worse for black reporters. Indeed, it is astonishing that South African journalism has during the past half century been able to attract and retain as many able journalists as it has. How, then, is the enterprise of journalism likely to emerge as the postapartheid society unfolds? Three points deserve attention: the place of journalism as a professional or quasiprofessional activity, the training of journalists, and their trade unions.

As in the United States and many other Western nations, journalists in South Africa are not licensed by the state. No one path to acquiring the title of "journalist" is prescribed, although several typical routes can be identified. Moreover, unless future government policy decrees otherwise, journalists of tomorrow are likely to acquire that title in a manner as laissez faire and diverse as they do now.

The newspeople referred to here are of course only one segment of a much larger pool of journalists. Excluded are the sizable news staff of the SABC; journalists working on consumer, trade, or other specialized periodicals; journalists on suburban or small-town newspapers beyond the scope of this study; freelance writers; and so on. As this list suggests, journalism in South Africa is an enterprise as diverse as that in countless other countries with highly developed mass media. One would expect that such a widely divergent group of individuals would have little sense of cohesion. In South Africa, though, this lack of cohesion extends even to those journalists working on the daily and weekly papers examined in this study. Ideological, racial, and organizational barriers have prevented these journalists from developing a unified sense of identity or purpose. This theme is examined presently. A prior question, of course, is, How does one get to be a journalist in South Africa?

Journalists on the mainstream and alternative press obtain their positions via one of four avenues. One is the country's handful of college- or university-level journalism programs. Rhodes University, in Grahamstown, offers undergraduate and graduate training in journalism and media studies, and Stellenbosch University offers an intensive graduate-level program. Their programs are supplemented by those at the Pretoria, Natal, and Cape Peninsula Technikons. Formerly known as technical colleges, the technikons are tertiary educational institutions that took on an especial importance in the government's educational strategy in the 1980s. Both the university and technikon programs are important conduits to the mainstream and alternative papers as well as to other media. With the crumbling of apartheid in higher education, a more racially diverse mix of students is being trained. Another tertiary institution offering journalism courses is the University of South Africa, a highly regarded correspondence institution. Several Afrikaans universities and some black universities offer programs in communication studies but with typically limited training in journalism.

A second channel that an aspirant journalist could pursue would be to seek training with the Argus group, which for several decades has conducted its own intensive "cadet" school. This highly competitive program lasts about six months and is limited to about twelve to fifteen students each year, most of whom are women or blacks.[25] The program is conducted at the *Star*, in Johannesburg and serves the various papers in the Argus group. Part of the rationale for the Argus course is the company's desire to train its own people, who are given an intensive course in basics of reporting, including a rigorous course in shorthand.

The fact that the cadet program has continued, despite the increasing supply of graduates in recent years, reflects the misgivings many editors have about the value of the university or technikon training these students receive. Most cadet trainees are university graduates but even those who have journalism degrees are typically required to undergo the Argus program. Over the years, the Argus school has fed a steady stream of journalists into its own but also other South African papers.

The third option facing an aspirant journalist in South Africa lies with the alternative papers, which have made a concerted effort to train journalists and others. Adopting what is a combination of an internship and an apprenticeship program, several alternative papers have taken on trainees for varying lengths of time and with equally diverse levels of structure. As a group, the alternative editors have spoken much about the need for training the journalists their papers need. These editors also recognize the need to staff alternative publications that may be launched in the future. They have addressed the problem by providing hands-on training for aspirant journalists as well as for those seeking to work in areas like advertising and management. Yet the training they offer, by the admission of several editors, tends to be skimpy, unstructured, and fragmented. With the pressure of day-to-day journalism being especially acute for the alternative papers, which are typically short of staff and other resources, these papers' editors and reporters have little time to do the one-on-one instruction and nurturing they would like. Moreover, the approach of these papers lacks the systematic, formal attention to content that marks the Argus cadet school and the universities and technikons. Consequently, the alternative press's emphasis on training, commendable though it was, was characterized more by good intentions than effectiveness.

The fourth route to a journalism job is the informal one, in which someone without specific training or experience in journalism would be hired and trained on the job. Afrikaans newspapers have often relied on this approach, hiring bright liberal arts graduates who were able to learn quickly the conventions of newswriting. In addition to these four traditional career paths, a potential fifth avenue was added in 1992 with the establishment of the Institute for the Advancement of Journalism in Johannesburg. Under the directorship of former *Rand Daily Mail* editor Allister Sparks, this multiracial organization is designed to offer training for midcareer journalists as well as recruit young people into the profession. The institute is modeled after the Poynter Institute for Media Studies in St. Petersburg, Florida, which was instrumental in founding the organization.

Earlier chapters referred to the gulf between journalists on the English papers and their managements. This deep rift, often marked by deep-seated mutual antagonism and suspicion, inevitably led to a union-management framework for dealings between these journalists and their employers. It is no surprise, therefore, that the largest professional journalists' interest group, the South African Society of Journalists, has as its primary role the quest for better salaries and benefits for its members. It also seeks to advance other interests of its members, including press freedom.

The SASJ presently has some 800 members. Because of the traditional preponderance of white journalists on the English papers, the SASJ has been an overwhelmingly white organization. As political awareness grew rapidly among the black population in the 1970s, black journalists formed the Union of Black Journalists, which was banned in 1977. Later, as more blacks began to reject the SASJ as an appropriate vehicle for expressing their interests and concerns, these journalists together with other blacks in the media formed the Media Workers Association of Southern Africa in 1980.[26] MWASA continues to be a significant media voice.

Then, in 1989, a third group was launched: Democratic Journalists of South Africa. This group is multiracial in membership. Politically to the left of the SASJ, it draws more support from the alternative press than the SASJ does.

The range of views reflected in these three groups and their memberships, which have some overlap, symbolize the fractured nature of South African journalism. This quality is sure to continue for the next decade or so. What is less certain is the status journalists will enjoy, the caliber of people they will attract to their ranks, or the quality of initial and ongoing training they will receive. These and other aspects of the profession, like so much associated with the press's future, are contingent on what else happens in South African society.

THE LEGAL FOUNDATION

Regardless of how the people producing tomorrow's news are trained or organized, they will continue to operate within the limits journalists everywhere must face, such as organizational and economic constraints. In South Africa, however, a particularly important factor will be the legal environment in which the press functions. Chapter 5 described how the legal system greatly limited the press's capacity to portray its society accurately. If the press is to thrive in the postapartheid era, fundamental changes must occur in the country's legal framework. These changes fall into two categories: removing barriers and installing safeguards.

The first type is easily described. A review of the legislation described in Chapter 5 indicates which laws present most difficulty. Obvious candidates for scrapping or amendment are the Internal Security Act, the Police Act, and the Prisons Act. By mid-1992, the government had begun reevaluating much of this and other problematic legislation and the legal arena was undergoing more rapid change than perhaps any other area analyzed in this study.

Listing offensive security laws is easy enough; it is also easy to make the mistake of seeking to throw out all restrictive legislation. Law professor Anthony Mathews cautioned against this approach, stressing the need to accept the *legitimate* security needs of a future South African government. His concern was that the society balance these needs with the demands of generally accepted legal principles.[27] Applying his argument to the press, one must avoid the simplistic and, in the long run, unworkable approach of seeking to scrap all restrictive legislation. More helpful is to identify some rights to which the press can aspire, both during and after South Africa's shift from its apartheid legacy.

The press, like any individual in the society, ought to be guaranteed the due process of law. This would include access to legal counsel, being charged with criminal offenses only under clearly defined statutes, and the right to a public trial before an independent court in accordance with normal legal standards and practices. Especially important in this connection for the press would be the need to drop provisions in the law that permit administrative action essentially beyond question by the courts. Also, the press ought to be accorded the presumption of innocence in legal proceedings and the onus of proving guilt should lie with the authorities.

Tied to the first point should be an assumption that the press is indeed entitled to gather and disseminate information freely. This right, like the others just listed, is of course not sought for the press alone but for all in the society. Other legal rights, regarded as standard in many other societies but disregarded in varying degrees in South Africa in the past, are detailed in the various examples of a bill of rights that several groups in South Africa have proposed. These documents indicate the legal criteria against which state conduct against the press should be evaluated.[28]

How the society moves toward securing such rights is another issue.[29] There is little point in attempting here to predict how this might happen. More important is to note that the prospect of a bill of rights has already generated considerable interest in South Africa. It is argued here that such a document, with a clause assuring freedom of expression, could greatly help the press.

The value of a bill of rights is not universally accepted in South Africa. Individuals and groups on various parts of the political spectrum have raised objections to the idea. Some blacks have contended that a bill of rights would simply entrench white benefits, and some conservative Afrikaans groups have argued that only individual and not group rights are protected or that a bill of rights would undermine state security.[30]

The arguments surrounding a bill of rights, as one would expect of such a fundamentally important question, are complex and have implications for all facets of the society. For our purposes it is important simply to recognize that such a document offers no guarantees of protection for the press or for any other agencies or individuals in the absence of a broad-based commitment in the society to implementing it. Because South Africa is a society weak in traditions of tolerance and dissent, constitutional promises of press freedom admittedly invite skepticism. Yet having such assurances built into a bill of rights, it is argued, constitutes a significant advance over the present situation.

It is crucial that for a bill of rights or other constitutional protections to succeed they would have to be introduced into a context of other fundamental, positive developments in the society. Writing in 1984, at the height of the unrest, Mathews argued against the premature introduction of a bill of rights into a society so unstable and repressive that it was incapable of implementing it. Rather, he said:

> We need to work for the acceptance of two related major propositions: first, full civil rights, while remaining an admirable goal, are the product of a just and stable order rather than the means to achieve it; and second, that a partial programme of civil rights, which takes account of both the requirements of political stability and the goal of human freedom, is needed for societies that lack social justice and political stability but are committed to the achievement of both.[31]

Far from defending the government's record on maintaining political stability, of which he was harshly critical, Mathews makes the important point that in the absence of other commitments to a socially just society, a bill of rights could even be harmful.[32] It is therefore assumed here that if such constitutional protections emerge in South Africa they will do so in a political climate far healthier than the one in which Mathews made these comments.

Should postapartheid South Africa adopt a bill of rights, the wording will undoubtedly be subjected to intense haggling and protracted crafting. There is thus little point in offering at this stage any formulation of a provision to protect free expression. Rather, the emphasis here is that such a provision should be included, a recognition that already typically characterizes the various bill of rights proposals that have surfaced in South Africa's political debate.

Two such examples bear mentioning here. The South African Law Commission[33] has proposed a bill of rights that guarantees "the right to freedom of speech and to obtain and disseminate information."[34] The ANC, in its Constitutional Guidelines of 1988, said the new constitution should include a bill of rights that guarantees "the basic rights and freedoms, such as freedom of association, expression, thought, worship and the press." Not all speech would be protected, however: "The advocacy or practice of racism, fascism, naziism or the incitement of ethnic or regional exclusiveness or hatred shall be outlawed."[35]

Legal scholar John Dugard addressed the fear that without such a protection conservative whites would exploit a free-expression clause to preach racist views. After noting how the U.S. Bill of Rights has been held to permit the advocacy of racism, Dugard said this objection is easily surmounted in the South African context. "International human rights conventions outlaw racist propaganda. ... Although a Bill of Rights should guarantee freedom of speech it would not be unusual, judged by international standards, for it to restrict free speech in order to obstruct the re-emergence of racism of any kind."[36]

It is dangerous to underestimate the fragility that will mark a South Africa that continues its transition from apartheid. Yet if a bill of rights accompanies other positive steps toward a more just and stable social order, such a document can play a valuable role for the press and the society at large. But whether or not free expression receives some form of constitutional guarantee, South Africa's legal system will be pivotal in shaping the quality of life for the press as a whole. Press vigor, in other words, will largely be shaped by both specific provisions of the legal system as well as its overall disposition toward free expression. Just as the press will struggle to thrive if beset by economic weakness, so too a hospitable legal climate—possibly undergirded by some constitutional protection—will be another necessary but not a sufficient condition to guarantee a vigorous press.

TOWARD A NATIONAL MEDIA POLICY

As South Africa reaches a historical turning point, it will need to consider the merits of adopting a national media policy. Questions of press freedom and free speech are admittedly unlikely to appear on the agenda of a new administration's first cabinet meeting, but this issue will inevitably command attention early in the new government's tenure. Thus unless it had previously committed itself to a detailed and comprehensive national information policy, it will eventually have to decide whether devising one is a wise move. The argument here is that this option merits serious consideration.

Many who are now in political opposition are troubled by various aspects of the press, such as its highly monopolistic nature. ANC officials, for example, have said: "We shall have to find a mechanism to provide many more papers for the people—African language papers, for instance. The mechanism could be state papers; party or community papers; perhaps subsidized media as in Europe."[37] Most mainstream editors wince when presented with prospects like these. For under the guise of providing a wider distribution of and access to information, a government could easily steer subsidies or full funding to publications serving its own, narrower interests.

A future government can make a strong case for intervening to address a white-dominated, highly monopolistic press. But unless it does so with extreme care and with a neutrality that would require great restraint, the worthwhile objective of creating greater newspaper diversity could soon backfire. The result could easily be a cynicism over government double standards rather than a fostering of respect and support for press freedom.

A national media policy could serve as an instrument for addressing present wrongs or avoiding future ones. As with a bill of rights, having such a policy would not guarantee its implementation or necessarily protect press freedom. Yet a well-conceived, viable policy commanding wide public support could greatly foster the cause of press freedom. What should such a policy contain? Five suggestions are that it should:

1. Identify a philosophy or framework, appropriate for South Africa's present needs, on which a national policy including all media could be built
2. Pursue appropriate constitutional protections for freedom of expression, as suggested previously, and ensure the press full access to the courts in disputes between the government and the press
3. Actively promote a culture of tolerance and acceptance of free expression within the country
4. Establish an independent, standing agency to play a mediating role between the press and the government or between other parties aggrieved by the press (the present Media Council already

fills this role well, and it might make sense to seek ways of increasing its acceptance outside the mainstream press)

5. Address the present financial structure of the press, possibly by
establishing an independent board, with the intent of increasing
media diversity and access.

For these objectives to be attained, and others affecting media other
than the press, the policy would require a high level of government and
public support as well as sustained, comprehensive implementation.
The mandate necessary to make these changes work could, in turn,
come from a broad-based commission of enquiry into the kind of media
a postapartheid South Africa ought to have.

No such policy has ever been implemented in South Africa. Nor
could one have succeeded given the polarization of opinion in the country and the white dominance of political power. Now the chances are
much improved of putting together a widely representative task force motivated to devise a workable, principled national media policy that would
command wide national credibility and support. Admittedly, many aspects of such a policy would be controversial. But despite the opposition any media policy would face, a systematic attempt at addressing
the overall media needs and problems would afford several benefits.

One would be the clarity and direction for the country on the kinds
of issues that have surfaced in this study. For example, a national policy
would make explicit where the country should head with respect to
subsidies of the press, the extent to which the press should be seen as a
partner in helping to build a postapartheid society, or what mechanisms
ought to exist to help balance the society's need to be informed with the
government's legitimate security needs. All these issues would need to
be addressed in the context of an ideological or philosophical framework, a foundational and of course highly contentious starting point for
whatever policies might be recommended.

The political climate in the immediate postapartheid era may make
it impossible to devise a national policy with the level of consensus
needed to make it work. The issues needing attention could be addressed instead on an ad hoc basis. Although this approach would lack
the benefits of a systematic plan, a piecemeal approach to addressing
media policy questions at least helps avoid the dangers inherent in a formal policy. If the government ignored the warning given here to seek a
broad base of support and adopted instead a policy reflecting a narrower,
more partisan agenda, any consequent national media plan would start
life fatally flawed. Far from offering considerable potential benefit for
the society, an ill-conceived, narrowly construed policy could do more
harm than good.

CONCLUSION

Whether or not the various issues discussed in this chapter, and those described earlier, are addressed in a formal policy, all have to be re-solved—even if only by default. Depending on the energy, imagination, courage, and integrity South Africans bring to these questions, the country's press faces a wide range of possible identities it could acquire in the future. Examining some of these possibilities is this study's final task.

10

Rewriting the Map

THE SOUTH AFRICAN WRITER Andre Brink recounted the possibly apocryphal story of a man, known only as Corporal Martens, living near Cape Town in the late 1700s. Having had the chance to travel to the virtually uncharted interior, he drew a map of the country and sent it to the authorities in the hope of receiving some reward. Instead, he was warned that if he ever drew another he would get thirty years in prison. Apparently undeterred, Martens then secretly spent his days continuing his project.

Brink related Martens's experience to that of South African writers two centuries later:

> The parallel is startlingly obvious. The strange territory explored and mapped for the first time; the assiduous cartographer offering his map to the world and threatened, to his dismay, with thirty years in chains should he disclose it; and the long lonely years afterwards, during which he continues to draw and redraw his map, refining it all the time in order to correspond more and more closely to the land he has explored. Here is the writer slaving away in his ceaseless attempt to draw the map of his vision of truth, risking his liberty in order to offer to the world a view of itself. And, opposing him, is a government prepared to go to any extremes to keep the truth locked away.[1]

Journalists too are mapmakers. As contemporary cartographers, they describe the lie of the land as they see it, perhaps inaccurately describing some chunks of territory or completely overlooking others. Usually, though, they provide reasonably close representations of reality, at times irritating, embarrassing, or angering the authorities. That is, if their maps are made available freely. Much of the South African press's recent history was shaped by government's attempts to control the content and distribution of its presentations or interpretations of reality.

216

As South Africa's newspapers approach the postapartheid era they will be called upon to draw maps that differ as their land continues to change. Likewise, the ground rules by which the authorities let them operate will also constitute new territory. How South Africa's sociopolitical map will be redrawn in the 1990s and beyond is cause for growing speculation as apartheid loosens its grip. That broader task, however, must be left to others. More significant here are the implications these changes will have for the press. The new shape of the press, and the directions that journalism and newspapering could pursue, will be determined by two factors: the environment in which the press is permitted to function and the choices that journalists themselves make as they practice their craft.

WHAT KIND OF PRESS?

Media scholars divide different countries' "styles" or "philosophies" of mass media systems into various categories. One classic fourfold study divided media into what were called the authoritarian, libertarian, social responsibility, and Soviet Communist theories of the press.[2] A more accurate term, however, would be to call them approaches because they were presented as descriptions rather than actual theories. More recently, the "developmental journalism" approach has secured a place in the literature. Denis McQuail termed these concepts "ideas of how the media *ought* to, or can be *expected* to, operate under a prevailing set of conditions and values."[3] In applying these five notions to South Africa's future, one could quickly eliminate the libertarian and Soviet Communist approaches, which are described more fully elsewhere, because each has minimal prospect of being embraced. The authoritarian, social responsibility, and developmental approaches merit closer attention.[4] A brief description of each is appropriate.

McQuail has summarized the key principles of each of these approaches. The authoritarian view, which increasingly dominated South Africa in the 1980s and then began receding in importance, holds that:

- Media should do nothing which could undermine established authority
- Media should always (or ultimately) be subordinate to established authority
- Media should avoid offence to majority, or dominant, moral and political values
- Censorship can be justified to enforce these principles
- Unacceptable attacks on authority, deviations from official policy, or offenses against moral codes should be criminal offences.[5]

These principles could well have been written specifically to describe the South African press in recent years. Of course, journalists in many other nations would see the same ready applicability to their own situations. In South Africa the question is, Given the shift away from an especially heavy-handed authoritarianism in the 1980s, how likely is this approach to the press to dominate in the future?

But first, a look at the two other contenders. The social responsibility view, which is most typical of the Western media systems, holds that:

- Media should accept and fulfill certain obligations to society
- These obligations are mainly to be met by setting high or professional standards of informativeness, truth, accuracy, objectivity, and balance
- In accepting and applying these obligations, media should be self-regulating within the framework of the law and established institutions
- The media should avoid whatever might lead to crime, violence, or civil disorder or give offence to ethnic or religious minorities
- The media as a whole should be pluralist and reflect the diversity of their society, giving access to various points of view and to rights of reply
- Society and the public, following the first named principle, have a right to expect high standards of performance and intervention can be justified to secure the, or a, public good.[6]

The social responsibility approach best matches the standard to which most English-language papers have aspired. Laboring though they did for a long while under an increasingly authoritarian media model, editors of English papers, and more recently alternative and Afrikaans editors too, have generally looked to the social responsibility approach as the one they most desired for their society.

Most recently, especially as black opposition groups have regained certain freedom of expression, the prospect of a developmental model has also received attention. According to this approach,

- Media should accept and carry out positive development tasks in line with nationally established policy
- Freedom of the media should be open to restriction according to (1) economic priorities and (2) development needs of society
- Media should give priority in their content to the national culture and language
- Media should give priority in news and information to links with other developing countries which are close geographically, culturally, or politically
- Journalists and other media workers have responsibilities as well as freedoms in their information gathering and dissemination tasks

- In the interest of development ends, the state has a right to intervene in, or restrict, media operations and devices of censorship, subsidy and direct control can be justified.[7]

Given the various developments and trends in newspapers predicted in Chapters 8 and 9, which—if any—of these three models is likely to dominate? These models are not mutually exclusive; elements of two or all three could be combined. The actual system that emerges will correlate highly with the kind of political change that occurs in South Africa. Undoubtedly, if the movement toward a more democratic society falters, for whatever reason, and white South Africa returns to its previously defensive, security-based style of government, a return to a full-blown authoritarian approach could easily result. A similar course could well be pursued by a black majority government facing what it perceived as great instability. Given the precedents of press restrictions from the state of emergency and statutory law generally, a new government could quickly embrace authoritarian measures (or continue ones in force at the time it took office). Another scenario could entail a right-wing white government coming to power in a military coup, in which case authoritarian or even military rule and severe media restrictions would certainly result.

A black government might also promote developmental journalism, seeking to use the press with some level of compulsion to advance government policies, especially on economic and racial or ethnic issues. Because of South Africa's apartheid history, a black government might well forbid the media from carrying racist material, however that might be defined. Proactively, the government might implement subsidies to benefit some financially weaker papers.

But the developmental system is highly unlikely to become preeminent. This is because the traditions of an already established mainstream press put these papers at odds with many elements of development journalism, especially because this approach entails abdicating varying degrees of editorial autonomy to government officials. The strong orientation to the social responsibility approach held by the most powerful papers will make it difficult for any government to promote developmental journalism beyond modest levels.

The social responsibility system is likely to dominate, although certainly not to the degree that marks most Western societies. This system can flourish only in liberal democratic societies, which are marked by high levels of tolerance, democratic political activity, and internal stability. Lawrence Schlemmer, who has written extensively on change in South Africa, described numerous factors that would make it difficult for South Africa to become a fully fledged liberal democratic society. Among these are its ethnic diversity and lack of values accepted widely across groups. He wrote that "South Africa has a number of features that powerfully militate against the establishment of democratic institutions. Because of a long history of social segregation and institutional separation, the different races have few political and social interests in common."[8] He added: "Enormous difficulties thus lie ahead in establishing a minimum consensus on overall socioeconomic goals and a sustained process of democratization."[9]

Given this sober assessment, only the most naive would expect South Africa to move rapidly and smoothly toward a markedly more open and democratic society. Not only is that unlikely to occur soon, but the press is equally unlikely in the near future to enjoy the freedoms typically marking most Western societies. The press is thus likely to function under more of a hybrid model, largely influenced by the tenets of the social responsibility approach but adapted to South Africa's realities. For the country is itself a strange hybrid, with a mix of First World and Third World components. Accordingly, its press system reflects the tensions of many papers aspiring to follow the social responsibility system while operating in a clearly predemocratic society. Because the country has not yet embraced democratic standards, various factors lead the society to incorporate authoritarian and developmental aspects into the way the press functions. Most recently, the basic social responsibility model was most diluted by elements of the authoritarian approach. In the future, the basic approach may instead be marked by a greater developmental emphasis.

One crucial factor underlies how the exact mix of these three models will take shape. Will the press be regarded—by the government, the public, and perhaps the press itself—as primarily a First World or a Third World institution? Journalism professor Arnold de Beer described the split between the First World and the Third World in South Africa as it affects foreign news coverage of the country. He argued that First World standards of media freedom cannot be universally applied to countries like South Africa, which also have significant Third World components. Writing during the state of emergency, de Beer contended that it was unrealistic for international media to expect South Africa to allow coverage according to First World media standards.[10] His argument would not be universally accepted by journalists in South Africa and beyond. They and others would say that the government opportunistically and hypocritically exploits the country's mix of First World and Third World components. Thus the government boasts of its First World economic standards, technology, and infrastructure yet pleads Third World status when evaluated on how it handles its sociopolitical problems, for example. Of course, each of these positions has validity. When it comes to the press, however, it seems that editors and journalists desperately hope that they can maintain what has primarily been a First World model, knowing that papers might increasingly operate as if they were running according to Third World standards.

This concern over standards stems not from an arrogant, Western ethnocentricism that contends that its ways of doing things are better than anything the Third World can produce. Rather, it arises from the sheer reality that whites are increasingly losing the economic and other advantages they have held. From their point of view, standards are indeed dropping. Whites see qualities that are prized in Western industrial society, such as efficiency, productivity, political and economic stability, and relatively limited government corruption, slipping increasingly from their grasp. In addition, the major items on the country's postapartheid agenda will intensify its Third World character: It faces massive population growth and the accompanying problems of needing to provide adequate housing, employment, education, and social and health benefits as well as stable, sustained political and economic development.[11]

If those in the press conceded that it was indeed changing into a Third World institution, it would be virtually impossible to adhere to its previous standards. Worse still, if editors openly acknowledged that their papers could be evaluated according to Third World standards, that would open the way to and even legitimize a wide range of government antipress actions. Government officials could say, "We always said you people in the press had unrealistic expectations; now that you've admitted our country's Third World needs and special circumstances, these are the ways we all need to work together for the national good." Such a development is not only a logical step for any government to take, but it would also greatly curtail independent journalism in South Africa.

Journalists have much unhappy experience with recent government authoritarianism toward the press. Their fears of an imposed developmental approach are based on what they have seen elsewhere. And whatever benefits this system may offer, the price it exacts is seen as prohibitive. Veteran Africa correspondent David Lamb assessed the toll that development journalism has taken on the continent. African nations, he said, contend that all they want

> from the Western media is objective reporting, and given that, [they] will accept exposés along with favorable stories. The argument is not convincing. What Africa really wants is boosterism, a style of advocacy journalism that concentrates on the opening of civic centers and ignores the warts. It wants a new set of guidelines for covering the underdeveloped world, one which, if used in the West, would tell journalists to disregard the Watergates and Charles Mansons and concentrate only on the posi-

tive and uplifting. ... To write about only what is good does not mean that
what is bad will simply evaporate. To contend that truth is only that
which promotes national causes is to deny the validity of other causes
and the necessity to re-evaluate them. It leaves a people in need of hearing a voice other than their own.[12]

Mainstream journalists in particular fear that developmental journalism could introduce the type of thinking experienced in the Republic of Somalia, for example. That country's government contended that
"it is the function of the nation's mass communication media to weld
the entire community into a single entity, a people of the same mind
and possessed of the same determination to safeguard the national interests."[13] Or, worse still, there is the danger typified by a Somali official who said: "Truth is whatever promotes your government. If
something is not favorable to your country, then it isn't true and you
should not publish falsehoods."[14]

This is not to suggest that the social responsibility model has served
South Africa flawlessly in the past and should continue unchanged in
the future. This study has shown that this is far from the case. Nor is it
to ignore the substantial body of literature on the weaknesses and failings in the Western, objective model of journalism.[15] Sharing as it does
the main tenets of this style of journalism, the mainstream press in
South Africa is prone to the weaknesses and flaws of Western journalism generally. The point here, however, is that despite the South African press's evident and ample shortcomings, whether in the
mainstream or alternative segments, developmental journalism *as a
whole* offers little to redress these weaknesses. Elements of developmental journalism are indeed likely to be incorporated into tomorrow's
press and ought to be welcomed. But any future government that de-
creed this approach to be the marching orders for the press would not
only be misguided but would meet intense resistance. Opposition from
the mainstream papers and presumably elements in the alternative
press would make fully fledged implementation of developmental journalism highly unlikely.

As a whole, then, the press is likely to cling to the social responsibility approach and First World standards for as long as possible, as indeed
it should. Should the society as a whole move toward liberal democracy, it will be easier for the press to maintain its allegiance to and practice of First World standards. By contrast, should the society move
further from liberal democracy, maintaining its present orientation
would be increasingly difficult.

As noted earlier, South Africa faces numerous barriers en route to a
liberal democratic society. Not the least of these is that traditional lib-

eral values have found little support among the country's blacks. More-over, most Afrikaners have long viewed liberalism in South Africa with intense distrust. Even among the English-speaking population that has traditionally been the home of South African liberal democratic values, such support has hardly flourished in recent years. As legal scholar John Dugard wrote, "In modern South Africa it has become fashionable to discredit liberals and liberalism. Political forces on both the right and the left dismiss the values and ideals of liberalism as irrelevant to the future of South Africa."[16] South African liberals have been attacked for being "members of the establishment complicit in maintaining apart-heid and ... peripheral idealists with no political constituency and a long record of failure in producing reform."[17] Both Afrikaners and crit-ics on the political left find fault with liberalism's emphasis on the indi-vidual as the basic unit of social analysis and its failure to consider adequately concepts like class, groups, and ethnicity.[18]

Despite these criticisms, Dugard argued that "the institutions and principles of liberal democracies offer the best hope for a new South Af-rica."[19] And that is the position adopted here. If the press is to operate at its fullest potential in postapartheid South Africa, it must be assured the freedom of expression that typifies most liberal democracies. To the extent that it receives that freedom, the press will both reflect the health of the emerging society and equip it to move increasingly toward a more just and humane order. It is not as if Western liberal democracies provide "the final answer to problems of human development. How-ever, no alternative systems presently appears to offer a superior combi-nation of general quality of life, freedom of expression, and protection from state oppression or bureaucratic constraints."[20] So too with the press, whose potential to flourish has never been greater than in liberal democracies.

The liberal democratic model may be an ideal that is unattainable in South Africa, as some have argued.[21] Yet even if this were so, the press ought to set its sights on no less a target because of the protections that a liberal democratic view of the press provides. Some Afrikaans and al-ternative press editors would undoubtedly resist being associated with the agenda of democratic liberalism's political agenda as it has been ad-vocated in South Africa. Yet liberalism cannot claim a monopoly over the principles proposed below; rooted though they are in that tradition, these principles are undoubtedly compatible with other value systems. In addition, a distinction must be made between the history of South African liberalism and its broader political agenda and the narrower im-plications this agenda holds for the press. It is argued here that the vari-ous groups of South Africa's newspapers are already advocates and practitioners of what is essentially a liberal democratic view of the press. In addition, to the extent that they are able to publish freely, these papers are also beneficiaries of a liberal democratic view of the press—admittedly undermined and abused, but a liberal democratic view nevertheless.

Many Afrikaans or alternative journalists would resist the idea of being associated with democratic liberalism generally and might see little applicability of this approach for their work in the press. Yet it is contended here that regardless of the problems associated with South Africa's liberal tradition, a wide range of journalists regard the *fundamental* values of democratic liberalism as not merely tolerable but meriting enthusiastic adoption. These values can provide the basis for a viable and coherent framework that is, potentially, broadly acceptable to South Africa's various press factions, who could promote this framework with integrity. Providing the outline of such a perspective is the final task of this study.

TOWARD A COMMITTED JOURNALISM— SOUTH AFRICAN STYLE

During a 1986 conference on the future of South African liberalism, Schlemmer correctly noted that:

> if South African liberals are to promote the processes which will yield a democratic outcome, they will need a more indigenous social theory of liberalism than they have had so far. Without a rigorous liberal theory, fully applicable to South African conditions, liberals will remain vulnerable to attack from the hitherto far more systematic white nationalists on the one hand and the revisionist or materialist intelligentsia on the other.[22]

It is not the intention here to provide the overall theory for which Schlemmer called. Rather, a more modest task is attempted: to offer a framework, rooted in a liberal democratic rationale, by which tomorrow's press can chart its course in South Africa. Whereas the government, the public, and other institutions in society will mostly determine the rules by which tomorrow's press will operate, journalists too will significantly influence how they practice their craft. They will not be helpless puppets, utterly subject to forces outside their control. They will have the rare opportunity, because the press and the whole society are now so highly malleable, to reconsider their approach to and practice of their craft. Regardless of the society in which South Africa's journalists will work tomorrow, they too have the chance—indeed, the duty—at this time of flux to reexamine the values underlying what they do. What, in other words, *is* their raison d'être as journalists?

Astonishingly, surveying the literature on the South African press and talking to those who work in it yield no clearly understood, explicitly stated, or widely accepted rationale for being a journalist. The culture of the press lacks any concise articulation of its journalistic mission or what is expected of journalists. Elements of such a statement may exist, perhaps in a paper's statement of philosophy, or in an individual editor's column or editorial here or there. Eloquent defenses of press freedom have emerged over the years but the call here is for something more fundamental: What ought journalism to be accomplishing in the first place and according to which values ought it be practiced?

One central reason for journalism's lack of a clearly defined philosophy or mission is the press's recent preoccupation with government pressure. Conflicts between the government and the press and questions of press freedom have consistently claimed priority in discussions about the press, and understandably so. Yet fundamental though press freedom is, thoughtful journalism everywhere faces other ethical or value-related issues. In South Africa, however, discussion of issues like privacy, news-gathering techniques, dealing with confidential sources, and so on is minimal. Again, one could argue that with the question of press survival dominating the agenda, journalists had little time to reflect on these other issues. With the ship taking on water fast, one does not spend time discussing health standards of the galley.

But the problem goes deeper. Even if journalists had had the time to examine other issues, as a group they appear ill equipped to do so. They lack any clear, common philosophical base or value system that could inform them in making difficult judgments. Inevitably, to guide their thinking they rely on their personal value systems, and perhaps especially on their political philosophies, as well as on a vaguely defined, amorphous cluster of beliefs about what good journalism would call for in a given situation.

The contention here, therefore, is that there is a dearth of careful thinking on the nature of journalism, except for press freedom issues. Those more thoughtful practitioners and papers that do wrestle with the implications of their craft are singularly ill equipped to do so in the absence of a clearly defined, coherent set of values that could direct and justify their thinking.

Undoubtedly, whatever stands South African journalists take on difficult issues—whether concerning police demands to reveal a source's identity or how to report with sensitivity a particularly tragic news story—their decisions do not emerge from a vacuum. As media ethicist

Edmund Lambeth has written, "Journalism is not a disembodied occupation." Referring to U.S. journalism, he added: "Conceived in the Renaissance, born in the Enlightenment, and nurtured to robust life in the modern west, journalism inherits the legacy of the larger society: the principles of truth, justice, freedom, humaneness, and individual responsibility."[23] This remark applies to the South African situation too, as do the principles in Lambeth's concept of "Committed Journalism." This concept offers a helpful starting point in filling the void just described. It provides a brief but clear set of ethical principles to guide South African journalists in all aspects of thinking about their work.

Lambeth's call was for a system of journalistic ethics that embodies the values of Judeo-Christian civilization.[24] Notwithstanding the pluralistic cultural traditions in South Africa, the values undergirding that country's press are unquestionably also rooted in this tradition. In the future, one can expect the country's journalists to continue adapting a journalism "nurtured to robust life in the modern west" to South Africa's indigenous, non-Western qualities. For now, though, the principles that Lambeth presents are utterly in harmony with the spirit of South African journalism. These principles also offer the rationale or raison d'être for journalists that, it was contended earlier, is presently lacking. Lambeth based his ethical framework on five values.

The Principle of Truth Telling

Lambeth identified several dimensions of truth. One is the need for journalism to stress factual accuracy. Another is for a journalist to dig behind the facts to understand their context. Linked to this idea, Lambeth said the reporter responsible for covering more specialized or technical material has an obligation to acquire the skills needed to understand his or her field. "It is not that a reporter is unethical if he fails to understand statistics, econometrics, or computer programming," for example. "The point is that without one or more of these skills he or she may come far less close to the truth in his work, may fail to realize his potential as a moral agent, as a truth teller."[25]

Lambeth emphasized too the need for truthfulness in the news-gathering process. Although conceding that deceptive means of gathering news may on rare occasions be justified, he said newsgathering should generally exemplify the highest standards of truthfulness.[26]

The Principle of Justice

"At the day-to-day operating level," Lambeth wrote, "the principle of justice is reflected in the journalist's concern for fairness."[27] Achieving such fairness "requires more than individual reporters observing a few simple rules."[28] In addition, the ethos of the newsroom and the corporate culture in which reporters work are also crucial in setting a climate that would foster high ethical standards.

The journalist ought not only to be concerned with acting justly, however. The journalist is also charged with attending to injustice in society, whatever its source. This focus on injustice "is a staple, occupational orientation of American and most western journalism."[29]

The Principle of Freedom

The journalist ought to be concerned with at least two facets of freedom, Lambeth said. One is to "guard that particular freedom under which he enjoys protection," which in the United States is the First Amendment.[30] In other words, the journalist must seek freedom to practice. The second facet concerns a freedom to be autonomous, or the need to be independent of interest groups. Maintaining an appropriate distance from one's sources is vital, lest reporters lose their critical perspective and risk becoming co-opted by sources.[31]

The Principle of Humaneness

This principle requires journalists to remember that despite their occupational commitments, they have a higher commitment to other people. Therefore, "other things being equal," journalists should "give assistance to another in need. Likewise, journalists should do no direct, intentional harm to others, and should prevent suffering where possible."[32]

The Principle of Stewardship

This principle is closely linked to the social responsibility model of the media described earlier. It contends that journalists are entrusted with a particular authority in society and as beneficiaries of that trust they have an obligation to honor and safeguard the power granted them. As Lambeth put it, a journalist

> is in a unique position to *help* keep the wells of public discourse unpoisoned, if not wholly clean. From the vantage points which his occupation gives him, he is in a better position than many citizens to monitor the condition of justice within or between institutions. As a special beneficiary of the First Amendment, the journalist has a material motive to *protect a protection* meant for all. It is his responsibility to do all of this, for he is a steward of free expression.[33]

How do these principles fit together? "To describe the ethical journalist as a humane truth teller who seeks justice and protects freedom as a faithful steward of his craft may well invite incredulity. To modern, late twentieth century eyes such an occupational portrait may seem to exude hubris and vibrate with impracticality."[34] Anticipating this charge, Lambeth then applied these principles to the contemporary United States, demonstrating their value as beacons to mark the way for a thoughtful, ethically sound journalism. Nor does he blindly believe that classical liberalism is without flaws. For example, he noted that "with its emphasis on individual rights and limitations on government, classical liberalism has often failed to develop a perspective that recognizes the common good, especially when doing so entails sacrifice or mutual restraint."[35]

But Lambeth is sufficiently confident in the enduring strength of these principles, and their applicability across time and national boundaries, to invite journalists to commit themselves to following them. Journalists should do so not in a void but cognizant of classical liberalism's weaknesses and ready to apply it to their own environment. His concern was to offer a foundation, not provide an all-encompassing ethical code to govern the diverse issues that journalists must address as individuals and collectively. Similarly, the purpose in applying these regulations to the South African situation is not to set up rules or a code of ethics. The contention is simply that these five principles can serve as a common foundation for South African journalists as they continue reshaping their craft in the 1990s and beyond. This list admittedly offers only the rudiments of a philosophical framework for discussing what postapartheid journalism should be like. But that is precisely the point, for it is the practitioners themselves who will flesh out a new approach to practicing journalism in South Africa. Depending on the degree of thought put into the exercise, a relatively sophisticated raison d'être or "professional ethic" of journalism could emerge. Alternatively, journalists and media scholars could, by default, let the present understanding of what drives South African journalism continue.

The principles listed here offer several advances over what has prevailed until now. One advance is to make explicit the values from which South African journalism, to a large degree, already flows as well as to point to those in which it ought to be rooted. Another is to provide values that transcend the highly divisive political values of the day. Journalists can thus reexamine their mission according to a set of easily understood and essentially noncontroversial principles. Of course, exactly how these general principles ought to be applied in specific situations, or how conflicting principles ought to be balanced, leads to endless debate. Agreeing on value-related controversies in the newsroom can be extraordinarily difficult, even among journalists with similar views. It would be much more difficult to expect agreement among those at opposite ends of the ideological spectrum. The point, though, is not to seek a philosophy of journalism that leads to some bland consensus. That would be ridiculous to expect, and dangerous to seek, in South Africa—or anywhere else. Rather, the concern is to offer these guidelines as a foundation from which discussion can proceed and serve as a touchstone for evaluating all aspects of journalism. In other words, journalists from all sectors of the press could point to these principles and say, *"That's* why I'm in journalism—and those are the criteria by which my colleagues and I should be evaluated." Despite countless differences in how they applied these principles, journalists would share at least the common ground of agreeing that together these principles constituted a raison d'être for their work.

These principles also offer a broader understanding of how journalism ought to be conceived in South Africa. Because of their recent history, many journalists have tended to view their task largely through adversarial lenses. But there is more to newspapering than clashes between the press and the government, whether with today's administration or tomorrow's. Truth, for example, has been an especially important pursuit of the opposition papers in their quest to hold government accountable. Crucial though the standard of truth is for journalists, that should not be the only impetus to their work. A study of recent South African journalism might well demonstrate far less concern with the principles of humaneness or stewardship, for example.

The need therefore is for a more holistic understanding of the ethical demands made of journalists. Of course reporters need to continue monitoring government performance and challenging its policies in editorials. But newspapers do not live by political coverage alone; journalism's mandate is to monitor *all* of society, at home and abroad, and to do so with integrity. If taken seriously in the South African context, Lambeth's principles would require much stretching of perspective in the country's newsrooms. Quite simply, journalists would have to measure a wider range of their occupational norms and practices, and the resulting stories, by the touchstone of these principles.

Any of these principles can be imperilled by pressures to make profits or simply survive financially. Hence the temptation to value greater circulation above a scrupulous adherence to the truth. Or, as has happened countless times before, the filter of ideology or party loyalty can subtly or brazenly distort the selection and presentation of facts, and journalists in any sector of the press might encounter pressures to compromise the truth to favor a particular political view. Journalists can act on whatever commitment they have to a journalism of integrity only to the degree that their managements let them. Organizational as well as personal pressures thus raise numerous issues that could be thoughtfully addressed using the five-part framework proposed here.

What then are we to make of the journalist whose primary rationale is an ideological agenda? The view of one journalist from the political left, Howard Barrell, is illustrative: "There is a role for all of us in the struggle for our emancipation; and the role of journalists is more easily defined than it is for many other of the professions. ... For, we are the guerillas [sic] of ideology; we go over the top or into action every day."[36] Such an individual is more properly regarded as a propagandist, in the strict, nonpejorative sense of that term. Being a propagandist, for one platform or another, political or not, may be perfectly respectable. Such advocates deserve the same freedoms claimed here for the journalist. Yet individuals who owe their first loyalty to an ideological stance cannot also faithfully adhere to the principles Lambeth said constitute the core of ethical journalism. Of course, the committed journalist—as defined here—could embrace any ideological position provided he or she was able to give first loyalty to truth or humaneness, for example, when ideological interests might suggest otherwise. The journalist of integrity is thus able to swallow hard, if necessary, and write a story harmful to or in conflict with his or her own political views.

The view of Glenn Moss, a journalist speaking from a perspective similar to that of Barrell's, is pertinent here. Moss said that the "progressive journalist has a duty and a responsibility to an interpretive and a factual truth that of its nature cannot be used to protect sectional or limited interests."[37]

The claim here is that journalists with widely divergent ideological commitments can work with skill and integrity. Doing so, however, requires a commitment to a common core of journalistic values, like those proposed here. The intent is not to offer another defense of journalistic objectivity. Nor is it to argue that journalism is a value-free enterprise. On the contrary, it is especially laden with ideological implications. Even proposing the five principles outlined here itself represents an ideological position. But the call is for journalists to view themselves as journalists first and ideological advocates second—perhaps a close second at times, but second nevertheless.

The principles are intended to help direct the discussions that will surround the reshaping of South African journalism in the years ahead. The hope is that including these principles in the discussion will lead to a clearer, more forceful articulation of South African journalism's raison d'être, acceptable to a wide range of the country's practitioners. At the very least, introducing these ideas will advance a step or two the present understanding of journalism's reason for being beyond its present rudimentary level.

This section has proposed a cluster of core values around which postapartheid journalism can define itself. How these values will be accepted by journalists and media scholars is another matter. But whether this framework is adopted, or whether it helps usher in a different one, South African journalism undoubtedly needs a far sharper self-concept than it presently has. Its present sense of purpose is vaguely conceived, highly politicized, and ideologically fragmented. Adopting the kind of values framework suggested here will equip South African journalists to overcome these weaknesses. United in a clear sense of their mission, though admitting irreconcilable differences on how this mission should be lived out, these journalists would be far better equipped to face tomorrow's challenges. Thus, despite the ideological differences of English, Afrikaans, or alternative papers, their journalists need common ground from which they can pursue their common good—and the benefits they can offer their society. As it is, this study has demonstrated how formidable are the challenges they face in preserving and expanding the duties of the press. Without that common ground, their task would be all the harder.

CONCLUSION

The tasks facing South African journalism are onerous indeed. Journalists and newspaper managements must ensure their papers' survival, without which all else becomes irrelevant. They must also seek constantly to educate their society to win the most favorable climate possible in which to practice. This includes securing greater legal protection from the state, both on free expression issues and, more generally, in regaining the rule of law. And in the broader society lies the challenge of heightening the regard for free expression and establishing a culture of tolerance for diverse views. Individual papers will need to steer between being ritualistically hostile to the government and offering it equally uncritical support.

Richard Steyn, editor of the *Star*, noted several other responsibilities facing the press. Writing in 1987, he said that the press ought to maintain standards, not an easy duty in view of the myriad pressures newspapers face, and to "guard against the 'monopolisation' of the truth."[38] As he said, "A vigorous press is ... sceptical of all conventional wisdoms and the certainties of officialdom."[39]

Next, he pointed to the need for the press to act as a channel of communication throughout the society.[40] With its unique capacity to cut across many of South Africa's diverse races, language groups, and classes, a newspaper has considerable potential for good or harm. Discovering how to exercise that power responsibly in as brittle and ideologically fragmented a society as South Africa is inordinately difficult.

Finally, Steyn said the press should hold up the vision of a better society. "A truly responsible newspaper," he said, "seeks not to nourish the prejudices of readers, but to break down prejudices and stereotypes and to emphasize the values and ideals that bring people together, not those that drive them apart. This is particularly important in a society where liberal and democratic values have been under assault for decades."[41]

These duties illustrate the magnitude of the changes facing South Africa's press. But just as these typify the daunting agenda facing the country itself, so too do South Africa and its press approach the postapartheid era with important forces working in their favor. For the press, these forces include well-established papers rooted in a long tradition of vigorous, independent journalism; two centuries of experience in newspapering; hundreds of talented, proficient, and often courageous people; a sophisticated, complex consumer economy to sustain its activities; and a burgeoning population needing its services.

As the press seeks to attain its potential, it must also fulfill a special onus it holds in this transitional era: convincing the society that freedom of expression is vital if South Africa is to continue moving closer to democracy. The press's present task, in other words, is to push exceptionally hard at setting the expectations for postapartheid press freedom. Moreover, the press, with all its diversity, must persuade South Africans that it ought to be entrusted with the liberty it seeks.

Journalists will not secure a hospitable climate of freedom without help. Hence *Sunday Times* editor Ken Owen's argument: "For the Press to play the kind of role which it can and should play ... will require a dedication to excellence that must involve business leaders, university faculties, politicians and readers. In the end, the quality of any society's Press depends on the quality of its elite."[42] Thus South Africa's press, like any nation's, can reach only as high as its society allows. But its practitioners will also bear much responsibility in attaining that potential.

How well newspapers and journalists use these strengths to their advantage and how badly they stumble over the obstacles en route will soon become clear. Whatever qualities characterize the postapartheid press, its overall shape will reflect the uniquely South African conditions it faces. Probably it will function according to a predominantly social responsibility model, yet it is likely to contain elements of the authoritarian and the developmental models. Given South Africa's dualistic First World/Third World character, one can confidently predict that its press will not resemble those of countries like the United States or Britain. Yet it is hoped that the First World, social responsibility elements will dominate the future mix. Moreover, it is hoped that South Africa's bruised and often beleaguered liberal democratic legacy will in large measure color the philosophy by which tomorrow's journalists practice their craft.

Although the benefits of liberal democracy will not soon be realized, if ever, in South Africa, its journalists ought to demand nothing less than the generous protections that such an approach assures them. Nor ought the press to settle for less than offering its society the high quality of journalism needed for liberal democratic societies to function optimally. Calling for such standards, let alone meeting them, may seem to be demanding First World performance in a society often facing Third World constraints. But as best it is able, the press should insist on the standards for which it has striven thus far.

Indeed, as Lambeth said of U.S. journalists, they

> could do worse than ... heed the call of the classical liberal tradition placed in the modern context. It is for a journalism of commitment and of humane truth telling. It is for a journalism watchful of its own ways but also alert to report injustice. It is for a journalism that respects its own independence, as well as that of others. It takes seriously its stewardship of free expression, and searches for better ways to report, and, therefore, help build the very community which can assure its survival in a free society.[43]

South African journalists should offer their society nothing less. Their call is to apply this tradition in their own context, revering classical liberalism's strengths and countering its weaknesses. The craftsmanship and integrity that journalists bring to their work, and the respect it merits and receives from the society, will together significantly shape the topography of postapartheid South Africa.

Because the 1990s are a time of unprecedented change in South Africa, the country has a unique opportunity to act on the observation by Albert Camus: "A free press can of course be good or bad, but almost certainly without freedom it will never be anything but bad. ... Freedom is nothing else but a chance to be better, whereas enslavement is a certainty of the worse."[44]

After four decades of apartheid and the concomitant stunting of freedom that it wrought, South Africa must now choose the level and quality of free expression it wants tomorrow. Perhaps its newspapers will receive, and act upon, the "chance to be better" that they have so long sought. Should that happen, South Africa's press will start making the maps that the country and its people deserve—and on which they can depend as they journey into the postapartheid era.

Appendix

PROCLAMATION
by the State President of the Republic of South Africa
No. R. 88, 1989

PUBLIC SAFETY ACT, 1953
MEDIA EMERGENCY REGULATIONS

Under the powers vested in me by section 3 of the Public Safety Act, 1953 (Act No. 3 of 1953), I hereby make the regulations contained in the Schedule with effect from 9 June 1989.

Given under my Hand and the Seal of the Republic of South Africa at Cape Town this Eighth day of June, One thousand Nine hundred and Eighty-nine.
P. W. BOTHA,
State President.
By Order of the State President-in-Cabinet:
J. C. G. BOTHA,
Minister of the Cabinet.

SCHEDULE

Definitions

1. In these regulations, unless the context otherwise indicates—

"Commissioner" means the Commissioner of the South African Police, and for the purposes of the application of a provision of these regulations in or in respect of—

(a) a division as defined in section 1 of the Police Act, 1958 (Act No. 7 of 1958), means the said Commissioner or the Divisional Commissioner designated under that Act for that division; or

(b) a self-governing territory, means the said Commissioner or the Commissioner or other officer in charge of the police force of the Government of that self-governing territory;

"film recording" means any substance, film, magnetic tape or any other material on which the visual images (with or without an associated sound

Government Gazette Staatskoerant, Vol. 288, No. 11948, Pretoria, 9 June 1989.

track) of a film as defined in section 47 of the Publications Act, 1974 (Act No. 42 of 1974), are recorded;

"firm" includes a State controlled or financed or other public undertaking;

"gathering" means a gathering, concourse or procession of any number of persons;

"local authority" means—

(a) an institution or body contemplated in section 84 (1) (f) of the Provincial Government Act, 1961 (Act No. 32 of 1961);

(b) a local authority as defined in section 1 of the Black Local Authorities Act, 1982 (Act No. 102 of 1982);

(c) a regional services council established under the Regional Services Councils Act, 1985 (Act No. 109 of 1985);

(d) a local government body established or deemed to be established under section 30 of the Black Administration Act, 1927 (Act No. 38 of 1927); or

(e) a board of management as defined in section 1 of the Rural Areas Act (House of Representatives), 1987 (Act No. 9 of 1987);

"Minister" for the purpose of the application of—

(a) a provision of regulation 3 or 9, means the Minister of Law and Order; or

(b) any other provision of these regulations, means the Minister of Home Affairs;

"office-bearer", in relation to an organisation, means a member of the governing or executive body of—

(a) the organisation; or

(b) a branch or division of the organisation;

"organisation" includes any association or body of persons irrespective of whether or not any such association or body has been incorporated and whether or not it has been established or registered in accordance with any law;

"periodical" means a publication issued either at regular or irregular intervals;

"previous media regulations" means the regulations published by Proclamation No. R. 97 of 1987, as amended by Proclamations Nos. R. 123 of 1987 and R. 7 of 1988;

"publication" means a newspaper, book, magazine, pamphlet, news letter, brochure, poster, handbill or sticker or part thereof or addendum thereto;

"public place" includes—

(a) any premises occupied by the State, a local authority or an educational institution or the controlling body of an educational institution; or

(b) any premises or place to which members of the public ordinarily or at specific times have access, irrespective of whether or not the right of admission to such premises or place is reserved and whether or not payment for such admission is required;

"publish", in relation to a publication, television recording, film recording or sound recording, means any act whereby the publication or the television, film or sound recording—

(a) is sold or leased, or is provided or made available free of charge, to a member of the public or is offered for sale, for hire or free of charge to such a member;

(b) is sent through the post to a member of the public, irrespective of whether or not that member has subscribed thereto; or

(c) is taken personally or is sent by post or courier out of the Republic or is transmitted or sent from the Republic by whatever means of telecommunication,

and further includes, in relation to—

(i) a publication, any act whereby such publication is posted up, exhibited, handed out or scattered at or in a public place or is displayed in such a way as to be visible from a public place;

(ii) a television or sound recording, any act whereby such television or sound recording—

(aa) is shown or played at or in a public place or is shown or played in such a way as to be visible or audible from a public place; or

(bb) is broadcast in a way which enables a member of the public to receive it by means of a radio or television set;

(iii) a film recording, any act whereby such film recording is shown at or in a public place or is shown in such a way as to be visible from a public place;

"registered periodical" means a periodical registered in terms of the Newspaper and Imprint Registration Act, 1971 (Act No. 63 of 1971);

"restricted gathering" means a gathering in respect of which a condition has been determined under section 46 (1) (ii) of the Internal Security Act, 1982 (Act No. 74 of 1982), or in respect of which a condition, prohibition or requirement has been imposed or is in force under regulation 10 (1) (d) of the Security Emergency Regulations, 1989;

"security action" means any of the following actions by a security force or a member of a security force, namely—

(a) any action to terminate any unrest;

(b) any action to protect life or property in consequence of any unrest;

(c) any follow-up action after any unrest has been terminated or has ended;

(d) any action under regulation 2 of the Security Emergency Regulations, 1989; or

(e) any action whereby a person is arrested—

(i) on a charge for an offence under these regulations or any other regulations made under the Public Safety Act, 1953 (Act No. 3 of 1953);

(ii) on a charge for an offence mentioned in the definition of "unrest" or committed in the course of any unrest or of any incident arising from unrest or connected therewith; or

(iii) under regulation 3 (1) of the Security Emergency Regulations, 1989;

"security force" means—

(a) the South African Police referred to in the definition of "the Force" in section 1 of the Police Act, 1958 (Act No. 7 of 1958);

(b) a part of the said South African Police of which the control, organisation and administration have been transferred to the Government of a self-governing territory;

(c) a police force established by or under a law of a self-governing territory;

(d) the South African Defence Force referred to in section 5 of the Defence Act, 1957 (Act No. 44 of 1957);

(e) the Prisons Service established by section 2 of the Prisons Act, 1959 (Act No. 8 of 1959); or

(f) a police force under the control of a local authority,

and also any part of a force referred to in paragraph (a) to (f) or any combination of two or more of such forces or of parts of such forces;

"self-governing territory" means a territory declared under section 26 of the National States Constitution Act, 1971 (Act No. 21 of 1971), to be a self-governing territory within the Republic;

"series of issues", in relation to—

(a) a periodical which is a daily newspaper, means at least six, or in the case of regulation 7 (3) or (4) at least two, different issues of that newspaper whether or not issued on consecutive days;

(b) a periodical, other than a daily newspaper, which is ordinarily issued at intervals of 10 days or less, means at least three, or in the case of regulation 7 (3) or (4) at least two, different issues of that periodical whether or not issued during consecutive intervals;

(c) a periodical which is ordinarily issued at intervals in excess of 10 days, means at least two different issues of that periodical whether or not issued during consecutive intervals;

"sound recording" means a disc, cassette, tape, perforated roll or other device in or on which sounds are embodied so as to be capable of being reproduced therefrom;

"subversive statement" means a statement—

(a) in which members of the public are incited or encouraged or which is calculated to have the effect of inciting or encouraging members of the public—

(i) to take part in an activity or to commit an act mentioned in paragraph (a), (b) or (c) of the definition of "unrest";

(ii) to resist or oppose a member of the Cabinet, or of a Ministers' Council, or another member of the Government or an official of the Republic or a member of the Government of a self-governing territory or an official of a self-governing territory or a member of a security force in the exercise or performance by such a member or official of a power or function in terms of a provision of a regulation made under the Public Safety Act, 1953 (Act No. 3 of 1953), or of a law regulating the safety of the public or the maintenance of public order;

(iii) to take part in a boycott action—

(aa) against a particular firm or against firms of a particular nature, class or kind, either by not making purchases at or doing other business with or making use of services rendered by that particular firm or any firms of that particular nature, class or kind or by making purchases only at or doing other business only with or making use only of services rendered by firms other than that particular firm or other than firms of that particular nature, class or kind;

(bb) against a particular product or article or against products or articles of a particular nature, class or kind, by not purchasing that particular product or article or any products or articles of that particular nature, class or kind; or

(cc) against a particular educational institution or against educational institutions of a particular nature, class or kind, by refusing to attend classes or to participate in other activities at that particular institution or at any institutions of that particular nature, class or kind;

(iv) to take part in an act of civil disobedience—

(aa) by refusing to comply with a provision of, or requirement under, any law or by contravening such a provision or requirement; or

(bb) by refusing to comply with an obligation towards a local authority in respect of rent or a municipal service;

(v) to stay away from work or to strike in contravention of the provisions of any law, or to support such a stayaway action or strike;

(vi) to attend or to take part in a restricted gathering;

(vii) to take part in any activities of or to join or to support an organisation in terms of the Internal Security Act, 1982 (Act No. 74 of 1982), or to take part in, or to support, any of such an organisation's campaigns, projects, programmes or actions of violence or resistance against, or subversion of, the authority of the State or any local authorities, or of violence against, or intimidation of, any persons or persons belonging to a particular category of persons;

(viii) to exert power and authority in specific areas by way of structures purporting to be structures of local government and acting as such in an unlawful manner, or to establish such structures, or to support such structures, or to subject themselves to the authority of such structures, or to make payments which are due to local authorities to such structures;

(ix) to prosecute, to try or to punish persons by way of unlawful structures, procedures or methods purporting to be judicial structures, procedures or methods, or to support such structures, procedures or methods, or to subject themselves to the authority of such structures, procedures or methods;

(x) to boycott or not to take part in an election of members of a local authority or to commit any act whereby such an election is prevented, frustrated or impeded: Provided that this subparagraph shall not prevent a political party registered under section 36 of the Electoral Act, 1979 (Act No. 45 of 1979), or an organisation, whether it is a political party or not, having candidates representing such organisation in such an election, from encouraging its supporters not to vote in such election or in any particular electoral division thereof; or

(xi) to commit any other act or omission identified by the Commissioner by notice in the *Gazette* as an act or omission which has the effect of threatening the safety of the public or the maintenance of public order or of delaying the termination of the state of emergency; or

(b) by which the system of compulsory military service is discredited or undermined;

"television recording" means a cassette, tape or other device in or on which visual images (with or without an associated sound track) are embodied in such a way so as to be capable of being reproduced on a television set and, in so far as a film recording is capable of being used for television broadcasts, also a film recording;

"unrest" means—

(a) any gathering in contravention of an order under regulation 10 (1) (c) or (d) of the Security Emergency Regulations, 1989, or of a provision of another law or of any prohibition, direction or other requirement under such an order or provision;

(b) any physical attack by a group of persons on a security force or on a member of a security force or on a member of a local authority or on the house or family of a member of a security force or local authority; or

(c) any conduct which constitutes sedition, public violence or a contravention of section 1 (1) (a) of the Intimidation Act, 1982 (Act No. 72 of 1982).

Presence of journalists, etc., at unrest, restricted gatherings or security actions

2. (1) Subject to subregulation (2) no journalist, news reporter, news commentator, news correspondent, newspaper or magazine photographer, operator of a television or other camera or of any television, sound, film or other recording equipment, person carrying or assisting in the conveyance or operation of such camera or equipment, or other person covering events for the purpose of gathering news material for the distribution or publication thereof in the Republic or elsewhere, shall, without the prior consent of the Commissioner or of a member of a security force who serves as a commissioned officer in that force, be at the scene of any unrest, restricted gathering or security action or at a place from where any unrest, restricted gathering or security action is within sight.

(2) The provisions of subregulation (1)—

(a) shall not apply to a person mentioned therein who—

(i) at the commencement of any unrest, restricted gathering or security action happens to be at the scene of that unrest, gathering or action or at a place from where that unrest, gathering or action is within sight; or

(ii) after the commencement of any unrest, restricted gathering or security action happens to arrive at the scene of that unrest, gathering or action, or at a place from where that unrest, gathering or action is within sight, for a reason other than to cover that unrest, gathering or action for the gathering of news material

provided such a person immediately leaves the scene of that unrest, gathering or action or the said place and removes himself within such time as is reasonably required under the circumstances to a place where that unrest, gathering or action is out of sight; or

(b) shall not prevent a person mentioned therein from being in his residence or on the premises where he ordinarily works or on his way to or from his residence or any such premises.

Publication of certain material prohibited

3. (1) Subject to subregulation (6) no person shall publish or cause to be published any publication, television recording, film recording or sound recording containing any news, comment or advertisement on or in connection with—

(a) any security action, including any security action referred to in regulation 3 (1) (a) of the previous media regulations or in regulation 3 (1) (a) of the Media Emergency Regulations, 1988;

(b) any deployment of a security force, or of vehicles, armaments, equipment or other appliances, for the purpose of security action;

(c) any restricted gathering, in so far as such news, comment or advertisement discloses at any time before the gathering takes place the time, date, place and purpose of such gathering, or gives an account of a speech, statement or remark of a speaker who performed at the gathering in contravention of a condition, prohibition or requirement determined or imposed under a law mentioned in the definition of "restricted gathering";

(d) any action, strike or boycott by members of the public which is an action, strike or boycott referred to in paragraph (a) (iii), (iv) or (v) of the definition of "subversive statement", in so far as such news, comment or advertisement discloses particulars of the extent to which such action, strike or boycott is successful or of the manner in which members of the public are intimidated, incited or encouraged to take part in or to support such action, strike or boycott or gives an account of any incidents in connection with such intimidation, incitement or encouragement;

(e) any structures referred to in paragraph (a) (viii) or (ix) of the definition of "subversive statement", in so far as such news, comment or advertisement discloses particulars of the manner in which members of the public are intimidated, incited or encouraged to support such structures or to subject themselves to the authority of such structures;

(f) any speech, statement or remark of a person in respect of whom steps under a provision of Chapter 3 of the Internal Security Act, 1982 (Act No. 74 of 1982), or regulation 3 (8) (b) or 8 of the Security Emergency Regulations, 1989, are in force or of a person intimating or of whom it is commonly known that he is an office-bearer or spokesman of an organisation which is an unlawful organisation in terms of the said Act or in respect of which an order under regulation 7 (1) (a) of the said Security Emergency Regulations is in force, in so far as any such speech, statement or remark has the effect, or is calculated to have the effect, of threatening the safety of the public or the maintenance of public order or of delaying the termination of the state of emergency;

(g) the circumstances of, or treatment in, detention of a person, who is or was detained under regulation 3 of the Security Emergency Regulations,

1989, or who at any time prior to the commencement of these regulations was detained under a regulation made under the Public Safety Act, 1953 (Act No. 3 of 1953); or

(h) the release of a person who is detained under the said regulation 3 of the Security Emergency Regulations, 1989.

(2) No person shall publish or cause to be published a publication containing an advertisement on or in connection with an organisation which is an unlawful organisation in terms of the Internal Security Act, 1982, or in respect of which an order under regulation 7 (1) (a) of the Security Emergency Regulations, 1989, is in force, defending, praising, or endeavouring to justify such organisation or any of such organisation's campaigns, projects, programmes, actions or policies of violence or resistance against, or of subversion of, the authority of the State or any local authorities, or of violence against, or of intimidation of, any persons or persons belonging to a particular category of persons.

(3) (a) The Commissioner may, for the purpose of the safety of the public, the maintenance of public order or the termination of the state of emergency, and without prior notice to any person and without hearing any person, issue an order not inconsistent with a provision of these regulations, prohibiting a publication, television recording, film recording or sound recording containing any news, comment or advertisement on or in connection with a matter specified in the order, to be published.

(b) For the purposes of paragraph (a) the provisions of regulations 10 (2) and (4) and 11 of the Security Emergency Regulations, 1989, shall *mutatis mutandis* apply.

(4) Subject to subregulation (6) no person shall broadcast any news, comment or advertisement on or in connection with a matter specified in subregulation (1) live on any television or radio service.

(5) No person shall publish or cause to be published a publication–

(a) in which any blank space or any obliteration, deletion or indication of an omission of part of the text of a report or of a photograph or part of a photograph appears if that blank space, obliteration, deletion or indication of an omission, as may appear from an express statement or a sign or symbol in that publication or from the specific context in which that blank space, obliteration, deletion or indication of an omission appears, is intended to be understood as a reference to the effect of these regulations; or

(b) in which any material appears which, as may appear from an express statement or a sign or symbol in that publication or from the specific context in which that material appears, is intended to be understood as material which would have been published by another publication if it were not for the fact that an order under regulation 7 (3) (i) or (ii) was published in respect of that other publication.

(6) The provisions of this regulation shall not prevent—

(a) a person from publishing a publication or a television, film or sound recording containing any news, comment or advertisement on or in connection with a matter specified in subregulation (1) in so far as particulars of such a matter—

(i) are disclosed, announced or released, or authorised for publication, by a member of the Cabinet or of a Ministers' Council, a Deputy Minister or a spokesman of the Government;

(ii) appear from debates, documents or proceedings of Parliament or the President's Council; or

(iii) appear from judicial proceedings, excluding proceedings in which evidence was submitted or given, whether by way of affidavit or *viva voce*, relating to the circumstances or manner of arrest or the circumstances of, or the treatment in, detention of a person who is or was detained under regulation 3 of the Security Emergency Regulations, 1989, or who at any time prior to the commencement of these regulations was detained under a regulation made under the Public Safety Act, 1953, and in which the court concerned has not yet given a final judgment; or

(b) a *bona fide* library from lending to a member of the public in the normal course of its activities a publication containing any news, comment or advertisement on or in connection with any such matter.

(7) The Minister may make rules prescribing the procedure by which and the authority or person through whom any authorisation referred to in subregulation (6) (a) (i) may be obtained.

(8) for the purposes of subregulations (4) and (6) a reference therein to a matter specified in subregulation (1) shall be construed as a reference also to a matter specified in an order under subregulation (3) (a).

Taking of photographs, etc., of unrest or security actions

4. (1) No person shall without the prior consent of the Commissioner or of a member of a security force serving as a commissioned officer in that force take any photograph or make or produce any television recording, film recording, drawing or other depiction—

(a) of any unrest or security action or of any incident occurring in the course thereof, including the damaging or destruction of property or the injuring or killing of persons; or

(b) of any damaged or destroyed property or injured or dead persons or other visible signs of violence at the scene where unrest or security action is taking or has taken place or of any injuries sustained by any person in or during unrest or security action.

(2) No person shall without the prior consent of the Commissioner or of a member of a security force serving as a commissioned officer in that force make any sound recording of any unrest or security action or of any incident occurring in the course thereof, including the damaging or destruction of property or the injuring or killing of persons.

(3) No person shall publish—

(a) a publication containing any photograph, drawing or other depiction; or

(b) a television, film or sound recording,

taken, made or produced in contravention of a provision of subregulation (1) or (2) of this regulation or of a provision of a regulation made under the Public Safety Act, 1953 (Act No. 3 of 1953), which was in force at any time during the period 12 June 1986 until immediately prior to the commencement of these regulations.

Making, publishing, etc., of subversive statements

5. No person shall—

(a) whether orally or in writing make a subversive statement or cause such a statement to be made;

(b) produce a publication in which a subversive statement appears or cause such a publication to be produced;

(c) produce a television, film or sound recording in which a subversive statement is recorded or cause such a television, film or sound recording to be produced; or

(d) publish or import into the Republic a publication or a television, film or sound recording containing a subversive statement or cause such a publication or such a television, film or sound recording to be published or imported into the Republic.

Prohibition of production, importation, or publishing of certain periodicals

6. (1) If the Minister is of the opinion that it is necessary for the safety of the public, the maintenance of public order or the termination of the state of emergency, he may, subject to subregulation (2), issue an order by notice in the *Gazette* prohibiting the production, importation into the Republic or publishing of all further issues of a periodical specified in the order for such period as may be specified in the order, but not exceeding three months at a time, in the case of a registered periodical, or six months at a time, in the case of any other periodical.

(2) No order under subregulation (1) shall be issued in respect of a periodical unless—

(a) an issue of that periodical was produced, imported or published in contravention of a provision of regulation 3 (1) or (2), 4 (3) or 5 (b) or (d), or of a provision of an order under regulation 3 (3); and

(b) the Minister has by notice in the *Gazette* requested all persons concerned in the production, importation or publishing of that periodical to ensure that no further issue of that periodical is produced, imported or published in contravention of any such provision; and

(c) a further issue of that periodical was produced, imported or published in contravention of any such provision after the publication of the notice referred to in paragraph (b); and

(d) the Minister, after a further issue referred to in paragraph (c) was produced, imported or published in contravention of any such provision—

(i) has given notice in writing to the publisher or importer of that periodical of the fact that action under subregulation (1) is being considered, stating the grounds for the proposed action; and

(ii) has given that publisher or importer the opportunity of submitting to him in writing, within a period of two weeks, representations in connection with the proposed action.

(3) The provisions of subregulations (1) and (2) may be applied irrespective of whether an issue referred to in paragraph (a) or (c) or the said subregulation (2) has been seized under regulation 9 (1) and irrespective of whether any person is prosecuted in consequence of the production, importation or publishing of such an issue.

(4) Compliance with an order issued under subregulation (1) shall not affect the continuation of the registration (if any) of the periodical concerned as a newspaper in terms of the Newspaper and Imprint Registration Act, 1971 (Act No. 63 of 1971).

Systematic or repetitive publishing of subversive propaganda

7. (1) If the Minister is in respect of a periodical which has not previously been the subject of a warning under this subregulation, regulation 7A (1) of the previous media regulations or regulation 7 (1) (a) of the media Emergency Regulations, 1988, or of an order under subregulation (3) of this regulation, regulation 7A (3) of the previous media regulations or regulation 7 (3) of the Media Emergency Regulations, 1988, of the opinion, solely on examination of a series of issues of that periodical—

(a) that there is in that periodical a systematic or repetitive publishing of matter, or a systematic or repetitive publishing of matter in a way, which, in his opinion, has, or is calculated to have, the effect—

(i) of promoting or fomenting revolution or uprisings in the Republic or other acts aimed at the overthrow of the Government otherwise than by constitutional means;

(ii) of promoting, fomenting or sparking the perpetration of acts referred to in paragraph (b) or (c) of the definition of "unrest";

(iii) of promoting or fomenting the breaking down of public order in the Republic or in any area of the Republic or in any community;

(iv) of stirring up or fomenting feelings of hatred or hostility in members of the public towards a local authority or a security force, or towards members or employees of a local authority or members of a security force, or towards members of any population group or section of the public;

(v) of promoting the public image or esteem of an organisation which is an unlawful organisation in terms of the Internal Security Act, 1982 (Act No. 74 of 1982), or in respect of which an order under regulation 7 (1) (a) of the Security Emergency Regulations, 1989, is in force;

(vi) of promoting the establishment or activities of structures referred to in paragraph (a) (viii) or (ix) of the definition of "subversive statement"; or

(vii) of promoting, fomenting or sparking actions, strikes or boycotts referred to in paragraph (a) (iii), (iv), (v) or (x) of the definition of "subversive statement"; and

(b) that the said effect which such systematic or repetitive publishing in his opinion has, or is calculated to have, is causing a threat to the safety of

the public or to the maintenance of public order or is causing a delay in the termination of the state of emergency,
he may, by notice in the *Gazette*, issue a warning to persons concerned in the production, importation, compilation or publishing of issues of that periodical that the matter published in that periodical or the way in which matter is published in that periodical, in his opinion, is causing a threat to the safety of the public or to the maintenance of public order or is causing a delay in the termination of the state of emergency.

(2) In an examination under subregulation (1) of a series of issues of a periodical, such series may include any issue of that periodical published before the commencement of these regulations but after 11 April 1989.

(3) If the Minister is in respect of a periodical which previously, whether under its present or any previous name, was the subject of—

(a) a warning under subregulation (1) of this regulation;

(b) a warning under regulation 7A (1) of the previous media regulations or regulation 7 (1) of the Media Emergency Regulations, 1988;

(c) an order under this subregulation; or

(d) an order under regulation 7A (3) of the previous media regulations or regulation 7 (3) of the Media Emergency Regulations, 1988,

of the opinion, solely on examination of a series of issues of that periodical, that there is in that periodical a systematic or repetitive publishing of matter, or a systematic or repetitive publishing of matter in a way, which, in his opinion, has, or is calculated to have, an effect described in paragraph (a) of subregulation (1) of this regulation, and that the said effect which such systematic or repetitive publishing, in his opinion, has or is calculated to have, is causing a threat to the safety of the public or to the maintenance of public order or is causing a delay in the termination of the state of emergency, he may, by notice in the *Gazette*, issue an order—

(i) whereby the publishing, during such period as may be specified in the order (but not exceeding three months at a time, in the case of a registered periodical, or six months at a time, in the case of any other periodical), of all further issues of that periodical is prohibited unless the matter to be published therein and the way in which it is to be published therein has previously been approved for publication by a person specified in the order; or

(ii) whereby the production, importation into the Republic or publishing, during such period as may be specified in the order (but not exceeding three months at a time, in the case of a registered periodical, or six months at a time, in the case of any other periodical), of all further issues of that periodical is totally prohibited.

(4) No issue of a periodical shall, for the purposes of an examination under subregulation (3) of a series of issues of that periodical, be included in such a series unless such issue was—

(a) in the case of a periodical contemplated in paragraph (a) of the said subregulation (3), published after publication of the warning referred to in that paragraph;

(b) in the case of a periodical contemplated in paragraph (b) of the said subregulation (3), published after the commencement of these regulations;

(c) in the case of a periodical contemplated in paragraph (c) of the said subregulation (3), published after the termination of the period for which the order referred to in that paragraph was issued; or

(d) in the case of a periodical contemplated in paragraph (d) of the said subregulation (3), published after the commencement of these regulations,

(5) No warning under subregulation (1) and no order under subregulation (3) shall be published unless the Minister—

(a) has given notice in writing to the publisher or importer of the periodical concerned of the fact that an examination under subregulation (1) or (3), as the case may be, is being conducted in respect of that periodical, stating the grounds of such examination; and

(b) has given that publisher or importer the opportunity of submitting to him in writing, within a period of two weeks, representations in connection with such examination.

(6) Subregulation (5) (a), in so far as the Minister is in terms of that subregulation required to state the grounds of any examination in respect of a periodical to the publisher or importer of that periodical, shall not be construed as if the Minister is obliged to disclose to such publisher or importer anything other than the following, namely—

(a) a list indicating the reports, comments, articles, photographs, drawings, depictions, advertisements, letters and other items published in that periodical and which are being taken into account against the periodical by the Minister in such examination for the purpose of establishing whether, in his opinion, there is in that periodical a systematic or repetitive publishing of matter, or a systematic or repetitive publishing of matter in a way, which, in his opinion, has, or is calculated to have, an effect described in paragraph (a) of subregulation (1); and

(b) an indication why each such item is being taken into account for such purpose.

(7) Save in so far as is required in subregulation (5), read with subregulation (6), the Minister shall not be obliged to give notice to any person of any examination, or any proposed action, under this regulation or to give any person a hearing when conducting such an examination or considering any such proposed action.

(8) The provisions of regulation 6 (4) shall *mutatis mutandis* apply in respect of a periodical in respect of which an order under subregulation (3) (ii) of this regulation has been issued.

Continuation of prohibited periodicals

8. If the Minister is of the opinion that a periodical, whether or not under another name, is a continuation of or substitution for any periodical the production, importation into the Republic or publishing of which was prohibited under regulation 6 (1) or 7 (3) (ii), he may, without prior notice to any person and without hearing any person, issue an order by notice in the *Gazette* prohibiting the production, importation or publishing of all further issues of the first-men-

tioned periodical for such period as may be specified in the order, but not exceeding a period equal to the remaining portion of the period for which the last-mentioned periodical was prohibited under the said regulation.

Seizure of certain publications or recordings

9. (1) If a publication or a television, film or sound recording is produced, published or imported into the Republic in contravention of a provision of regulation 3 (1) or (2), 4 (3) or 5 (b), (c) or (d) or of a provision of an order under regulation 3 (3), 6 (1), 7 (3) or 8, the Minister or the Commissioner may, without prior notice to any person and without hearing any person, issue an order under his hand ordering the seizure of that publication or television, film or sound recording.

If the Minister or the Commissioner is of the opinion—

(a) that the publishing of a publication (excluding a registered periodical) or a television, film or sound recording has, or is calculated to have, the effect—

(i) of promoting or fomenting revolution or uprisings in the Republic or other acts aimed at the overthrow of the Government otherwise than by constitutional means;

(ii) of promoting, fomenting or sparking the perpetration of acts referred to in paragraph (b) or (c) of the definition of "unrest";

(iii) of promoting or fomenting the breaking down of public order in the Republic or in any area of the Republic or in any community;

(iv) of stirring up or fomenting feelings of hatred or hostility in members of the public towards a local authority or a security force, or towards members or employees of a local authority or members of a security force, or towards members of any population group or section of the public;

(v) of promoting the public image or esteem of an organisation which is an unlawful organisation in terms of the Internal Security Act, 1982 (Act No. 74 of 1982), or in respect of which an order under regulation 7 (1) (a) of the Security Emergency Regulations, 1989, is in force;

(vi) of promoting the establishment or activities of structures referred to in paragraph (a) (viii) or (ix) of the definition of "subversive statement"; or

(vii) of promoting, fomenting or sparking actions, strikes or boycotts referred to in paragraph (a) (iii), (iv), (v) or (x) of the definition of "subversive statement"; and

(b) that the said effect which the publishing of such publication or television, film or sound recording has, or is calculated to have, is causing a threat to the safety of the public or to the maintenance of public order or is causing a delay in the termination of the state of emergency,

he may, without prior notice to any person and without hearing any person, issue an order under his hand ordering the seizure of that publication or television, film or sound recording.

(3) An order under subregulation (1) or (2) shall, unless otherwise specified in the order, be carried out in respect of all copies or reproductions of the pub-

lication or television, film or sound recording to which the order relates.

(4) An order under subregulation (1) or (2) shall be carried out by a member of a security force in possession of a document being or purporting to be such an order or a copy or reproduction thereof, and such a member may for the purposes of such seizure—

(a) enter any vehicle, vessel, aircraft or premises in or on which the publication or recording, or copy or reproduction thereof, to which the order relates, is or is suspected by him to be found; and

(b) in or on that vehicle, vessel or aircraft or those premises do all such things as are reasonably necessary to carry out the order.

(5) A document referred to in subregulation (4) shall be produced to a person affected thereby, at his request.

(6) A publication or recording, or any copies or reproductions thereof, seized under this regulation shall be dealt with in accordance with the direction of the Minister which may be issued by him at his discretion with a view to the safety of the public, the maintenance of public order or the termination of the state of emergency, either generally or with reference to a particular seizure.

(7) The provisions of this regulation may be applied irrespective of whether any person is prosecuted in consequence of the production, publishing or importation of a publication or a television, film or sound recording in contravention of a provision referred to in subregulation (1).

Compulsory deposit of periodicals

10. (1) If the Minister is of the opinion that it is necessary for the proper administration of a provision of these regulations he may, by order under his hand, direct the publisher or importer of a periodical to supply an official of the Department of Home Affairs, and at an address, specified in the order, free of charge with one copy of each issue of that periodical which is published in the Republic during a period specified in the order.

(2) A copy of an issue of a periodical which in pursuance of an order under subregulation (1) is required to be supplied to the said official, shall be sent to him within one day of the day on which that issue is published in the Republic.

(3) In this regulation "issue", in relation to a periodical issuing different editions on the same day, means each edition of that periodical which is so issued.

Offences and penalties

11. (1) Any person who—

(a) wilfully contravenes a provision of regulation 2 (1), 3 (4) or (5), 4 (1) or (2) or 5 or a provision of an order under regulation 6 (1), 7 (3) or 8; or

(b) either wilfully or negligently contravenes a provision of regulation 3 (1) or (2) or 4 (3) or a provision of an order under regulation 3 (3); or

(c) wilfully hinders or obstructs a member of a security force in the performance of his functions in terms of regulation 9 (4), shall be guilty of an offence and on conviction be liable to a fine not exceeding R20 000 or to imprisonment for a period not exceeding 10 years or to that imprisonment without the option of a fine.

(2) Any person who either wilfully or negligently fails to comply with an order under regulation 10 (1), shall be guilty of an offence and on conviction be liable to a fine not exceeding R500.

Direction of Attorney-General

12. No prosecution for an offence under these regulations shall be instituted except by the express direction of the Attorney-General having jurisdiction in respect of that prosecution.

Short title

13. These regulations shall be called the Media Emergency Regulations, 1989.

Notes

Chapter 1

1. Joel Mervis, "Can press freedom survive in South Africa?" in *South African Conference on the Survival of the Press and Education for Journalism* (Grahamstown, South Africa: Department of Journalism, Rhodes University, 1979), no pp.

2. Ibid.

3. See for example, Denis McQuail, *Mass Communication Theory* (London: Sage, 1983).

4. A lone exception was the *Citizen*, a progovernment paper that was the product of the notorious Muldergate scandal of the late 1970s, which is described in Chapter 2.

5. Elaine Potter, *The Press as Opposition: The Political Role of South African Newspapers* (Totowa, N.J.: Rowman and Littlefield, 1985).

6. See for example William A. Hachten and C. Anthony Giffard, *Total Onslaught: The South African Press Under Attack* (Johannesburg: Macmillan, 1984), chap. 9.

7. See for example Gavin Stewart, "Policom 1987: political news on South African television during the May election," in *South African Election 1987: Context, Process and Prospect*, ed. D. J. van Vuuren, L. Schlemmer, H. C. Marais, and J. Latakgomo (Pinetown, South Africa: Owen Burgess, 1987), 139–151. Toward the end of the 1980s, and especially in the early 1990s, however, many commentators noted that the SABC became considerably more relaxed in allowing more controversial material and greater political diversity on the airwaves.

8. John Grogan. Interview with author. Grahamstown, South Africa, 10 August 1989.

9. Mike Leahy and Paul Voice, eds., *SARAD Media Yearbook 1989* (Johannesburg: WTH Publications, 1989), 59.

10. Ibid., 59, 99, and 116.

11. Readership figures are based on the All Media Product Surveys, or AMPS. By definition, these are estimated levels of readership.

12. Circulation figures are based on reports conducted by the Audit Bureau of Circulations, or ABC. These reports verify the accuracy of newspapers' claims concerning their precise sales figures.

13. Untitled address given by Louis Raubenheimer, of the SABC, at the South African Communication Organization Conference, Grahamstown, South Africa, July 1989.

14. Zac de Beer, "Batten down the budgets," advertising supplement to *Financial Mail*, 22 August 1986, 56.

15. AMPS 1987–1988 figures.

16. P. Eric Louw, "The libertarian theory of the press: How appropriate in the South African context?" *Communicatio* 10 (1984), 33.

17. See for example Jo-Anne Collinge, Herbert Mabuza, Glenn Moss, and David Niddrie, "What the papers don't say," *Index on Censorship*, 17 (March 1988), 27–36; and Ameen Akhalwaya, "The role of the alternative press," *Nieman Reports* 42 (Winter 1988), 14–18.

18. See for example Louw, "The libertarian theory of the press."

19. Bob Steyn. Interview with the author. Grahamstown, South Africa, 19 July 1989.

20. Quoted in Gavin Stewart and Charles Riddle, "Three years on: The state of press freedom in South Africa" (Paper delivered at the Congress of the South African Society of Journalists, in Port Elizabeth, South Africa, 5 May 1989), 5.

21. Ibid., 5.

22. See for example Anthony S. Mathews, *The Darker Reaches of Government* (Cape Town: Juta; Berkeley and Los Angeles: University of California Press, 1978), and Anthony S. Mathews, "Censorship, access to information and public debate," *Theoria* 55 (1980), 21–31.

23. Stewart and Riddle, "Three years on," 5.

24. Joel Mervis, *The Fourth Estate: A Newspaper Story* (Johannesburg: Jonathan Ball, 1989), 552.

25. Corrie Faure, "Koerantsubsidies, persvryheid en M-net" (Newspaper subsidies, press freedom, and M-Net), *Communicatio* (Pretoria) 13 (1987), 31–44.

26. *Beeld*, 19 August 1988.

27. Quoted in John Grogan and Charles Riddle, "South Africa's press in the eighties: Darkness descends," *Gazette* 39 (1987), 3.

28. Anthony Heard, "The media blackout," *Africa Report* 31 (March/April 1986), 57.

29. Ibid., 58.

30. Grogan and Riddle, "South Africa's press," 14.

31. See for example Stewart and Riddle, "Three years on," 3–4.

32. Ibid., 6.

33. Grogan and Riddle, "South Africa's press," 3.

Chapter 2

1. Francis Williams, *The Right to Know: The Rise of the World Press* (London: Longmans, Green and Co., 1969), 1.

2. Ibid.

3. See for example Peter L. Berger and Bobby Godsell, eds., *A Future South Africa: Visions, Strategies and Realities* (Boulder, Colo.: Westview Press, 1988); Hermann Giliomee and Lawrence Schlemmer, *Negotiating South Africa's Future* (Cape Town: Oxford University Press, 1989); Anthony Lemon, *Apartheid*

in Transition (Boulder, Colo.: Westview Press, 1987); Martin Murray, *South Africa: Time of Agony, Time of Destiny* (London: Verso, 1987); and Robert Schrire, ed., *Critical Choices for South Africa: An Agenda for the* 1990s (Cape Town: Oxford University Press, 1990).

4. William A. Hachten and C. Anthony Giffard, *Total Onslaught: The South African Press Under Attack* (Johannesburg: Macmillan, 1984), 22.

5. Ibid., 23.

6. Rene de Villiers, "Threats to press freedom in South Africa," *Janus* (1979), 2.

7. Ibid.

8. Ibid.

9. See for example Chenhamo Chimutengwende, *South Africa: The Press and Politics of Liberation* (London: Barbican Books, 1979); Hachten and Giffard, *Total Onslaught;* John M. Phelan, *Apartheid Media: Disinformation and Dissent in South Africa* (Westport, Conn.: Lawrence Hill, 1987); Richard Pollak, *Up Against Apartheid: The Role and Plight of the Press in South Africa* (Carbondale: Southern Illinois University Press, 1981); and Elaine Potter, *The Press as Opposition: The Political Role of South African Newspapers* (Totowa, New Jersey: Rowman and Littlefield, 1975).

10. Harvey Tyson, "The future of an opposition press in South Africa," in *South African Conference on the Survival of the Press and Education for Journalism* (Grahamstown, South Africa: Department of Journalism, Rhodes University, 1979), no pp.

11. Quoted in Hachten and Giffard, *Total Onslaught,* 52.

12. For more details on the *Rand Daily Mail* trial and the Prisons Act, see Chapter 5.

13. Quoted in John Seiler, "A government against the world," *Africa Report* 22 (September/October 1979), 9.

14. See Hachten and Giffard, *Total Onslaught,* 72–75.

15. For detailed studies of the Muldergate scandal, see Hachten and Giffard *Total Onslaught,* chap. 1, and Mervyn Rees and Chris Day, *Muldergate: The Story of the Info Scandal* (Johannesburg: Macmillan, 1980).

16. Hachten and Giffard cite the figure of $74 million, which at the exchange rate prevailing at the time translated into R64 million. *Total Onslaught,* 6–7.

17. Ibid., 250–251.

18. Patrick O'Meara, "South Africa's Watergate: The Muldergate scandals," *American Universities Field Staff Reports,* no. 43, 1979, 7.

19. Philip Frankel, "Race and counter-revolution: South Africa's 'Total Strategy,'" *Journal of Commonwealth and Comparative Politics* 18 (November 1980): 275.

20. Lemon, *Apartheid in Transition,* 342.

21. For a more extended analysis of the importance of the role of the "Total Onslaught" concept, see Graeme Addison, "Total Strategy as total propaganda: The socialization of danger," paper presented at the Association for Sociology in Southern Africa conference, Maseru, Lesotho, June 1980; Frankel, "Race and counter-revolution"; and Les Switzer, "Steyn Commission I: The press and Total Strategy," *Critical Arts* 1:4 (February 1981): 41–45.

22. Addison, "Total Strategy," 6.

23. Hachten and Giffard, *Total Onslaught*, 77.

24. Quoted in Ibid.

25. *Report of the Commission of Inquiry into the Reporting of Security News from South African Defence Force and Police*, PR 52 (Pretoria: Government Printer, 1980). For a fuller treatment on the two Steyn Commissions see *Distrust in Democracy: A Lawyers for Human Rights Commentary on the Report of the Steyn Commission of Inquiry into the Mass Media* (N.p.: Lawyers for Human Rights, 1982); Andre du Toit, "The Steyn Commission and the theory of the Total Onslaught," *South African Outlook* 112 (April 1982): 51–54; Hachten and Giffard, *Total Onslaught*, chap. 4; K. Roelofse, *Towards Rational Discourse: An Analysis of the Steyn Commission of Enquiry into the Media* (Pretoria: Van Schaik, 1983); Gavin Stewart, "The South African press and the Steyn Report: A critical appraisal," *South Africa International* 12 (April 1982), 500–507; and Switzer, "Steyn Commission I."

26. *Report of the Commission of Inquiry into the Mass Media*, PR 89, 3 vols. (Pretoria: Government Printer, 1981).

27. Ibid., 945.

28. W.H.B. Dean, "The Commission's response to the 'Total Onslaught,'" in *Distrust in Democracy*, 66.

29. M. J. Richman, preface to *Distrust in Democracy*, 1.

30. D. M. Davis, "Steyn Commission—Methodology," in *Distrust in Democracy*, 33; and Helen Zille, "Judging the judge by his own code," *South African Outlook* 112 (April 1982), 57.

31. "The Steyn Commission," editorial in *South African Outlook* 112 (April 1982), 50.

32. Hansard, 2 February 1982, cols. 101–102.

33. Harvey Tyson, "Report on South Africa" *Editor and Publisher*, 10 July 1982, 40.

34. The Newspaper and Imprint Registration Act of 1971, discussed in Chapter 5.

35. Registration of Newspapers Amendment Bill, No. 98 of 1982, section 3. Parentheses in original. The law and its implications are discussed in Chapter 5.

36. *S.A. Digest*, 4 March 1983, 9.

37. John Allen, "Examining the workings of the Media Council," *Journalist*, September 1983, 6.

38. South African Media Council Constitution, section 1.

39. Bob Steyn. Interview with the author. Grahamstown, 19 July 1989.

40. Tony Heard, "The media blackout," *Africa Report*, 31 (March/April 1986), 58.

41. See for example John Brewer, "The police in South African politics," in *South Africa: No Turning Back* ed. Shaun Johnson (Bloomington and Indianapolis: Indiana University Press, 1989), 258–279; Kenneth W. Grundy, *The Militarization of South African Politics* (Bloomington: Indiana University Press, 1986); and J. E. Spence, "The military in South African politics," in *South Africa: No Turning Back*, 240–257.

42. *Southern Africa Report*, 27 October 1989, 4.

43. *Star*, 13 November 1989.

44. Lemon, *Apartheid in Transition*, 342.

45. Ibid., 343.

46. Don Pinnock, "Popularize, organize, educate and mobilize: Some reflections on South Africa's left-wing press in the 1980's," paper presented to the conference of the Association for Sociology in South Africa, Johannesburg, July 1989, 6.

47. Ibid., 5. Italics in original.

48. Ibid., 8.

49. Ibid., 9.

50. Mike Leahy and Paul Voice, eds., *SARAD Media Yearbook* 1989 (Johannesburg: WTH Publications, 1989), 5, 7.

51. Ibid., 7.

52. William A. Hachten, "Mass media in South Africa: The view from without," in *English-Speaking South Africa Today*, ed. Andre de Villiers (Cape Town: Oxford University Press, 1976), 337.

53. In the early 1990s the circulations of almost all the daily and weekly papers dropped by about 5 to 10 percent in response to the country's severe economic recession. The figures noted here, the latest available, are the first reflecting this decline.

54. Potter, *The Press as Opposition*.

55. Quoted in Willem Wepener, "The role of the Afrikaans press," in *South African Conference on the Survival of the Press and Education for Journalism* (Grahamstown, South Africa: Department of Journalism, Rhodes University, 1979), no pp.

56. James McClurg, "Toeing the line," *Leadership SA* 5 (1986), 76–77.

57. Ibid., 79.

58. See for example note 9 above.

59. P. Eric Louw, "The emergence of a progressive-alternative press in South Africa with specific reference to *Grassroots*," *Communicatio* 15:2 (1989), 27.

60. For more on the SABC see for example William A. Hachten, "Policies and performance of South African television," *Journal of Communication* 29 (Summer 1979): 62–72; Hachten and Giffard, *Total Onslaught*, chap. 9; Gordon Jackson, "TV2: The introduction of television for blacks in South Africa," *Gazette* 29 (1982): 155–171; *South Africa 1989–1990: Official Yearbook of the Republic of South Africa* (Pretoria: Bureau for Information, 1989), chap. 36; and Keyan Tomaselli, Ruth Tomaselli, and Johan Muller, *Currents of Power: State Broadcasting in South Africa* (Bellville, South Africa: Anthropos, 1989).

61. The external broadcast programming was extensively cut in 1990.

62. Hachten, "Policies and performance," 63.

63. Gavin Stewart, "Policom 1987: Political news on South African television during the May election," in *South African Election 1987: Context, Process and Prospect*, ed. D. J. van Vuuren, L. Schlemmer, H. C. Marais, and J. Latakgomo (Pinetown, South Africa: Owen Burgess, 1987), 148.

64. Ibid., 147.

65. Ibid., 150.

66. Quoted in Ken Owen, "The way forward: The press in South Africa," in *South Africa: The Road Ahead,* ed. G. F. Jacobs (Johannesburg: Jonathan Ball, 1986), 244.

67. Under the de Klerk administration, signs of increasing openness in the SABC emerged. A vivid example of this occurred in May 1991, when SATV broadcast a debate between Joe Slovo, head of the South African Communist Party, and editor Ken Owen, a leading champion of capitalism.

68. Owen, "The way forward," 232.

69. Willem de Klerk, "The press and political change in South Africa," in *Change in South Africa,* ed. D. J. van Vuuren (Durban: Butterworths, 1983), 334.

70. Nasionale Pers's publication section is now known as "Nasionale Media," but for simplicity's sake the better-known name is used here.

71. John Grogan and Charles Riddle, "South Africa's press in the eighties: Darkness descends," *Gazette* 39 (1987), 9.

72. Ibid.

73. One possible exception is that Johannesburg has two morning English dailies, *Business Day* and the *Citizen,* yet because of the former paper's specialized audience of business readers they can hardly be seen as direct competitors.

74. Grogan and Riddle, "South Africa's press," 10.

75. Ken Owen, "Of broadsides and broadsheets," *Leadership SA* 3 (1984), 47.

76. See for example Pallo Jordan, "Monopoly capitalism, racism and mass media in South Africa," *Sechaba,* May 1985, pp. 2–9; and R. W. McGregor, *Who Owns Who in the Newspaper Industry* (Cape Town: Purdy Press, 1982).

77. Paul Bell, "A winter's tale," *Leadership SA* 8, no. 5 (1989), 21.

78. Ibid.

79. "Structural analysis," say Keyan and Ruth Tomaselli, entails interpreting the press as part of "the broader political economy of the South African society." (Ruth Tomaselli and Keyan Tomaselli, "The political economy of the South African press," in *Narrating the Crisis: Hegemony and the South African Press,* ed. Keyan Tomaselli, Ruth Tomaselli, and Johan Muller [Johannesburg: Richard Lyon, 1987], 42.) The term is used in this study to refer specifically to one of several theoretical approaches to the study of the South African press. For examinations of these main approaches, see Gordon Jackson, "The Secular and the sacred: A comparative study of the daily and religous press in South Africa" (PhD dissertation, Indiana University, Bloomington, 1983), pp. 55–67, and 80–90; and Tomaselli, Tomaselli, and Muller, *Narrating the Crisis,* chap. 1 and pp. 39–42.

80. Tomaselli and Tomaselli, "The political economy of the South African press," 57.

81. Bell, "A winter's tale," 21.

82. Ken Owen. Interview with the author. Johannesburg, 15 September 1989.

83. Gerald Shaw, "The English-language press," in *Democratic Liberalism in South Africa: Its History and Prospect,* ed. Jeffrey Butler, Richard Elphick and David Welsh (Middletown, Conn.: Wesleyan University Press, and Cape Town: David Philip; 1987), 288–300.

84. This question is examined in Chapter 7.

85. Ton Vosloo, in Jack Foisie et al., "Update: The press in South Africa," *Nieman Reports* 36 (Summer 1982), 28.

86. Trevor Brown, "Free press fair game for South Africa's government," *Journalism Quarterly* 48 (Spring 1971), 121.

87. Quoted in D.A.S. Herbst, "The role of the press in the political process," in *Political Alternatives for South Africa*, ed. D. J. van Vuuren and D. J. Kriek (Durban: Butterworths, 1983), 396–397.

88. de Klerk, "The press and political change in South Africa," 338.

89. See for example James McClurg, "The one-eyed watchdog," *Ecquid Novi* 3 (1982), and Owen, "The way forward."

90. Howard Barrell, "From fringe to formative intervention in the South African press," paper presented at the Cultural Alternatives for South Africa Conference, Amsterdam, 1987. Jo-Anne Collinge, Herbert Mabuza, Glenn Moss, and David Niddrie, "What the papers don't say," *Index on Censorship* 17 (March 1988), 27–36; Rob Davies, Dan O'Meara, and Sipho Dlamini, *The Struggle for South Africa: A Reference Guide to Movements, Organizations and Institutions*, vol. 2 (London: Zed Books, 1984): 406–416; Julie Frederikse, "South Africa's media: The commercial press and the seedlings of the future," *Third World Quarterly* 9 (April 1987), 638–656; P. Eric Louw, "The emergence of a progressive-alternative press," and "The English and Afrikaans press in South Africa: One press or two?" *Communicatio* 9 (1983): 14–16; Tomaselli, Tomaselli, and Muller, *Narrating the Crisis*. See also various articles by Keyan and Ruth Tomaselli in the Bibliography.

91. Rob Davies et al., *The Struggle for South Africa*, 406.

92. Louw, "The English and Afrikaans press, " 16.

93. Frederikse, "South Africa's media," 640.

94. Ameen Akhalwaya, "The role of the alternative press," *Nieman Reports* 42 (Winter 1988): 16.

95. Ibid.

Chapter 3

1. As noted in the Preface, the alternative press is now commonly known in South Africa as the independent press. However, because this chapter was based on writings and interviews marked by the earlier term, the use of "alternative press" throughout this book more faithfully reflects those sources. Also, as the emphasis of this study is on the period 1976–1990, it is more historically accurate to use the term that was current during that time.

2. *Grassroots* subsequently ceased publication. For more on *Grassroots*, see for example P. Eric Louw, "The emergence of a progressive-alternative press in South Africa with specific reference to *Grassroots*," *Communicatio* 15:2 (1989): 26–32.

3. Roger Thurow, "At one newspaper, gunshots and fires cover the reporters," *Wall Street Journal*, 10 August 1988.

4. Anthony Heard, "How I was fired," *Index on Censorship* 16 (November/December 1987): 11.

5. Leila Patel, "How small media can organize communities," *Media Development* 32 (Summer 1985): 12.

6. Anton Harber. Interview with the author. Johannesburg, 19 September 1989.

7. Ibid.

8. See for example the remarks of the minister of home affairs in Parliament, 19 May 1988, Hansard cols. 10347–10348.

9. Ameen Akhalwaya, "The role of the alternative press," *Nieman Reports* 42 (Winter 1988): 14.

10. Ameen Akhalwaya. Interview with the author. Johannesburg, 13 September 1989.

11. Ibid.

12. Shaun Johnson, "Barometers of the liberation movement: A history of South Africa's alternative press," *Media Development* 32 (Summer 1985): 21.

13. Anton Harber, "The press and the battle for the right of expression in South Africa today," *Monitor,* special edition titled "Human rights in South Africa 1988," 1989, 70.

14. See for example Johnson, "Barometers of the liberation movement."

15. Akhalwaya, "Role of the alternative press," 15.

16. Mansoor Jaffer, untitled address to the annual congress of the South African Society of Journalists, 13 May 1988, 5.

17. Louw, "The emergence of a progressive-alternative press," 7.

18. Patel, "How small media can organize communities," 14.

19. Akhalwaya, "Role of the alternative press," 15.

20. Harber interview.

21. Howard Barrell, "From fringe to formative intervention in the South African press," paper presented at the Cultural Alternatives for South Africa Conference, Amsterdam, 1987, 6.

22. Clive Emdon, citing Makanjee (who is not further identified), "Alternative media in the region: Durban newspaper group and ADJ projects 1986–88," paper presented to workshop "Regionalism and restructuring in Natal," University of Natal, Durban, 28–31 January 1988, 5.

23. Jaffer, untitled address, 4.

24. Riaan de Villiers, "Zwelakhe Sisulu," *Leadership SA* 5 (1986): 86.

25. Joe Latakgomo, "Caught in the middle," in "Issue," supplement to *Frontline,* Spring 1982, 27.

26. The larger debate over the possibility of objective reporting has a long and sometimes fiery history. The outworking of that debate in South Africa is examined in Chapter 9.

27. Allan Boesak and Rashid Seria, Proposal for a weekly newspaper project and a journalism training project, no date, 3.

28. Patel, "How small media can organize communities," 12.

29. Jaffer, untitled address, 4.

30. Patel, "How small media can organize communities," 12.

31. Akhalwaya, "Role of the alternative press," 17.

32. Moegsien Williams. Interview with the author. Cape Town, 20 October 1989.

33. Akhalwaya interview.

34. Max du Preez. Interview with the author. Johannesburg, 11 September 1989.

35. See for example the remarks of Stoffel Botha, minister of home affairs, reported in Harvey Tyson, ed., *Conflict and the Press: Proceedings of the* Star's *Centennial Conference on the Role of the Press in a Divided Society* (Johannesburg: Argus, 1987), 134–146.

36. Akhalwaya interview.

37. Akhalwaya, "Role of the alternative press," 15–16.

38. Louw, "The emergence of a progressive-alternative press," 3.

39. Du Preez interview.

40. See for example Gordon Jackson, "The secular and the sacred: A comparative study of the daily and religious press in South Africa," PhD dissertation, Indiana University, Bloomington, 1983.

41. *Weekly Mail*, 18 August 1988.

42. Du Preez interview.

43. Williams interview.

44. Louise Flanagan. Interview with author. East London, 26 August 1989.

45. Chris Louw, "Afrikaanse koerante in 'n noodtoestand" (Afrikaans papers in a crisis), *Die Suid-Afrikaan*, February 1989, 21. My translation.

46. "Editor pays record deposit for right to publish newest opposition newspaper," *IPI Report*, February 1989, 6.

47. Minutes of meeting of the alternative press leaders held in Johannesburg, 25 July 1989.

48. Louw, "The emergence of a progressive-alternative press," 6.

49. Ibid.

50. Barrell, "From fringe to formative intervention," 11.

51. Harber interview.

52. Audit Bureau of Circulations report, July–December 1991.

53. Du Preez interview.

54. Williams interview.

55. Akhalwaya interview.

56. "Countdown to closure," *South*, 10 May 1988.

57. Patel, "How small media can organize communities," 14.

58. Andrew Drysdale. Interview with the author. Cape Town, 9 October 1989.

59. Kosie Viviers. Interview with the author. Cape Town, 9 October 1989.

60. Akhalwaya, "Role of the alternative press," 16.

61. Almost every editor of a mainstream paper interviewed had high regard for the *Weekly Mail*.

62. An exception was the *Weekly Mail*, which for a short while published daily.

63. Akhalwaya, "Role of the alternative press," 15.

64. Du Preez interview.

65. Pat Sidley. Interview with the author. Johannesburg, 23 September 1989.

66. Patel, "How small media can organize communities," 12.

67. Ibid.

68. Akhalwaya interview.

69. ABC figures for July to December 1991.

70. Barrell, "From fringe to formative intervention," 5.

71. Williams interview.

72. Du Preez interview.

73. Michael Massing, "Letter from South Africa," *Columbia Journalism Review* 25 (January/February 1987), 38.

Chapter 4

1. Raymond Louw. Interview with the author. Johannesburg, 18 September 1989.

2. Quoted in Henry Catto, "End of the line: South Africa's defunct *Rand Daily Mail,*" *Washington Journalism Review*, September 1985, 23.

3. See Chapter 5 for a brief account of the Prisons Act.

4. See Mervyn Rees and Chris Day, *Muldergate: The Story of the Info Scandal* (Johannesburg: Macmillan, 1980), for an account by two *Mail* reporters of their coverage of the scandal.

5. Benjamin Pogrund, "Paying the price for being brave," *Journalist*, April 1985, 11.

6. Raymond Louw, "Remember the days when a newspaper told us the news?" *Weekly Mail*, 20 December 1985, 9.

7. Paul Bell, "A winter's tale," *Leadership SA* 8:5 (1989), 21.

8. Ibid.; Laurence Gandar, "The *Mail* died but it did not have to die," *Journalist*, February/March 1987, 24; Anton Harber, "Behind closed doors: Media murders," *Work in Progress* 35 (April 1985), 3–6; Joel Mervis, *The Fourth Estate: A Newspaper Story* (Johannesburg: Jonathan Ball, 1989); Koos Roelofse, "*Rand Daily Mail:* Die dood in perspektief" (*Rand Daily Mail:* The death in perspective), *Communicatio* 11 (1985), 30–37; Gavin Stewart, "Going the whole hog: The *Rand Daily Mail*, 1957–1985" (unpublished paper, Department of Journalism and Media Studies, Rhodes University, Grahamstown, South Africa, 1988); Keyan Tomaselli, Ruth Tomaselli, and Johan Muller, *Narrating the Crisis: Hegemony and the South African Press* (Johannesburg: Richard Lyon, 1987), 79–86.

9. Gandar, "The *Mail* died," 24.

10. Not-for-attribution information provided in an interview with the author.

11. Mervis, *The Fourth Estate*, 521.

12. Ibid., 520 ff.

13. Bell, "Winter's tale," 21.

14. Mervis, *The Fourth Estate*, 461.

15. Ibid., 470.

16. Ibid., 474.

17. Ibid., 521.

18. Ibid., 460.

19. Quoted in ibid., 459.

20. Ibid., 460.

21. Ibid., 504–505.

22. Ibid., 544.

23. William A. Hachten and C. Anthony Giffard, *Total Onslaught: The South African Press Under Attack* (Johannesburg: Macmillan 1984), 7.

24. Hachten and Giffard, *Total Onslaught*, 241.

25. Quoted in Catto, "End of the line," 23.

26. Mervis, *The Fourth Estate*, 453.

27. Stewart, "Going the whole hog," 10.

28. Quoted in Catto, "End of the line," 23.

29. Stewart, "Going the whole hog," 7–8.

30. Ibid., 8.

31. "Grey readership," *Financial Mail*, 7 October 1988, 92.

32. The explanation for the high proportion of black readers of a progovernment paper is at least twofold. The *Citizen* is regarded as having particularly good hard-news coverage and it is the only English-language morning daily available in Johannesburg except for the specialized *Business Day*.

33. "Grey readership," 92.

34. Stewart, "Going the whole hog," 8.

35. Mervis, *The Fourth Estate*, 477.

36. Catto, "End of the line," 23.

37. Ibid.

38. Ken Owen. Interview with the author. Johannesburg, 15 September 1989.

39. Mervis, *The Fourth Estate*, 496.

40. Ibid., 498.

41. Ibid.

42. Hugh Murray, "Blueblood blues," *Leadership SA* 6 (1987), 54.

43. Gandar, "The *Mail* died," 24.

44. Catto, "End of the line," 23.

45. Bell, "Winter's tale."

46. ABC Report, July-December 1991. All subsequent circulation figures are based on this or an earlier ABC Report.

47. Bell, "Winter's tale," 27.

48. Mervis, *The Fourth Estate*, 536.

49. Ibid.

50. Ibid., 537.

51. Ibid., 521.

52. Bell, "Winter's tale," 27.

53. Ibid., 27.

54. Mervis, *The Fourth Estate*, 548.

55. Sue Lewis, "Stephen Mulholland: A man of action," *Marketing Mix*, May 1989, 12.

56. For details see Bell, "Winter's tale, " 27.

57. Ibid., 29.

58. Lewis, "Stephen Mulholland," 14.

59. Bell, "Winter's tale," 27.

60. Mervis, *The Fourth Estate*, 542.

61. Bell, "Winter's tale," 41.

62. Lewis, "Stephen Mulholland," 14.

63. Bell, "Winter's tale," 41.

64. Jeanette Minnie. Interview with the author. Johannesburg, 18 January 1990.

65. Group discussion between several Johannesburg journalists and author. Johannesburg, 20 September 1989.

66. Lee, "Gentlemen of the press," 86.

67. Mervis, *The Fourth Estate,* 543.

68. Bell, "Winter's tale," 19.

69. Mike Leahy and Paul Voice, eds., *SARAD Media Yearbook 1989* (Johannesburg: WTH Publications, 1989), 59.

70. Ibid., 4–5.

71. Dawid de Villiers, "The state of the press," *Leadership SA* 2 (1983), 38–48.

72. The 1976 license fee of R36 was increased to R42 in 1982–83, and to R46.20 in 1984–85. Subsequent rapid increases came in 1986–87, to R60; in 1987–88, to R72; in 1988–89, to R80; in 1990–91, to R120; and in 1991–92, to R150. Letter from Eric van der Merwe, SABC, 9 September 1991.

73. De Villiers, "The state of the press, " 43.

74. Leahy and Voice, *SARAD Media Yearbook 1989,* 98.

75. Ibid.

76. Ibid.

77. Syd Pote. Interview with the author. Johannesburg, 19 January 1991.

78. Leahy and Voice, *SARAD Media Yearbook 1989,* 105.

79. Ibid., 73.

80. Ibid.

81. Although the suburban press and the country press are grouped together for reporting purposes, the growth indicated here is overwhelmingly attributable to the suburban papers, as the *SARAD Yearbook* notes on p. 73. Separated out, the figures for the suburban papers would be even more striking.

82. Lee, "Gentlemen of the press," 90.

83. Ibid.

84. Noel Coburn. Interview with the author. Johannesburg, 22 January 1990.

85. Quoted in William L. Rivers, Wilbur Schramm, and Clifford G. Christians, *Responsibility in Mass Communication,* 3rd ed. (New York: Harper and Row, 1980), 107.

86. *A Way to Win: Strategies to Evaluate and Improve Your Readership and Circulation* (Washington, D.C.: American Newspaper Publishers Association, 1990), 43.

87. Conrad Fink, *Strategic Newspaper Management* (Belmont, Calif.: Wadsworth, 1988), 185.

88. Leahy and Voice, *SARAD Yearbook 1989,* 63.

89. Figures taken from *Business Futures,* 72. The calculations are based on rounded figures, taken from the 1960 census and from projections for 1990. The percentage increase is based on these figures, not the shortened versions mentioned here.

90. Coburn interview.

91. For a more complete account of economic developments in the period under review, see the annual issues of the *Survey of Race Relations*. More detailed economic data are available in the reports of the South African Reserve Bank.

92. Bell, "Winter's tale," 31.

93. Mervis, *The Fourth Estate*, 481.

94. Zac de Beer, "Batten down the budgets," advertising supplement to *Financial Mail*, 22 August 1986, 54.

95. The struggle between these two companies is described in detail in Tomaselli, Tomaselli, and Muller, *Narrating the Crisis*, 133–138.

96. Rob Davies, Dan O'Meara, and Sipho Dlamini, *The Struggle for South Africa: A Reference Guide to Movements, Organizations and Institutions*, vol. 2 (London: Zed Books, 1984), 411.

97. The *Transvaler* subsequently moved back to Johannesburg but continued to run at a loss as an afternoon paper.

98. Anthony Heard, "Don't forget who pays you … ," *Journalist*, December 1984, 11.

99. "Sunday, bloody Sunday … " *Financial Mail*, 27 July 1984, 31.

100. Mervis, *The Fourth Estate*, 502.

101. John Grogan and Charles Riddle, "South Africa's press in the eighties: Darkness descends," *Gazette* 39 (1987): 10.

102. Derek Smith, editor of the *Eastern Province Herald*, and Neville Woudberg, editor of the *Evening Post*, respectively. Interviews with the author. Port Elizabeth, 21 August 1989.

103. Quoted in *Journalist*, November 1985, 13.

104. Pierre van Manen. Interview with the author. Port Elizabeth, 18 August 1989.

105. Jolyon Nuttall. Interview with the author. Johannesburg, 25 September 1989.

106. M-Net is an entertainment service, specializing in movies and sports programming. The service's license originally prohibited it from broadcasting news but the government subsequently removed this constraint and M-Net began moving toward introducing a news service. For more on M-Net, see Mike Leahy and Paul Voice, eds., *SARAD Media Yearbook 1989* (Johannesburg: WTH Publications, 1989), 107–109; and Corrie Faure, "Koerantsubsidies, persvryheid en M-net" (Newspaper subsidies, press freedom, and M-Net), *Communicatio* 13 (1987): 31–44.

107. *Star*, 15 September 1989.

108. *South Africa Statistics: 1990* (Pretoria: Central Statistical Services, 1990), 7.6.

109. Leahy and Voice, *SARAD Media Yearbook 1989*, 108.

110. P. Eric Louw, "The English and Afrikaans press in South Africa: One press or two?" *Communicatio* 9 (1983): 14–16.

111. Conversation with the author. Durban, 28 August 1989.

112. Examples of this rapprochement included the meeting between government and business leaders at the Carlton Hotel in Johannesburg, in November 1979, and the Good Hope Conference in Cape Town, in November 1981.

113. See for example Tomaselli, Tomaselli, and Muller, *Narrating the Crisis*, 79–86.

114. Heard, "Don't forget who pays you ...," 11.

115. Stephen Mulholland. Interview with the author. Johannesburg, 22 September 1989.

116. See for example Fink, *Strategic Newspaper Management*, chap. 1.

117. Mary A. Anderson, "Newspaper marketing," *presstime*, January 1989, 26.

118. Bell, "Winter's tale," 38.

119. Ton Vosloo. Interview with the author. Cape Town, 29 November 1989.

120. Peter McLean. Interview with the author. Johannesburg, 25 January 1990.

121. Quoted in Karl Albrecht, *Brain Power* (New York: Prentice-Hall, 1980), 36.

Chapter 5

1. *Race Relations Survey 1984* (Johannesburg: South African Institute of Race Relations, 1985), 886.

2. As this chapter is being written, many of the laws affecting the press are also being eased or dropped. For simplicity's sake, this chapter is thus written in the past tense to indicate which laws were in effect during the period examined in this book. Many of these are likely to have been eased or completely removed by the time this study is published.

3. Anthony Heard, "The media blackout," *Africa Report* 31 (March/April 1986): 57.

4. See S. A. Strauss, M. J. Strydom, and J. C. van der Walt, *Mediareg* (Media law), 4th ed., by H. B. Klopper (Pretoria: Van Schaik, 1987), and Kelsey Stuart and Bell, Dewar and Hall, *Newspaperman's Guide to the Law*, 5th ed. (Durban: Butterworths, 1990), for details on these and numerous other areas.

5. Stuart, *A Newspaperman's Guide to the Law*.

6. Gilbert Marcus, "Blacks treated more severely," *Index on Censorship* 13 (December 1984), 15.

7. Justice Rumpff, in Publications Control Board v. William Heinemann Ltd (1965), quoted in Marcus, "Blacks treated more severely," 15.

8. Justice Van Zijl, in State v. Turrell (1973), quoted in ibid.

9. Yvonne M. Burns, "Freedom of the Press in South Africa," in *South Africa: A Plural Society in Transition*, ed. D. J. van Vuuren (Durban: Butterworths, 1985), 223.

10. Many judges have been sympathetic to the goals of the government. For this reason, as well as the tradition of legal positivism in South Africa that requires judges to avoid judicial activism and injecting their own moral values into judgments, judges have shown little inclination to challenge laws like those described in this chapter. See Anthony Mathews, *Freedom, State Security and the Rule of Law: Dilemmas of the Apartheid Society* (Cape Town: Juta, 1986), 296–302.

11. John Grogan, *The Media Emergency Regulations, 1988: A Guide for Journalists,* Occasional paper no. 2, Grahamstown, South Africa: Department of Journalism and Media Studies, Rhodes University, 1988, 5; Burns, "Freedom of the press in South Africa" (also, "Freedom of the press: a comparative legal study," LLD dissertation, University of South Africa, 1984); William A. Hachten and C. Anthony Giffard, *Total Onslaught: The South African Press Under Attack* (Johannesburg: Macmillan 1984), chap. 5; Mathews, *Freedom, State Security and the Rule of Law* (also, *The Darker Reaches of Government* [Cape Town: Juta, and Berkeley and Los Angeles: University of California Press, 1978]).

12. Stuart, *A Newspaperman's Guide to the Law.*

13. *Vrye Weekblad* experienced other difficulties in obtaining registration and its editor was subsequently charged with publishing an unregistered paper.

14. Anti-Censorship Action Group newsletter, March 1989, 2.

15. Mathews, *Freedom, State Security and the Rule of Law,* 150.

16. Ibid., 250.

17. Anti-Censorship Action Group newsletter, March 1989, 4.

18. Mathews, *Freedom, State Security and the Rule of Law,* 150.

19. Anti-Censorship Action Group newsletter, March 1989, 4.

20. In 1962 banned papers were prevented from appearing under a new name.

21. See section 5 (1) of the Act.

22. Published annually by the South African Institute of Race Relations, Johannesburg.

23. Published by the Anti-Censorship Action Group, PO Box 260425, Excom 2023, Transvaal.

24. See for example occasional surveys in *Index on Censorship,* such as those by Gavin Stewart, "Intimidation and prosecution of journalists," *Index on Censorship* 14 (July 1986): 24–40.

25. John Dugard, *Human Rights and the South African Legal Order* (Princeton: Princeton University Press, 1978), 183.

26. Anti-Censorship Action Group newsletter, August 1989, 2.

27. Burns, "Freedom of the press in South Africa," 227–228.

28. *Star,* 31 August 1989.

29. Ibid.

30. Anti-Censorship Action Group newsletter, August 1989, 2.

31. The text of the interview is contained in Anthony Heard, *The Cape of Storms: A Personal History of the Crisis in South Africa* (Fayetteville and London: University of Arkansas Press, 1990): 231–244.

32. Anthony Heard, "How I was fired," *Index on Censorship* 16 (November/December 1987), 10.

33. Heard was later fired as editor. For his detailed account of his firing see Heard, "How I was fired. "

34. Section 118 of the act.

35. Mathews, *Freedom, State Security and the Rule of Law,* 158.

36. Ibid., 159.

37. Ibid.

38. Ibid., 160.

39. Section 101 of the act.
40. Act 64 of 1979.
41. *Race Relations Survey 1987*, 833–834.
42. Ibid., 834–835.
43. Mathews, *Freedom, State Security and the Rule of Law*, 155.
44. However, for more on the role of the police see John Brewer, "The police in South African politics," in *South Africa: No Turning Back*, edited by Shaun Johnson (Bloomington and Indianapolis: Indiana University Press, 1989), 258–279.
45. G. E. Devenish, "Critical review of inroads into press freedom in South Africa," *Business SA* 15 (May 1980), 31–32.
46. Mathews, *Freedom, State Security and the Rule of Law*, 151.
47. See Stuart, *Newspaperman's Guide to the Law*, chap. 11.
48. See for example Mathews, *Freedom, State Security and the Rule of Law*, 168.
49. Devenish, "Critical review," 34.
50. Ibid., 30.
51. Section 4 of the act.
52. Mathews, *Freedom, State Security and the Rule of Law*, 162.
53. Ibid., 165.
54. *Survey of Race Relations 1983*, 211.
55. Mathews, *Freedom, State Security and the Rule of Law*, 172.
56. Hachten and Giffard, *Total Onslaught*, 123.
57. Anti-Censorship Action Group newsletter, May 1989, 2.
58. Anthony Heard, "Risking life and liberty in South Africa," *Washington Journalism Review*, January 1986, 39.
59. See for example Branzburg v. Hayes, 408 U.S. 665 (1972). Especially important were the safeguards for journalists that Justice Potter Stewart described in his concurring opinion, which has had much influence on subsequent court decisions.
60. Anti-Censorship Action Group newsletter, May 1989, 2.
61. *Star*, 1 June 1989.
62. Ibid.
63. Ibid.
64. See Stuart, *Newspaperman's Guide to the Law*, chap. 7, and Hachten and Giffard, *Total Onslaught*, chap. 7, for relatively brief but comprehensive overviews of the act. J.C.W. van Rooyen, *Censorship in South Africa* (Cape Town: Juta, 1987), provides an in-depth legal analysis of the act and its operation.
65. Anthony Mathews, "Censorship, access to information and public debate," *Theoria* (Pietermaritzburg) 55 (October 1980), 23.
66. The description and discussion of this act draw heavily upon chap. 7 in Hachten and Giffard, *Total Onslaught*, and on Gilbert Marcus's essay, "Reasonable Censorship?" in *Essays on Law and Social Practice in South Africa*, ed. Hugh Corder (Cape Town: Juta, 1988), 349–360.
67. The Publications and Entertainment Act (Act 26 of 1963).
68. Section 47 (2).

69. Marcus, "Blacks treated more severely, " 16.
70. Section 47 (2).
71. Marcus, "Reasonable censorship?" 351–352.
72. U.S. newspaper publisher Josephus Daniels; citation unknown.
73. Marcus, "Blacks treated more severely, " 16.
74. Board decisions may of course be challenged on procedural grounds.
75. Jo-Anne Collinge, Herbert Mabuza, Glenn Moss, and David Niddrie, "What the papers don't say," *Index on Censorship* 17 (March 1988), 27.
76. Marcus, "Reasonable censorship?" 359.
77. One reason for this was the legal expense involved; another was the refusal of some authors to participate in a system they saw as abhorrent.
78. Marcus, "Blacks treated more severely, " 16.
79. Marcus, "Reasonable censorship?"
80. Ibid., 358.
81. For details on the introduction of the act, and the controversy it caused, see *Survey of Race Relations 1982*, 269–270.
82. For a fuller discussion of the Newspaper Bill, see Hachten and Giffard, *Total Onslaught*, 72ff.
83. Mathews, *Freedom, State Security and the Rule of Law*, chap. 13.
84. Ibid., 272.
85. Anthony Mathews, "National security, freedom and reform," in *Critical Choices for South Africa: An Agenda for the 1990s*, ed. Robert Schrire (Cape Town: Oxford University Press, 1990), 76.
86. John Grogan, "News control by decree: An examination of the South African government's power to control information by administrative action," *South African Law Journal* 103 (February 1986), 133.
87. See for example Mathews, *Freedom, State Security and the Rule of Law*, 297ff.
88. Grogan, "News control by decree," 134.
89. Ibid., 126–127.
90. Ibid., 130.
91. Hachten and Giffard, *Total Onslaught*, 118.
92. Max du Preez. Interview with the author. Johannesburg, 11 September 1989.
93. Dugard, *Human Rights*, 186.

Chapter 6

1. Justin Whittle and Richard Kenin, eds. *Dictionary of Biographical Quotation of British and American Subjects* (London: Routledge and Kegan Paul, 1979), 334.
2. The state of emergency is in fact a succession of separate states of emergency, as will be explained. For simplicity's sake, and because it accurately reflects the continuous nature of the declared emergency except for one brief gap, the term "state of emergency" is used here.
3. Proclamation R 120 of 1985.
4. Act 3 of 1953.

5. John Grogan, "News control by decree: An examination of the South African government's power to control information by administrative action," *South African Law Journal* 103 (February 1986), 125.

6. Regulation 4(b) of Proclamation R 121 of 1985.

7. Proclamation R 208 of 1985.

8. *Race Relations Survey 1987* (Johannesburg: South African Institute of Race Relations, 1988), 813.

9. Proclamation R 224 of 1986.

10. *Race Relations Survey 1987*, 818.

11. The media regulations were formally ended on 3 February 1990, by Proclamation R 19 of 1990, the day after President de Klerk's speech in Parliament announcing the release of Nelson Mandela, the unbanning of the ANC, and other changes.

12. Providing a detailed, article-by-article description of the media regulations would be a lengthy task. The enthusiastic reader can examine the last set of regulations in full. Similarly, a detailed analysis of each step in the process that led to the regulations in their "polished" form would have legal and historical interest but is of limited value for our discussion. For a more detailed analysis of the specific regulations enacted on the dates listed earlier, the loopholes that emerged, and how the government closed them, see the applicable issues of *Race Relations Survey*.

13. This analysis relies heavily on Grogan's excellent guide to the emergency regulations, *The Media Emergency Regulations, 1988: A Guide for Journalists*, Occasional paper no. 2 (Grahamstown, South Africa: Department of Journalism and Media Studies, Rhodes University, 1988).

14. For such an analysis, see Grogan, *Media Emergency Regulations*, for example.

15. Section 4(3)(a).

16. Under section 6.

17. All those appearing monthly or more often had to be registered. See Chapter 5 for details on registration.

18. Section 7(3)(d)(i).

19. Grogan, *Media Emergency Regulations*, 22.

20. Anti-Censorship Action Group newsletter, March 1989, 1.

21. 1988 Regulations, Section 11(5).

22. Anton Harber, "The register of news agencies," *Index on Censorship* 17 (August 1988), 26.

23. Grogan, *Media Emergency Regulations*, 24.

24. Anton Harber, "Soul of the white ant, " *Leadership SA* 7 (1988), 93.

25. Quoted in Harber, "Register of news agencies," 25. Italics in original.

26. Ibid., 26.

27. Grogan, *Media Emergency Regulations*, 10.

28. Section 3(1)(b).

29. Section 3(1)(f).

30. "Although detentions are included among 'security actions,' the definition of that term is limited to 'any action whereby a person is arrested' under

the emergency regulations. The mere fact of an arrest is not an *action* whereby an arrest is effected." Grogan, *Media Emergency Regulations*, 12.

31. Grogan pointed out that this regulation was an apparent anomaly because one was not prevented from reporting the original arrest. Grogan, *Media Emergency Regulations*, 12.

32. Section 3(2).

33. Section 5(d).

34. Definition of "subversive statement," under Section 1(a)(xi).

35. Grogan, *Media Emergency Regulations*, 15.

36. Section 2.

37. Section 2(2)(b).

38. Quoted in Cameron Duodo, "*Cape Times:* Editor faces imprisonment after breaking censorship rule," *Index on Censorship* 15 (January 1986), 9.

39. Gilbert Marcus, "The gagging writs," *Reality* 19 (May 1987), 8.

40. *Star*, 7 October 1987.

41. For an imaginative assessment of the U. S. media coverage of South Africa in the wake of Pretoria's public relations efforts and domestic violence, see Jarol B. Manheim and Robert B. Albritton, "Insurgent violence versus image management: The struggle for national images in Southern Africa," *British Journal of Political Science* 17 (1987): 201–218.

42. For an example of the impact in the United States, see Manheim and Albritton, "Insurgent Violence," 218.

43. William A. Hachten and C. Anthony Giffard, *Total Onslaught: The South African Press Under Attack* (Johannesburg: Macmillan, 1984), 278.

44. *Weekly Mail*, 8 November 1985.

45. Ibid.

46. Ibid.

47. The author wrote to the minister of law and order, asking him to provide evidence of examples where foreign journalists had acted unprofessionally. No evidence was provided.

48. Quoted in *Race Relations Survey* 1985, 460.

49. In Harvey Tyson, ed., *Conflict and the Press: Proceedings of the* Star*'s Centennial Conference on the Role of the Press in a Divided Society* (Johannesburg: Argus, 1987), 136–137.

50. Tyson, *Conflict and the Press*, 78.

51. Anti-Censorship Action Group newsletter, August 1989, 8.

52. Manheim and Albritton, "Insurgent violence," 205.

53. Ibid., 205–206.

54. Ibid., 215.

55. Tyson, *Conflict and the Press*, 64–65.

56. Grogan, *Media Emergency Regulations*, 1.

57. Anton Harber, "Even bigger scissors," *Index on Censorship* 16 (November/December 1987), 13.

58. Grogan, *Media Emergency Regulations*, 2. See also David Dison, "Tightening the screw," *Leadership SA* 6 (1987): 15–19.

59. See Omar v. Minister of Law and Order 1987 (3) SA 859 (A), and Minister of Law and Order v. Dempsey 1988 (3) SA 19(A).

60. Grogan, *Media Emergency Regulations*, 3.

61. *Star*, 7 October 1985.

62. Tyson, *Conflict and the Press*, 144–145.

63. Quoted in *RSA Policy Review* 2 (March 1989), 100.

64. Gilbert Marcus, "Fine distinctions: Scientific censorship and the courts," *South African Journal on Human Rights* 4 (1988), 83.

65. Marcus, "Fine distinctions," 83.

66. Ibid.

67. Quoted in ibid.

68. Anthony Mathews, "Crossing the threshold," *Leadership SA* 5 (1986), 52; italics in original.

69. Jo-Anne Collinge, Herbert Mabuza, Glenn Moss, and David Niddrie, "What the papers don't say," *Index on Censorship* 17 (March 1988), 33.

70. Gavin Stewart, "The Walls of Jericho," *Sunday Tribune*, 10 November 1985.

71. Anthony Heard, "Caution is the watchword," *Index on Censorship* 15 (August 1986), 8.

72. Collinge, "What the papers don't say," 34.

73. Richard Manning, *They Cannot Kill Us All: An Eyewitness Account of South Africa Today* (Boston: Houghton-Mifflin, 1987), 133.

74. Quoted in *South African Journal on Human Rights* 2 (1986), 252.

75. Collinge, "What the papers don't say," 33.

76. John Grogan and Charles Riddle, "South Africa's press in the eighties: Darkness descends," *Gazette* 39 (1987), 5.

77. Collinge, "What the papers don't say," 33.

78. W. du Plessis and N.J.J. Olivier, "Persvryheid: Quo vadis?" (Press freedom: Quo vadis?), *Ecquid Novi* 9 (1988), 48.

79. Gilbert Marcus, "Fanning revolution, unrest and violence: A case study of censorship under the emergency," *Harvard Human Rights Yearbook* 2 (Spring 1989): 125–135.

80. The minister said the problematic articles were, in the language of the regulations, "fomenting revolution," "promoting the breakdown of public order," "fanning hatred toward the South African security forces," and "promoting the image of an outlawed organization."

81. Marcus, "Fanning revolution," 131.

82. Ibid., 129.

83. See the section on the Internal Security Act in Chapter 5.

84. Tyson, *Conflict and the Press*, 314.

85. Marcus, "Fanning revolution," 131.

86. *Star*, 17 November 1987.

87. Ibid.

88. Gilbert Marcus. Interview with the author. Johannesburg, 27 September 1989.

89. Anti-Censorship Action Group newsletter, May 1989, 6.

90. Quoted in *Race Relations Survey 1987*, 829.

91. A "briefing paper" by the editors of alternative newspapers, September 1989.

92. Anti-Censorship Action Group newsletter, August 1989, 8.

93. *Weekly Mail*, 18 August 1989.

94. For details on the outcome of this and other emergency-related media trials, see the appropriate issue of *Race Relations Survey*.

95. *Weekly Mail*, 18 August 1989.

96. Gavin Stewart and Charles Riddle, "Three years on: The state of press freedom in South Africa," updated version of paper presented to the Congress of the South African Society of Journalists, Port Elizabeth, 5 May 1989, 2.

97. *IPI Report*, December 1987, 23–24.

98. Jeanette Minnie. Interview with the author. Johannesburg, 18 January 1990.

99. "Standing on the Truth," leaflet published by the Association of Democratic Journalists, September 1989.

100. Ibid.

101. Ibid.

102. Dison, "Tightening the screw," 19.

103. Collinge, "What the papers don't say," 30.

104. Ibid., 31.

105. Stewart and Riddle, "Three years on," 2.

106. Ibid.

107. Ibid.

108. Ibid.

109. Ibid.

110. Richard Steyn. Interview with the author. Pietermaritzburg, 30 August 1989.

111. Kosie Viviers. Interview with the author. Cape Town, 9 October 1989.

112. Salie de Swardt. Interview with the author. Johannesburg, 22 September 1989.

113. Denis Beckett. Interview with the author. Johannesburg, 28 September 1989.

114. Louise Flanagan. Interview with the author. East London, 26 August 1989.

115. Rex Gibson. Interview with the author. Johannesburg, 21 September 1989.

116. Arnold de Beer. Interview with the author. Grahamstown, 6 July 1989.

117. Gisele W. Aymes, "The newspaper: where to from here?" *Marketing Mix*, October 1989, 56.

118. Michael Green. Interview with the author. Durban, 28 August 1989.

119. Steyn interview.

120. Andrew Drysdale. Interview with the author. Cape Town, 9 October 1989.

121. De Swardt interview.

122. Ibid.

123. Marcus, "Gagging writs," 10.

124. Not-for-attribution information provided in an interview with a media source who had held discussions with the government on the regulations.

125. Quoted in *Speaking of a Free Press: 200 Years of Notable Quotations About Press Freedoms* (Washington, D.C.: American Newspaper Publishers Association Foundation, 1987), 13.

Chapter 7

1. Bob Steyn. Interview with the author. Grahamstown, South Africa, 19 July 1989.

2. Speech delivered at Rhodes University, Grahamstown, South Africa, 19 July 1989.

3. Steyn speech.

4. Ken Owen, "Like a sapper into a minefield," in *Issue*, a supplement to *Frontline*, Spring 1982, 18.

5. Ibid., 19.

6. Richard Manning, *They Cannot Kill Us All: An Eyewitness Account of South Africa Today* (Boston: Houghton-Mifflin, 1987), 135–136.

7. Ibid., 136.

8. Ibid., 145–146.

9. Harvey Tyson, ed. *Conflict and the Press: Proceedings of the Star's Centennial Conference on the Role of the Press in a Divided Society* (Johannesburg: Argus, 1987), 156.

10. Ibid., 157.

11. Ken Owen, "The way forward: The press in South Africa," in *South Africa: The Road Ahead*, ed. G. F. Jacobs (Johannesburg: Jonathan Ball, 1986), 239.

12. Gilbert Marcus, "Reasonable censorship?" in *Essays on Law and Social Practice in South Africa*, ed. Hugh Corder (Cape Town: Juta, 1988), 350.

13. T. S. Eliot, "Burnt Norton," in *T. S. Eliot: The Complete Poems and Plays, 1909–1950* (San Diego and New York: Harcourt Brace Jovanovich, 1952), 118.

14. Richard Steyn, "The press's responsibility in a polarised society," *Theoria*, May 1987, 22.

15. See Chapter 2, note 9.

16. Anthony Mathews, *The Darker Reaches of Government* (Cape Town: Juta, and Berkeley and Los Angeles: University of California Press, 1978).

17. See also Anthony Mathews, "Censorship, access to information and public debate," *Theoria* 55 (October 1980), 21–31; *Freedom, State Security and the Rule of Law: Dilemmas of the Apartheid Society* (Cape Town: Juta, 1986); and "Legislation and civil liberties in South Africa," *Optima* 32 (March 1984), 11–15.

18. See for example Gavin Stewart, "History of press control," *South African Outlook* 112 (April 1982), 67–68.

19. Amanda Armstrong, "'Hear no evil, see no evil, speak no evil': Media restrictions and the state of emergency," in *South African Review No. 4*, eds. Glenn Moss and Ingrid Obery (Johannesburg: Ravan Press, 1987), 212.

20. Ibid., 211.

21. Theo Coggin, "A liberal perspective on freedom of speech," address given to the Institute for a Democratic Alternative for South Africa, Durban, 5 November 1988.

22. Mathews, "Censorship, access to information," 22.

23. Gilbert Marcus: "The gagging writs," *Reality* 19 (May 1987), 10.

24. Yvonne Burns, "Freedom of the press in the realm of state security," *De Jure* 18 (June 1985), 65.

25. Anton Harber, "The press and the battle for the right of expression in South Africa today," *Monitor*, special edition titled "Human rights in South Africa 1988," 1989, 67.

26. See for example Yvonne Burns, "Freedom of the press in South Africa," in *South Africa: A Plural Society in Transition*, ed. D. J. van Vuuren, (Durban: Butterworths, 1985), 244.

27. Charlotte Bauer, "Disinvited," *Index on Censorship* 17 (November/December 1988), 33.

28. Ibid.

29. Harber, "The press and the battle," 70.

30. Bauer, "Disinvited," 33.

31. "Censorship," *Reality* 21 (January 1989), 3.

32. Coggin, "A liberal perspective."

33. Ibid.

34. Ibid.

35. For more detailed accounts of the difficulties facing black journalists, see William Finnegan, *Dateline Soweto* (New York: Harper and Row, 1988), and *Mau-Mauing the Media: New Censorship for the New South Africa* (Johannesburg: South African Institute of Race Relations, 1991).

36. The proceedings of the conference were published as *Mau-Mauing the Media*.

37. *Sunday Times*, 27 August 1989.

38. Ibid.

39. Lester Venter, "Propaganda: The nasty things that others do," *Frontline*, October/November 1987, 19.

40. For a fuller discussion of these laws see Chapter 5.

41. Mathews, "Censorship, access to information," 24.

42. Association of Democratic Journalists constitution, 1.

43. Moegsien Williams. Interview with the author. Cape Town, 20 October 1989.

Chapter 8

1. Quoted in Richard Steyn, "The press's responsibility in a polarised society," *Theoria* (May 1987), 26.

2. *Survey of Race Relations 1978* (Johannesburg: South African Institute of Race Relations, 1979), 134.

3. Quoted in *Speaking of a Free Press: 200 Years of Notable Quotations About Press Freedoms* (Washington, D.C.: American Newspaper Publishers Association Foundation, 1987), 22.

4. Lord McGregor, "Opening remarks," in *Conflict and the Press: Proceedings of the* Star's *Centennial Conference on the Role of the Press in a Divided Society*, ed. Harvey Tyson (Johannesburg: Argus, 1987), 19.

5. See for example Samuel P. Huntington, *Political Order in Changing Societies* (New Haven, Conn.: Yale University Press, 1968), and Samuel P. Huntington and Joan Nelson, *No Easy Choice: Political Participation in Developing Countries* (Cambridge: Harvard University Press, 1976).

6. See for example Everette E. Dennis and John C. Merrill, *Basic Issues in Mass Communication* (New York: Macmillan, 1984), chap. 1.

7. This definition closely parallels that of the Commission on Freedom of the Press. See note 21 below.

8. Quoted in Tyson, *Conflict and the Press*, 54.

9. Quoted in Harald Pakendorf, "Kortvat van die pers: 'N sekere onheilspad" (Disciplining the press: a sure road to disaster) *Woord en Daad*, November 1988, 4.

10. For examples of such lists see publications like the *Index on Censorship*; the *IPI Report*; the newsletter of the Anti-Censorship Action Group, based in Johannesburg; and the South African Institute of Race Relations' annual *Race Relations Survey*.

11. *South*, 10 May 1989.

12. These incidents are described in a memo by Franz Krüger, at the ELNews news bureau in East London, sent to the *Weekly Mail* on 8 October 1987.

13. Ibid.

14. Louise Flanagan. Interview with the author. East London, 26 August 1989.

15. Anti-Censorship Action Group Newsletter, August 1989, 4.

16. Ibid., 4–5.

17. Peter Auf der Heyde. Interview with the author. Grahamstown, 23 August 1989.

18. Ibid.

19. Denis McQuail, *Mass Communication Theory* (London: Sage, 1983), 89–90.

20. John Grogan, *The media emergency regulations, 1988: A guide for journalists*, Occasional paper no. 2 (Grahamstown, South Africa: Department of Journalism and Media Studies, Rhodes University, 1988), 5.

21. William Hocking, *Freedom of the Press: A Framework of Principle* (Chicago: University of Chicago Press, 1947), 195.

22. Moegsien Williams. Interview with the author. Cape Town, 20 October 1989.

23. Rhoda E. Howard, *Human Rights in Commonwealth Africa* (Totowa, N.J.: Rowman and Littlefield, 1986), 212.

24. David Lamb, "Endangered species," *Nieman Reports* 36 (Autumn 1982), 22.

25. Ibid., 23.

26. Salie de Swardt. Interview with the author. Johannesburg, 22 September 1989.

27. Anthony Mathews, *The Darker Reaches of Government* (Cape Town: Juta; Berkeley and Los Angeles: University of California Press, 1978).

28. Anthony Heard, "The press in South Africa: Twilight of freedom?" in *The South African Quagmire*, ed. S. Prakash Sethi (Cambridge, Mass.: Ballinger, 1987), 261.

29. Quoted in Steyn, "The press's responsibility," 26.

30. Denis Beckett. Interview with the author. Johannesburg, 28 September 1989.

31. Heard, "The press in South Africa," 261.

32. P. Eric Louw, "The libertarian theory of the press: How appropriate in the South African context?" *Communicatio* 10 (1984), 36.

33. Constitutional Guidelines of the African National Congress. Published in the *South African Journal on Human Rights* 5 (1989), 131.

34. *Pretoria News*, 7 July 1989.

35. Brian Bunting, "South African journalists in the front line," *Sechaba*, April 1989, 15.

36. Anton Harber. Interview with the author. Johannesburg, 19 September 1989.

37. Constitutional Guidelines, 131.

38. Williams interview.

39. See for example the editorial in the *Cape Times*, 14 March 1991, titled "Press-bashing can end in bloodshed."

40. Frank Meintjies, "SA's press arrives at a strange crossroad of darkness and light," Supplement to the *Weekly Mail*, 30 May 1991.

41. Lawrence Peter, *Peter's Quotations* (London: Methuen, 1982), 203.

Chapter 9

1. Constitutional Guidelines of the African National Congress. Published in the *South African Journal on Human Rights* 5 (1989), 129–132.

2. Max du Preez and Anton Harber. Interviews with the author. Johannesburg, 11 September 1989 and 19 September 1989 respectively.

3. Pallo Jordan, "Monopoly capitalism, racism and mass media in South Africa," *Sechaba*, May 1985, 8.

4. Ibid., 9.

5. Jo-Anne Collinge, Herbert Mabuza, Glenn Moss, and David Niddrie, "What the papers don't say," *Index on Censorship* 17 (March 1988), 36.

6. Jonathan Hobday. Untitled speech, delivered in Durban, August 1990.

7. See for example Göran Hedebro, "Communication policy in Sweden: An experiment in state intervention," in *Communication Policy in Developed Countries*, ed. Patricia Edgar and Syed A. Rahim (London: Kegan Paul International, 1983), 137–165.

8. Richard Steyn, "Media freedom in a liberal-democratic South Africa," *Reality* 21 (May 1989), 6–7.

9. Collinge et al., "What the papers don't say," 36.

10. *Business Futures* 1989 (Bellville, South Africa: Institute for Futures Research: 1989), 526.

11. Quoted in Michael D. McGrath, "Income redistribution: The economic challenge of the 1990s," in *Critical Choices for South Africa: An Agenda for the 1990s*, ed. Robert Schrire (Cape Town: Oxford University Press, 1990), 95. Note that the figure is quoted for "Indians," not "Asians," the customary grouping that also includes South Africans of Chinese extraction.

12. Hobday speech.

13. Ibid.

14. Ibid.

15. Ibid.

16. Peter McLean. Interview with the author. Johannesburg, 25 January 1990.

17. *Business Futures 1989*, 72. These figures include the homeland populations.

18. Mike Leahy and Paul Voice, eds., *SARAD Media Yearbook 1989* (Johannesburg: WTH Publications, 1989), 63.

19. "Is print the advertising medium suitable for you?" *Marketing Mix*, November–December 1987, 34.

20. Ibid.

21. "Is print the advertising medium," 34.

22. Quoted in John Battersby, "When we look at the world, do we all see it the same way?" *Journalist*, March 1981, 6.

23. Ibid.

24. Ken Owen, "The way forward: The press in South Africa," in *South Africa: The Road Ahead*, ed. G. F. Jacobs (Johannesburg: Jonathan Ball, 1986), 239.

25. John Patten. Interview with the author. Johannesburg, 25 January 1990.

26. For more on MWASA see for example Ameen Akhalwaya, "Why senior black journalists are leaving," *Journalist*, February/March 1987, 12–13; Denis Beckett, "Beneath the surface of the MWASA strike," *Ecquid Novi* 2 (1981), 38–48; "What comes after BC?" *Journalist*, March 1984, 7.

27. Anthony Mathews, "National security, freedom and reform," in *Critical Choices for South Africa: An agenda for the* 1990s, ed. Robert Schrire (Cape Town: Oxford University Press, 1990), 57–76.

28. Nic Olivier, "A bill of rights," in *Critical Choices for South Africa: An Agenda for the* 1990s, ed. Robert Schrire (Cape Town: Oxford University Press, 1990), 31–56.

29. See for example South African Law Commission, *Project 58: Group and Human Rights* (Pretoria: South African Law Commission, 1989), chap. 16.

30. See for example John Dugard, "The quest for a liberal democracy in South Africa," *Acta Juridica* (1987), 237–258; and South African Law Commission, *Project 58*, 213–214.

31. Anthony S. Mathews, "Legislation and civil liberties in South Africa," *Optima* 32 (March 1984), 12–13.

32. Ibid., 12.

33. The Commission is a quasiofficial group that "consists of judges, members of the Bar and Law Society, academics and officials of the Department of Justice." Olivier, "A bill of rights," 40.

34. Ibid., 43.

35. ANC Constitutional Guidelines, 131.

36. Dugard, "Quest for liberal democracy," 254.

37. *Pretoria News*, 7 July 1989.

Chapter 10

1. Andre Brink, *Mapmakers: Writing in a State of Siege* (London and Boston: Faber and Faber, 1983), 166–167.

2. Fred S. Siebert, Theodore Peterson, and Wilbur Schramm, *Four Theories of the Press* (Urbana: University of Illinois Press, 1956).

3. Denis McQuail, *Mass Communication Theory: An Introduction* (London and Beverly Hills: Sage, 1983), 84.

4. For an analysis of these theories to the South African situation, and an evaluation of their applicability, see Arnold S. de Beer, "Mass media coverage of developing countries: A functional approach," *Politikon* 14 (December 1987), 70–78.

5. McQuail, *Mass Communication Theory*, 86.

6. Ibid., 91–92.

7. Ibid., 95–96.

8. Lawrence Schlemmer, "Prospects for a liberal society in South Africa," in *Democratic Liberalism in South Africa: Its History and Prospect*, ed. Jeffrey Butler, Richard Elphick, and David Welsh (Middletown, Conn.: Wesleyan University Press, and Cape Town: David Philip, 1987), 389.

9. Ibid., 391.

10. De Beer, "Mass media coverage."

11. For statistics on needs in these areas, see for example *Business Futures 1989* (Bellville, South Africa: Institute for Futures Research, 1989).

12. David Lamb, *The Africans* (New York: Vintage Books, 1984), 252–253.

13. Ibid., 245.

14. Ibid., 243.

15. For a useful introduction to some of the literature on this issue see McQuail, *Mass Communication Theory*.

16. John Dugard, "The quest for a liberal democracy in South Africa," *Acta Juridica* (1987), 237.

17. Jeffrey Butler, Richard Elphick, and David Welsh, eds., "Editors' Introduction," in *Democratic Liberalism in South Africa*, 11.

18. James Leatt, Theo Kniefel, and Klaus Nürnberger, eds., *Contending Ideologies in South Africa* (Cape Town: David Philip, 1986), 62–63.

19. Dugard, "The quest for a liberal democracy," 237.

20. Schlemmer, "Prospects for a liberal society," 396–397.

21. See for example Pierre van den Berghe, "The impossibility of a liberal solution in South Africa," in *The Liberal Dilemma in South Africa*, ed. Pierre van den Berghe (London: Croom Helm, 1979), 56–67.

22. Schlemmer, "Prospects for a liberal society," 397–398.

23. Edmund Lambeth, *Committed Journalism* (Bloomington: Indiana University Press, 1986), 27.

24. Ibid.

25. Ibid., 30.

26. Ibid., 31.

27. Ibid.

28. Ibid., 32.

29. Ibid., 33.

30. Ibid., 34.

31. Ibid., 35.

32. Ibid.

33. Ibid., 37.

34. Ibid., 38.

35. Ibid., 177.

36. Howard Barrell, "From fringe to formative intervention in the South African press," paper presented at the Culture for Another South Africa conference in Amsterdam, December 1987, 10.

37. Glenn Moss. Transcript of an address titled "Progressive and advocacy journalism," given to the Association of Democratic Journalists (Transvaal), 8 March 1988, p. 2.

38. Richard Steyn, "The press's responsibility in a polarised society," *Theoria* (May 1987), 22.

39. Ibid., 23.

40. Ibid.

41. Ibid.

42. Ken Owen, "The way forward: The press in South Africa," in *South Africa: The Road Ahead*, ed. G. F. Jacobs (Johannesburg: Jonathan Ball, 1986), 250.

43. Lambeth, *Committed Journalism*, 179.

44. Quoted in *Speaking of a Free Press: 200 Years of Notable Quotations About Press Freedoms* (Washington, D.C.: American Newspaper Publishers Association Foundation, 1987), 11.

Bibliography

Addison, Graeme. "Total Strategy as total propaganda: The socialization of danger." Paper presented at the Association for Sociology in Southern Africa conference, Maseru, Lesotho, June 1980.

Akhalwaya, Ameen. "The role of the alternative press." *Nieman Reports* 42 (Winter 1988): 14–18.

―――. "Through the loopholes." *Index on Censorship* 17 (March 1988): 24–26.

―――. "Why senior black journalists are leaving." *Journalist*, February/March 1987, pp. 12–13.

Allen, John. "Examining the workings of the Media Council." *Journalist*, September 1983, pp. 4–6.

Anderson, Mary A. "Newspaper marketing." *presstime*, January 1989, pp. 26–29.

Armour, Denise. "*Mail:* What now?" *Journalist*, February/March 1987, p. 1.

Armstrong, Amanda. "'Hear no evil, see no evil, speak no evil': Media restrictions and the state of emergency." In *South African Review No. 4*, edited by Glenn Moss and Ingrid Obery, pp. 199–214. Johannesburg: Ravan Press, 1987.

Aymes, Gisele W. "The newspaper: Where to from here?" *Marketing Mix*, October 1989, pp. 53–56.

Barrell, Howard. "From fringe to formative intervention in the South African press." Paper presented at the Culture for Another South Africa conference, Amsterdam, 1987.

Barton, Frank. *The Press in Africa: Persecution and Perseverance*. New York: Africana, 1979.

Battersby, John. "When we look at the world, do we all see it the same way?" *Journalist*, March 1981, pp. 6–7.

Bauer, Charlotte. "Disinvited." *Index on Censorship* 17 (November/December 1988): 33.

Beckett, Denis. "Beneath the surface of the MWASA strike." *Ecquid Novi* 2 (1981): 38–48.

Bell, Paul. "Turn of the tide." *Leadership SA* 9:6 (August 1990): 38–40.

―――. "A winter's tale." *Leadership SA* 8:5 (1989): 19–41.

Berger, Peter L., and Bobby Godsell, eds. *A Future South Africa: Visions, Strategies and Realities*. Boulder, Colo.: Westview Press, 1988.

Bleazard, David. "The Media Council dilemma." *Journalist*, October 1983, pp. 4–5.

Boesak, Allan, and Rashid Seria. Proposal for a weekly newspaper project and a journalism training project. No date.

Brewer, John. "The police in South African politics." In *South Africa: No Turning Back*, edited by Shaun Johnson, pp. 258–279. Bloomington and Indianapolis: Indiana University Press, 1989.

Brink, Andre. *Mapmakers: Writing in a State of Siege*. London and Boston: Faber and Faber, 1983.

Broughton, Morris. *Press and Politics of South Africa*. Cape Town: Purnell and Sons, 1960.

Brown, Trevor. "Free press fair game for South Africa's government." *Journalism Quarterly* 48 (Spring 1971): 120–127.

Bundy, Colin. "Waarvoor is Stoffel bang?" (What is Stoffel afraid of?) *Die Suid-Afrikaan*, August 1988, pp. 38–39.

Bunting, Brian. "South African journalists in the front line." *Sechaba*, April 1989, pp. 8–15.

Burns, Y. M. "Freedom of the press: A comparative legal study." LLD thesis, University of South Africa, 1984.

———. "Freedom of the press in South Africa." In *South Africa: A Plural Society in Transition*, edited by D. J. van Vuuren, pp. 221–256. Durban: Butterworths, 1985.

———. "Freedom of the press in the realm of state security." *De Jure* 18 (June 1985): 60–69.

Business Futures 1989. Bellville, South Africa: Institute for Futures Research, 1989.

Butler, Jeffrey, Richard Elphick, and David Welsh, eds. *Democratic Liberalism in South Africa: Its History and Prospect*. Middletown, Conn.: Wesleyan University Press, and Cape Town: David Philip, 1987.

Catto, Henry. "End of the line: South Africa's defunct *Rand Daily Mail*." *Washington Journalism Review*, September 1985, pp. 20–23.

"Censorship." *Reality* 21 (January 1989): 3.

Chimutengwende, Chenhamo. *South Africa: The Press and Politics of Liberation*. London: Barbican Books, 1979.

Coggin, Theo. "A liberal perspective on freedom of speech." Address to the Institute for a Democratic Alternative for South Africa, Durban, 5 November 1988.

———. ed. *Censorship*. Johannesburg: South African Institute of Race Relations, 1983.

Collinge, Jo-Anne, Herbert Mabuza, Glenn Moss, and David Niddrie, "What the papers don't say." *Index on Censorship* 17 (March 1988): 27–36.

Constitutional Guidelines of the African National Congress. Published in the *South African Journal on Human Rights* 5 (1989): 131–132.

Davies, Rob, Dan O'Meara, and Sipho Dlamini. *The Struggle for South Africa: A Reference Guide to Movements, Organizations and Institutions*. Vol. 2. London: Zed Books, 1984.

Davis, D. M. "Steyn Commission—Methodology." In *Distrust in Democracy: A Lawyers for Human Rights Commentary on the Report of the Steyn Commission of Inquiry into the Mass Media*, pp. 23–41. N.p.: Lawyers for Human Rights, 1982.

Dean, W.H.B. "The Commission's response to the 'Total Onslaught.'" In *Distrust in Democracy: A Lawyers for Human Rights Commentary on the Report of the Steyn Commission of Inquiry into the Mass Media*, pp. 57–75. N.p.: Lawyers for Human Rights, 1982.

de Beer, Arnold S. "Mass media coverage of developing countries: A functional approach." *Politikon* (Stellenbosch) 14 (December 1987): 70–77.

_____ . "Pers en party: 'N huwelik of 'n heilige koei?" (Press and party: A marriage or a sacred cow?) *Aambeeld* (Johannesburg) 15 (June 1987): 23–25.

_____ . "The press in post-apartheid South Africa: A functional analysis." *Communicare* 8 (1989): 29–39.

_____ . "Die professionaliseering van die joernalistieke koerantberoep in Suid-Afrika." (The professionalization of newspaper journalism in South Africa.) *Communicatio* 3 (1977): 9–14.

de Beer, Cedric, and Daryl Glaser. "Debating liberalism in the 1980s." *Work in Progress* 31 (May 1984): 4–13.

de Beer, Zac. "Batten down the budgets." In "Advertising," supplement to *Financial Mail*, 22 August 1986, pp. 54–57.

de Klerk, Willem. "Etiek en die pers" (Ethics and the press). *Ecquid Novi* 3 (1982): 45–51.

_____ . "Newspapers need to be more patriotic." In "Issue," supplement to *Frontline*, Spring 1982, pp. 8–10.

_____ . "The press and political change in South Africa." In *Change in South Africa*, edited by D. J. van Vuuren, pp. 334–344. Durban: Butterworths, 1983.

de Kock, Wessel. *A Manner of Speaking: The Origins of the Press in South Africa.* Cape Town: Saayman and Weber, 1982.

Dennis, Everette E., and John Merrill. *Basic Issues in Mass Communication.* New York: Macmillan, 1984.

de Villiers, Dawid. "The state of the press." *Leadership SA* 2 (1983): 38–48.

de Villiers, Rene. "Threats to press freedom in South Africa." *Janus* (Cape Town) (1979): 1–13.

de Villiers, Riaan. "Zwelakhe Sisulu." *Leadership SA* 5 (1986): 84–92.

Devenish, G. E. "A critical review of inroads into press freedom in South Africa." *Business SA* 15 (May 1980): 30–35.

Diamond, Edwin, and Steven Bram with Karen Wishod. "Has South Africa won its battle to control the news?" *TV Guide*, 10 May 1986, pp. 4–10.

Different Realities: A HAP Focus Comparing the Star Africa and City Late Editions. N.p.: Human Awareness Project, 1985.

Dison, David. "Tightening the screw." *Leadership SA* 6 (1987): 15–19.

Distrust in Democracy: A Lawyers for Human Rights Commentary on the Report of the Steyn Commission of Inquiry into the Mass Media. N.p.: Lawyers for Human Rights, 1982.

Dommisse, Ebbe. "The changing role of the Afrikaans press." In *The Afrikaners*, edited by Edwin S. Munger, pp. 95–106. Cape Town: Tafelberg, 1979.

Dugard, John. *Human Rights and the South African Legal Order.* Princeton: Princeton University Press, 1978.

———— . "The quest for a liberal democracy in South Africa." *Acta Juridica* (Cape Town), 1987: 237–258.

Duodo, Cameron. "*Cape Times:* Editor faces imprisonment after breaking censorship rule." *Index on Censorship* 15 (January 1986): 8–10.

———— . "South Africa cracks down on foreign journalists." *Index on Censorship* 14 (December 1985): inside back cover.

du Plessis, Sylvia. "*Rand Daily Mail* chronology." Mimeographed. Department of Journalism and Media Studies, Rhodes University, 1988.

du Plessis, W., and N.J.J. Olivier. "Persvryheid: Quo vadis?" (Press freedom: Quo vadis?). *Ecquid Novi* 9 (1988): 33–51.

du Toit, Andre. "The Steyn Commission and the theory of the Total Onslaught." *South African Outlook* 112 (April 1982): 51–54.

"Editor pays record deposit for right to publish newest opposition paper." *IPI Report,* February 1989, p. 6.

Emdon, Clive. "Alternative media in the region: Durban newspaper group and ADJ projects 1986–88." Paper presented to workshop "Regionalism and restructuring in Natal," University of Natal, Durban, 28–31 January 1988.

Faure, Corrie. "Koerantsubsidies, persvryheid en M-net." (Newspaper subsidies, press freedom, and M-net) *Communicatio* 13 (1987): 31–44.

Fink, Conrad. *Strategic Newspaper Management.* Belmont, Calif.: Wadsworth, 1988.

Finnegan, William. *Dateline Soweto.* New York: Harper and Row, 1988.

Fitzgerald, Mark. "Survey: South Africa's restrictions result in less U.S. coverage." *Editor and Publisher,* 28 December 1985, p. 13.

Foisie, Jack, John G. Ryan, Ameen Akhalwaya, and Ton Vosloo, "Update: The press in South Africa." *Nieman Reports* 36 (Summer 1982): 23–28.

Frankel, Philip. "Race and counter-revolution: South Africa's 'Total Strategy.'" *Journal of Commonwealth and Comparative Politics* 18 (November 1980): 272–292.

Franks, Peter E. "Perceptual dynamics in South Africa: A textual analysis of the press coverage during the 1987 election." In *South African Election 1987,* edited by D. J. van Vuuren, L. Schlemmer, H. C. Marais, and J. Latakgomo, pp. 167–186. Pinetown: Owen Burgess, 1987.

Frederikse, Julie. "South Africa's media: The commercial press and the seedlings of the future." *Third World Quarterly* 9 (April 1987): 638–656.

"The Freedom Charter of South Africa." Reprinted in *Mission to South Africa: The Commonwealth Report,* pp. 157–160. Harmondsworth: Penguin, 1986.

Gandar, Laurence. "The giant sleeps on." Reprinted in *Journalist,* April 1985, p. 12.

———— . "The *Mail* died but it did not have to die." *Journalist,* February/March 1987, p. 24.

Gibson, Rex. "The press we deserve." In "Issue," supplement to *Frontline,* Spring 1982, pp. 20–22.

Giffard, C. A. "Circulation trends in South Africa." *Journalism Quarterly* 57 (Spring 1980): 86–91.

―――― . "The impact of television on South African daily newspapers." *Journalism Quarterly* 57 (Summer 1980): 216–223.

―――― . "The role of the media in a changing South Africa." *Gazette* 46 (1990): 143–153.

―――― . "South African attitudes toward news media." *Journalism Quarterly* 53 (Winter 1976): 653–660.

Giliomee, Hermann, and Lawrence Schlemmer. *Negotiating South Africa's Future.* Cape Town: Oxford University Press, 1989.

Gillwald, A. " 'A black coup': Inkatha and the sale of *Ilanga.*" *Transformation* (Durban) 7 (1988): 27–36.

Glaser, Daryl. "Liberalism in the 1980s." *Work in Progress* 30 (February 1984): 12–19.

Graaf, Michael, ed. *Hawks and Doves: The Pro- and Anti-Conscription Press in South Africa.* Durban: Contemporary Cultural Studies Unit, University of Natal, 1988.

Greenblo, Allan. "Press in a squeeze." *Finance Week,* 30 September 1982, pp. 9–13.

―――― . "Rather be damned: Assessing when to publish and when not." *Finance Week,* 22 August 1985, pp. 580–581.

―――― . "Star wars: Argus prepares to take on the *Sunday Times.*" *Finance Week,* 26 July 1984, pp. 179–180.

Grey, Madi. "Coercion, control and censorship." *Media Development* 32 (1985): 25–28.

"Grey readership." *Financial Mail,* 7 October 1988, p. 92.

Grogan, John. *The Media Emergency Regulations, 1988: A Guide for Journalists.* Occasional paper no. 2. Grahamstown, South Africa: Department of Journalism and Media Studies, Rhodes University, 1988.

―――― . "News control by decree: An examination of the South African government's power to control information by administrative action." *South African Law Journal* 103 (February 1986): 118–135.

Grogan, John, and Charles Riddle. "South Africa's press in the eighties: Darkness descends." *Gazette* 39 (1987): 3–16.

Grundy, Kenneth W. *The Militarization of South African Politics.* Bloomington: Indiana University Press, 1986.

Hachten, William. "Black journalists under apartheid." *Index on Censorship* 8 (May/June 1979): 43–48.

―――― . "Mass media in South Africa: The view from without." In *English-Speaking South Africa Today,* edited by Andre de Villiers, pp. 331–341. Cape Town: Oxford University Press, 1976.

―――― . *Muffled Drums: The News Media in Africa.* Ames: Iowa State University Press, 1971.

―――― . "Policies and performance of South African television." *Journal of Communication* 29 (Summer 1979): 62–72.

Hachten, William, and C. A. Giffard. *The Press and Apartheid: Repression and Propaganda in South Africa.* Madison: University of Wisconsin Press, 1984. Also published as *Total Onslaught: The South African Press Under Attack.* Johannesburg: Macmillan, 1984.

Harber, Anton. "Behind closed doors: Media murders." *Work in Progress* 35 (April 1985): 3–6.

———. "Even bigger scissors." *Index on Censorship* 16 (November/December 1987): 13–14.

———. "Finding the loopholes." *Index on Censorship* 16 (April 1987): 22–24.

———. "The press and the battle for the right of expression in South Africa today." *Monitor*, special edition titled "Human rights in South Africa 1988," 1989, pp. 67–70.

———. "The register of news agencies." *Index on Censorship* 17 (August 1988): 25–27.

———. "Soul of the white ant." *Leadership SA* 7 (1988): 93–94.

Heard, Anthony H. *The Cape of Storms: A Personal History of the Crisis in South Africa.* Fayetteville and London: University of Arkansas Press, 1990.

———. "Caution is the watchword." *Index on Censorship* 15 (August 1986): 7–8.

———. "Don't forget who pays you . . ." *Journalist*, December 1984, p. 11.

———. "How I was fired." *Index on Censorship* 16 (November/December 1987): 9–12.

———. "The media blackout." *Africa Report* 31 (March/April 1986): 57–59.

———. "New emergency regulations." *South African Outlook* 117 (July 1987): 75–76.

———. "The press in South Africa: Twilight of freedom?" In *The South African Quagmire*, edited by S. Prakash Sethi, pp. 253–262. Cambridge, Mass.: Ballinger, 1987.

———. "Risking life and liberty in South Africa." *Washington Journalism Review*, January 1986, pp. 34–39.

Hedebro, Göran. "Communication policy in Sweden: An experiment in state intervention." In *Communication Policy in Developed Countries*, edited by Patricia Edgar and Syed A. Rahim, pp. 137–165. London: Kegan Paul International, 1983.

Herbst, D.A.S. "The role of the press in the political process." In *Political Alternatives for South Africa*, edited by D. J. van Vuuren and D. J. Kriek, pp. 384–399. Durban: Butterworths, 1983.

Hobday, Jonathan. Untitled address, delivered in Durban, August 1990.

Hocking, William. *Freedom of the Press: A Framework of Principle.* Chicago: University of Chicago Press, 1947.

Howard, Rhoda E. *Human Rights in Commonwealth Africa.* Totowa, N.J.: Rowman and Littlefield, 1986.

"How to mix the marketing mix—A debate on how to reach buying power in South Africa." *Marketing Mix*, November/December 1987, pp. 10–20.

Human Rights Commission. "Banning and restriction of organizations." Fact paper no. 2. Human Rights Commission, Braamfontein, January 1989.

Huntington, Samuel P. *Political Order in Changing Societies.* New Haven, Conn.: Yale University Press, 1968.

Huntington, Samuel P., and Joan Nelson. *No Easy Choice: Political Participation in Developing Countries.* Cambridge: Harvard University Press, 1976.

"Is print the advertising medium suitable for you?" *Marketing Mix*, November/December 1987, p. 34.

Jackson, Gordon S. *The Prison Exposés and Muldergate: A Case Study in Changing Government-Press Relations in South Africa*. Bloomington: African Studies Program, Indiana University, 1980.

―――― . "The secular and the sacred: A comparative study of the daily and religious press in South Africa." PhD dissertation. Indiana University, Bloomington, Indiana, 1983.

―――― . "TV2: The introduction of television for blacks in South Africa." *Gazette* 29 (1982): 155–171.

Jaffar, Mansoor. Untitled address to the annual congress of the South African Society of Journalists. N.p., 13 May 1988.

Johnson, Shaun. "Barometers of the liberation movement: A history of South Africa's alternative press." *Media Development* 32 (Summer 1985): 18–21.

Jordan, Pallo. "Monopoly capitalism, racism and mass media in South Africa." *Sechaba*, May 1985, pp. 2–9.

Kenyon, Roger. "No wonder people have stopped reading newspapers." Reprinted in *Journalist*, November 1986, p. 12.

"Kill the messenger." *Financial Mail*, 1 November 1985, pp. 43–44.

Klaaste, Aggrey. "MWASA and the Steyn Commission." *South African Outlook* 112 (April 1982): 54–56.

Krüger, Rosa Thelma. "Die krisis van die dagbladpers" (The crisis of the daily newspaper). MA thesis, Rand Afrikaans University, Johannesburg, 1985.

Krüger, R., W. De Klerk, and N. Overton. "Die krisis van die dagbladpers: Ontleding van bepaalde faktore wat die hedendaagse dagblad beinvloed" (The crisis of the daily newspaper: Analysis of specific factors that influence the present-day daily). *Communicare* 5 (1986): 34–52.

Lacob, Miriam. "South Africa: Battling the ban." *Columbia Journalism Review*, March/April 1986, pp. 13–15.

―――― . "South Africa's 'free' press." *Columbia Journalism Review*, November/December 1982, pp. 49–56.

Lamb, David. *The Africans*. New York: Vintage Books, 1984.

―――― . "Endangered species." *Nieman Reports* 36 (Autumn 1982): 22–23.

Lambeth, Edmund. *Committed Journalism*. Bloomington: Indiana University Press, 1986.

Latakgomo, Joe. "Caught in the middle." In "Issue," supplement to *Frontline*, Spring 1982, pp. 26–27.

Leahy, Mike, and Paul Voice, eds. *SARAD Media Yearbook 1989*. Johannesburg: WTH Publications, 1989.

Leatt, James, Theo Kniefel, and Klaus Nürnberger, eds. *Contending Ideologies in South Africa*. Cape Town: David Philip, 1986.

Lee, Patrick. "Gentlemen of the press . . ." *Leadership SA* 4 (1985): 82–97.

Lefort, Rene. "The 'Black' press in South Africa." *International Social Sciences Journal* 33 (1981): 99–121.

Lemon, Anthony. *Apartheid in Transition*. Boulder, Colo.: Westview Press, 1987.

Lewis, Sue. "Stephen Mulholland: A man of action." *Marketing Mix*, May 1989, pp. 12–14.

Louw, Chris. "Afrikaanse koerante in 'n noodtoestand" (Afrikaans papers in a crisis). *Die Suid-Afrikaan*, February 1989, pp. 18–21.

Louw, Nick. "Do newspapers rate? How much longer can they keep charging more for less?" *Marketing Mix*, July 1986, pp. 26–29.

Louw, P. Eric. "'Consensus journalism': A critique with reference to the dialectical paradigm." *Communicatio* 11 (1985): 60–63.

––––––. "The emergence of a progressive-alternative press in South Africa with specific reference to *Grassroots*." *Communicatio* 15:2 (1989): 26–32.

––––––. "The English and Afrikaans press in South Africa: One press or two?" *Communicatio* 9 (1983): 14–16.

––––––. "The libertarian theory of the press: How appropriate in the South African context?" *Communicatio* 10 (1984): 31–37.

Louw, Raymond. "Remember the days when a newspaper told us the news?" *Weekly Mail*, 20 December 1985, p. 9.

McClurg, James. "The one-eyed watchdog." *Ecquid Novi* 3 (1982): 31–35.

––––––. "Toeing the line." *Leadership SA* 5 (1986): 76–79.

McGrath, Michael D. "Income redistribution: The economic challenges of the 1990s." In *Critical Choices for South Africa: An Agenda for the* 1990s, edited by Robert Schrire, pp. 92–108. Cape Town: Oxford University Press, 1990.

McGregor, R. W. *Who Owns Who in the Newspaper Industry*. Cape Town: Purdy Press, 1982.

McQuail, Denis. *Mass Communication Theory: An Introduction*. London and Beverly Hills: Sage, 1983.

Manheim, Jarol B., and Robert B. Albritton. "Insurgent violence versus image management: The struggle for national images in Southern Africa." *British Journal of Political Science* 17 (1987): 201–218.

Manning, Richard. *They Cannot Kill Us All: An Eyewitness Account of South Africa Today*. Boston: Houghton-Mifflin, 1987.

Manoim, Irwin. "Getting the press to do its own dirty work." *Critical Arts* 2 (1982): iv–ix.

Marcus, Gilbert. "Blacks treated more severely." *Index on Censorship* 13 (December 1984): 14–21.

––––––. "Fanning revolution, unrest and violence: A case study of censorship under the emergency." *Harvard Human Rights Yearbook* 2 (Spring 1989): 125–135.

––––––. "Fine distinctions: Scientific censorship and the courts." *South African Journal on Human Rights* 4 (1988): 82–86.

––––––. "The gagging writs." *Reality* 19 (May 1987): 8–10.

––––––. "Reasonable censorship?" In *Essays on Law and Social Practice in South Africa*, edited by Hugh Corder, pp. 349–360. Cape Town: Juta, 1988.

Massing, Michael. "Letter from South Africa." *Columbia Journalism Review* 25 (January/February 1987), pp. 35–39.

Mathews, Anthony S. "Censorship, access to information and public debate." *Theoria* (Pietermaritzburg) 55 (October 1980): 21–31.

_____ . "Crossing the threshold." *Leadership SA* 5 (1986): 49–55.

_____ . *The Darker Reaches of Government*. Cape Town: Juta, and Berkeley and Los Angeles: University of California Press, 1978.

_____ . *Freedom, State Security and the Rule of Law: Dilemmas of the Apartheid Society*. Cape Town: Juta, 1986.

_____ . "Legislation and civil liberties in South Africa." *Optima* 32 (March 1984): 11–15.

_____ . "National security, freedom and reform." In *Critical Choices for South Africa: An Agenda for the 1990s*, edited by Robert Schrire, pp. 57–76. Cape Town: Oxford University Press, 1990.

Mau-Mauing the Media: New Censorship for the New South Africa. Johannesburg: South African Institute of Race Relations, 1991.

"The media policy debate." *Rhodes University Journalism Review* 1:1 (November 1990): 33–58.

Meintjies, Frank. "SA's press arrives at a strange crossroad of darkness and light." Supplement to the *Weekly Mail*, 30 May 1991.

Mervis, Joel. "Can press freedom survive in South Africa?" In *South African Conference on the Survival of the Press and Education for Journalism*. Grahamstown, South Africa: Department of Journalism, Rhodes University, 1979; no page numbers.

_____ . "Case for a free press." *South African Outlook* 112 (April 1982): 62–64.

_____ . "Editors and politics." *Leadership SA* 3 (1984): 66–72.

_____ . *The Fourth Estate: A Newspaper Story*. Johannesburg: Jonathan Ball, 1989.

_____ . "The shadow over press freedom and the light in the darkness." *Ecquid Novi* 3 (1982): 26–30.

Mische, Annemarie. "Koerantapartheid en die onluste" (Newspaper apartheid and the unrest). *Die Suid-Afrikaan*, Summer 1985, pp. 8–10.

Mission to South Africa: The Commonwealth Report. Harmondsworth: Penguin, 1986.

Moche, Victor. "Towards a democratic post-apartheid media." Paper presented at the Cultural Alternatives for South Africa Conference, Amsterdam, December 1987.

Moseki, M. "Black journalists under apartheid." *Index on Censorship* 17 (August 1988): 22–24.

Moss, Glenn. "Progressive and advocacy journalism." Talk given to Association of Democratic Journalists (Transvaal), Johannesburg, 8 March 1988.

Motau, Sejamothopo. "Writing for black readers: Responsibilities, obligations and problems of the black journalist in South Africa." *Communicare* 2 (1981): 40–47.

Muller, P. J. "The media and security forces: Is a joint strategy possible?" *Communicare* 5 (1986): 29–33.

Murray, Hugh. "Blueblood blues." *Leadership SA* 6 (1987): 53–54.

Murray, Martin. *South Africa: Time of Agony, Time of Destiny*. London: Verso, 1987.

Nadel, Laura, and Aryeh Neier. *South Africa and Zimbabwe: The Freest Presses in Africa?* New York: Committee to Protect Journalists, Inc., 1983.

Nel, Louis. "The freedom of the press and the freedom of television." *Ecquid Novi* 8 (1987): 73–77.

"Newspapers 'still versatile.'" *Marketing Mix*, June 1985, p. 39.

Niddrie, David. "The commercial press: Selling up or selling out?" *Work in Progress* 48 (July 1987): 23–27.

Niddrie, David, and Howard Barrell. "The South African mass media in a post-apartheid society." Paper presented at the conference "The Southern African economy after apartheid," at the University of York, 29 September to 2 October 1986.

O'Connor, H. E. "Fairburn memorial address to Southern Africa Society of Journalists." Address given in Port Elizabeth, 4 May 1989.

Olivier, Nic. "A bill of rights." In *Critical Choices for South Africa: An Agenda for the 1990s*, edited by Robert Schrire, pp. 31–56. Cape Town: Oxford University Press, 1990.

Omar, Dullah. "The role of the independent press." *South African Outlook* 118 (February 1988): 26–27.

O'Meara, Patrick. "South Africa's Watergate: The Muldergate scandals." American Universities Field Staff Reports, No. 43, 1979.

Owen, Ken. "Like a sapper into a minefield." In "Issue," supplement to *Frontline*, Spring 1982, pp. 16–19.

―――. "Of broadsides and broadsheets." *Leadership SA* 3 (1984): 46–55.

―――. "The way forward: The press in South Africa." In *South Africa: The Road Ahead*, edited by G. F. Jacobs, pp. 231–250. Johannesburg: Jonathan Ball, 1986.

―――. "Whose ox is gored?" *Communicare* 7 (1988): 67–69.

Pakendorf, Harald. "The Afrikaner press: Free to a degree." In *The South African Quagmire*, edited by S. Prakash Sethi, pp. 263–267. Cambridge, Mass.: Ballinger, 1987.

―――. "Kortvat van die pers: 'N seker onheilspad" (Disciplining the press: A sure road to disaster). *Woord en Daad*, November 1988, pp. 4–5.

Patel, Leila. "How small media can organize communities." *Media Development* 32 (Summer 1985): 12–14.

Phelan, John M. *Apartheid Media: Disinformation and Dissent in South Africa*. Westport, Conn.: Lawrence Hill, 1987.

Pinnock, Don. "Popularize, organize, educate and mobilize: Some reflections on South Africa's left-wing press in the 1980's." Paper presented to the conference of the Association for Sociology in South Africa, Johannesburg, July 1989.

"P is for press war." *Work in Progress* 33 (1984): 13–16.

Pogrund, Benjamin. "Paying the price for being brave." *Journalist*, April 1985, pp. 10–11.

Pollak, Richard. *Up Against Apartheid: The Role and Plight of the Press in South Africa*. Carbondale: Southern Illinois University Press, 1981.

Potter, Elaine. *The Press as Opposition: The Political Role of South African Newspapers*. Totowa, N.J.: Rowman and Littlefield, 1975.

"The press." *Work in Progress* 12 (1980): 30–33.

"The press: A response." *Work in Progress* 13 (July 1980): 62–64.

Race Relations Survey (from 1984; previously titled *Survey of Race Relations*). Johannesburg: South African Institute of Race Relations; annual.

Reed, Dick. "It's larger than life! Television towers above other media in ad-spend growth rate." *Marketing Mix,* June 1986, pp. 14–16.

Rees, Mervyn, and Chris Day. *Muldergate: The Story of the Info Scandal.* Johannesburg: Macmillan, 1980.

Report on the launch of *New Nation.* Unpublished report.

Republic of South Africa. *Report of the Commission of Inquiry into the Mass Media,* PR 89, 3 volumes. Pretoria: Government Printer, 1981.

———. *Report of the Commission of Inquiry into the Reporting of Security News from South African Defence Force and Police,* PR 52. Pretoria: Government Printer, 1980.

———. The South African Competition Board, Report No. 16. *Acquisition by Argus Printing and Publishing Company Limited of the Newspaper Interests of Robinson and Company (Pty) Limited.* Pretoria: Government Printer, 1986.

———. *Supplementary Report of Commission of Inquiry into the Mass Media,* PR 13. Pretoria: Government Printer, 1982.

Roelofse, K. "*Rand Daily Mail:* Die dood in perspektief" (*Rand Daily Mail:* The death in perspective). *Communicatio* 11 (1985): 30–37.

———. *Towards Rational Discourse: An Analysis of the Steyn Commission of Enquiry into the Media.* Pretoria: Van Schaik, 1983.

Rubin, Barry. "The uncertain future of South Africa's press." *Washington Journalism Review,* November 1980, pp. 41–45.

Rubin, Bernard. "Afrikaner view of press and government." *Nieman Reports* 36 (Winter 1982): 37–42.

Schechter, Danny. "South Africa: Where did the story go?" *Africa Report* 33 (March/April 1988): 27–31.

Schlemmer, Lawrence. "Prospects for a liberal society in South Africa." In *Democratic Liberalism in South Africa: Its History and Prospect,* edited by Jeffrey Butler, Richard Elphick, and David Welsh, pp. 384–398. Middletown, Conn.: Wesleyan University Press, and Cape Town: David Philip, 1987.

Schrire, Robert, ed. *Critical Choices for South Africa: An Agenda for the 1990s.* Cape Town: Oxford University Press, 1990.

Seiler, John. "A government against the world." *Africa Report* 22 (September/October 1979): 9–15.

Shaw, Gerald. "The English-language press." In *Democratic Liberalism in South Africa: Its History and Prospect,* edited by Jeffrey Butler, Richard Elphick, and David Welsh, pp. 288–300. Middletown, Conn.: Wesleyan University Press, and Cape Town: David Philip, 1987.

Siebert, Fred S., Theodore Peterson, and Wilbur Schramm. *Four Theories of the Press.* Urbana: University of Illinois Press, 1956.

Silber, Gus. "State of submergency." *Frontline,* August 1986, p. 17.

Simon, Alan. "Rhodesian immigrants in South Africa: Government, media and a lesson for South Africa." *African Affairs* 87 (1988): 53–68.

Singer, Eleanor, and Jacob Ludwig. "South Africa's press restrictions: Effects on press coverage and public opinion toward South Africa." *Public Opinion Quarterly* 51 (1987): 315–334.

Smith, H. Lindsay. *Behind the Press in South Africa.* Cape Town: Stewart, 1945.

"South Africa and the news: Conference report." *Nieman Reports* 40 (Autumn 1986): 25–28.

"South Africa: Controlling the news. Report of the media conference." *Nieman Reports* 42 (Autumn 1988): 38–49.

South African Conference on the Survival of the Press and Education for Journalism. Grahamstown, South Africa: Department of Journalism, Rhodes University, 1979.

"South African editor is arrested for publishing interview." *Editor and Publisher,* 16 November 1985, p. 20.

South Africa 1989–1990: Official Yearbook of the Republic of South Africa. Pretoria: Bureau for Information, 1989.

South African Law Commission. *Project 58: Group and Human Rights.* Pretoria: South African Law Commission, 1989.

"South African media: Who owns whom?" *Marketing Mix,* January 1984, pp. 50–51.

Sparks, Allister. "Closing of the *Rand Daily Mail.*" *Nieman Reports* 39 (Summer 1985): 17–19.

Speaking of a Free Press: 200 Years of Notable Quotations About Press Freedom. Washington, D.C.: American Newspaper Publishers Association Foundation, 1987.

Spence, J. E. "The military in South African politics." In *South Africa: No Turning Back,* edited by Shaun Johnson, pp. 240–257. Bloomington and Indianapolis: Indiana University Press, 1989.

Stewart, Gavin. "Demographics of the South African daily newspaper." Mimeographed. Grahamstown, South Africa: Department of Journalism and Media Studies, Rhodes University, 1985.

———. "Going the whole hog: The *Rand Daily Mail,* 1957–1985." Unpublished paper. Grahamstown, South Africa: Department of Journalism and Media Studies, Rhodes University, 1988.

———. "History of press control." *South African Outlook* 112 (April 1982): 67–68.

———. "Intimidation and prosecution of journalists." *Index on Censorship* 14 (July 1986): 24–40.

———. "Media as instruments of change in South Africa." Unpublished paper. Grahamstown, South Africa: Department of Journalism and Media Studies, Rhodes University, 1989.

———. "'Perfecting the free flow of information': Media control in South Africa, 12 June to 18 November 1986." *Index on Censorship* 15 (January 1987): 29–38.

———. "Policom 1987: Political news on South African television during the May election." In *South African Election 1987: Context, Process and Prospect,* edited by D. J. van Vuuren, L. Schlemmer, H. C. Marais, and J. Latakgomo, pp. 139–151. Pinetown: Owen Burgess, 1987.

_____ . "Propaganda, communication and the contest for power in South Africa." Unpublished paper. Grahamstown, South Africa: Department of Journalism and Media Studies, Rhodes University, 1987.

_____ . "Serving the governors." *South African Outlook* 110 (June 1980): 2–4.

_____ . "The South African press and the Steyn Report: A critical appraisal." *South Africa International* 12 (April 1982): 500–507.

_____ . "Trends in media use in South Africa: 1975–1984." Unpublished paper. Grahamstown, South Africa: Department of Journalism and Media Studies, Rhodes University, 1985.

_____ . "The Walls of Jericho," *Sunday Tribune*, 10 November 1985.

Stewart, Gavin, and Charles Riddle. "Three years on: The state of press freedom in South Africa." Updated version of paper presented to the Congress of the South African Society of Journalists, Port Elizabeth, 5 May 1989.

Steyn, Richard S. "An address at the graduation ceremony, University of Natal Pietermaritzburg, 1987." *Reality* 19 (July 1987): 15–17.

_____ . "Media freedom in a liberal-democratic South Africa." *Reality* 21 (May 1989): 6–7.

_____ . "The press and the right to know." Address to IDASA (Institute for a Democratic Alternative for South Africa) conference, Durban. 4 November 1988.

_____ . "The press's responsibility in a polarised society." *Theoria* (May 1987): 15–27.

Steyn, Robert C. "Media Council: Restoring the balance." Speech delivered at Rhodes University, 19 July 1989.

"The Steyn Commission." Editorial in *South African Outlook* 112 (April 1982): 50.

Strauss, S. A., M. J. Strydom, and J. C. van der Walt. *Mediareg* (Media law). 4th ed. by H. B. Klopper. Pretoria: Van Schaik, 1987.

Stuart, Kelsey, and Bell, Dewar and Hall. *Newspaperman's Guide to the Law.* 5th ed. Durban: Butterworths, 1990.

"Sunday, bloody Sunday . . ." *Financial Mail*, 27 July 1984, p. 31.

Switzer, Les. "Steyn Commission I: The press and Total Strategy." *Critical Arts* 1:4 (February 1981): 41–45.

Switzer, Les, and Donna Switzer. *The Black Press in South Africa and Lesotho.* Boston: Hall, 1979.

Thurow, Roger. "At one newspaper, gunshots and fires cover the reporters." *Wall Street Journal*, 10 August 1988.

Tomaselli, Keyan. "Community and the Progressive Press: A case study in finding our way." *Journal of Communication Enquiry* 12 (Winter 1988): 26–44.

_____ . "Die duiwel van verwoesting" (The devil of destruction). *Die Suid-Afrikaan*, February 1988, pp. 36–37.

_____ . "Race class and the South African progressive press." *International Journal of Intercultural Relations* 10 (1986): 53–74.

_____ . "The struggle for meaning." *Media Development* 32 (1985): 9–11.

Tomaselli, Keyan, and P. Eric Louw. "Crushing South Africa's alternative press." *Index on Censorship* 16 (February 1987): 2.

———— . "Moves toward the registration of South African journalists: An overview from a critical point of view." *Ecquid Novi* 10 (1989): 95–112.

———— . "The South African progressive press under emergency: 1986–1988." *Ecquid Novi* 10 (1989): 70–94.

———— . "*Vrye Weekblad* and post-apartheid mania: What to do with the press." *Communicare* 9:1 (1990): 87–92.

Tomaselli, Keyan, Ruth Tomaselli, and Johan Muller. *Currents of Power: State Broadcasting in South Africa*. Bellville, South Africa: Anthropos, 1989.

———— . "Ideology/culture/hegemony and mass media in South Africa: A literature survey." *Critical Arts* 2 (1981): 1–25.

———— . *The Limits of Dissent: Resistance, Community and the Press*. Johannesburg: Richard Lyon, 1986.

———— . *Narrating the Crisis: Hegemony and the South African Press*. Johannesburg: Richard Lyon, 1987.

Tomaselli, Ruth. "A pressing emergency." *Indicator SA* 4 (Summer 1987): 19–22.

———— . "The limitations to information under the state of emergency." Paper presented at "Rethinking Freedom of the Press in Europe Workshop," London, November 1988.

Tomaselli, Ruth, and Keyan Tomaselli. "From news management to control." *Die Suid-Afrikaan*, Winter 1986, pp. 53–55.

———— . *Ideology, Culture and the South African Mass Media*. Johannesburg: Jonathan Ball, 1984.

Tyson, Harvey. "The future of an opposition press in South Africa." In *South African Conference on the Survival of the Press and Education for Journalism*. Grahamstown, South Africa: Department of Journalism, Rhodes University, 1979; no page numbers.

———— . "Press, censorship, and communication in South Africa." *Ecquid Novi* 8 (1987): 140–151.

———— . "Report on South Africa." *Editor and Publisher*, 10 July 1982, pp. 40ff.

———— . "The South African press and the international image of South Africa." In *The Marketing of the International Image of South Africa*, edited by G.H.G. Lucas and G. J. de J. Cronje, pp. 219–228. Pretoria: University of South Africa, 1978.

Tyson, Harvey, ed. *Conflict and the Press: Proceedings of the Star's Centennial Conference on the Role of the Press in a Divided Society*. Johannesburg: Argus, 1987.

Vale, C. A. "South Africa's communication crisis." *ISSUP Strategic Review* (Pretoria), October 1986, pp. 1–16.

van den Berghe, Pierre, ed. *The Liberal Dilemma in South Africa*. London: Croom Helm, 1979.

van der Ross, Richard Ernest. "The alternative press: The rationale." *Communicatio* 16:2 (1990): 2–8.

van Rooyen, J.C.W. *Censorship in South Africa*. Cape Town: Juta, 1987.

van Zyl, Mikki. "Chronology of South African media." Mimeographed. Grahamstown, South Africa: Department of Journalism and Media Studies, Rhodes University, 1982.

Venter, Lester. "Propaganda: The nasty things that others do." *Frontline*, October/November 1987, p. 18–19.

Walker, Tony. "A comparative study of the circulation of the *Rand Daily Mail*, 1947–1985." Unpublished paper. Grahamstown, South Africa: Department of Journalism and Media Studies, Rhodes University, 1988.

A Way to Win: Strategies to Evaluate and Improve Your Readership and Circulation. Washington, D.C.: American Newspaper Publishers Association, 1990.

Wepener, Willem. "The role of the Afrikaans press." In *South African Conference on the Survival of the Press and Education for Journalism*. Grahamstown, South Africa: Department of Journalism, Rhodes University, 1979; no page numbers.

"What comes after BC [Black Consciousness]?" *Journalist*, March 1984, p. 7.

Williams, Francis. *The Right to Know: The Rise of the World Press*. London: Longmans, Green and Co., 1969.

Winship, Thomas. "It's time to help South Africa's emerging press." *ASNE Bulletin*, December 1987, p. 26.

Woods, Donald. "Press freedom must be safeguarded in the new South Africa." *Rhodes University Journalism Review* 1:1 (November 1990): 7–9.

———. "South Africa: Black editors out." *Index on Censorship* 10 (June 1981): 32–34.

Zille, Helen. "Judging the judge by his own code." *South African Outlook* 112 (April 1982): 56ff.

———. "The 'little press' flexes its muscles." *Frontline*, September 1983, pp. 17–19.

———. "What kind of reporting would Judge Steyn like to keep out of the newspapers?" *South African Outlook* 112 (April 1982): 64–65.

About the Book and Author

A COMPREHENSIVE REVIEW of the press in South Africa since 1976—the year the Soweto riots triggered nationwide protests against white domination—this book examines the role the press has played in reflecting and shaping both apartheid and its undoing. Beginning with a survey of the social and political changes occurring during the period, Gordon Jackson goes on to examine the overall structure of the newspaper industry in South Africa.

Jackson offers an in-depth analysis of the economic difficulties facing journalism, including the impact of television's increasing share of the advertising market. He gives special attention to the alternative press, which arose in the mid-1980s at the height of the government's crackdown on dissent, and explores the origins and impacts of regulations imposed under the State of Emergency, in effect from 1985 to 1990, which included massive restrictions on the media.

In closing, Jackson considers how the press confronted obstacles in order to survive in a political climate that brought freedom of the press to the brink of extinction and looks at how the press is changing now that the South African government itself has rejected apartheid. He concludes by examining the forces favoring the success of a free press under a black majority government and assessing the desirability of a national media policy.

Gordon S. Jackson is professor of communication studies at Whitworth College in Spokane, Washington.

Index

Advertising
  advertising-reader equation, 8
  and alternative press, 52, 59–61
  future of, 200
  inflation, 8, 75, 93
  and radio, 7
  and *Rand Daily Mail,* 75, 77–78
  sales tax on, 8, 93
  spending, 7, 8
  and suburban press, 87–88
  and "synergy" studies, 86–87
  and television, 7, 75, 84–87, 98, 102
Advocacy journalism, 9, 54, 56, 66–
    67, 203–204
  and ethical demands on journalists,
    230
  and objective journalism, 230
  and propaganda, 230
  See also Objectivity
Advocate-General Act, 115–116
Africa, press in, 37, 181–182, 185,
    186, 221–222. *See also individual*
    countries
African National Congress, 28, 47,
    49, 103, 140, 148, 182, 189
  censorship of, 170
  and Constitutional Guidelines,
    189, 190, 195, 212
  coverage of, 53, 55, 65, 110
  and economic structure of the
    press, 195–197, 213
  guerrilla activity, 22, 113, 148
  and Inkatha, 13, 27
  negotiation with government, 30
  and *New Nation,* 47
  opposition to government, 20

  and press freedom, 190–191
  unbanning of, 3, 30, 130, 166, 189
Afrikaans-language press, 5, 10, 15,
    54, 196, 208, 218
  and alternative press, 50–57
  and English-language press, 10–11,
    41, 42
  future of, 186, 196, 204, 205
  as government critic, 33
  as government supporter, 33
  and market penetration, 89
  and M-Net, 98–99
  and press freedom, 183–184
  as voice of Afrikanerdom, 17–18,
    33, 41–42
  See also Nasionale Pers;
    Newspapers; Objectivity;
    Perskor; Press
Akhalwaya, Ameen, 43, 49, 51, 52,
    56, 57, 59–60, 62, 63–64, 67, 69
Al Qalam, 149
Albany News Agency, 179
Albritton, Robert, 141
Allen, John, 25
Allied Distributors, 75
Alternative press, 6, 15, 26, 36, 44,
    119, 122, 170, 185, 191, 195–196,
    204, 218
  and advocacy journalism, 9, 54–56,
    203
  circulation, 48(table)
  compared with Afrikaans and
    English press, 9, 50–57
  compared with press in Western
    Europe, 49
  contribution of, 63–67

criticisms of, 68–69
definition of, 257(n1)
diversity of, 47, 48, 57–58
and extraparliamentary movement,
    49–50, 50–51
funding of, 59–61
future of, 204, 205–206
as government critic, 34
government response to, 46, 47–48,
    58, 61–62, 69
history of, 28–30, 50–52
impact on mainstream press, 8–9
independent ownership, 186
limitations of, 62–63
and new technology, 29, 31
and news coverage, 55–56, 63–64
non-commercial orientation, 52–53
number of papers, 48
and press freedom, 66, 183
and state of emergency, 138, 141,
    147, 149, 150, 153
and training of journalists, 66, 208
vulnerability of, 58–59
See also Advertising; Advocacy
    journalism; Objectivity;
    Newspapers; Press; State of
    emergency
Amnesty International, 27
ANC. See African National Congress
Anglo-American Corporation, 38, 39,
    61, 73
Angola, 19, 30, 111, 161
Anti-Censorship Action Group,
    newsletter, 109, 147
Argus, The, 8, 82, 95, 201
    joint operating agreement, 82, 95,
        201
Argus Company, 36, 37, 84, 95, 97,
    100, 101, 103, 133
    cadet school, 16, 207–208
    and Caxton Limited, 88
    and editorial autonomy, 39–40, 74
    financial aspects, 38
    and joint operating agreements, 80,
        82, 95, 201
    and M-Net, 82, 98–99

and nationalization, 197, 200
    and SAAN/TML, 38, 75, 80, 94
Armstrong, Amanda, 164–165
Army. See South African Defence
    Force; State of emergency
Associated Press, 132
Association of Democratic
    Journalists, 44, 150, 171, 209
Atex Computer System, 96
Audit Bureau of Circulations, 61
Auf der Heyde, Peter, 179
Australia
    advertising in, 31
    press freedom in, 183
    recruiting of journalists, 96–97
Australian, The, 97
Authoritarian approach to the media,
    217–218, 220
    applicability to South Africa, 217–
        218
Azanian Peoples' Organization, 35
AZAPO. See Azanian Peoples'
    Organization

Baily, Jim, 101
Banned persons. See Internal Security
    Act
Barrell, Howard, 41, 53, 60–61, 68,
    230
Battersby, John, 203–204
Beckett, Denis, 153, 186
Beeld, 11, 31, 64, 93, 94, 97, 101, 148,
    201
Bell, Paul, 38, 39, 72, 80, 81, 82, 84,
    101
Biko, Steve, 19
Bill of Rights, 124, 200, 210–212. See
    also United States, Bill of Rights
Boesak, Alan, 203
Bop TV, 86
Botha, Pik, 11
Botha, P. W., 11, 20, 21, 24, 27, 30, 91,
    99, 101, 129, 137, 139, 178
Botha, Stoffel, 140, 142, 143, 144,
    146, 150, 157
Brink, Andre, 216

Britain, 31, 183, 233
  advertising in, 31
  Official Secrets Act, 116
  press funding from, 199
  secrecy in, 164
British Broadcasting Corporation,
  150, 198
Broadcasting, 15, 36, 54, 201–202
  future of, 195
  state control of, 5
  See also Advertising; Radio;
  Television
Brown, Trevor, 41
Budd, Zola, 55–56
Bunting, Brian, 190
Bureau of Information, 145–146
Burger, Die, 33, 90, 97
Burns, Yvonne, 106
Business Day, 55, 80, 83, 91, 186

Camus, Albert, 233
Canada
  advertising in, 31
  press freedom in, 183
  press funding from, 59, 199
Cape Times, The, 8, 43, 113, 152, 159
  and joint operating agreement, 82,
  95, 201
*Cape Town Gazette and African
  Advertiser,* 16
Caxton Limited, 87–88, 98
Censorship, 131–132, 164, 170–171,
  216–217
  and apathy, 163
  distinctive power of, 166–167
  self-censorship, 12, 152, 155
  See also Internal Security Act,
  Intolerance; Publications Control
  Act, and other *individual acts;*
  Secrecy; State of emergency
Chile, press in, 197
Citizen, The, 20, 32, 38, 75–76, 77,
  77(n32), 148
City Press, 101
Coburn, Noel, 87–88
Coggin, Theo, 165, 168

Collinge, Jo-Anne, 41, 121, 146, 197
Commissioner of Police
  power under State of emergency,
  130–132, 135, 142
Committed journalism, 206
  five elements of, 226–228
Common law. *See* Law and
  Legislation
Communism/Communist, 30, 109,
  125, 126, 138. *See also* South
  African Communist Party;
  Suppression of Communism Act
Communist Party. *See* Communism;
  South African Communist Party
Conference on Culture for Another
  South Africa, 190
Conflict and the Press Conference,
  141–142, 143, 162, 176
Congress of South African Writers,
  167–168
Conservative Party, 33, 34, 195
Constitutional change of 1983, 21–22
Corruption, coverage of. *See*
  Advocate-General Act
COSAW. *See* Congress of South
  African Writers
Criminal Procedure Act, 117–119,
  126

Daily Dispatch, 37, 98
Daily News, The, 8
  and joint operating agreement, 95
Daily Telegraph, 189
Davies, Rob, 41
De Beer, Arnold, 220
De Kiewiet, C. W., 19
De Klerk, Frederik W., 3, 12, 30, 126,
  157, 164, 165, 177, 182, 187, 195.
  See also National Party/
  Nationalist government
De Klerk, Willem, 36, 41
De Swardt, Salie, 153, 155, 182
De Villiers, Dawid, 85, 102
Dean, W.H.B., 24
Defence Act, 111–112

Democracy
  and limited flow of information,
    164–167
  See also Liberal democracy
Developmental approach to the
    media, 204, 217, 218–219, 220,
    221
  journalists' fear of, 221–222
Directorate of Media Relations, 138,
    143, 144
Directorate of Publications, 120–121
Dison, David, 151
Disraeli, Benjamin, 128
Dlamini, Sipho, 41
Drum, 101
Drysdale, Andrew, 63, 155
Dugard, John, 127, 212, 223
Du Preez, Max, 57, 58, 60, 61, 64, 69

Eastern Cape News Agencies, 59,
    108, 178, 179
Eastern Europe, 30
Eastern Province Herald, 95–96, 113,
    152
Eksteen, Adriaan, 35
Eliot, T. S., 163
Emdon, Clive, 53
Emergency, State of. *See* State of
    emergency
Engelbrecht, Andries, 138
English-language press, 204, 218
  and Afrikaans press, 10–11, 40, 41–
    42
  apathy, 160–162
  compared with alternative press,
    50–57
  conflict between journalists and
    management, 43–44, 154, 209
  credibility of, 37, 39–43
  editorial autonomy, 39–40
  future of, 196, 204–205
  independent ownership, 186
  and market penetration, 89, 201
  and M-Net, 98–99
  as opposition press, 5, 9, 18, 32–33,
    40–41, 46, 196
  and press freedom, 183–184

and State of emergency, 138, 147
  See also Argus Company;
    Newspapers; Objectivity; Press;
    South African Associated
    Newspapers; Times Media
    Limited
English-speaking whites
  apathy of, 160–161
Ethics. *See* Journalism, ethics
Evening Post, 95–96
Extraparliamentary movement, 9, 28,
    42, 49–50, 53, 60, 67, 68, 169,
    188, 190, 196. *See also* Mass
    Democratic Movement; United
    Democratic Front

Fair Lady, 98
Fairbairn, John, 17
Faure, Abraham, 17
Finance Week, 61
Financial Mail, 81, 82, 83
Fink, Conrad, 89
First Amendment, 227
Flanagan, Louise, 153, 178
Foreign Correspondents Association,
    139
Frankel, Philip, 21
Frederikse, Julie, 41–42
Freedom Charter, 195–197
Freedom of speech. *See* Press freedom
Freedom of the press. *See* Press
    freedom
Friend, The, 6, 11, 95
Frog analogy, 159, 165

Gandar, Laurence, 71, 72, 76, 80
Gibson, Rex, 74, 154
Giffard, C. Anthony, 16, 18, 22, 106
Government Gazette, 110
Government-press relations. *See*
    National Party/Nationalist
    government; Press, history of;
    Press freedom
Grassroots, 6, 29, 47, 51, 56, 57, 149
Green, Michael, 155
Greig, George, 17

Grogan, John, 12, 106, 107, 125–126, 131, 133, 134, 136, 142
Guardian (Britain), 189
Guardian (South Africa), 29, 109
Gwala, Harry, 110

Hachten, William, 16, 18, 22, 31, 34, 106
Harber, Anton, 48–49, 50, 52, 61, 72, 133, 142, 166–167, 190
Heard, Tony, 11, 26, 48, 93, 100, 110–111, 118, 184, 187
Hobday, Jonathan, 197, 200
Hoofstad, 93
Howard, Rhoda, 181
Huisgenoot, 98
Hutchins Commission on Freedom of the Press, 180

Ilanga, 32
Imvo Zabantsundu, 32
Independent, The, 189
Independent press. *See* Alternative press
Indicator, 47, 59, 62, 68
Inflation, 92(table)
Information Scandal, 20, 21, 72, 75, 76, 78, 115
Inkatha, 182, 189
and ANC, 13, 27
Institute for the Advancement of Journalism, 208–209
Internal Security Act, 103, 107–111, 116, 126, 134, 135, 137, 210
International Commission of Jurists, 166
International Federation of Journalists, 59, 127
Intolerance, 164, 167–169, 170–171. *See also* Censorship; Secrecy
IPI Report, 147
Israel
compared with South Africa, 162

Jaffer, Mansoor, 51, 53, 55–56
Jordan, Pallo, 197

Johannesburg Consolidated Investments, 38, 39
and closing of *Rand Daily Mail*, 73, 81
Joint operating agreements
between Argus and TML, 80, 82, 95, 201
in United States, 82
Journalism, 38
ethics, 139, 225–231
future of, 202–209, 231–234
lack of philosophy or mission, 225, 231
proposed philosophical framework, 225–231
western model of, 13
See also Advocacy journalism; *individual countries*; Journalists; Newspapers; Objectivity; Press
Journalists
black journalists' difficulties, 168–169
detention of, 109, 177
diversity of, 204
future of, 4, 224–225
harassment of, 144, 149–150, 177–178, 206
ideological differences among, 13, 229–230
licensing of, 23
and management, 13, 43–44, 154, 209
salaries of, 83, 206
status of, 206
task of, 216–217, 231–232
training of, 44, 66, 83, 207–209
See also Journalism
Judiciary. *See* Law and legislation

Kennnedy, John, 157
Khomeini, Ayatollah, 167
Kinsley, Clive, 74, 75
Kuper, Jocelyn, 154

Lamb, David, 181, 221–222

Lambeth, Edmund, 226, 233
  and Committed journalism, 226–
    228
Latakgomo, Joe, 54
Law and legislation, 20
  as basis for apartheid, 18, 104
  common law, 105
  due process, 210
  future legal foundations, 209–212
  legal costs, 126–127
  limitations on judiciary, 124–125
  sovereignty of parliament, 106, 124
  unobjectionable laws, 105
  See also individual acts; State of
    emergency
Lee, Patrick, 70, 88
Le Grange, Louis, 139–140, 176
Liberal democracy
  applicability to press, 198, 223
  limited support for, 222–223
  obstacles to, 219–220, 222–223
  and press freedom, 223
  and Social responsibility approach
    to the media, 219
  and standards for journalism, 222,
    233
  values meriting adoption, 223–224
  See also Liberalism; Press freedom
Liberalism
  applicability to journalism, 228
  criticisms of, 224, 228
  viewed with distrust, 222–223, 224
  See also Liberal democracy
Libertarian approach to the media,
    188, 217
Liddy, G. Gordon, 176
Lindberg, Dawn, 169
Litani, Yehudi, 162
Literacy, 8
Louw, Gene, 157
Louw, P. Eric, 34, 41, 51, 57–58, 60,
    99, 188–189
Louw, Raymond, 71, 72, 75, 144

Mabuza, Herbert, 41, 121, 197
Macaulay, Thomas, 193
Magazines, 34. *See also* Press

Mainstream press. *See* Afrikaans-
    language press; English-language
    press; Newspapers; Press
Mandela, Nelson, 30, 54
Manheim, Jarol, 141
Manning, Richard, 161–162
Marcus, Gilbert, 105, 120–122, 147–
    148, 156–157, 163, 166
Marketing and Media Research, 100
Martens, Corporal, 216
Maslow, Abraham, 101
Mass Democratic Movement, 8–9,
    10, 28
  and cultural desk, 169
  and State of emergency, 140
  See also Extraparliamentary
    movement
Mass media
  consumption by race group,
    90(table)
  and effects on society, 16
  See also Broadcasting; Journalism;
    Press; Radio; Television
Mathews, Anthony, 106, 108, 112,
    116, 119, 124, 164, 166, 170, 183,
    210, 211
McClurg, James, 33
McGregor, Lord, 176
McLean, Peter, 101, 200
McQuail, Denis
  and media systems, 217–218
  and press freedom, 179
MDM. *See* Mass Democratic
    Movement
Media. *See* Mass media
Media Council, 24–26, 119, 123, 129,
    213–214
Media emergency regulations. *See*
    State of emergency
Media systems. *See individual
    systems*
Media Workers Association of South
    Africa, 44, 209
  opposition to Media Council, 25
Mellet, Leon, 140
Mervis, Joel, 4, 7, 11, 14, 71, 73, 74–
    76, 81, 83, 92, 94

Minister of Defence, 112, 117
Minister of Economic Affairs, 119
Minister of Home Affairs, 7, 107–108, 122–123, 133, 147–149
  power under State of emergency, 130–132, 143–144
  See also Botha, Stoffel
Minister of Law and Order, 7, 109, 139–140
Minnie, Jeanette, 83, 150
M-Net, 98(n106)
  formation of, 10, 86, 98–99
  and *Rand Daily Mail*, 73
Moolman, Terry, 87–88
Moss, Glenn, 41, 121, 197, 230
Mozambique, 19, 161
Mugabe, Robert, 161, 187
Muldergate. *See* Information scandal
Mulholland, Stephen, 81–88, 100
Muller, Johan, 41, 72
Muslim community
  reaction to Salman Rushdie visit, 167
Myburgh, Tertius, 75, 78–79

Namibia, 19, 30
Nasionale Pers, 37, 84, 97, 101
  conflict with Perskor, 93–94
  and M-Net, 98–99
Natal Mercury, 152
  and joint operating agreement, 95
Natal Witness, 37, 98, 149
National Key Points Act, 117, 164
National Party/Nationalist
  government, 3, 10, 17, 19, 26, 33, 35, 38, 40, 41, 50, 64, 71, 76, 105, 106, 124, 161, 164, 177, 181, 182, 188, 196, 205. *See also* De Klerk, F. W.
National security, 105, 107–115, 116, 117, 120, 121, 123–125, 126, 210, 214
Nederduitsch Zuid-Afrikaansch Tijdschrift, 17
Nel, Louis, 80
New African, 47, 108, 179
New Era, 149

New Nation, 6, 29, 47, 52, 57, 58, 59, 61, 68, 147–148, 179, 196
New York Times, 150
News agencies
  and State of emergency, 132–133
  See also individual agencies
Newspaper and Imprint Registration Act, 107
  and *New African*, 108
  and *Vrye Weekblad*, 60, 108
Newspaper Press Bill, 123
Newspaper Press Union, 44, 119, 123, 176
  agreement with police, 113
  agreement with prison service, 114
  agreement with South African Defence Force, 112
  and Media Council, 24–25
  and State of emergency, 129, 141
  and "synergy" studies, 86–87
Newspapers
  circulation of, 8, 31–32, 32(table), 33(table), 48(table), 255(n53)
  compared with broadcasting, 7–8, 201–202
  competition between, 37–39
  defined under Internal Security Act, 107
  defined under State of emergency, 130–131
  future of, 202–203, 231–234
  lack of national distribution, 31
  market penetration, 87–91
  morning publication, 97
  political influence of, 5
  readership of, 8, 31–32, 201–202
  registration of, 107–108, 122–123
  and technology, 29, 31
  See also Advertising; *individual newspapers*; Journalism; Journalists; Press
New Zealand
  and press freedom, 183
Niddrie, David, 41, 121, 197
Northern Ireland
  compared with South Africa, 162

Nuttall, Jolyon, 97

Objectivity, 9, 39, 54, 56, 66–67, 203.
    See also Advocacy journalism;
    Social responsibility approach to
    the media
O'Brien, Conor Cruise, 167, 168
Observer, The, 137
Oggendblad, 93
O'Meara, Dan, 41
O'Meara, Patrick, 20
Oosterlig, Die, 97
Oppenheimer, Harry, 74
Out of Step, 149
Owen, Ken, 35(n67), 36, 38, 39, 78,
    160, 162, 185, 206, 232

Pan-Africanist Congress
    censorship of, 170
    opposition to government, 20
Patel, Leila, 48, 52, 56, 62–63, 65, 67
Perskor, 37, 84, 97, 100
    conflict with Nasionale Pers, 93–
    94
    and M-Net, 82, 98–99
Petroleum Products Act, 117
Pinnock, Don, 28–29
Pogrund, Benjamin, 72
Police, 166, 170
    action against journalists, 144,
    149–151, 177–178
    agreement with Newspaper Press
    Union, 113
    See also State of emergency
Police Act, 111, 112–114, 126, 210
Port Elizabeth News Agency, 179
Potter, Elaine, 5, 32–33
Poynter Institute for Media Studies,
    209
Press, 15
    advertising pressure on, 8
    alternative press pressure on, 8–9
    compared with West and Third
    World, 37, 220
    compared with United States, 31,
    37, 39, 202, 207
    control of, 36

credibility and State of emergency,
    154
credibility of, 36, 39–43, 181
distinctive features of, 30–31, 36–
    45
and diversification, 97–99
fractured character, 43–44
future of, 12–14, 44–45, 65–66, 171,
    217–224
economic cutbacks, 95–97
economic pressure on, 7–8, 11, 91–
    93
government pressure on, 6–7
history of, 16–30, 50–52
influence on politics, 36
monopolistic control of, 37–39
nationalization of, 196, 200, 204
national media policy, 198, 212–
    214
openness to change, 44–45
and problems (general), 6
provincial press, 34, 35, 59
public pressure on, 9–10
religious press, 59
responsibilities of, 232
specialized press, 5
subsidy of, 197–199, 213–214
suburban press, 34, 35, 87–88
television pressure on, 7–8, 100,
    102, 201
thinking differently, 100–101
white domination of, 36–37
    See also Advertising; Africa;
    Afrikaans-language press;
    Alternative press; Democracy;
    English-language press;
    *individual countries; individual
    laws;* Journalism; Journalists;
    Newspaper Press Union;
    Newspapers
Press Commission, 18
Press Council, 25
Press freedom, 4, 171, 212–213
    absolutist approach to, 177
    access rights, 106, 111, 124, 136–
    137
    and alternative press, 66

and apathy, 9–10, 160, 184
and bill of rights, 211
and common law, 105–106
and credibility, 181
definition of, 177
and democracy, 175–176, 232
editorial autonomy, 83, 106, 109–
   111, 124, 133–136, 186
expectations concerning, 186–187
factors favoring, 183–187
factors impeding, 187–191
as foundation for other freedoms,
   175
foundation rights, 106, 107–109,
   124, 130–132
government record on, 188
government views on, 11, 177–178
history of, 16–30, 163–165, 183–
   184
and Hutchins Commission on
   Freedom of the Press, 180
and ideological diversity, 186
impact of independent ownership
   on, 187
impact on political process, 165–
   167
legal foundations of, 105–106
and liberal democracies, 223
limits on, 177
main elements of, 179–181
neccesary conditions needed for,
   182–183
and political stability, 175, 182–
   183, 187–188
practicing rights, 106, 109, 124,
   132–133
roots in Western Europe, 177, 188
and security needs, 177, 183
seen as a luxury, 176
and State of emergency, 140
and subsidization, 199
support from other sectors in
   society, 184–185, 189–191
See also Censorship; Intolerance;
   Law and legislation; National
   security; Press; Secrecy
Press Ordinance, 17

Presstime, 100
Pretoria News, 82, 101
Pringle, Thomas, 17
Prisons, 170
   agreement with Newspaper Press
      Union, 114
   coverage of, 71, 114–115, 126
   See also Prisons Act
Prisons Act, 111, 114–115, 126, 210
   and *Rand Daily Mail,* 18, 71
Progressive Federal Party, 33, 35, 43,
   74
Protection of Information Act, 116
Public Safety Act
   and State of emergency, 128–129,
      138
Publications Appeal Board, 121
Publications Control Act, 25, 119–
   122

Qoboza, Percy, 71, 101
Quoting banned persons. *See* Internal
   Security Act

Race Relations Survey, 109, 147
Radio
   and advertising, 7
   importance in South Africa, 5, 34–
      35
Radio South Africa, 34
Rand, value of, 92(table)
Rand Daily Mail, 8, 41, 59, 83, 94,
   116, 204
   advertising profile, 77–78
   and *The Citizen,* 75–76
   closing of, 6, 11, 63–64, 70–80, 81,
      95, 96
   editorial weaknesses, 78–79
   as government critic, 6, 43, 71
   impact on society, 71
   and Information scandal, 72, 75,
      76, 78
   management errors, 75–78
   and M-Net, 73, 99
   as pioneer in journalism, 71–72
   and prison exposés, 18, 71, 114, 126

racism at, 43
readership, 76–77
Rapport, 11, 36, 116
Reality, 168, 169
Registration of Newspapers
    Amendment Act, 24, 122–123
Relly, Gavin, 73, 74
Reuters, 132
Rhodes University, 207
Rhodesia. *See* Zimbabwe
Riddle, Charles, 12, 152
Roelofse, Koos, 72
Roman Catholic Church, 59
Rushdie, Salman, 167–168

Saamstaan, 47, 56, 57, 58, 68, 149
SABC. *See* South African
    Broadcasting Corporation
Saspu National, 48
SATV, 5–6, 84–86, 98, 138. *See also*
    Advertising; South African
    Broadcasting Corporation
Save the Press Campaign, 66
Schlemmer, Lawrence, 219–220, 224
Scope, 133
Sechaba, 190
Secrecy, 157, 164, 169–171. *See also*
    Censorship; Intolerance
Serfontein, Hennie, 41
Seria, Rashid, 149
Seychelles coup attempt, 116
Shaw, Gerald, 39
Shield laws, 117
Shell Oil Company, 61
Sidley, Pat, 65
Sisulu, Zwelakhe, 54, 69, 109
Slabbert, Van Zyl, 74
Slovo, Joe, 35(n67), 126–127
Smith, Derek, 95–96
Smith, Ian, 187
Social responsibility approach to the
    media, 217, 218–220, 222, 233
    applicability to South Africa, 222
    See also Liberal democracy
Sokotu, Brian, 132
Somalia, 222
Somerset, Lord Charles, 17

South, 6, 29, 47, 52, 54, 57, 59, 62,
    68–69, 149, 177
South Africa
    as closed society, 157, 164
    international coverage and image
        of, 138–139, 139–141, 156, 165,
        220
    mix of First and Third World
        qualities, 220–221, 233
    population projections, 202(table)
    social problems facing, 221
South African Associated
    Newspapers, 72, 73
    conflict with Argus Company, 75,
        94
    and editorial autonomy, 74
    financial problems, 81
    financial recovery, 81–82
    joint operating agreement, 80
    and M-Net, 82
    See also Rand Daily Mail, Times
        Media Limited
South African Broadcasting
    Corporation, 5–6, 10, 34–35,
        35(n67), 57, 84–87, 98, 103, 154,
        207, 251(n7)
    and M-Net, 98
*South African Commercial
    Advertiser,* 17
South African Communist Party, 140
    censorship of, 170
    unbanning of, 3
South African Defence Force, 53, 166,
    170
    agreement with Newspaper Press
        Union, 112
    See also Defence Act; State of
        emergency
South African Institute of Race
    Relations, 169
South African Journal, 17
South African Law Commission
    and bill of rights, 212
South African Press Association, 31,
    110, 132
South African Society of Journalists,
    44, 83, 209

opposition to Media Council, 25
and press freedom, 209
and State of emergency, 150
Sovereignty of parliament. *See* Law
and legislation
Soviet Communist approach to the
the media, 217
Soviet Union, 30
Sowetan, The, 31, 32, 36, 68, 89, 148,
149, 154, 201
Soweto riots, 19–20, 109
anniversary of, 155
coverage of, 72
Sparks, Allister, 74, 208–209
Staffrider, 48
Star, The, 8, 32, 43, 77, 78, 89, 94, 96,
97, 103, 104, 133, 139, 148, 152–
153, 191, 201, 204, 208
State of emergency, 6–7, 28, 106, 123,
128–158, 159, 160, 164
abuse of, 146–151
definitions of key concepts, 134–
136
government powers under, 130–
131, 145–146
impact of, 28, 151–156
legal challenges to, 129–130, 143,
154
weakness as law, 142–144
Stellenbosch University, 207
Stem, Die, 149
Stewart, Gavin, 35, 72, 76, 77, 145,
152
Steyn, Bob, 9–10, 159–160
Steyn Commission, 22–24
criticisms of, 23–24
first report, 23
government response to, 24
press opposition to, 23
second report, 23
and Total Onslaught, 22, 26
Steyn, Marthinus, 23
Steyn, Richard, 153, 155, 163, 198,
199, 231–232
Structuralist perspective on the
press, 38–39, 39(n79), 41–43
Stuart, Kelsey, 106

Suburban press. *See* Press
Sun, 189
Sunday Express, 38, 72, 73, 74, 81,
83, 94, 95, 96, 206
and M-Net, 99
Sunday Star, 96, 118–119
Sunday Times, 31, 78, 83, 92, 98, 110,
116
Sunshine journalism, 12
Suppression of Communism Act,
125, 138. *See also* Internal
Security Act
Survival of the Press Conference, 4
Sweden
subsidy of press in, 197–198, 199

Tambo, Oliver, 103, 110–111, 148
Technikons, journalism training at,
207
Technology, 29, 31
Television
credibility of, 8, 84–87
impact on press, 84–87
importance in South Africa, 5, 31,
34–35
power of, 7–8, 85
and State of emergency, 139
See also Advertising; Broadcasting;
South African Broadcasting
Corporation
Third World. *See* Africa;
Developmental approach to the
media
Thloloe, Joe, 168–169
Thomson, Lord, 88
Times Media Limited, 10, 37, 110
and the Argus Company, 38
financial aspects, 38
and financial turnaround of SAAN,
10, 80, 81–83, 95–97
and joint operating agreements, 82,
95, 202
and M-Net, 98–99
and nationalization, 200
See also South African Associated
Newspapers
TML. *See* Times Media Limited

Tomaselli, Keyan, 39, 41, 72, 99
Tomaselli, Ruth, 39, 41, 72
Total Onslaught, 22–24, 26, 27, 166
  press response to, 22
  and State of emergency, 137
  "Total Strategy" as response to, 22
Transvaler, Die, 36, 93, 94, 100
Trelford, Donald, 175
True Love, 101
Tutu, Desmond, 53
Tyson, Harvey, 17, 24, 96, 103, 110,
  118–119, 133, 189

Union of Black Journalists, 209
United Democratic Front, 28, 35,
  168. *See also* Extraparliamentary
  movement
United Kingdom. *See* Britain
United Nations
  arms embargo, 19
United Press International, 132
United States, 16, 37, 82, 100
  advertising in, 31
  Bill of Rights, 212
  and Hutchins Commission on
    Freedom of the Press, 180
  journalism in, 226, 233
  and Lambeth's principles, 226, 228
  market penetration in, 89
  newspaper layout and design, 202
  political system, 124
  press freedom in, 183
  press in, 8, 31, 183, 233,
  and protection of sources, 118
  and sanctions, 91
  secrecy in, 164, 183
  as source of news, 97
  South African public relations
    efforts in, 141
  television in, 31
  See also First Amendment; Press,
    compared with United States
University of South Africa, 207

UPITN, 20

Vaderland, 93
Van der Merwe, Stoffel, 140, 141–142
Van Manen, Pierre, 97
Van Rooyen, J.C.W., 121
Verwoerd, Hendrik, 177
Viviers, Kosie, 63, 153
Vorster, John, 20
Vosloo, Ton, 40, 101
Vrye Weekblad, 47, 56–62, 64, 68,
  108, 126–127, 149, 196

Waddell, Gordon, 73, 74, 79, 81
Washington Star, 20
Weaver, Tony, 113
Weekend World, 109
Weekly Mail, The, 6, 29, 47, 52, 56–
  59, 62, 64, 68, 149, 167–168, 191,
  196, 204
  daily paper, 200
  and desktop publishing, 29
Western Europe
  and press freedom, 183
  press in, 16, 31, 213
  and sanctions, 91
  as source of press funding, 59
  as source of press values, 37, 177,
    185
  See also individual countries
Western media, 8, 30, 37, 107, 176,
  179, 181, 207, 218, 219, 222
Williams, Francis, 15, 16
Williams, Moegsien, 56–57, 62, 68–
  69, 171, 180–181, 190
Work in Progress, 48, 149
World, 109
World Council of Churches, 19
Woudberg, Neville, 95–96
Writers Association of South Africa,
  51

Zimbabwe, 19, 186, 187, 188